Being-in-the-World

Being-in-the-World

A Commentary on Heidegger's Being and Time, *Division I*

Hubert L. Dreyfus

The MIT Press
Cambridge, Massachusetts
London, England

For Stephen and Gabrielle

© 1991 Massachusetts Institute of Technology

Quotations from *Being and Time* by Martin Heidegger, translated by John Macquarrie and Edward Robinson, ©1962 by SCM Press Ltd., are used here by permission of SCM Press Ltd. and Harper & Row, Publishers, Inc.

This book was set in New Baskerville by The MIT Press and printed and bound in the United States of America.

Library of Congress Cataloging-in-Publication Data

Dreyfus, Hubert L
    Being-in-the-world : a commentary on Heidegger's being and time, division I / Hubert L. Dreyfus.
        p. cm.
    Includes bibliographical references.
    ISBN-13 978-0-262-04106-5 – ISBN-13 978-0-262-54056-8 (pbk.)
    ISBN 0-262-04106-5 – ISBN 0-262-54056-8 (pbk.)
    1. Heidegger, Martin, 1889–1976. Sein und Zeit. 2. Ontology.
3. Space and time. I. Title.
B3279.H48S462   1990
111—dc20   89-38812
                                        CIP

20 19

Contents

Preface

This commentary has been circulating in gradually changing versions for over twenty years. It started in 1968 as a set of "Fybate Lecture Notes" transcribed from my course on *Being and Time* at the University of California, Berkeley. In 1975 I started circulating my updated lecture notes to students and anyone else who was interested. For a decade thereafter I revised the notes each year, incorporating and responding to what I learned from my students and teaching assistants. By 1985 there were so many requests for "The Heidegger Transcripts" that I was encouraged to transform them into a book. The first draft of the book was finished in time for a 1988 NEH Summer Institute held at the University of California, Santa Cruz. On the basis of what I learned from colleagues and participants there and during the following summer, when I taught a course on *Being and Time* at the University of Frankfurt, I did one final revision for this MIT Press edition.

About all that has stayed constant over twenty years of revising has been my decision to limit the notes to Division I of Part One of *Being and Time*. I still consider this the most original and important section of the work, for it is in Division I that Heidegger works out his account of being-in-the-world and uses it to ground a profound critique of traditional ontology and epistemology. Division II of Part One, which makes up the rest of what we have of Heidegger's proposed two-part book (Division III of Part One and all of Part Two were never published), divides into two somewhat independent enterprises. First, there is the "existentialist" side of Heidegger's thought, which focuses on anxiety, death, guilt, and resoluteness and which, although highly influential on its own and in its Sartrian version in *Being and Nothingness*, was, for good reasons, later abandoned by Heidegger himself. And second, there is the laying out of the temporality of human being and of the world, and the grounding of both of these in a more originary temporality whose past, present, and future dimensions are not to be thought of as successive.

Although the chapters on originary temporality are an essential part of Heidegger's project, his account leads him so far from the phenomenon of everyday temporality that I did not feel I could give a satisfactory interpretation of the material. Moreover, the whole of Division II seemed to me much less carefully worked out than Division I and, indeed, to have some errors so serious as to block any consistent reading. (I subsequently learned that when Heidegger was up for the equivalent of tenure, he submitted only Division I for publication, but the Ministry of Education considered it "insufficient." He agreed, in exchange for tenure, to publish a hastily finished version of Division II.)

In the end, thanks to two of my former students, the book has turned out somewhat differently than I had originally planned. Jane Rubin, who was then teaching the Kierkegaard course at Berkeley, agreed to collaborate with me on an article on Kierkegaard's influence on early Heidegger. At roughly the same time, Berkeley went on the semester system, at which time I decided to add Division II to my *Being and Time* course. Under these conditions I became more and more involved in sorting out the existentialist side of Heidegger, and our article grew into the appendix of this book.

With regard to the very difficult chapters on time, I was saved by William Blattner, who, after working on Heidegger as an undergraduate at Berkeley, wrote his doctoral dissertation with John Haugeland at Pittsburgh on temporality in Kant and Heidegger. His account of temporality in *Being and Time* pinpoints and corrects Heidegger's confusions and makes sense of even the most difficult passages. When Blattner publishes his work, it will be an important contribution to an understanding of Heidegger on time and can be thought of as completing this commentary.

Another event that required radically revising the transcripts was the posthumous publication of Heidegger's lecture courses, including those from the years immediately preceding and following the publication of *Being and Time* in 1927. *History of the Concept of Time* (1925), *The Basic Problems of Phenomenology* (1927), and *The Metaphysical Foundations of Logic* (1928) cast floods of new light on Heidegger's magnum opus. Many passages that are unintelligible in *Being and Time* are spelled out in clear and simple terms in the lectures. These new publications also confirmed a hypothesis John

Haugeland and I had made in 1978 that *Being and Time* could be understood as a systematic critique of Husserl's phenomenology, even though Husserl and his basic concept, intentionality, are hardly mentioned in the book. The appearance of *Basic Problems*, which explicitly undertakes "the task of . . . interpreting more radically the phenomena of intentionality and transcendence" seemed a confirmation of our approach. It also justified my emphasis on the *nonmentalistic* approach to intentionality in *Being and Time*, which, thanks to the constant friendly opposition of John Searle, already figured prominently in my commentary.

When *Being and Time* was published in 1927, it was immediately recognized as a classic. Perhaps for this reason Heidegger never made any substantive changes to the text, although he did make small stylistic changes in the fourteen subsequent reprintings. He also kept several copies of the book in which he made notes correcting passages that had been or could be misunderstood and criticizing the book's substantive claims from the perspective of his later thought. (Heidegger's writings are divided by him into two periods: those dating roughly from before 1930, and those written from 1930 on.)

Quotations from *Being and Time* in this book are followed by two sets of page numbers; the first (in parentheses) refers to a page of the standard English translation, the second (in brackets) to a page of the standard German. When I quote from Heidegger's marginal notes, I cite the page number from *Sein & Zeit* in the *Gesamtausgabe* [Collected works] edition in braces. Chapters in *Being and Time* are cited with roman numerals, chapters in this book with arabic numerals (and a lower-case *c* for clarity).

Being and Time is notoriously hard to translate. Heidegger was determined to avoid the mistaken ontology built into traditional philosophical terms, but he was also convinced that ordinary language was inevitably misleading and had contributed to and reciprocally been corrupted by philosophy. He therefore made up many of his own technical terms. Heidegger's translators have struggled with this problem with varying degrees of success. In the Macquarrie-Robinson translation of *Being and Time*, which is the only one in English, Heidegger's prose is generally well rendered, but many of the technical terms have been translated into English terms that either lack the connotations Heidegger is relying on to get his point across or, worse, have just the connotations Heidegger is trying to avoid. In some cases the translators of the three volumes of lectures from the period of *Being and Time* have come up with better terms, but their diverse ideas only further complicate matters when one needs to assemble quotations from all four texts.

In the face of these problems, and in the hope of ultimately decreasing rather than augmenting the number of English variations in print for each German term, John Haugeland, William Blattner, and I have made an attempt to standardize our terminology. I have tried to keep to this agreement, though in some contexts I have felt forced to strike out on my own. Thus the occasional use of the word "I" in the following list of modifications of the standard translations:

Augenblick means literally "the glance of an eye." It is Luther's translation of the biblical "twinkling of an eye" in which "we shall be changed." Kierkegaard uses *Oieblik* as a technical term that is translated as "the moment"; since Heidegger derives his usage from Kierkegaard, I shall translate *Augenblick* not as "the moment of vision" but simply as *the moment.*

Ausrichtung can mean "directionality," but in context *orientation* seems more appropriate.

Befindlichkeit is not an ordinary German word but is constructed out of an idiom. In chapter 10 I explain why the standard translation, "state of mind," is misleading and why, after much discussion and without great enthusiasm, we have chosen *affectedness.*

Begegnen means "to encounter." As Heidegger uses the term, things encounter us, but in the standard translation, we encounter things. In most cases, "things *show up* for us" captures Heidegger's meaning.

Durchsichtig, if translated as "transparent," could be taken to mean invisible; for Heidegger, it always means *clear* or *perspicuous,* and that is how I shall translate it.

Ent-fernung is another term that Heidegger has constructed, this time by taking apart the ordinary word for "distance." The standard translation, "de-severance," is unnecessarily strange. Heidegger's word play can be captured exactly by taking the normal translation for *Entfernung*, "distance," and writing it *dis-stance*. For an explanation see chapter 7.

Ganzheit can be rendered "totality," but Heidegger's holism is better captured by translating it as *whole* (see chapter 4).

Innerweltlich. Intraworldly is often simpler than the standard "within-the-world." I have used each term where it fits best.

Das Man. It is misleading to translate this term as "the They," since this suggests that we are not part of *Das Man.* For reasons given in detail at the beginning of chapter 8, we have chosen *the one.*

Rede literally means talk, but "discourse" is too formal and too linguistic for what Heidegger includes under this term. For reasons given in chapter 12, we use *telling.*

Sein will be translated as *being* (with a lower-case *b*). Being is "that on the basis of which beings are already understood." Being is not a substance, a process, an event, or anything that we normally come across; rather, it is a fundamental aspect of entities, viz. their intelligibility (see chapter 1). There are two basic ways of being. Being-human, which Heidegger calls Dasein, and nonhuman being. The latter divides into two categories: *Zuhandenheit* and *Vorhandenheit.* These terms are standardly translated as "readiness-to-hand" and "presence-at-hand." To convey a sense of the two modes of intelligibility that Heidegger is singling out, we have chosen *availableness* and *occurrentness.* The entities that have these ways of being are called *available* and *occurrent.*

Sein bei, as Heidegger uses the term, does not mean "being-alongside" but *being-amidst.*

Ein Seinendes is standardly translated as "an entity." When Heidegger is describing everyday contexts, however, it is preferable to use *a being.* In abstract philosophical contexts, and where "a being" is likely to be confused with "being," I have retained *an entity.*

Seinkönnen. The standard translation, "potentiality-for-being," is both awkward and misleading, since *können* signifies a know-how, not just a potentiality. We use *ability-to-be.*

Sinn is usually translated as "meaning," but that makes phrases like "the meaning of being" sound too definitional. We use *sense*.

Unheimlich, usually translated as "uncanny," is meant to call attention to the sense human beings have of not being at home in the world. For this reason we propose *unsettled*.

Ursprunglich is always translated "primordial" in the standard translation. This is appropriate when Heidegger is speaking of the "more primordial," meaning closer to the source. When, however, *ursprunglich* is used to mean *being* the source, I translate it as *originary*.

Verfassung in *Seinsverfassung* and *Grundverfassung* is usually translated as "constitution," but this is a Husserlian term and is therefore misleading in this context. We prefer *makeup*.

Vorlaufen. The standard translation, "anticipating," sounds too intentionalistic. Moreover, it has connotations of looking forward to something. As in the case of other nonintentionalistic notions such as the toward-which, we need a technical term and will simply use the literal translation *forerun*.

Weltlichkeit. The German literally means world*liness* not world*hood*. Worldliness, understood as the way of being of the world, is in no way connected with the ordinary sense of worldliness as a way of life opposed to the spiritual.

Woraufhin is an important and difficult technical term, translated as "the upon-which" and also in many other ways in the standard translation. It refers to the background *on the basis of which*, or to the *structure* of the background *in terms of which*, things are intelligible. I translate it *that in terms of which* or *that on the basis of which*, depending on the context.

Zunächst und zumeist are a common pair, like "by and large." More exactly, they mean *primarily and usually*.

Zusammenhang could be translated "context," but *nexus* is less ambiguous.

I have tried to use the above terms consistently in citing *Being and Time* and the lectures. I have also felt free to revise the standard translations when I saw a way to sharpen the point Heidegger was trying to make. In addition to adding italics to stress the relation of a term or phrase to my argument, I have in most cases deleted all or part of Heidegger's own italics. Italics in general are used more freely in German than in English; moreover, Heidegger's italics often make sense only in the context of the surrounding pages.

Most of those who read Heidegger in German or English are at first put off by his strange new language, but after passing through a stage of trying to put what he says into more familiar terms, they come to feel that Heidegger's vocabulary is rigorous, illuminating, and even indispensable for talking about the phenomenon he wants to reveal. If, thanks to Heidegger's language, the reader comes to see the phenomenon of world, which is so obvious that it has been passed over for 2,500 years, and learns to think and talk about being-in it, *Being and Time* and this commentary will have done their job.

Acknowledgments

Over the past two decades I have incurred an enormous debt to successive generations of students and teaching assistants who have contributed to my understanding of *Being and Time*. The corps of gifted teaching assistants, many of whom are now active Heidegger scholars in their own right, includes Charles Guignon, Carol White, John Richardson, Corbin Collins, Theodore Schatzki, and Charles Spinosa. Although there are ideas in what follows that one or another of them has been trying to talk me out of for years, this book is as much theirs as mine.

John Haugeland is in a category by himself. As my student, then teaching assistant, collaborator, and finally colleague, his influence on this commentary is pervasive. Although we disagree almost totally about the existentialist Heidegger in Division II and would perhaps emphasize different aspects of Division I, many of the basic ideas presented here have been hammered out in our two decades of intense Heidegger discussions.

Former students and colleagues at other universities have also helped immensely by sharply and creatively criticizing various versions of my transcripts. The detailed objections and suggestions from Dorothea Frede, William Blattner, Charles Taylor, Joseph Rouse, Piotr Hoffman, and Randall Havas have been especially distressing and valuable. They have delayed publication for several years, but without their help the following pages would have been harder to understand and less help in understanding Heidegger.

I am grateful to Denise Dennison, David Blake, and Andrew Cross for their detailed and helpful stylistic suggestions. And I am especially grateful to my dedicated editor Larry Cohen, who has deciphered and improved many versions of this commentary.

The most sustained work of transforming the transcripts into this book was done during 1985, when I was a Guggenheim Fellow. I am grateful to the Guggenheim Foundation for this support.

Finally, for taking over the transcripts and seeing them through all their changes, as typewriters gave way to word processors and copiers to print, I want especially to thank my wife, Geneviève.

Introduction
Why Study **Being and Time** *?*

What Martin Heidegger is after in *Being and Time* is nothing less than deepening our understanding of what it means for something (things, people, abstractions, language, etc.) to be. He wants to distinguish several different ways of being and then show how they are all related to human being and ultimately to temporality.

Heidegger claims that the tradition has misdescribed and misinterpreted human being. Therefore, as a first step in his project he attempts to work out a fresh analysis of what it is to be human. Obviously the results, if sound, are important for anyone who wants to understand what sort of being he or she is. Heidegger's conclusions are also crucial for the human sciences, for it should be obvious that one cannot understand something unless one has an accurate account of what it is one is trying to understand. Thus, for example, if one thinks of man as a rational animal, solving problems and acting on the basis of beliefs and desires, as the tradition has done since Aristotle, one will develop a theory of mind, decision-making, rule-following, etc., to account for this way of being. If this description of human reality turns out to be superficial, all that hard work will have been in vain.

The traditional misunderstanding of human being starts with Plato's fascination with theory. The idea that one could understand the universe in a detached way, by discovering the principles that underlie the profusion of phenomena, was, indeed, the most powerful and exciting idea since fire and language. But Plato and our tradition got off on the wrong track by thinking that one could have a theory of everything—even human beings and their world— and that the way human beings relate to things is to have an implicit theory about them.

Heidegger is not against theory. He thinks it is powerful and important—but limited. Basically he seeks to show that one cannot have a theory of what makes theory possible. If he is right about this,

his analysis calls into question one of the deepest and most pervasive assumptions accepted by traditional philosophers from Plato to Descartes to Kant to Edmund Husserl, Heidegger's own mentor. Since this assumption plays a crucial role in our thinking, questioning it implies questioning current work in philosophy and in all other disciplines that study human beings. In linguistics, anthropology, psychology, sociology, literary criticism, political science, and economics, for example, the tradition underlies the current quest for formal models. Researchers in each of these disciplines attempt to find context-free elements, cues, attributes, features, factors, primitives, etc., and relate them through covering laws, as in natural science and in behaviorism, or through rules and programs, as in structuralism and cognitivism.

While there is great interest in these formal approaches—especially the so-called information-processing model of the mind—there is already a growing sense that they have not worked out as well as had been hoped. Structuralism is out of favor, and there are more and more phenomena being investigated in the human sciences, such as the role of prototypes in psychology or self-interpreting social practices in anthropology, that do not fit well with the information-processing model. As researchers are coming to question the role of theory in their disciplines, they are becoming interested in interpretive methods that take into account meaning and context.

Such approaches draw, whether consciously or not, on the hermeneutic method of *Being and Time.* Heidegger followed Wilhelm Dilthey in generalizing hermeneutics from a method for the study of sacred texts to a way of studying all human activities. Indeed, Heidegger introduced the hermeneutic method into modern philosophy through his elaboration of the necessity of interpretation in the study of human being and of the circular structure such an interpretation must have.

Heidegger developed his *hermeneutic* phenomenology in opposition to Husserl's *transcendental* phenomenology. Husserl had reacted to an earlier crisis in the foundations of the human sciences by arguing that the human sciences failed because they did not take into account intentionality—the way the individual mind is directed at objects by virtue of some mental content that represents them. He developed an account of man as essentially a consciousness with self-contained meanings, which he called intentional content. According to Husserl, this mental content gives intelligibility to everything people encounter. Heidegger countered that there was a more basic form of intentionality than that of a self-sufficient individual subject directed at the world by means of its mental content. At the foundation of Heidegger's new approach is a phenomenology of "mindless" everyday coping skills as the basis of all intelligibility.

Since Descartes, philosophers have been stuck with the *epistemological* problem of explaining how the ideas in our mind can be true of the external world. Heidegger shows that this subject/object epistemology presupposes a background of everyday practices into which we are socialized but that we do not represent in our minds. Since he calls this more fundamental way of making sense of things our understanding of being, he claims that he is doing *ontology*, that is, asking about the nature of this understanding of being that we do not *know*—that is not a representation in the mind corresponding to the world—but that we simply *are*.

Thus Heidegger breaks with Husserl and the Cartesian tradition by substituting for *epistemological* questions concerning the relation of the knower and the known *ontological* questions concerning what sort of beings we are and how our being is bound up with the intelligibility of the world. Following Kierkegaard, he holds that Descartes's famous starting point should be reversed, becoming "I am therefore I think." As Heidegger puts it:

With the *"cogito sum"* Descartes had claimed that he was putting philosophy on a new and firm footing. But what he left undetermined when he began in this "radical" way was the kind of being which belongs to the *res cogitans*, or—more precisely—the *sense of the being of the "sum."* (46) [24] [1]

Heidegger, like the cognitivists and structuralists, seeks to minimize the role of the conscious subject in his analysis of human being. For this reason he is sometimes confused with the structuralists. But his critique of Husserl and the Cartesian tradition is more radical. Unlike the formalizers, Heidegger introduces an analysis of intentionality or meaning that leads him to question both meaningless formal models and the traditional claim that the basic relation of the mind to the world is a relation of a subject to objects by way of mental meanings.

Heidegger's hermeneutic phenomenology thus calls into question both the Platonic assumption that human activity can be explained in terms of theory and the central place the Cartesian tradition assigns to the conscious subject. We can distinguish five traditional assumptions that Heidegger seeks to clear away to make room for his interpretation of human being and his account of being in general.

1. *Explicitness.* Western thinkers from Socrates to Kant to Jürgen Habermas have assumed that we know and act by applying principles and have concluded that we should get clear about these presuppositions so that we can gain enlightened control of our lives. Heidegger questions both the possibility and the desirability of making our everyday understanding totally explicit. He introduces the idea that the shared everyday skills, discriminations, and practices into which we are socialized provide the conditions necessary for people to pick out objects, to understand themselves as subjects, and, generally, to make sense of the world and of their lives. He then argues that these practices can function only if they remain in the background. Critical reflection is necessary in some situations where our ordinary way of coping is insufficient, but such reflection cannot and should not play the central role it has played in the philosophical tradition. If all were clear about our "presuppositions," our actions would lack seriousness. As Heidegger says in a later work, "Every decision . . . bases itself on something not mastered, something concealed, confusing; else it would never be a decision."[2] Thus what is most important and meaningful in our lives is not and should not be accessible to critical reflection. Critical reflection presupposes something that cannot be fully articulated.

Heidegger calls this nonexplicitable background that enables us to make sense of things "the understanding of being." His hermeneutic method is an alternative to the tradition of critical reflection in that it seeks to point out and describe our understanding of being from within that understanding without attempting to make our grasp of entities theoretically clear. Heidegger points out how background practices function in every aspect of our lives: encountering objects and people, using language, doing science, etc. But he can only *point out* the background practices and how they work to people who already share them—who, as he would say, dwell in them. He cannot *spell out* these practices in so definite and context-free a way that they could be communicated to any rational being or represented in a computer. In Heidegger's terms, this means that one must always do hermeneutics from within a hermeneutic circle.

2. *Mental Representation.* To the classic assumption that beliefs and desires underlie and explain human behavior, Descartes adds that in order for us to perceive, act, and, in general, relate to objects, there must be some content in our minds—some internal representation—that enables us to direct our minds toward each object. This "intentional content" of consciousness has been investigated in the first half of this century by Husserl[3] and more recently by John Searle.[4]

Heidegger questions the view that experience is always and most basically a relation between a self-contained subject with mental content (the inner) and an independent object (the outer). Heidegger does not deny that we sometimes experience ourselves as conscious subjects relating to objects by way of intentional states such as desires, beliefs, perceptions, intentions, etc., but he thinks of this as a derivative and intermittent condition that presupposes a more fundamental way of being-in-the-world that cannot be understood in subject/object terms.

Cognitivism, or the information-processing model of the mind, is the latest and strongest version of the mental-representation idea. It introduces the idea of *formal* representations and thus seeks to explain human activity in terms of a complex combination of logically independent symbols representing elements, attributes, or primitives in the world. This approach underlies decision analysis, transformational grammar, functional anthropology, and cognitive psychology, as well as the belief in the possibility of programming digital computers to exhibit intelligence. Heidegger's view on the nonrepresentable and nonformalizable nature of being-in-the-world doubly calls into question this computer model of the mind.

3. *Theoretical Holism.* Plato's view that everything human beings do that makes any sense at all is based on an implicit theory, combined with the Descartes/Husserl view that this theory is represented in our minds as intentional states and rules for relating them, leads to the view that even if a background of shared practices is necessary for intelligibility, one can rest assured that one will be able to analyze that background in terms of further mental states. Insofar as background practices contain knowledge, they must be based on implicit beliefs; insofar as they are skills, they must be generated by tacit rules. This leads to the notion of a holistic network of intentional states, a tacit belief system, that is supposed to underlie every aspect of orderly human activity, even everyday background

practices. Tacit knowledge—what Husserl calls "horizontal intentionality" in his answer to *Being and Time*[5]—has always been the
fallback position of consistent cognitivists.

—Heidegger opposes this philosophical move. He denies the traditional assumption that there must be a theory of every orderly
domain—specifically that there can be a theory of the commonsense
world. He insists we return to the phenomenon of everyday human
activity and stop ringing changes on the traditional oppositions of
immanent/transcendent, representation/represented, subject/
object, as well as such oppositions within the subject as conscious/
unconscious, explicit/tacit, reflective/unreflective. Heidegger is
definitely not saying what Peter Strawson rather condescendingly
finds "plausible" in Heidegger's works, namely, that we each have
an "*unreflective* and largely unconscious grasp of the basic general
structure of interconnected *concepts* or *categories* in terms of which
we *think about* the world and ourselves."[6] This would make our
understanding of the world into a belief system entertained by a
subject, exactly the view that Husserl and all cognitivists hold and
that Heidegger rejects.

4. *Detachment and Objectivity.* From the Greeks we inherit not only
our assumption that we can obtain theoretical knowledge of every
domain, even human activities, but also our assumption that the
detached theoretical viewpoint is superior to the involved practical
viewpoint. According to the philosophical tradition, whether rationalist or empiricist, it is only by means of detached contemplation that we discover reality. From Plato's theoretical dialectic,
which turns the mind away from the everyday world of "shadows,"
to Descartes's preparation for philosophy by shutting himself up in
a warm room where he is free from involvement and passion, to
Hume's strange analytical discoveries in his study, which he forgets
when he goes out to play billiards, philosophers have supposed that
only by withdrawing from everyday practical concerns before
describing things and people can they discover how things really
are.

The pragmatists questioned this view, and in this sense Heidegger
can be viewed as radicalizing the insights already contained in the
writings of such pragmatists as Nietzsche, Peirce, James, and Dewey.
Heidegger, along with his fellow student Georg Lukács, quite likely
was exposed to American Pragmatism through Emil Lask.[7]

5. *Methodological Individualism.* Heidegger follows Wilhelm Dilthey in emphasizing that the meaning and organization of a culture must be taken as the basic given in the social sciences and philosophy and cannot be traced back to the activity of individual subjects. Thus Heidegger rejects the methodological individualism that extends from Descartes to Husserl to existentialists such as the pre-Marxist Sartre and many contemporary American social philosophers. In his emphasis on the social context as the ultimate foundation of intelligibility, Heidegger is similar to that other twentieth-century critic of the philosophical tradition, Ludwig Wittgenstein. They share the view that most philosophical problems can be (dis)solved by a description of everyday social practices.

At this point someone is sure to object that in spite of his interest in our shared, everyday practices, Heidegger, unlike Wittgenstein, uses very unordinary language. Why does Heidegger need a special, technical language to talk about common sense? The answer is illuminating.

To begin with, Heidegger and Wittgenstein have a very different understanding of the background of everyday activity. Wittgenstein is convinced that the practices that make up the human form of life are a hopeless tangle.

How could human behavior be described? Surely only by showing the actions of a variety of humans, as they are all mixed up together. Not what *one* man is doing *now*, but the whole hurly-burly, is the background against which we see an action, and it determines our judgment, our concepts, and our reactions.[8]

Wittgenstein warns against any attempt to systematize this hurly-burly. "*Not* to explain, but to *accept* the psychological phenomenon—that is what is difficult."[9]

Heidegger, on the contrary, thinks that the commonsense background has an elaborate structure that it is the job of an existential analytic to lay out. This background, however, is not what we usually deal with and have words for, so to talk of it requires a special vocabulary. Searle faces the same problem when he tries to talk about the background.

There is a real difficulty in finding ordinary language terms to describe the Background: one speaks vaguely of "practices," "capacities," and "stances" or one speaks suggestively but misleadingly of "assumptions" and "presuppositions." These latter terms must be literally wrong, because they imply the apparatus of representation . . . . The fact that we have no natural vocabulary for discussing the phenomena in question and the fact that we tend to lapse into an Intentionalistic vocabulary ought to arouse our interest. . . . There simply is no first-order vocabulary for the Background, because the Background is as invisible to Intentionality as the eye which sees is invisible to itself.[10]

When, for example, Heidegger substitutes such technical terms as "worldliness," the "toward-which," and the "for-the-sake-of-which" for such everyday terms as "context," "goal," and "purpose," he is wrestling with this very problem.

Heidegger struggles to free himself from traditional assumptions and our everyday vocabulary in his attempt to return to the phenomena. Among traditional philosophers he most admired Aristotle, who was, he says, "the last of the great philosophers who had eyes to see and, what is still more decisive, the energy and tenacity to continue to force inquiry back to the phenomena . . . and to mistrust from the ground up all wild and windy speculations, no matter how close to the heart of common sense" (BP, 232).[11] But even Aristotle was under the influence of Plato and so was not radical enough. Heidegger therefore proposes to start again with the understanding in the shared everyday activities in which we dwell, an understanding that he says is closest to us yet farthest away. *Being and Time* is supposed to make manifest what we are already familiar with (although not to make it so explicit that a Martian or computer could come to know it) and in so doing to modify our understanding of ourselves and so transform our very way of being.

This would be reason enough to study *Being and Time*, but Heidegger does not simply want to clear the ground of traditional distortions and pseudoproblems. He has a positive account of authentic human being and a positive methodological proposal for how human being should be systematically studied. Both his understanding of human existence and his interpretive method for studying human being-in-the-world have had an enormous influence on contemporary life and thought. Wherever people understand themselves and their work in an atomistic, formal, subjective, or objective way, Heidegger's thought has enabled them to recognize appropriate alternative practices and ways of understanding and acting available but neglected in our culture. At an international conference in Berkeley commemorating the hundredth anniversary of Heidegger's birth, not only philosophers but also doctors, nurses, psychotherapists, theologians, management consultants, educators, lawyers, and computer scientists took part in a discussion of the way Heidegger's thought had affected their work.[12]

Most of the leading thinkers in the humanities and social sciences also acknowledge a debt to Heidegger. Michel Foucault has said, "For me Heidegger has always been the essential philosopher. . . . My entire philosophical development was determined by my reading of Heidegger."[13] Early in his career, Jacques Derrida doubted that he could write anything that had not already been thought by Heidegger. Pierre Bourdieu says that in philosophy Heidegger was his "first love." His own important concept of the social field is indirectly indebted to Heidegger by way of Maurice Merleau-Ponty, who acknowledged the influence of *Being and Time* on his *Phenomenology of Perception*. Even Habermas, who started out under Heidegger's influence but has distanced himself from Heidegger and developed a more traditional philosophical line, judges *Being and Time* to be "probably the most profound turning point in German philosophy since Hegel."[14]

In the course of studying and teaching *Being and Time* for twenty-five years—trying to clarify Heidegger's theses, checking them against the phenomena, and defending them against opposed positions in contemporary continental and analytic philosophy—I have come to the conclusion that such praise is justified. The commentary that follows is meant to enable readers to decide for themselves.

1

Heidegger's Substantive Introduction

I. Questioning the Nature of Being

Heidegger's primary concern is to raise the question of being—to make sense of our ability to make sense of things—and to reawaken in people a feeling for the importance of this very obscure question. Moreover, he wants to answer it "concretely" (19) [1]. He begins by noting three ways in which the nature of being has traditionally been misconstrued, ways that nonetheless contain hints of what he considers the real issues. (Remember through this difficult section that what Heidegger has in mind when he talks about being is the intelligibility correlative with our everyday background practices.)

1. *Being is the most universal concept.* On this mistaken view, "beingness" (as Heidegger puts it in his marginal corrections to *Being and Time*){4}[1] is a property like any other, except that it is the most general property. It is arrived at by abstraction. We look at oaks, maples, firs, etc., and abstract treeness. Then from trees and bushes and flowers we abstract plantness. Then we get to the "livingness" of all living things. Finally we arrive at entities that have in common only beingness.

Aristotle, however, already saw a problem in this approach. "Being" does not behave like a very general predicate. For example, the being of numbers seems not to be the same as, but at best only analogous to, the being of objects, and the being of real objects differs from the being of imaginary objects such as unicorns. Aristotle says that being is predicated analogously. Since being transcends the universality of a class or genus the Scholastics called it a *transcendens*. Heidegger concludes that being is clearly no ordinary predicate.

2. *An abstract notion like being is indefinable.* In rejecting being as a most general predicate, philosophers have said that it is an empty concept. Since it cannot be contrasted with anything else, "being" does not refer to anything. According to Heidegger, this warns us that being is not an entity (23) [4].

If one writes Being with a capital *B* in English, it suggests some entity; indeed, it suggests a supreme Being, the ultimate entity. I have therefore decided to translate *Sein* by "being" with a lower-case *b*. But this attempt to make "being" look more like a form of the verb "to be" than like a noun has its own risks. One might get the mistaken idea that being for Heidegger is not an entity but some sort of event or process. Many commentators make this mistake. For example, Joseph Kockelmans gets his book on Heidegger off to a very bad start by noting, "Heidegger is never concerned with beings or things, but with meaning and Being; never with stable entities, but with events."[2] Heidegger must have been aware of this danger, since at the point where he says being is not an entity, he writes in the margin of his copy of *Being and Time*, "No! One cannot make sense of being with the help of these sorts of concepts." To think of being in terms of concepts like entity, or process, or event is equally misleading.

3. *The nature of being must be self-evident, since every proposition can be analyzed as including the copula "is."* But for Heidegger this supposed self-evidence poses a problem: "The very fact that we already live in an understanding of being and that the sense of being is still veiled in darkness proves that it is necessary in principle to raise this question again" (23) [4]. We can raise the question on the basis of this obscure experience, since "we always conduct our activities in an understanding of being." Although "we do not even know the horizon in terms of which that sense is to be grasped and fixed, ... this vague average understanding of being is still a fact" (25) [5].

The understanding of being is in our background practices;[3] an account of this sense of being is what our investigation is to produce. It must lay out the structure of our access to entities and account for our ability to make sense of making sense.

We always conduct our activities in an understanding of being. Out of this understanding arise both the explicit question of the sense of being and the tendency that leads us toward its conception. (25) [5]

II. Approaching the Question of Being by Way of Dasein

Heidegger thinks that the tradition never succeeded in correctly formulating the being-question. The nearest it came is captured by Heidegger in a formula that is sufficiently ambiguous to cover some sort of supreme Being, a constituting activity like that of a transcendental ego, and the intelligibility revealed by our background practices.

What is asked about is being—that which determines beings as beings, that on the basis of which beings are already understood. (25–26) [6]

Heidegger is explicit, however, that his account will differ radically from the traditional one "in not defining entities as entities by tracing them back in their origin to some other entities, as if being had the character of some possible entity" (26) [6].

If one is to avoid being trapped by the traditional approach, the way in which one raises the question of being is of paramount importance:

When we come to what is to be interrogated, the question of being requires that the right way of access to beings shall have been obtained and secured in advance. But there are many things which we designate as "being," and we do so in various senses . . . . Being lies in the fact that something is, and in its being as it is; in reality; in occurrentness; in subsistence; in validity; in Dasein; in the "there is." In *which* beings is the sense of being to be discerned? . . . Which entity shall we take for our example, and in what sense does it have priority? (26) [6–7]

Heidegger wants to avoid what he sees as the recurrent structure of traditional ontology, namely, grounding all kinds of being in a causally self-sufficient source. (He later calls this structural mistake ontotheology.) He proposes, nonetheless, to show that all beings gain their intelligibility in terms of the structure of one sort of being. In Section 2 of Part I of the introduction to *Being and Time* we get a glimpse of the course Heidegger's investigation is going to take.

To work out the question of being adequately, we must make a being—the inquirer—perspicuous in his own being. . . . This being which each of us is himself and which includes inquiring as one of the possibilities of its being, we shall denote by the term "Dasein." (27) [7]

A. *Dasein Is Not a Conscious Subject*

Since, as Heidegger holds, getting the right approach is crucial, we must stop here to get the right approach to Dasein. "Dasein" in colloquial German can mean "everyday human existence," and so Heidegger uses the term to refer to human being. But we are not to think of Dasein as a conscious subject. Many interpreters make just this mistake. They see Heidegger as an "existential phenomenologist," which means to them an edifying elaboration of Husserl. The most famous version of this mistake is Sartre's brilliant but misguided reformulation of *Being and Time* into a theory of consciousness in *Being and Nothingness*. Other interpreters have followed the same line. Dagfinn Føllesdal, one of the best interpreters of Husserl, justifies his Husserlian reading of *Being and Time* by pointing out that while Heidegger was working on the book, he wrote Husserl: "The constituting subject is not nothing, hence it is something and has being . . . . The inquiry into the mode of being of the constituting subject is not to be evaded."[4] Heidegger, however, warns explicitly against thinking of Dasein as a Husserlian meaning-giving transcendental subject: "One of our first tasks will be to prove that if we posit an 'I' or subject as that which is primarily given, we shall completely miss the phenomenal content of Dasein" (72) [46].

In 1943 Heidegger was still trying to ward off the misunderstanding of *Being and Time* dictated by the Cartesian tradition. He reminds the reader that he was from the start concerned with being, and then he continues:

But how could this . . . become an explicit question before every attempt had been made to liberate the determination of human nature from the concept of subjectivity. . . . To characterize with a single term both the involvement of being in human nature and the essential relation of man to the openness ("there") of being as such, the name of "being there [*Dasein*]" was chosen . . . . Any attempt, therefore, to rethink *Being and Time* is thwarted as long as one is satisfied with the observation that, in this study, the term "being there" is used in place of "consciousness."[5]

Dasein must be understood to be more basic than mental states and their intentionality. In a footnote toward the end of *Being and Time* Heidegger says, "The intentionality of 'consciousness' is grounded in the ecstatical temporality of Dasein" (498) [363].

In bending over backward to avoid the Sartre/Føllesdal mistake of identifying Dasein with the conscious subject central to Husserlian phenomenology, interpreters such as John Haugeland have claimed that Dasein is not to be understood as an individual person at all.[6] Dasein, according to Haugeland, is a mass term. People, General Motors, and Cincinnati are all cases of Dasein. While Haugeland has presented a well-motivated and well-argued corrective to the almost universal misunderstanding of Dasein as an autonomous, individual subject—a self-sufficient source of all meaning and intelligibility—Haugeland's interpretation runs up against many passages that make it clear that for Heidegger Dasein designates exclusively entities like each of us, that is, individual persons. For example, "Because Dasein has in each case mineness one must always use a *personal* pronoun when one addresses it: 'I am,' 'you are'" (68) [42].

The best way to understand what Heidegger means by Dasein is to think of our term "human being," which can refer to a way of being that is characteristic of all people or to a specific person—a human being. Roughly, in Division I Heidegger is interested in the human *way of being*, which he calls "being-there" or Dasein. In Division II he is interested in individual human beings and speaks more often of *a* Dasein. I will switch back and forth between "human being" and "a human being," as Heidegger does between "Dasein" and "a Dasein," using whichever term brings out Heidegger's meaning at a particular point in his analysis. The challenge is to do justice to the fact that Dasein names beings like you and me, while at the same time preserving the strategy of *Being and Time*, which is to reverse the Cartesian tradition by making the individual subject somehow dependent upon shared social practices.

B. Dasein's Way of Being: Existence

The way to do justice to the fact that Dasein is Heidegger's name for us and yet avoid the centrality of human individuals is to see that what is to be studied in *Being and Time* ultimately is not Dasein but *Dasein's way of being*. "When we designate this entity with the term 'Dasein,' we are expressing not its 'what' (as if it were a table, house, or tree) but its being" (67) [42]. The whole question of whether Dasein is a general term or the name for a specific entity is undercut by Heidegger's more basic interest in the way of being that human beings, cultures, and institutions share. Human beings, it will turn out, are special kinds of beings in that their way of being embodies an understanding of what it is to be. "These beings, in their being, comport themselves towards their being" (67) [41]. Dasein's activity—its way of being—manifests a stand it is taking on what it is to be Dasein. "Its ownmost being is such that it has an understanding of that being, and already maintains itself in each case in a certain interpretedness of its being" (36) [15]. Heidegger calls this self-interpreting way of being *existence.* "That kind of being towards which Dasein can comport itself in one way or another, and always does comport itself somehow, we call 'existence'" (32) [12]. For Heidegger, existence does not mean simply to be real. Stones and even God do not exist in his sense of the term. Only self-interpreting beings exist.

Heidegger is not interested in giving the necessary and sufficient conditions for existing in his sense. He is only interested in the de facto structure of this way of being. Yet he is clear that to be a conscious subject or self is neither necessary nor sufficient for human existence, rather the reverse: "The existential nature of man is the reason why man can represent beings as such, and why he can be conscious of them. All consciousness presupposes . . . existence as the *essentia* of man."[7]

Cultures as well as human beings exist; their practices contain an interpretation of what it means to be a culture. Heidegger tells us that institutions such as science have existence as their way of being too (32) [11], and in discussing language he comments, "Language is not identical with the sum total of all the words printed in a dictionary; instead . . . language is as Dasein is . . . it exists" (BP, 208).

Heidegger calls *Being and Time* an *existential* analytic, but only at the end of Division I of *Being and Time* does he make it clear that existence has been his concern from the start.

What have we gained by our preparatory analysis of Dasein, and what are we seeking? . . . When we came to analyze this being, we took as our clue existence, which, in anticipation, we had designated as the essence of Dasein. . . . By working out the phenomenon of care, we have given ourselves an insight into *the concrete makeup of existence.* (274, my italics) [231]

To arrive at a description of the basic structures of the way of being called existence, shared by cultures, institutions, and human beings, Heidegger proposes to describe in detail the various activities of Dasein that are specific manifestations of these general existential structures.

Looking at something, understanding and conceiving it, choosing access to it—all these ways of behaving are constitutive for our inquiry, and therefore are modes of being for those particular entities which we, the inquirers, are ourselves. (26–27) [7]

Heidegger thus devotes Division I of *Being and Time* to Dasein's ways of acting—its different stances vis-à-vis itself, things, and others—and the kinds of being these stances reveal. We shall see what these basic stances are and what mode of intelligibility shows up for each stance. This is what Heidegger calls "the ontological task of a genealogy of the different possible ways of being" (31) [11].

Such a study reveals the basis for doing science and for doing philosophy.

The question of being aims therefore at ascertaining the a priori conditions not only for the possibility of the sciences which examine beings as beings of such and such a type, and, in doing so, already operate with an understanding of being, but also for the possibility of those ontologies themselves which are prior to the ontical sciences and which provide their foundations. (31) [11]

The need for such a study becomes clear whenever a normal science is in crisis, and it is also required by sciences that are unclear about their method and subject matter, as are the sciences of man. It is also necessary to save philosophy from its recurrent "problems" and "solutions" and give it a proper subject matter.

C. Dasein's Preontological Understanding of Being

Since its way of being is existence, a human being always embodies an understanding of its being. "Dasein has grown up both into and in a traditional way of interpreting itself: in terms of this it understands itself primarily and, within a certain range, constantly" (41) [20]. This understanding of being is Dasein's unique characteristic. "Understanding of being is itself a definite characteristic of Dasein's being. Dasein is ontically distinctive in that it is ontological" (32) [12].

Since the notion that our social practices embody an ontology is an unfamiliar idea, we need a specific illustration. Because Heidegger does not provide one, we have to bring one in from outside. To start with, we need an example of how the understanding of being human in an individual's activity is the result of being socialized into practices that contain an interpretation not exhaustively contained in the mental states of individuals. A striking example can be drawn from the contrasting child-rearing practices in the United States and Japan. (It does not matter for this example whether the following description is accurate.)

A Japanese baby seems passive . . . . He lies quietly . . . while his mother, in her care, does [a great deal of] lulling, carrying, and rocking of her baby. She seems to try to soothe and quiet the child, and to communicate with him physically rather than verbally. On the other hand, the American infant is more active . . . and exploring of his environment, and his mother, in her care, does more looking at and chatting to her baby. She seems to stimulate the baby to activity and vocal response. It is as if the American mother wanted to have a vocal, active baby, and the Japanese mother wanted to have a quiet, contented baby. In terms of styles of caretaking of the mothers in the two cultures, they get what they apparently want . . . . A great deal of cultural learning has taken place by three to four months of age . . . babies have learned by this time to be Japanese and American babies.[8]

To draw the moral that an ontology need not be represented in a mind, I turn to the French anthropologist Pierre Bourdieu. Bourdieu gives an excellent general description of the process of socialization that forms public intelligibility and even private experience.

A whole group and a whole symbolically structured environment . . . exerts an anonymous, pervasive pedagogic action. . . . The essential part of the modus operandi which defines practical mastery is transmitted in practice, in its practical state, without attaining the level of discourse. The child imitates not "models" but other people's actions. Body *hexis* speaks directly to the motor function, in the form of a pattern of postures that is both individual and systematic, because linked to a whole system of techniques involving the body and tools, and charged with a host of social meanings and values: in all societies, children are particularly attentive to the gestures and postures which, in their eyes, express everything that goes to make an accomplished adult—a way of walking, a tilt of the head, facial expressions, ways of sitting and of using implements, always associated with a tone of voice, a style of speech, and (how could it be otherwise?) a certain subjective experience.[9]

Bourdieu sees that our practices embody pervasive responses, discriminations, motor skills, etc., which add up to an interpretation of what it is to be a person, an object, an institution, etc. To use an example from later Heidegger, our culture has entered a phase in which we deal with things as "standing reserve." This means in part that we treat them as resources to be used efficiently and then disposed of when no longer needed. A styrofoam cup is a perfect example. When we want a hot or cold drink it does its job, and when we are through with it, we simply throw it away. How different is a delicate Japanese teacup, preserved from generation to generation for its beauty and its social meaning.

Note that our hypothetical Japanese understanding of what it is to be a human being (passive, contented, gentle, social, etc.) fits with an understanding of what it is to be a thing (delicate, beautiful, traditional, etc.). It would make no sense for Americans, who we are supposing to be active, independent, and aggressive—constantly striving to cultivate and satisfy their desires—to relate to things the way the Japanese do, or for the Japanese (before their understanding of being was interfered with by ours) to invent and prefer styrofoam tea cups. In the same vein, Americans tend to think of politics as the negotiation of individual desires, whereas the Japanese seek consensus. In sum, the practices containing an interpretation of what it is to be a person, an object, and a society fit together. They are all aspects of what Heidegger calls an understanding of being. Such an understanding is contained in our knowing-how-to-cope in various domains rather than in a set of beliefs that such and such is the case. Thus we embody an understanding of being that no one has in mind. We have an ontology without knowing it.

Another example that brings out the anticognitivism implicit in Heidegger's view even more strikingly is our distance-standing practices. We all have learned to stand the appropriate distance from strangers, intimates, and colleagues for a conversation. Each culture has a different "feel" for the appropriate distances. In North Africa people stand closer and have more body contact than in Scandinavia, for example. These practices are not taught by the parents. They do not know that there is any pattern to what they are doing, or even that they are doing anything. Rather, the children, always imitating the adults without even trying, simply pick up the pattern. There is no reason to think that there are any rules involved; rather, we have a skilled understanding of our culture. Indeed, if one tried to state the rules for distance-standing, one would require further rules, such as stand closer if there is noise in the background, or further away if the other person has the flu, and the application of these rules would in turn require further rules, and so on, always leading us back to further everyday, taken-for-granted practices. Distance-standing practices are simply something that we do. Of course, learning to do it changes our brain, but there is no evidence and no argument that rules or principles or beliefs are involved. Moreover, this is not an isolated practice; how close one stands goes with an understanding of bodies, intimacy, sociality, and finally reflects an understanding of what it is to be a human being.

We can now see why Heidegger holds that Dasein's understanding of being is not a belief system implicit in the minds of individual subjects, as Cartesian philosophers have generally held. Again, Bourdieu gives a Heideggerian account of the nonmental nature of everyday practices and of their importance:

Principles em-bodied . . . are placed beyond the grasp of consciousness, and hence cannot be touched by voluntary, deliberate transformation, cannot even be made explicit; nothing seems more ineffable, more incommunicable, more inimitable, and, therefore, more precious, than the values given body, made body by the transubstantiation achieved by the hidden persuasion of an implicit pedagogy, capable of instilling a whole cosmology, an ethic, a metaphysic, a political philosophy, through injunctions as insignificant as "stand up straight" or "don't hold your knife in your left hand."[10]

As Bourdieu notes, only those who study but do not share a specific social understanding think of it as a system of rules.

The anthropologist is condemned to adopt unwittingly for his own use the representation of action which is forced on agents or groups when they lack practical mastery of a highly valued competence and have to provide themselves with an explicit and at least semi-formalized substitute for it in the form of a *repertoire of rules.*[11]

Heidegger would differ from Bourdieu, however, in holding that Dasein's shared ways of behaving are not mere facts to be studied *objectively* by a "scientific" discipline such as anthropology or sociology (although they are that too). Rather, because they contain an understanding of being they must be studied as an *interpretation.*

Heidegger calls the shared agreement in our practices as to what entities can show up as a *preontological* or *pretheoretical* understanding of being. (This distinction between preontological and ontological must not be confused with the distinction between the *ontic* and the *ontological,* between that which concerns beings and that which concerns ways of being. See Table 1.)

Table 1
Terminology of various investigations and kinds of understanding.
(The body of the table shows what is to be discovered in the investigation.)

	Kind of investigation	
What is investigated	Ontic (apophantic) concerns beings	Ontological (hermeneutic) concerns ways of being
A "who"—a being with the character of Dasein (i.e., that exists)	(Factical) possible ways to be (roles) (e.g., being a student, being gay) and structures thereof	Existentials and structures thereof (e.g., being-with, facticity)
A "what"—a being of any other kind	(Factual) properties (e.g., being orange, being prime) and structures thereof (scientific laws, etc.)	Categories and structures thereof (e.g., quality, quantity)

Kinds of understanding

Existential understanding is a worked-out understanding of the ontological structures of existence, that is, of what it is to be Dasein.

Existentiell understanding is an individual's understanding of his or her own way to be, that is, of what he or she is.

Examples:

•A psychologist's understanding of his or her own role is existentiell.
•The psychologist's clients' understandings of their own roles are existentiell.
•The psychologist's understanding of his or her clients' various roles and possible roles is ontic (neither existential nor existentiell).
•If the psychologist (or anyone) does fundamental ontology and understands what it is to be Dasein in general, that understanding is existential. (It will turn out that for an individual to do fundamental ontology, his or her existentiell understanding of himself or herself must be authentic.)

If we reserve the term "ontology" for that theoretical inquiry which is explicitly devoted to the being [i.e., intelligibility] of beings, then what we have had in mind in speaking of Dasein's "being ontological" is to be designated as something "preontological." It does not signify simply "being-ontical," however, but rather "being in such a way that one has an understanding of being." (32) [12]

Thanks to our preontological understanding of being, what shows up for us shows up *as* something. As Heidegger puts it, using "actuality" this time instead of "being":

We must be able to understand actuality *before* all factual experience of actual beings. This understanding of actuality or of being in the widest sense as over against the experience of beings is in a certain sense *earlier* than the experience of beings. To say that the understanding of being precedes all factual experience of beings does not mean that we would first need to have an explicit concept of being in order to experience beings theoretically or practically. We must understand being—being, which may no longer itself be called a being, being, which does not occur as a being among other beings but which nevertheless must be given and in fact is given in the understanding of being. (BP, 11)

But when we try to make the preontological understanding we in fact possess explicit, we find that it is by no means obvious:

In demonstrating that Dasein is ontico-ontologically prior, we may have misled the reader into supposing that this being must also be what is given as ontico-ontologically primary not only in the sense that it can itself be grasped "immediately," but also in that the kind of being which it possesses is presented just as "immediately." Ontically, of course, Dasein is not only close to us—even that which is closest: we *are* it, each of us, we ourselves. In spite of this, or rather for just this reason, it is ontologically that which is farthest. (36) [15]

That is, Dasein in its concerned activity just is a stand on its being and the being of all entities ("Dasein is ontically closest to itself"), but we cannot explicitly grasp this stand (it is also "ontologically farthest")—and yet Dasein has a dim understanding that it is interpreting itself and entities ("preontologically it is surely not a stranger") (37) [16].

In consciousness-raising groups, for example, one learns that the understanding one can make explicit is just the tip of the iceberg. Our most pervasive interpretation of being masculine and feminine, for example, is in our bodies, our perceptions, our language, and generally in our skills for dealing with the same and the opposite sex. We can to some extent *light up* that understanding, that is, point it out to those who share it, but we cannot *spell it out*, that is, make it understandable even to those who do not share it. Moreover, what we can get clear about is only what is least pervasive and embodied. Heidegger has the sense that the more important some aspect of our understanding of being is, the less we can get at it.

If this difficulty resulted from the *holism* of our network of beliefs, we might try to jump out of our belief system all at once and contemplate it. This is exactly what Husserl claims to do in *Crisis*. Or if this were impossible because we always presuppose a network of beliefs in order to make sense of anything, we could at least make any particular beliefs and principles explicit while leaving the rest of the belief system in the background. Wittgenstein sometimes talks this way, and this idea is central to Habermas's proposal for a critical rationality. But Heidegger has a more radical reason for saying that we cannot get clear about the "beliefs" about being we seem to be taking for granted. There are no beliefs to get clear about; there are only skills and practices. These practices do not arise from beliefs, rules, or principles, and so there is nothing to make explicit or spell out. We can only give an interpretation of the interpretation already in the practices. This is why Heidegger says in Introduction II that since phenomenology deals with our understanding of being, it must be hermeneutic. To sum up, an explication of our understanding of being can never be complete because we dwell in it—that is, it is so pervasive as to be both nearest to us and farthest away—and also because there are no beliefs to get clear about.

Ontology, then, cannot be a Kantian transcendental analytics nor a Husserlian eidetic science. Hermeneutic ontology must be practiced on the background of an horizon of intelligibility in which the ontologist must dwell. It is always unfinished and subject to error. Heidegger cautions in *Basic Problems* concerning his own temporal interpretation of being:

Faulty interpretations of the basic relationship of Dasein to beings and to itself are no mere defects of thought or acumen. They have their reason and their necessity in Dasein's own historical existence. . . . Without our knowing where the faulty interpretation lies, we can be quietly persuaded that there is also a faulty interpretation concealed within the temporal interpretation of being as such, and again no arbitrary one. (BP, 322)

Heidegger may well be the first philosopher to have had a critical sense of the inevitability of unknowable limitations on his own enterprise—the first philosopher of finitude, as he would put it.

III. Dasein as Self-Interpreting

We are now in a position to draw out the implications of Dasein's special way of being, which is existence. Cultures and cultural institutions have existence as their way of being, and so does each of us. To exist is to take a stand on what is essential about one's being and to be defined by that stand. Thus Dasein is what, in its social activity, it interprets itself to be. Human beings do not already have some specific nature. It makes no sense to ask whether we are essentially rational animals, creatures of God, organisms with built-in needs, sexual beings, or complex computers. Human beings can interpret themselves in any of these ways and many more, and they can, in varying degrees, become any of these things, but to be human is not to be *essentially* any of them. Human being is essentially simply self-interpreting.

We cannot define Dasein's essence by citing a "what" of the kind that pertains to a subject matter, . . . its essence lies rather in the fact that in each case it has its being to be. (32–33) [12]

The "essence" of Dasein lies in its existence. (67) [42]

As we saw in the example of the Japanese baby, human beings begin to exist in Heidegger's special sense of existence only after the first few weeks. They begin to exist as they are socialized into the understanding of what it is to be a human being that is already contained in social practices. In his 1925 lecture, Heidegger notes, "This common world, which is there primarily and into which every maturing Dasein first grows, as the public world, governs every interpretation of the world and of Dasein."[12] But he is not interested in when and how a human organism gets existence as its way of being or in what specific understanding of being it gets. Such questions, about specific cases not general structures, Heidegger calls *existentielle*. Heidegger wants rather to describe the *structure* of the self-interpreting way of being that we, and other entities such as cultures, are. (See Table 1.)

The question about that structure aims at the analysis of what makes up existence. The nexus of such structures we call *"existentiality."* Its analytic has the character of an understanding which is not existentiell, but rather *existential.* (33)[12][13]

In speaking of existence as the self-interpreting way of being in our practices, Heidegger is not equating Dasein and human activity. To avoid this, he sometimes speaks of the Dasein *in* man.[14] Dasein's way of being (existence) is just the self-interpreting aspect of human being. There may be facts about *Homo sapiens* bodies that are the same in all cultures; but each culture has already taken over these facts and given them some specific meaning. Thus, for example, it is a fact that like any other animal, *Homo sapiens* is either male or female. This fact, however, is transformed into a social interpretation of human beings as either *masculine* or *feminine.* In Heidegger's terminology, we can say that *Homo sapiens* can be characterized by *factuality* (e.g., male or female), like any object, but that, because human beings "exist," have Dasein in them, they must be understood in their *facticity* as a gendered way of behaving, e.g., as masculine or feminine.[15]

"Man," I take it, is the name for whatever Dasein takes itself to be and thus is, in any given culture. If, as in ancient Greece, Dasein understands itself in terms of heroes and villains, men and women will be heroes and villains, but if, as in Christian times, Dasein understands itself in terms of saints and sinners, men and women will be not villains or heroes but rather sinners with the potential to be saints. There could be no saints in ancient Greece, not even undiscovered ones. There could at best be weak people who let others walk all over them. And in medieval times, any would-be hero who wanted to be a self-sufficient defender of mankind would at best be a prideful sinner. Each Dasein must understand itself within some culture that has already decided on specific possible ways to be human—on what human beings essentially are.

The most a Dasein can do is "raise its consciousness," that is, clarify the interpretation in the culture. For example, feminists try to become conscious of what it means to be feminine in our culture in order to modify our practices. Heidegger would be sympathetic to, and indeed provides the appropriate ontology for, those who are trying to get clear about what being feminine means. Heidegger would disagree, however, with people like Simone de Beauvoir who think we should get clear about our sex roles and thus get over them and simply be persons. As he puts it:

The everyday way in which things have been interpreted is one into which Dasein has grown in the first instance, with never a possibility of extrication. In it, out of it, and against it, all genuine understanding, interpreting, and communicating, all re-discovering and appropriating anew, are performed. In no case is a Dasein untouched and unseduced by this way in which things have been interpreted. (213) [169]

Dasein can never get clear *about* its facticity, so it can never get clear *of* its facticity and interpret things in a radically new way.

To sum up: *Homo sapiens* has factual characteristics, which constitute its factuality. *Man* is the result of a cultural interpretation; his culturally defined characteristics constitute his facticity. Now we will see that, precisely because Dasein's way of being makes facticity possible, it can never be defined by its facticity.

IV. Dasein as Self-Misinterpreting

Being essentially self-interpreting, Dasein has no nature. Yet Dasein always understands itself as having some specific essential nature. It grounds its actions in its understanding of human nature, and feels at home in belonging to a certain nation or a certain race. Thus Dasein's everyday preontological understanding of its own being necessarily involves a preontological misunderstanding. Understanding itself thus as an object with a fixed essence covers up Dasein's unsettledness and calms the anxiety occasioned by recognizing that Dasein is interpretation all the way down. Dasein's tendency to cover up its own preontological understanding accounts for the traditional misinterpretations of Dasein as some sort of object with a fixed nature. Heidegger calls this motivated misunderstanding "fleeing" and sees the "falling" it produces as an essential structure of human being.

V. Dasein's Three Modes of Existing

One last characteristic of Dasein must be mentioned. Heidegger says that Dasein always belongs to someone. It is owned.

We are ourselves the entities to be analyzed. The being of any such entity is *in each case mine.* (67) [41]

But this cannot mean that each Dasein has a private world of experience. Heidegger's "mineness" must be sharply distinguished from what Husserl calls "the sphere of ownness." When Heidegger describes Dasein as "owned" in a lecture course in 1923, he warns, "Dasein as its own does not mean an isolating relativization to . . . the individual (*solus ipse*), rather 'ownness' is a way of being."[16] Heidegger must do justice to the separatedness of human beings without cutting us off from knowing what is crucial about each other. Therefore my mineness cannot be like my private feelings such as my headache, the kinesthetic feeling of moving my body, or some private sense of who I am. For Heidegger, Dasein's mineness is the public stand it takes on itself—on what it is to be this Dasein— by way of its comportment.

Remember that a culture always takes its interpretation to be human nature. A particular Dasein can take a stand on itself by relating to this public understanding of human nature and its possibilities in three ways: "Dasein has either chosen these possibilities itself, or got itself into them, or grown up in them already" (33) [12]. That is, Dasein can *own up, disown,* or *fail to take a stand* on its unsettling way of being. To start with the last way, Dasein must first, as in the example of the Japanese baby, passively be formed by the public interpretation, since every person, in order to be a person at all, must be socialized into a particular cultural understanding of being. (At this stage, Dasein, which Heidegger later tells us is always anxious about its unsettledness, has presumably not focused its anxiety.) In this mode Dasein has not yet taken a stand on itself—or, better, since "Dasein has always made some sort of decision as to the way in which it is in each case mine" (68) [42], its stand is just what it picks up from the public collective way of not owning up to itself, of covering up its unsettledness.

Second, perhaps at adolescence, when its anxiety comes to be focused on the question, Who am I?, a particular Dasein can "get itself into" the public identities that are offered by its society as a way to flee its unsettledness. Instead of simply accepting passively the social role it grew up in, it actively identifies with some social role such as lawyer, father, or lover or some socially sanctioned identity such as victim or sacrificing mother, which allows it to disown, or cover up, its true self-interpreting structure. What in Erik Erikson's terms would be the resolution of an identity crisis, is for Heidegger only *seeming* to win oneself.

The owned mode, the third way of relating to ones own existence, is the subject of much of Division II of *Being and Time.* (See Appendix.) In this mode Dasein finally achieves individuality by realizing it can never find meaning by identifying with a role. Dasein then "chooses" the social possibilities available to it in such a way as to manifest in the style of its activity its understanding of the groundlessness of its own existence.

Thus Dasein can "'choose' itself and win itself [the third possibility above]; it can also lose itself and never win itself [the first possibility], or only 'seem' to do so [the second possibility]" (68) [42]. Heidegger calls choosing itself or owning up Dasein's authentic (*eigentlich*) way of being, and seeming to choose while disowning, Dasein's inauthentic (*uneigentlich*) way of being. He calls the third mode, in which Dasein exists most of the time, the undifferentiated mode.

We have defined the idea of existence as . . . an understanding ability to be, for which its own being is an issue. But this ability to be, as one which is in each case *mine*, is free either for authenticity or for inauthenticity or for a mode in which neither of these has been differentiated. (275) [232]

The possibility of existing in any one of these three modes is what Heidegger means by mineness. What makes my comportment *my* comportment is that it exhibits a particular stand on what it is to be Dasein—a specific way of owning up to or disowning unsettledness. That is what is most essential about me. Since whether I am fleeing or facing up is manifest in my comportment, what is essential about me is accessible to you. The story that each Dasein is an isolated individual giving meaning *to its own world* and then to other subjects and finally to a shared world is Husserl's and Sartre's account, not Heidegger's.

Division I deals with the undifferentiated mode:

At the outset of our analysis it is particularly important that Dasein should not be interpreted with the differentiated character of some definite way of existing, but that it should be uncovered in the undifferentiated character which it has primarily and usually. This undifferentiated character of Dasein's everydayness is *not nothing*, but a positive phenomenal characteristic of this entity. (69) [43]

By calling this mode "positive," Heidegger suggests that the undifferentiated mode is not inferior or derivative. Even when Heidegger sometimes calls this normal everyday mode of being inauthentic, he does not mean to denigrate it. He is clear about this in his lectures.

While we exist in the everyday, we understand ourselves in an everyday way or, as we can formulate it terminologically, *not authentically* in the strict sense of the word, not . . . from the . . . most extreme possibilities of our own existence, but *inauthentically*, . . . as we are not our own, as we have lost our self in things and human beings while we exist in the everyday. "Not authentically" means: not as we at bottom are *able* to own up to ourselves. Being lost, however, does not have a negative, depreciative significance but means something positive belonging to Dasein itself. . . . This everyday having of self within our factical, existent, passionate merging into things can surely be genuine. (BP, 160)

VI. The Primacy of Dasein

In concluding our discussion of Introduction I, let us summarize the reasoning by which Heidegger reaches the conclusion that the correct way to start the investigation of being is to examine the way of being (existence) of the being that raises the question. There seem to be three steps to the argument, none fully convincing:

1. Heidegger first establishes that it is Dasein who is trying to make sense of being (27)[7], and that in order to raise the question, Dasein must have in its "average understanding" a premonition of the answer.

2. He then says that this average understanding belongs to the essential makeup of Dasein (28)[8], that is, it is definitive of Dasein to take a stand on its being: "Dasein always understands itself in terms of its existence" (33)[12].

3. Heidegger then claims that Dasein's understanding of its being implies an understanding of all modes of being: "Dasein also possesses—as making up its understanding of existence—an understanding of the being of all beings of a character other than its own. Dasein has therefore a third priority as providing the ontico-ontological condition for the possibility of any ontologies" (34)[13]. Thus, by carrying out the existential analytic of Dasein, we are to arrive at a "fundamental ontology." We shall understand how every mode of intelligibility—the being of equipment, of objects, of institutions, of people, etc.—depends upon a fundamental way of being, namely, existence.

Heidegger concludes the first section of his introduction with an interesting comment about the relation of philosophical inquiry to ordinary life. "The question of being is nothing other than the radicalization of an essential tendency-of-being which belongs to

Dasein itself" (35) [16]. Dasein is constantly, in its activities, making sense of itself and everything else. Heidegger, in investigating the question of being, in seeking to understand the understanding of our practices, sees himself as doing thematically what every human being does unawares all the time.

As an investigation of being, this phenomenological interpretation brings to completion, autonomously and explicitly, that understanding of being which belongs already to Dasein and which "comes alive" in any of its dealings with beings. (96) [67]

2

Heidegger's Methodological Introduction

I. Heidegger's Conception of Phenomenology

In Section 7 Heidegger asks, What should someone do who wants to investigate being? His answer is phenomenology. And what is phenomenology? In answering, Heidegger succeeds in taking over Husserl's definition of phenomenology and totally transforming it for his own ends, making "phenomenology" mean exactly the opposite of Husserl's proposed method for spelling out the intentional contents of his own belief system and thereby arriving at indubitable evidence. In Heidegger's hands, phenomenology becomes a way of letting something shared that can never be totally articulated and for which there can be no indubitable evidence show itself.

A. The Phenomenon

The phenomenon in its ordinary conception is what shows itself directly, as when we say that natural science studies natural phenomena. "The bewildering multiplicity of 'phenomena' designated by the words 'phenomenon,' 'semblance,' 'appearance,' 'mere appearance,' cannot be disentangled unless the concept of the phenomenon is understood from the beginning as that which shows itself in itself" (54) [31]. The phenomenon, as something that shows itself, is the necessary condition for all the derivative kinds.

But this commonsense view of the phenomenon in turn presupposes a phenomenological conception. The phenomenon in the phenomenological sense is that which, although unnoticed (unthematized), accompanies and makes possible all that shows itself. "That which already shows itself in the appearance as prior to the 'phenomenon' as ordinarily understood and as accompanying it in every case, can, even though it thus shows itself unthematically, be brought thematically to show itself; and what thus shows itself in itself... will be the 'phenomena' of phenomenology" (54–55) [31]. It may begin to dawn on the attentive reader that Heidegger's phenomenon as understood by phenomenology bears a striking resemblance to what he calls Dasein's preontological understanding of being and the modes of intelligibility it reveals.

B. Logos

Logos means "letting something be seen in its *togetherness* with something—letting it be seen *as* something" (56) [31]. What shows itself to the phenomenologist as the basis of what ordinarily shows itself must be pointed out and laid out in a perspicuous way. Remember, there are no interpretation-free facts for the phenomenologist to describe, neither objective facts nor subjective ones like a system of beliefs, so the phenomenologist must interpret and organize the phenomena to reveal the understanding of being in which he already dwells, which lets anything show up *as* anything.

C. Phenomenology

Heidegger distinguishes three conceptions of phenomenology:

1. The *formal* conception of phenomenology is "to let that which shows itself be seen from itself in the very way in which it shows itself from itself" (58) [34]. This conception is broad enough to embrace both Husserl's and Heidegger's understanding of phenomenology. Even the formal conception, however, excludes deduction, dialectic, and transcendental arguments. It limits phenomenology to a study in which we directly reveal what we are talking about.

2. In the *ordinary* conception of phenomenology, any object may be the proper object of study, and the goal is to bring it as fully before consciousness as possible. "To have a science 'of' phenomena means to grasp its objects in such a way that everything about them which is up for discussion must be treated by exhibiting it directly" (59) [35]. Phenomenology is "concrete demonstration" (359) [311] in that it attempts to show each type of phenomenon in a way that brings forth the best possible evidence for it.

3. The *phenomenological* conception.

(a) Heidegger asks, "What is it that phenomenology is to 'let us see'? What is it that must be called a 'phenomenon' in a distinctive sense?" (59) [35]. And he answers that if phenomenology is letting something show itself, what phenomenology deals with must be something that is not already obvious: "It is something that primarily and usually does not show itself at all; it is something that lies *hidden*, in contrast to that which primarily and usually does show itself, and it [the hidden] belongs to it [that which shows itself] so essentially as to constitute its sense and its ground" (59) [35]. That which is necessarily hidden might be a Kantian thing-in-itself, a sort of thing, like measles, that never shows itself except in its effects. But this cannot be what phenomenology deals with. The subject of phenomenology must be something that does not show itself but can be made to show itself.

A perfect instance of what is concealed but can be revealed is "not just this being or that, but rather the *being* of beings" (59) [35], "that which determines beings as beings, that on the basis of which beings are already understood" (25–26) [6]. That is, the phenomenon par excellence is the modes of intelligibility of entities and the background understanding on the basis of which each sort of being can show up as what it is. "In the phenomenological conception of 'phenomenon' what one has in mind as that which shows itself is the being of beings, its sense, its modifications and derivatives. . . . Only as phenomenology is ontology possible" (60) [35].

(b) How does the phenomenon show itself? Husserl says that phenomenology should study only what can be made fully evident. Heidegger reverses Husserl's understanding of phenomenology on this point. Husserl's method, which aims at *adequate evidence* and complete freedom from prejudice, cannot be used when we wish to understand the background upon which all our understanding takes place. Our understanding of being is so pervasive in everything we think and do that we can never arrive at a clear presentation of it. Moreover, since it is not a belief system but is embodied in our skills, it is not the sort of thing we could ever get clear about.

We can only come to understand what Husserl called the "natural conception of the world," the understanding of the world that comes naturally to us, by looking at more and more aspects of our lives and trying to fit them into a more and more general and unified structure. Thus a phenomenology that wants to be what Husserl called "self-responsible" must give up Husserl's goal, and the goal of philosophy since Plato, of working out a presuppositionless science. Phenomenology, when correctly understood, turns out to be hermeneutic, that is, interpretative. "Our investigation itself will show that the meaning of phenomenological description as a method lies in *interpretation*" (61) [37].

II. Hermeneutics: Heidegger's Two-Stage Approach to the Analysis of Dasein

We have seen how Heidegger takes Husserl's phenomenology and turns it around. We are to investigate not consciousness but Dasein. Our method cannot be the inspection of self-evident meanings in our mind; the understanding of being is not mental, and besides, our understanding of being is covered up. Indeed, "just because the phenomena are . . . for the most part not given, there is need for phenomenology" (60) [36].

There are, Heidegger says, two kinds of covered-upness. The first is simply being *undiscovered* —"neither known nor unknown" (60) [36]. This is the kind of covered-upness we find when we investigate the background of everyday practices. The second is being *buried over.* "This means that [the phenomenon] has at some point been discovered but has deteriorated to the point of getting covered up again" (60) [36]. This is what happens when Dasein senses its unsettledness. Then Dasein attempts to pass off the phenomenon that has covered over the original phenomenon as itself the truth, in effect denying that anything has been covered up. Heidegger calls this cover-up *disguise,* which suggests that the covering up is motivated by not wanting to see the truth. He notes: "This covering up . . . is . . . the most dangerous, for here the possibilities of deceiving and misleading are especially stubborn" (60) [36].

Roughly, Divisions I and II of *Being and Time* are each concerned with one of these two kinds of hidden phenomena: Division I lays bare the obvious and unnoticed, and Division II breaks through to the disguised. According to Heidegger, the *world* and Dasein's absorption in it, the subject of Division I, are so obvious as to be unnoticed in the course of our everyday activity; Dasein's way of being, however, is so unsettling that, just because it is constantly sensed, it is constantly covered up. This unsettling way of being and its disguises are the subject of the first half of Division II.

The two forms of hiddenness also require two different kinds of phenomenological-hermeneutic inquiry. Each of these interpretive techniques has been pioneered by Heidegger and elaborated and applied by contemporary writers who call their work hermeneutic.

A. A Hermeneutics of Everydayness

In Division I Heidegger elaborates what he calls an interpretation of Dasein in its everydayness (38)[16]. The understanding in everyday practices and discourse, overlooked by the practitioners, has become the subject of much recent hermeneutic investigation. Harold Garfinkel[1] in sociology and Charles Taylor[2] in political science, each in a different way, pursue this type of hermeneutic concern. An offshoot of this sort of hermeneutics of the everyday is the application of the same method to other cultures, as in Clifford Geertz's brand of anthropology,[3] or to other epochs in our own culture, as in Thomas Kuhn's application of what he now explicitly calls the hermeneutic method to the understanding of nature presupposed by Aristotelian physics.[4]

Richard Rorty has defined hermeneutics as the attempt to make incommensurate discourses commensurable.[5] Anyone can define hermeneutics any way he or she pleases, but this definition is surely far from the one Heidegger introduced into contemporary philosophy. For Heidegger, hermeneutics begins at home in an interpretation of the structure of everydayness in which Dasein dwells. Heidegger would claim that in several ways, attempts to interpret *alien* discourse and practices, such as we find in Geertz and Kuhn, presuppose a hermeneutics of everydayness. In *On the Way to Language*, he quotes Schleiermacher's remark that hermeneutics is "the art of understanding rightly another man's language," and he notes that "broadened in the appropriate sense [hermeneutics] can mean the theory and methodology for every kind of interpretation." He then adds that "in *Being and Time* the term 'hermeneutics' is used in a *still* broader sense" to mean "the attempt first of all to define the nature of interpretation."[6] Heidegger thus claims to be doing a sort of hermeneutics that lays the basis for all other hermeneutics by showing that human beings *are* a set of meaningful social practices and how these practices give rise to intelligibility and themselves can be made intelligible. Moreover, Heidegger sees that this claim is itself an interpretation. He says that "hermeneutics, used as an adjunct word to 'phenomenology,' does not have its usual meaning, methodology of interpretation, but means the interpretation itself."[7]

Hermeneutic phenomenology, then, is an interpretation of human beings as essentially self-interpreting, thereby showing that interpretation is the proper method for studying human beings. Moreover, Heidegger's account, as we have seen, is supposed to be "transcendental" or, more exactly, existential, since he does not discuss what it means to be a human being in specific cultures or historical periods, but rather attempts by describing everyday life to lay out for us the general, cross-cultural, transhistorical structures of our self-interpreting way of being and how these structures account for all modes of intelligibility.

B. A Hermeneutics of Suspicion

We have already seen that our understanding of our being is never fully accessible since (1) it is embodied in skills and (2) we dwell in our understanding like fish in water. In Division II Heidegger focuses on a third problem: (3) Our understanding of being is distorted. Since everyday Dasein does not want to face up to its own interpretive activity and the consequent unsettledness of human being, it uses its everyday understanding to conceal the truth about itself.

Our being amidst the things with which we concern ourselves most closely in the "world"* . . . guides the everyday way in which Dasein is interpreted, and *covers up ontically* Dasein's authentic being, so that the ontology which is directed toward this entity is denied an appropriate basis. Therefore the primordial way in which this entity is presented as a phenomenon is anything but obvious, even if ontology primarily follows the course of the everyday interpretation of Dasein. (359, my italics) [311]

If Dasein hides from itself the truth about its own being, we cannot directly read off its way of being from its practices. Indeed, since Dasein's understanding of its being is noncognitive, pervasive, and distorted, there is no direct method by which Heidegger can proceed. He can begin only where we are, in the midst of Dasein's (mis)understanding of itself, and describe those aspects of Dasein's activities that are least distorted because they do not directly involve Dasein's making sense of its own being. Dasein must be described "as it is primarily and usually—in its average everydayness" (37–38)[16].

In this conception of phenomenology we can see one of the deep similarities between Heidegger's view of philosophy and Wittgenstein's. In his *Investigations*, Wittgenstein remarks:

The aspects of things that are more important for us are hidden because of their simplicity and familiarity. (One is unable to notice something because it is always before one's eyes.) The real foundations of his enquiry do not strike a man at all. Unless that fact has at some time struck him. And this means: we fail to be struck by what, once seen, is most striking and most powerful.[8]

But for Heidegger this can only be a beginning. Heidegger assumes that his preparatory analysis will yield insights on the basis of which he can then give a more primordial account.

> Our analysis of Dasein . . . is . . . *provisional.* It merely brings out the being of this entity, *without Interpreting its sense.* It is rather a preparatory procedure by which the horizon for the most primordial way of interpreting being may be laid bare. Once we have arrived at that horizon, this preparatory analytic of Dasein will have to be repeated on a higher and authentically ontological basis. (38, second italics mine)[17]

This approach gives special importance to the circular nature of hermeneutic analysis. In general, the so-called hermeneutic circle refers to the fact that in interpreting a text one must move back and forth between an overall interpretation and the details that a given reading lets stand out as significant. Since the new details can modify the overall interpretation, which can in turn reveal new details as significant, the circle is supposed to lead to a richer and richer understanding of the text. As introduced by Heidegger, even in Division I, however, the phenomenological-hermeneutic circle involves a stronger methodological claim: (1) Since we must begin our analysis from within the practices we seek to interpret, our choice of phenomena to interpret is already guided by our traditional understanding of being. (2) Since it deals with what is difficult to notice, this traditional understanding may well have passed over what is crucial, so we cannot take the traditional interpretation at face value. (3) Thus we must be prepared to revise radically the traditional account of objects, subjects, language, space, truth, reality, time, and so on, on the basis of the phenomena revealed by our interpretation.

The job of Division I is thus to call attention to those aspects of everyday activity that that activity itself makes it difficult for us to notice. Division II, however, goes further and does not take even the everyday ontological structures of Dasein revealed in Division I at face value. Rather, it sees them as a motivated masking of a painful truth. Dasein not only *covers up* its unsettling way of being; it uses the commonsense ontology to "close off" access to its structure. As Heidegger says in Division II:

Not only in exhibiting the most elemental structures of being-in-the-world, . . . but also, above all, in analyzing care, death, conscience, and guilt . . . we have shown how in Dasein itself concernful common sense has taken control of Dasein's ability to be and the disclosure of that ability—that is to say, *the closing of it off.* (359, second italics mine) [311]

Heidegger draws the following moral:

Dasein's *kind of being* thus demands that any ontological Interpretation which sets itself the goal of exhibiting the phenomena in their primordiality, should capture the being of this entity, in spite of this entity's own tendency to cover things up. Existential analysis, therefore, constantly has the character of *doing violence* whether to the claims of the everyday interpretation, or to its complacency and its tranquilized obviousness. (359) [311]

Transcendental-hermeneutic phenomenology, then, does not simply seek to lay out the general structure of self-interpreting being; it claims to force into view a substantive truth about human beings. Not only is human being interpretation all the way down, so that our practices can never be grounded in human nature, God's will, or the structure of rationality, but this condition is one of such radical rootlessness that everyone feels fundamentally unsettled (*unheimlich*), that is, senses that human beings can *never* be at home in the world. This, according to Heidegger, is why we plunge into trying to make ourselves at home and secure. Thus the conformist, everyday activities in which human beings seek to give their lives some stable meaning reveal to Heidegger a flight motivated by the preontological understanding each human being has of his or her ultimate ungroundedness.

It is clear that, especially in Division II, Heidegger's method turns into what Paul Ricoeur has called a hermeneutics of suspicion, violently exposing disguises.[9] In any such supposedly motivated distortion, whether one finds the concealed truth in the class struggle as revealed by Marx, or the twists and turns of the libido as uncovered by Freud, some authority who has already unmasked the truth (the Marxist theorist, the psychoanalyst) must lead the self-deluded participant to see it too. In *Being and Time* such an enlightened authority is already present in Dasein's sense of its own condition. Heidegger calls it the voice of conscience. Moreover, in any such case where the truth is repressed, the individual must confirm the truth of the deep interpretation by acknowledging it, and since the real problem is the restrictions erected as defenses against the truth, the participant's acknowledging the truth is supposed to bring some sort of liberation. Marx promises the power released by the realization that one's class is exploited, Freud offers the control gained from recovering the repressed secrets of one's sexuality, and Heidegger claims that the realization that nothing is grounded and that there are no guidelines for living gives Dasein increased openness, tenacity, and even gaiety. (This idea is developed further in the Appendix.)

III. Methodological Problems

Just as hermeneutic phenomenology, in its investigation of intelligibility, cannot start from what is self-evident as Descartes did, so it cannot arrive at what is self-evident, as Hegel claimed to do. When Heidegger gets to the "end" of this analysis in *Being and Time,* he will only have opened up a new background for investigation:

In any investigation in this field, where "the thing itself is deeply veiled" one must take pains not to overestimate the results. For in such an inquiry one is constantly compelled to face the possibility of disclosing an even more primordial and more universal horizon from which we may draw the answer to the question, "What is 'being'?" (49) [26]

But Heidegger is not always true to this insight. The plan of his book was to show that temporality made sense of Dasein's way of making sense and then to show that all other ways of being could be understood in terms of temporality. That would have completed the fundamental ontology promised as Part One of *Being and Time.* "The Interpretation of Dasein in terms of temporality, and the explication of time as *the* transcendental horizon for the question of being" (63, my italics) [39].

Heidegger's hesitation between being open to endless further interpretations and claiming to have found the final horizon is also evident at the end of Division I. There Heidegger asks:

What does it signify that being "is," where being is to be distinguished from every being? One can ask this concretely only if the sense of being and the full scope of the understanding of being have in general been clarified. Only then can one also analyze primordially what belongs to the concept of *a science of being as such,* and to its possibilities and its variations. (272, my italics) [230]

Here Heidegger seems to imply that his fundamental ontology in *Being and Time* will be a *full clarification* of the understanding of being, and even a *science of being as such.* This idea conflicts with the presuppositions of hermeneutics. Likewise, as we shall see, Heidegger's claim that ontology is a "theoretical inquiry" (32) [12] conflicts with this account of theory.

What in fact happened in his later work is just what Heidegger's notion of finding ever more encompassing horizons would lead one to expect. Each horizon for making sense of being turned out to exclude some ways of being. *Being and Time* leaves out the way of being of works of art. When Heidegger includes works of art in "The Origin of the Work of Art," he still leaves out spatial locality, and later he sees that he has not done justice to natural things like trees, which are neither equipment nor objects. Each interpretation accounts for some modes of intelligibility but leaves out others. Indeed, Heidegger never answered his original question concerning the sense of being. The issues raised by asking about our practices of making sense and the ways of being they reveal just kept getting broader and deeper. But Heidegger never gave up his basic idea that were it not for the clearing opened by the understanding of being in language, tradition, and other human practices, we could never encounter beings as beings at all.

3

A Preliminary Sketch of Being-in-the-World

I. Being-In

Heidegger calls the activity of existing, "being-in-the-world." With characteristic precision, in introducing this concept he stresses the importance of approaching this overlooked phenomenon in the right way. He emphasizes that the "being-in" in Dasein's being-in-the-world is not to be thought of as a characteristic of objects spatially located with respect to other objects.

The way of being of objects, understood as isolated, determinate, substances, Heidegger calls *Vorhandenheit*. This term is usually translated "presence-at-hand," but since there is no mention of presence in the German, and since Heidegger rarely makes use of the embedded word for hand, I shall use the translation "occurrentness." The most general characteristics of occurrent objects are called *categories*. Thus:

Being-occurrent "in" something which is likewise occurrent, and being occurrent-along-with in the sense of a definite location-relationship . . . are ontological characteristics which we call *categorial*: they are of such a sort as to belong to beings whose kind of being is not of the character of Dasein. (79) [54]

As we have seen, the most general characteristics of Dasein are called *existentials*.

Because Dasein's characters of being are defined in terms of existentiality, we call them "*existentials*." These are to be sharply distinguished from what we call "*categories*"—characteristics of being for beings whose character is not that of Dasein. (70) [44]

With this terminology in place, Heidegger then calls attention to Dasein's unique way of being-in which is totally different from the way one object can be in another.

Being-in . . . is a state of Dasein's being; it is an existentiale. So one cannot think of it as the being-occurrent of some corporeal thing (such as a human body) "in" a being which is occurrent. (79)[54]

Here, as in several other place in *Being and Time,* Heidegger seems to suggest that having a body does not belong to Dasein's essential structure, although he acknowledges that "This 'bodily nature' hides a whole problematic of its own" (143)[108]. It no doubt follows from the generality of Dasein's way of being as essentially self-interpreting activity that Dasein is not necessarily embodied. As Heidegger says in *The Metaphysical Foundations of Logic,* "The term 'man' was not used for that being which is the theme of the analysis. Instead, the neutral term Dasein was chosen. By this we designate the being for which its own proper mode of being in a definite sense is not indifferent. The peculiar 'neutrality' of the term 'Dasein' is essential, because the interpretation of this being must be carried out prior to every factual concretion" (136). But of course, "Neutral Dasein is never what exists; Dasein exists in each case only in its factical concretion" (137), and, "as factical, Dasein is, among other things, in each case dispersed in a body" (137).

Heidegger gives an illuminating description of the different way objects and people are in the world. This is a good illustration of revealing the phenomenon. We are not given an argument to show that there are several distinct senses of "in," nor is Heidegger doing linguistic analysis. Rather, "in these analyses the issue is one of *seeing* a primordial structure of Dasein's being" (81)[54]. Ordinarily we do not notice what is pointed out by the different senses of many of our prepositions and idioms just because we use them so transparently. Moreover, if we step back and think about the meaning of a preposition like "in," the first sense that comes to mind in detached reflection is the categorial sense, physical inclusion.

When someone calls our attention to the fact that "in" also has an existential sense which expresses *involvement,* as in being in love, being in business, or being in the theater, we tend to think of this as a metaphorical derivation from physical inclusion. This is just what one would expect if Heidegger is right that Dasein always (mis)interprets itself in terms of the objects with which it deals.

[Dasein] has a tendency [to understand its own being] in terms of that being toward which it comports itself primarily and in a way which is essentially constant—in terms of the "world" [the totality of objects]. In Dasein itself, and therefore in its own understanding of being, the way the world is understood is, as we shall show, reflected back ontologically upon the way in which Dasein itself gets interpreted. (36–37, my gloss in the third pair of brackets) [15–16]

Thus Dasein overlooks the directly given and fundamental experience of involvement. Here hermeneutics must call attention to the hidden as the "undiscovered," although there is also a hint that this overlooking is motivated and so results in a "disguise." To combat this tendency to overlook and cover up the phenomenon, Heidegger points out that "in" does not originally mean inclusion. The primordial sense of "in" was, rather, "to reside," "to dwell" (80) [54]. This is supposed to help us get over the idea that the "in" of inclusion, like chalk in a box, is basic.

But, one might well ask, why should these primitive meanings be more illuminating than later ones, since, according to Heidegger, Dasein *always* misunderstands itself in terms of the world? Heidegger would answer that "'primitive phenomena' are often less concealed and less complicated by extensive self-interpretation on the part of the Dasein in question" (76) [51]. The natural distortions of common sense have not been further covered up by philosophical distortions reflected back into everyday language. Thus, for example, in the early stages of our language, the detached and the involved senses of words have not yet separated out. Even now when we speak of being in the theater, we can mean both that someone is spatially in the theater and that the theater plays a crucial role in that person's self-interpretation—or better, we may mean something more simple than either of these alternatives. When we recall that "in" derives from "reside," it jars us out of our assumption that our objective, "literal" sense of "in" is basic.

Not that the metaphorical is supposed to be more basic than the literal, as some now try to argue. Heidegger is more radical than those who point out that metaphors are much more important than people ordinarily realize and that without metaphors like inside/outside that are based on spatial inclusion, as for example inside and outside our bodies, we could not think about more abstract involvement relations.[1] This still assumes that the spatial relation is the basic one from which we imaginatively project the others. On the contrary, Heidegger wants us to see that at an early stage of language the distinction metaphorical/literal has not yet emerged.

Heidegger's specific discussion of the senses of the preposition "in" will be illuminating only to those who know German. We can, however, capture his point in English. In English we also distinguish two senses of "in": a spatial sense ("in the box") and an existential sense ("in the army," "in love"). The first use expresses inclusion, the second conveys involvement. Table 2 illustrates further distinctions along these lines.

Being-in (with a hyphen) is essentially distinguished from *being in* because Dasein takes a stand on itself *by way of being occupied with things*. Being-in as being involved is definitive of Dasein.

From what we have been saying, it follows that being-in is not a "property" which Dasein sometimes has and sometimes does not have, and *without* which it could *be* just as well as it could with it. . . . Dasein is never "primarily" a being which is, so to speak, free from being-in, but which sometimes has the inclination to take up a "relationship" toward the

Table 2
Spatial and existential senses of some prepositions.

	Categorial sense (characterized by indifference)	Existential sense (characterized by concern)
In	In-clusion, being in.	In-volvement, being-in.
	Spatial inclusion ("She is in the house.")	Personal involvement ("He is in love." "She is in a good mood." "He is in business.")
	Logical inclusion, class membership ("She is in the working class [socioeconomically].")	Self-defining involvement, being-in-a-class ("He is in the working class [and class-conscious, in the sense of understanding himself in that role].")
At	"He is at work (at his place of work)."	"She is at (her) work (in the sense of being occupied by it)."
By	"He stood by (beside) his sister."	She stood by (remained faithful to) her brother."
To	"She turned to (turned to face) her friend."	"He turned (for help) to his friend."

world. Taking up relationships toward the world is possible only *because* Dasein, as being-in-the-world, is as it is. (84)[57]

Heidegger notes that, strictly speaking, objects cannot touch each other because they cannot encounter each other. (Here the use of "touch" for objective contact is, indeed, metaphorical.) We can make this distinction in English by noting that we have two senses of the word "touch." *Objects* can touch in the sense of physical contact (a metaphorical sense), but they cannot touch each other in the sense of mattering to each other (a literal sense). *Dasein* alone can be touched, that is, moved, by objects and other Daseins.

Heidegger adds that there are two ways in which Dasein itself can be treated like an object. One is that Dasein can be "occurrent 'in' the world, or, more exactly, can with some right and within certain limits be *taken* as merely occurrent" (82) [55]. Here again, Heidegger seems to be referring obliquely to Dasein's body.

The fact that "Dasein" can be taken as something which is occurrent and just occurrent is not to be confused with a certain way of '"occurrentness" which is Dasein's own. This latter kind of occurrentness becomes accessible not by disregarding Dasein's specific structures but only by understanding them in advance. Dasein understands its ownmost being in the sense of a certain "factual occurrentness." (82)[55–56]

This latter way has to do with Dasein's *facticity*. Not only is Dasein's activity conditioned by cultural interpretations of facts about its body, such as being male or female, but since Dasein must define itself in terms of social roles that require certain activities, and since its roles require equipment, Dasein is at the mercy of factual events and objects in its environment. "It has been delivered over to beings which it needs in order to be able to be as it is" (416) [364].

The concept of "facticity" implies that an "intraworldly" being has being-in-the-world in such a way that it can understand itself as bound up in its "destiny" with the being of those beings which it encounters within its own world. (82)[56]

The most important kind of being-in is *sein-bei*, which is very badly translated as "being alongside." The resulting phrase, "being-alongside-the-world," is as far from Heidegger as one can get, since Dasein is in-the-world, not next to it or outside it. Heidegger says directly: "There is no such thing as the 'side-by-side-ness' of an entity called 'Dasein' with another entity called 'world'" (81) [55].

But one cannot translate *sein-bei* as being-at-home, as would be most natural, since Heidegger holds that Dasein is *unheimlich*, that is, never truly at home in the world. I shall therefore translate *sein-bei* as *being-amidst.*

What Heidegger is getting at is a mode of being-in we might call "inhabiting." When we inhabit something, it is no longer an object for us but becomes part of us and pervades our relation to other objects in the world. Both Heidegger and Michael Polanyi call this way of being-in "dwelling." Polanyi points out that we dwell in our language; we feel at home in it and relate to objects and other people through it. Heidegger says the same for the world. Dwelling is Dasein's basic way of being-in-the-world. The relation between me and what I inhabit cannot be understood on the model of the relation between subject and object.

II. Heidegger's Critique of the Traditional Priority of Disinterested Knowledge

Traditional philosophy has, since the time of Plato, maintained that knowledge is gained by means of detached, disinterested inquiry. Since Descartes, the results of such detached inquiries are supposed to have consequences concerning the nature of the subject and object of knowledge, not just in these special circumstances but for the whole range of human activities. According to the tradition, we can, of course, pay attention to our involvement, as Heidegger is doing in *Being and Time*, and we then may find we are being-in. If, however, we step back from involved activity and become reflective, detached observers, we cannot help seeing ourselves as subjects contemplating objects. The whole array of philosophical distinctions between inner subjective experience and the outer object of experience, between perceiving and the perceived, and between appearance and reality arise at this point, and "it becomes the 'evident' point of departure for problems of epistemology or the 'metaphysics of knowledge'" (86) [59]. Only by exposing the derivative character of the detached, reflective stance, Heidegger holds, can we see the limits of subjective consciousness and the objects it knows.

To break out of the epistemological tradition, we must begin with everyday involved phenomena and then see where consciousness and its intentional content fit in. Heidegger holds that human *experience* (*Erfahrung*) discloses the world and discovers entities in it—and yet this does not entail the traditional conclusion that human beings relate to objects by means of their *experiences* (*Erlebnisse*), that is, by way of mental states. This view defies common sense and a long philosophical tradition.

> Being-amidst as existential is of course itself a problem. It is a problem precisely because of the seeming self-evidence of the premise of a subject-object relation. It is remarkable that the problem addressed by this claim cannot be budged. It is as old as philosophy and appears already in Parmenides. The view developed early and easily in the pre-philosophical understanding of Dasein that the soul, thinking and representing, consciousness, establishes a relationship to objects, or put conversely, that entities occur before and lie opposite to thinking, seeing, and representing. (MFL, 130)

Heidegger's opposition to this traditional view has much in common with that of Michael Polanyi[2] and Thomas Kuhn.[3] All three thinkers claim that the theoretical, disinterested knowledge that is correctly described in subject/object terms and has been held up as the best example of knowledge for the last 2500 years presupposes a practical and involved "know-how" that cannot be accounted for in terms of theoretical knowledge. According to these thinkers, theoretical knowledge depends on practical skills. (This, of course, does not imply that the objects discovered in theoretical reflection depend on these skills, although Kuhn, unlike Heidegger, seems to draw this conclusion.)[4]

A. Heidegger's Critique of Intentionality

The fundamental difference between Heidegger and the tradition of disinterested inquiry that culminates in Husserl is obvious in the sort of examples each chooses. Husserl talks, like Kant, about the mental "syntheses" required when, in the course of a lecture, he walks around a die and receives a succession of visual experiences of it.[5] It is on the basis of these syntheses that he perceives the die as an enduring object, and only then can he give it the meaning "something to throw." This shows, Husserl claims, that perception and action necessarily involve mental activity.

Heidegger's examples start with involved acting in the world, using things such as hammers and doorknobs. Heidegger seeks to demonstrate that what is thus revealed is exactly the opposite of what Descartes and Husserl claim. Rather than first perceiving perspectives, then synthesizing the perspectives into objects, and finally assigning these objects a function on the basis of their physical properties, we ordinarily manipulate tools that already have a meaning in a world that is organized in terms of purposes. To see this, we must first overcome the traditional interpretation that theory is prior to practice. Only then will we be ready to describe our involved, practical dealings with things and what they reveal. This requires a new phenomenological approach.

Those beings which serve phenomenologically as our preliminary theme—in this case, those which are used . . . become accessible when we put ourselves into the position of concerning ourselves with them in some way. Taken strictly, this talk about "putting ourselves into such a position" is misleading; for the kind of being which belongs to such concernful dealings is not one into which we need to put ourselves first. This is the way in which everyday Dasein always *is*: when I open the door, for instance, I use the doorknob. The achieving of phenomenological access to the beings which we encounter, consists rather in thrusting aside our interpretative tendencies, which keep thrusting themselves upon us and running along with us, and which conceal not only the phenomenon of such "concern," but even more those beings themselves *as* encountered of their own accord *in* our concern with them. (96) [67]

An extreme version of the attitude Heidegger is opposing appears in Sartre's novel *Nausea*, where the main character, Roquentin, succumbs to traditional "disinterestedness" to the point of psychosis. As he does so, Roquentin perceives a doorknob—Sartre's example too—as a cold, metal object pressing the palm of his hand. Sartre thinks (like Descartes and Husserl) that through his extreme detachment his hero is getting back to the pure perception of the basic being of things.

Heidegger would agree with Sartre that pure disinterestedness is an abnormal state, but he would give a completely different analysis of the philosophical significance of Sartre's case study. For Heidegger, unlike Descartes, Husserl, and Sartre, the object of mere staring, instead of being that which really is, is an impoverished residue of the equipment we directly manipulate. The bare objects of pure disinterested perception are not basic things we can subsequently use, but the debris of our everyday practical world left over when we inhibit action.

It looks like Heidegger thus inverts the tradition and sees detached contemplation as a privative modification of everyday involvement. He seems to be saying that the detached, meaning-giving, knowing subject that is at the center of Husserlian phenomenology must be replaced by an embodied, meaning-giving, *doing* subject. But if one simply inverts the tradition, one risks being misunderstood and reappropriated. Indeed, Dagfinn Føllesdal has been led to underestimate Heidegger's originality at just this point. In an article on the role of action in Husserl and Heidegger, he interprets Heidegger as holding that Husserl overemphasized detached contemplation, and he agrees with what he takes to be Heidegger's claim that embodied practical activity is the basic way subjects give meaning to objects.

It has commonly been held that practical activity presupposes theoretical understanding of the world. . . . Heidegger rejects this. He regards our practical ways of dealing with the world as more basic than the theoretical. . . . This idea of Heidegger's that all our human activity plays a role in our constitution of the world, and his analyses of how this happens, I regard . . . as Heidegger's main contribution to philosophy.[6]

Føllesdal reports that "after he came to Freiburg in 1916, in the late teens and especially in the early twenties, Husserl clearly became more and more aware that our practical activity is an important part of our relation to the world. . . . There is, according to Husserl, 'an infinite chain of goals, aims, and tasks' that our actions and their products relate to."[7] Føllesdal tries to determine who deserves credit for this new interest in the phenomenology of practical activity: "Husserl had ideas similar to those of Heidegger long before *Being and Time* was published. These ideas started appearing in Husserl shortly after he arrived in Freiburg and met Heidegger in 1916. It is possible that Husserl influenced Heidegger in this 'practical' direction. . . . However, it is also possible that it was Husserl who was influenced in this direction through his discussion with the younger Heidegger."[8]

Once one sees the depth of Heidegger's difference from Husserl and the tradition, however, one sees that Føllesdal's question, although interesting, is irrelevant. The real issue concerns intentionality. As used by Franz Brentano and then Husserl, "intentionality" names the fact that mental states such as perceiving, believing, desiring, fearing, and intending in its ordinary sense are always about something, that is, directed at some object under some description, whether that extramental object exists or not. The mental property that makes this directedness possible is called the representational or intentional content of the mental state. By focusing his discussion on the relative importance of involved action and disinterested contemplation, Føllesdal overlooks Heidegger's more radical point that the traditional account of both these ways of relating to the world presupposes but overlooks a more fundamental sort of intentionality.

Being-in is something quite different from a mere confrontation, whether by way of observation or by way of action; that is, it is not the being-occurrent-together of a subject and an object. (221, my italics) [176]

Heidegger does not want to make practical activity primary; he wants to show (pace Husserl) that neither practical activity nor contemplative knowing can be understood as a relation between a self-sufficient mind and an independent world. Føllesdal's failure to focus on Heidegger's true originality is natural, however, since Heidegger does argue that the involved stance and what it reveals is in some sense prior to the detached stance and what it reveals—that, as he puts it in the title of Section 13, knowing the world is a founded mode of being-in. Knowing is an exemplary subject/object relation, so that if one makes knowing basic, one is from the start locked into the intentionalistic picture of human beings as subjects with beliefs (justified and unjustified) about objects and states of affairs. Heidegger's strategy is first to reverse the usual priorities. But this *reversal* of the priority of knowing over doing only clears the ground for the *phenomenological* question: what is the way of being of intentionality?

Essentially the person exists only in the performance of intentional acts . . . . What, however, is the ontological meaning of "performance"? (73) [48]

The traditional view of practice, from Descartes on at least, is representational. Contemporary philosophers such as John Searle and Donald Davidson, who do not agree on much, do agree that action must be explained in terms of beliefs and desires, that is, mental states causing bodily movements. Heidegger's attempt to break out of the tradition is focused in his attempt to get beyond the subject/object distinction in all domains, including action. In a lecture he says, "My essential intention is to first pose the problem [of the subject/object relation] and work it out in such a way that the essentials of the entire Western tradition will be concentrated in the simplicity of a basic problem" (MFL, 132). The focal problem is thus not which kind of intentionality—theoretical or practical—is more basic, but how to get beyond the traditional account of intentionality altogether.

Already in his 1925 lectures—two years before *Being and Time*—Heidegger questions the traditional account of intentionality in order to go beyond it to undermine the priority of the subject/object relation in all its forms:

Intentionality is not an ultimate explanation of the psychic but an initial approach toward overcoming the uncritical application of traditionally defined realities such as the psychic, consciousness, continuity of lived experience, reason. (HCT, 47)

Everything, then, turns on Heidegger's critique of Husserl's theory of intentionality. As Heidegger says:

Here again we have a term and concept taken so much for granted that no one lingers with it for long and, even in a preparatory stage, assumes it is the solution to the problem, as if it were surely the key to all doors. On the contrary, we should make what is itself meant by the term into the problem. (MFL, 132)

Heidegger's objection is not that the theory of intentionality inserts a picture in the mind that comes between the subject and the object. Husserl explicitly rejected this view. To understand the issue focused around intentionality, one must know that early Husserl, like Searle, has a minimal notion of representation and intentional content. The mind is not directed toward some special object in it that in turn mirrors an object in the world. Speaking of intentional content is meant to capture the fact that perceptions, beliefs, desires, intentions, and so on can all be directed toward the same object under the same aspect. For example, I can *perceive* that I am driving to work, *believe* that I am driving to work, *desire* that I be driving to work, *intend* to be driving to work, and so on.

Heidegger sees, however, that such an account already introduces the subject/object distinction. It allows the separation of an intentional content that is mental from an objective world that may or may not be the way the mind takes it to be. Husserl defined phenomenology as the study of the intentional content remaining in the mind after the bracketing of the world.[9] Heidegger accepts intentional directedness as essential to human activity, but he denies that intentionality is mental, that it is, as Husserl (following Brentano) claimed, the distinguishing characteristic of *mental states.*

The usual conception of intentionality . . . misconstrues the structure of the self-directedness-toward, the intention. This misinterpretation lies in *an erroneous subjectivizing* of intentionality. An ego or subject is supposed, to whose so-called sphere intentional experiences are then supposed to belong. . . . The idea of a subject which has intentional experiences merely inside its own sphere and is . . . encapsulated within itself is an absurdity which misconstrues the basic ontological structure of the being that we ourselves are. (BP, 63–64)

To get the ontology right Heidegger introduces his own term for the way human beings relate to things, *Verhalten*, translated as "comportment."

Comportments have the structure of directing-oneself-toward, of being-directed-toward. Annexing a term from Scholasticism, phenomenology calls this structure *intentionality.* (BP, 58, first italics mine)

Heidegger uses "comportment" to refer to our directed activity, precisely because the term has no mentalistic overtones. He points out that the whole machinery of the mental is a construction of the theorist, not the result of phenomenological description. He thus takes comportment or intentionality as characteristic not merely of acts of consciousness, but of human activity in general. Intentionality is attributed not to *consciousness* but to *Dasein.*

Because the usual separation between a subject with its immanent sphere and an object with its transcendent sphere—because, in general, the distinction between an inner and an outer—is constructive and continually gives occasion for further constructions, we shall in the future no longer speak of a subject, of a subjective sphere, but shall understand the being to whom intentional comportments belong as *Dasein*, and indeed in such a way that it is precisely with the aid of *intentional comportment*, properly understood, that we attempt to characterize suitably the being of Dasein. (BP, 64)

Heidegger points out that Husserl's introduction of intentional content—an ideal structure that is supposed to be neither physical nor psychical—in order to explain the directedness of the mind and bridge the gap between subject and object, gives rise to more problems than it solves.

The more unequivocally one maintains that knowing is proximally and really "inside" and indeed has by no means the same kind of being as entities which are physical or psychical, the more one believes that one is presuppositionlessly making headway in the question of the essence of knowledge and in the clarification of the relationship between subject and object . . . [But] no matter how this inner sphere may get interpreted, if one does no more than ask how knowing makes its way "out of" it and achieves "transcendence," it becomes evident that the knowing which presents such enigmas will remain problematical unless one has previously clarified how it is and what it is. (87) [60-61]

Heidegger is thus clear that the priority of knowing in Husserl cannot simply be supplemented by action. Rather, the whole idea of transcending from the inner to the outer must be revised. Heidegger criticizes the traditional account of everyday intentionality, what he calls "ontic transcendence," for overlooking a more basic way of being.

We must . . . make intentionality itself into a problem. Intentionality is indeed related to beings themselves and, in this sense, is an ontic transcending comportment, but it does not primordially constitute this relating-to but is founded in a being-amidst beings. This being-amidst is, in its intrinsic possibility, in turn grounded in existence. In this way the limitations of the earlier interpretation and function of the concept of intentionality become clear, as does its fundamental significance. (MFL, 134)

Heidegger holds that all relations of mental states to their objects presuppose a more basic form of being-with-things which does not involve mental activity.

Intentionality belongs to the existence of Dasein . . . . To exist then means, among other things, to be as relating to oneself by comporting with beings. It belongs to the nature of Dasein to exist in such a way that it is always already with other beings. (BP, 157)

Heidegger's way of understanding Dasein enables him to see why in the tradition knowledge was mistakenly taken as basic, and why even action was interpreted as a kind of knowledge.

[Existence] not only brings a modification of the traditional concept of consciousness and of mind; the radical formulation of the intended phenomenon in an ontology of Dasein leads to a fundamental, "universal" overcoming of this position. From there the previous concept of intentionality proves to be a restricted conception. . . . Because of this restriction, intentionality is conceived primarily as "to take as" [as mean-ing-giving].... Thus *every act of directing oneself toward something receives the characteristic of knowing*, for example, in Husserl. (MFL, 134, my italics and my gloss in the second brackets)

The above quotation shows that in his lectures, a year after the publication of *Being and Time*, Heidegger feels he needs to explain that what he was getting at in Sections 12 and 13 goes far beyond reversing the priority of knowing and doing. It is worth quoting his new interpretation of these misleading sections at length since it is, in effect, Heidegger's most explicit account of the fundamental point of Division I of *Being and Time.*

Underneath the entire earlier problem of the "relation" of "subject" to "object" is the undiscussed problem of *transcendence*. ... The problem of transcendence as such is not at all identical with the problem of inten-tionality. As ontic transcendence, the latter is itself only possible on the basis of originary transcendence, on the basis of being-in-the-world. This primal transcendence makes possible every intentional relation to beings. ... The relation is based on a preliminary understanding of the being of beings. This understanding-of-being first secures the possibility of beings manifesting themselves as beings. (MFL, 135)

One of the main preparatory tasks of *Being and Time* is to bring this "re-lation" radically to light in its originary essence ... (cf. Sections 12 and 13 as the first introductory characterizations). (MFL, 131)

Heidegger returns again later in these lectures to these same sections of *Being and Time.* By calling attention to what is more basic than all intentional states whether they represent the world as it is (belief) or as one wants it to be (desire), he tries to avert the Husserl/Føllesdal misunderstanding that he is simply reversing the priority of theoretical to practical intentionality.

The central task in the ontology of Dasein is to go back behind those divisions into comportments to find their common root, a task that need not, of course, be easy. [Originary] transcendence precedes every possible mode of activity in general, prior to *noesis* [belief], but also prior to *orexis* [desire]. (MFL, 183)

Or, as he put it in his 1927 lectures:

In whatever way we conceive of knowing, it is ... a *comportment toward beings.* ... But all practical-technical commerce with beings is also a comport-ment toward beings. ... In all comportment toward beings—whether it is specifically cognitive, which is most frequently called theoretical, or whether it is practical-technical—an understanding of being is already involved. For a being can be encountered by us *as* a being only in the light of the understanding of being. (BP, 275)

Thus by 1928 the full import of Heidegger's rejection of *all* purely mentalistic forms of intentionality is fully explicit, as is his justification for beginning with what misleadingly seems like a reversal of priority between two subject/object relations, knowing and acting.

Inasmuch as Dasein exists qua being-in-the-world, it is already out there with beings; and even this manner of speaking is still imprecise since "already out there" presupposes Dasein is at some point on the inside. Even if I say, Dasein's intentional activity is always already open towards beings and for beings, there is still at bottom the supposition that it was once closed. What we mean by transcendence cannot be made compatible with the previous formulations of it and is very difficult to see, in light of the usual deadlocked version of the problem. Neither Bergson . . . nor Husserl sees the problem and the phenomenon. . . . We are required to try to clarify this basic make-up, first of all, by proceeding from the traditional concept of the epistemological subject-object relation. Thus the investigation in *Being and Time*, after the exposition and first chapter, begins with: "Being-in-the-world in general as the basic make-up of Dasein" and Sections 12 and 13 present an outline and a first acquaintance with the phenomenon. (MFL, 167)

The moral of Sections 12 and 13, then, is supposed to be that if we start with intentional states, whether receptive or active, even with tacit or prereflective mental states, we shall distort the phenomenon of everyday coping and be led back into all the old epistemological problems. Thus, before raising the question of the ontological and phenomenological status of consciousness, one must reinterpret Dasein's everyday way of being-in. Heidegger's analysis of the natural situation of everyday activities is meant to show that the traditional epistemic situation of a mind distinct from objects, *whether observing or acting upon them*, is a deficient mode of being-in-the-world and cannot, therefore, have the broad philosophical implications modern philosophers of mind have supposed.

B. The Contemporary Relevance of Heidegger's Critique

Before we can fully appreciate the difficulty of Heidegger's project and decide whether he succeeds, we have to sharpen as much as possible the Husserlian intentional theory of mind that he opposes. Just how is the subject/object distinction supposed to be built into all ways of relating to the world, whether they are knowing or acting? Since Heidegger focuses on action as the area in which it is easiest to see that our experience need not involve a mind/world split, I shall concentrate on an account of action. Since Husserl never worked out a theory of action, however, I shall turn to John Searle, who defends a detailed and convincing formulation of the intentionalist account Heidegger opposes. In order to appreciate the power and originality of Heidegger's attack on mentalistic intentionality, on which everything else turns, I must first spell out Searle's formulation of the way the mind/world split is built into the experience of acting.

It is generally agreed among analytic philosophers that our commonsense concepts of perception and action are causal concepts. Paul Grice showed that our concept of perception requires that we have an experience that is caused in the right way by the object perceived.[10] In the parallel case of acting, Searle and Davidson agree that our concept of an action is likewise causal—that an action is a bodily movement that has been caused in the right way by a mental state. Davidson thinks that it must be caused by a belief and a desire; Searle holds a more minimal view, claiming only that it must be caused by an intention.

Searle distinguishes two types of intentions that cause actions: prior intentions and intentions in action. As their names suggest, the prior intention is formed prior to the action, whereas the intention in action is simply concurrent with the action. Searle writes: "Actions thus necessarily contain intentions in action, but are not necessarily caused by prior intentions."[11] Spontaneous actions (jumping up and pacing while thinking is Searle's favorite example) do not involve forming a prior intention but must nonetheless be caused by an intention in action. Searle argues that both the prior intention and the intention in action are causally self-referential, in that they include in their conditions of satisfaction the requirement that the intention cause its conditions of satisfaction. (Conditions of satisfaction for Searle define what counts as the success of an intentional state, that is, what counts as a desire's being satisfied, an assertion's being true, a perception's being veridical, etc.) In the case of action, the conditions of satisfaction are more than that a certain bodily movement be performed. If the conditions of satisfaction *happen*, that is, if the body moves, but this is not *caused* in the right way, the intention has not been satisfied. Self-referentiality refers to the inclusion of the causal requirement that the intention cause the movement in the content of the intention itself. In short, an action is a bodily movement caused by my intention to perform it.

According to Searle, the intention in action is the experience of acting—what William James calls "the feeling of effort." James says:

> That we *have* a feeling of effort there can be no doubt. Popular language has sufficiently consecrated the fact by the institution of the word effort, and its synonyms exertion, striving, straining. The difference between a simply passive sensation, and one in which the elements of volition and attention are found, has also been recorded by popular speech in the difference between such verbs as to see and to look; to hear and to listen; to smell and to scent; to feel and to touch.[12]

On Searle's analysis, all acting is accompanied by an experience of acting, and this experience of effort has as its intentional content that it is causing my bodily movement. The mental experience of acting and the physical movement belong to totally separate domains. I can have the experience of acting even if I am deluded— for example, paralyzed—and the bodily movement is not taking place. Thus, according to Searle, the distinction between mind and world, between subject and object, is built directly into both the concept of action and the phenomenology of acting.

As we have seen, James associates attention, volition, and effort (Searle's experience of acting). We do often experience ourselves as attentive subjects and our conscious effort as causing our actions. Indeed, Heidegger would grant that the philosophical tradition has built self-referentiality into our concept of consciousness. In a seminar he asks, "Where does consciousness begin in philosophy?" And he answers, "With Descartes every consciousness of something is at the same time self-consciousness. . . . There is no consciousness without self-consciousness, which does not mean the self must become thematic. This is the universal structure of representation in Husserl's sense of consciousness of something."[13] Heidegger might well grant, too, that James and Searle have given an accurate description of the self-referential experience of deliberate action, and that a formal account of the intentional content of such an experience, as provided by Searle, for example, is a legitimate area of phenomenological analysis. Heidegger acknowledges that one can describe self-referential consciousness as Husserl does in his phenomenology:

The kind of "giving" we have here is the mere, formal, reflective awareness of the "I"; and perhaps what it gives is indeed evident. This insight even affords access to a phenomenological problematic in its own right, which has in principle the signification of providing a framework as a "formal phenomenology of consciousness." (151)[115]

But he hastens to ask, "Is it then obvious a priori that access to Dasein must be gained only by mere reflective awareness of the 'I' of actions?" (151)[115]

Certainly, such self-referential consciousness is not the subject matter of *Being and Time.* According to Heidegger, such consciousness is a special mode of revealing and a derivative one at that. Not all human activity is deliberate, and therefore not all activity is caused by a self-referential mental state. Nietzsche saw the same phenomenon:

We could think, feel, will, and remember, and we could also "act" in every sense of that word, and yet none of all this would have to "enter our consciousness" (as one says metaphorically). The whole of life would be possible, without, as it were, seeing itself in a mirror. Even now, for that matter, by far the greatest portion of our life actually takes place without this mirror effect; and this is true even of our thinking, feeling, and willing life.[14]

Yet, as Searle points out, there seems to be some sort of self-awareness in action since, if one is stopped and questioned while acting in a nondeliberate way, one can still say what one is doing. Searle claims that this shows that even in such nondeliberate activity our movements are being guided by a self-referential intention in action. Heidegger, like Wittgenstein, would no doubt respond that the ability to say what we are doing only shows a retroactive rationalization of our ongoing activity. It need not be based on the inspection of an internal mental cause. (See the exposition of Heidegger's discussion of the "toward-which" of activity in chapter 4.)

Notice that in trying to explain Heidegger, I have had to speak of *activity* rather than *action*, since Heidegger may well hold that the subject/object account of *action*, which is self-evident to common sense, does require that the movements that constitute the action be performed intentionally. Heidegger, however, is trying not to explicate our commonsense concept of action but to make a place for a sort of *comportment*, as he calls it, that has been overlooked both by common sense and a fortiori by the philosophical tradition. The tradition has been concerned either with explaining deliberate action (Aristotle) or with assigning moral responsibility (Kant). Such concerns lead either to a focus on the beliefs and desires leading to action (Davidson) or to the intention in action (Searle). Heidegger, however, wants to work out an account of everyday, nondeliberate, ongoing coping. In letting such comportment show itself as it is in itself, Heidegger has to free himself not only from the tradition but from our commonsense focus on deliberate action. As Heidegger says:

The most dangerous and stubborn prejudices relative to the understanding of intentionality are not the explicit ones in the form of philosophical theories but the implicit ones that arise from the natural apprehension and interpretation of things by the Dasein's everyday "good sense." These latter misinterpretations are exactly the ones that are least noticeable and hardest to repulse. (BP, 59)

Heidegger holds that the commonsense concept of action and consciousness misses the structure of our most basic mode of comportment. In opposition to the tradition, Heidegger wants to show that we are not normally thematically conscious of our ongoing everyday activity, and that where thematic self-referential consciousness does arise, it presupposes a nonthematic, non-self-referential mode of awareness.

In his critique of Kant's account of perception Heidegger suggests in *Basic Problems* that perception too is not self-referential in Grice's sense but is based on a non-self-referential openness to the world. Just as action absorbed in the world does not involve an experience of acting, a mental state self-referentially causing a bodily movement, so, perception does not involve a visual experience: I am simply fascinated by and drawn into the spectacle of the world. He remarks that "Perceivedness . . . is in a certain way objective, in a certain way subjective, and yet neither of the two" (BP, 314). It is Dasein's openness onto the world that makes possible the derivative experience of looking or trying to see, as for example in the extreme case of an eye examination, which could, perhaps, be described as involving a private visual experience caused by an object.[15]

Being and Time seeks to show that much of everyday activity, of the human way of being, can be described without recourse to deliberate, self-referential consciousness, and to show how such everyday activity can disclose the world and discover things in it without containing any explicit or implicit experience of the separation of the mental from the world of bodies and things.

The task of bringing to light Dasein's existential makeup leads first of all to the twofold task, intrinsically one, of *interpreting more radically the phenomena of intentionality and transcendence.* With this task—of bringing to view, along with the more originary conception of intentionality and transcendence, a basic determination of Dasein's whole existence—we also run up against a central problem that has remained unknown to all previous philosophy. (BP, 162)

Heidegger will seek to show that (1) intentionality without self-referential mental content is characteristic of the unimpeded mode of Dasein's everyday activity, whereas mental-state intentionality is a derivative mode, and (2) both these modes of directedness (ontic transcendence) presuppose being-in-the-world, a more originary transcendence.

It will turn out that intentionality is founded in Dasein's transcendence and is possible solely for this reason—that transcendence cannot conversely be explained in terms of intentionality. (BP, 162).

We can now understand why at the end of Section 13 Heidegger claims that "in knowing, Dasein achieves a new *being-stance* toward a world which has already been discovered in [sic] Dasein" (90, translation corrected) [62]. Here the word "in" must, of course, be understood not as though the world were to be found as an internal representation "inside" Dasein, but rather in the sense that the world is discovered in the everyday activity of Daseining, of being-there—in the activity called existing which is Dasein's way of being-in.

4

Availableness and Occurrentness

In approaching Chapter III it is important to keep in mind that for Heidegger there are two basic questions: (1) Which mode of being, that of mere objects or that of equipment, makes the other intelligible? and (2) What way of being makes possible *every* type of encountering, including encountering both objects and equipment? We shall see that Heidegger not only inverts the traditional interpretation that the disinterested attitude and the entities it reveals are more basic than the interested attitude and the entities it reveals, but he also changes the ontological question itself. It is no longer a question of which sorts of entities can be built up out of which other sorts of entities. This question makes sense only if ontology is a question of reduction, which assumes that entities are reducible to some basic substance or building blocks. Heidegger calls this whole traditional problematic into question. He describes two modes of being, which he calls availableness and occurrentness, and two modes of comportment, dealing with (*Umgang*) and cognition (*Erkennen*), that reveal them. He then asks which mode of being and which mode of comportment is directly intelligible to us and in what sense the other mode is a modification of the one which is most readily intelligible. But, even more basically, he points to a way of being called existing which accounts for *both* these ways of encountering beings and their priority relations.

The mode of argument will have to change along with the questions. Heidegger does not expect to prove his theses and thereby overcome the traditional subject/object distinction, or its more recent variations such as the internalist/externalist debate concerning meaning. "An analytic does not do any proving at all by the rules of the 'logic of consistency'" (363) [315]. But he does not think his inability to provide proofs results in a standoff, such as, for example, John Searle and Donald Davidson confronting each other over whether to do philosophy from a first-person, subjective or a third-person, objective perspective. Heidegger proposes to get out of this traditional Cartesian confrontation by focusing on the more basic way of being that he calls existence. He will seek to show that the traditional picture is prima facie implausible and will sketch out an alternative, viz. that subjects and objects can be understood only in terms of being-in-the-world. This alternative is to be "concretely demonstrated" (359) [311].

Heidegger proposes to demonstrate that the situated use of equipment is in some sense prior to just looking at things and that what is revealed by use is ontologically more fundamental than the substances with determinate, context-free properties revealed by detached contemplation. (This is the subject of this chapter.) But to see why the traditional model of self-sufficient subjects related to self-sufficient objects by means of mental content is never appropriate we need to look more deeply. Thus, Heidegger seeks to *supplant* the tradition by showing that the ways of being of equipment *and* substances, and of actors *and* contemplators, presuppose a background understanding of being—originary transcendence or being-in-the-world. (See chapter 5.)

To begin with, we need to recall that the stand Dasein takes on itself, its existence, is not some inner thought or experience; it is the way Dasein acts. (What makes a Japanese baby a *Japanese* baby is first and foremost what it does and how things show up for it, and only derivatively its thoughts, assuming it has any.) Dasein takes a stand on itself through its involvement with things and people.

In everyday terms, we understand ourselves and our existence by way of the activities we pursue and the things we take care of. (BP, 159) To exist then means, among other things, *relating to oneself by being with beings.* (BP, 157)

So Heidegger begins his phenomenological account of Dasein by turning to the beings with which Dasein is involved and the way in which it is involved with them.

I. Absorbed Intentionality as Prior to Representational Intentionality

A. Equipment—The Available
Since we cannot take the traditional account of subjects knowing objects for granted as the basis for our investigation of being-in-the-world, we must look instead at what we do in our everyday concernful coping.

The being of those beings which we encounter as closest to us can be exhibited phenomenologically if we take as our clue our everyday being-in-the-world, which we also call our *"dealings"* in the world and with intraworldly beings. (95) [66–67]

It is this mode of everyday coping which is constantly closest to us. "The kind of dealing which is closest to us is . . . not a bare perceptual cognition, but rather that kind of concern which manipulates things and puts them to use" (95) [67].

But, as we have noted, Heidegger does not want simply to privilege the practical; he wants to describe a more fundamental involvement of people with things than the traditional relation between self-referential mental content and objects outside the mind. He calls this more basic directedness "ontic transcendence" in *The Metaphysical Foundation of Logic,* "comportment-towards" in *Basic Problems* and "being-towards" in *Being and Time.*

Heidegger first notes that we do not usually encounter (use, talk about, deal with) "mere things," but rather we use the things at hand to get something done. These things he calls "equipment" [*Zeug*], in a broad enough sense to include whatever is useful: tools, materials, toys, clothing, dwellings, etc.

We shall call those entities which we encounter in concern *"equipment."* In our dealings we come across equipment for writing, sewing, working, transportation, measurement. The kind of being which equipment possesses must be exhibited. (97) [68]

The basic characteristic of equipment is that it is used for something. "Equipment is essentially 'something-in-order-to'" (97) [68]. It is important to note, however, that Heidegger is not defining equipment merely in terms of its in-order-to. A chimp using a stick in order to reach a banana is not using equipment. Equipment always refers to other equipment. "In the 'in-order.to' as a structure there lies an *assignment* or *reference* of something to something" (97) [68]. An "item" of equipment is what it is only insofar as it refers to other equipment and so fits in a certain way into an "equipmental whole."

Equipment—in accordance with its equipmentality—always is *in terms of* its belonging to other equipment: inkstand, pen, ink, paper, blotting pad, table, lamp, furniture, windows, doors, room. (97) [68]

For something to function as equipment in Heidegger's sense, then, there must be a nexus of other equipment in which this thing functions.

Taken strictly, there "is" no such thing as *an* equipment. To the being of any equipment there always belongs an equipmental whole, in which it can be this equipment that it is. (97)[68]

A piece of equipment is *defined* in terms of what one uses it for:

What and how it is as this entity, its *whatness* and *howness*, is constituted by this in-order-to as such, by its involvement. (BP, 293)

The functionality that goes with a chair, blackboard, window is exactly that which makes the thing what it is. (BP, 164)

Take a chair, for example. What do we know when we know what it is to be a chair? (a) We might just know some facts like the physical description of the shape, material, and the relations among the parts of those objects we call chairs. But chairs come in all sorts of shapes and materials. Think of bean-bag chairs. (b) We might have an image of a prototypical chair and compare other objects to it as more or less distant from the prototype. But would a traditional Japanese or a Bushman, who had this image and could use it to pick out similar objects, know what a chair was? (c) We could add a function predicate, such as a chair is a portable seat for one, but so is a bicycle seat. It is not just what a chair is for in some narrow sense but how it fits in with tables and all the rest of our activities which is crucial. We pick it out as a chair by recognizing its place in the whole:

The specific *thisness* of a piece of equipment, its *individuation* . . . is not determined primarily by space and time in the sense that it appears in a determinate space-and-time position. Instead, what determines a piece of equipment as an individual is its equipmental character and equipmental nexus. (BP, 292)

"The fact that it has such [an] involvement is ontologically definitive for the being of such an entity, and is not an ontical assertion about it" (116)[84]. Heidegger calls the way of being of those entities which are defined by their use in the whole, "*availableness*" (114)[83].

B. Dasein's Way of Encountering Equipment

1. Manipulation

We normally know what a thing is in terms of its functioning, but how can we study this functioning? Perception, when this means just staring at objects, cannot be our mode of access.

No matter how sharply we just *look* at the "outward appearance" of things in whatever form this takes, we cannot discover anything available. (98)[69]

Rather, since what a piece of equipment is is its place in a context of use, i.e., how it is used in order to accomplish something, our most basic way of understanding equipment is to use it.

Where something is put to use, our concern subordinates itself to the "in-order-to" which is constitutive for the equipment we are employing at the time; the less we just stare at the hammer-thing, and the more we seize hold of it and use it, the more primordial does our relationship to it become, and the more unveiledly is it encountered as that which it is— as equipment. (98)[69]

Heidegger calls this mode of understanding "manipulating."

Of course, we know what plows and crutches are without necessarily having used them. Heidegger would call this second-hand understanding "positive" but not "primordial." As becomes clear in Chapter IV, a piece of equipment like a chair is defined by what it is *normally* used for by a normal user in a culture where such objects have an established function. Thus actual use by someone is essential to a *primordial* understanding of what a piece of equipment is, but one can have a *positive* understanding of equipment if one is merely familiar with its normal function.

2. The Transparency of Equipment

When we are using equipment, it has a tendency to "disappear." We are not aware of it as having any characteristics at all.

The peculiarity of what is primarily available is that, in its availableness, it must, as it were, withdraw in order to be available quite authentically. That with which our everyday dealings primarily dwell is not the tools themselves. On the contrary, that with which we concern ourselves primarily is the task—that which is to be done at the time. (99)[69]

Consider the example (used by Wittgenstein, Polanyi, and Merleau-Ponty) of the blind man's cane. We hand the blind man a cane and ask him to tell us what properties it has. After hefting and feeling it, he tells us that it is light, smooth, about three feet long, and so on; it is occurrent for him. But when the man starts to manipulate the cane, he loses his awareness of the cane itself; he is aware only of the curb (or whatever object the cane touches); or, if all is going well, he is not even aware of that, but of his freedom to walk, or perhaps only what he is talking about with a friend. Precisely when it is most genuinely appropriated equipment becomes transparent. When hammering a nail, "The hammering itself uncovers the specific 'manipulability' of the hammer" (98)[69], but I am not aware of any determinate characteristics of the hammer or of the nail. All I am aware of is the task, or perhaps what I need to do when I finish:

We do not always and continually have explicit perception of the things surrounding us in a familiar environment, certainly not in such a way that we would be aware of them expressly as available . . . . In the indifferent imperturbability of our customary commerce with them, they become accessible precisely with regard to their unobtrusive presence. The presupposition for the possible equanimity of our dealing with things is, among others, the *uninterrupted quality* of that commerce. It must not be held up in its progress. (BP, 309)

Partly as a joke but also in dead seriousness Heidegger adds that this withdrawal or holding itself in is the way equipment is *in itself.* "It is in this that the phenomenal structure of the being-in-itself of entities which are available consists" (106)[75]. This is a provocative claim. Traditional philosophers from Plato to Husserl have been led to claim that the use-properties of things, their function as equipment, are interest-relative so precisely *not* in themselves. They reason that, since the same thing can be both a hammer and a door-stop, the thing *as it is in itself* cannot be either. There must be something that underlies these two subjective perspectives and their respective use-predicates, and that must be the thing as a substance, independent of our subjective projections. As Husserl puts it in an unpublished note called "This is against Heidegger":

Theoretical interest is concerned with what is; and that, everywhere, is what is identical through variation of subjects and their practical interests. . . . Anybody can verify (if he takes a theoretical attitude) that this thing here counts for subject A as such and such a piece of equipment, for B as quite a different one, that anything can be woven into equipmental nexus of many kinds, both for the same and for different subjects.... Whatever is cognized, it is a being that is cognized; and a being is something identical, something identifiable again and again.[1]

In chapter 6 we shall see how Heidegger would answer this objection. Roughly he would agree that in the theoretical attitude substances can be viewed in abstraction from their functioning as equipment, but he would argue that equipment cannot be made intelligible in terms of objective substances plus subjective use-predicates. Since equipment is in no way derivative, and since involvement is as genuine a mode of access as theory, we can say that equipment in use is equipment as it is in itself.

3. The Transparency of Dasein
Not only is equipment transparent; so is the user. Heidegger calls the user's grasp of his environment in his everyday way of getting around, "circumspection."[2] He describes for his class this everyday activity as a kind of "sight" which does not involve deliberate, thematic awareness:

The *equipmental nexus* of things, for example, the nexus of things as they surround us here, stands in view, but not for the contemplator as though we were sitting here in order to describe the things. . . . The view in which the equipmental nexus stands at first, completely unobtrusive and unthought, is the view and sight of practical *circumspection*, of our practical everyday orientation. "Unthought" means that it is not thematically apprehended for deliberate thinking about things; instead, in circum-spection, we find our bearings in regard to them. . . . When we enter here through the door, we do not apprehend the seats, and the same holds for the doorknob. Nevertheless, they are there in this peculiar way: we go by them circumspectly, avoid them circumspectly, . . . and the like. (BP, 163)

An extreme case of such nonthematic, non-self-referential awareness is the experience athletes sometime call flow, or playing out of their heads.

A person in the midst of the flow experience is both keenly aware of his or her own actions and oblivious to that awareness itself. One rock climber remarks, "You are so involved in what you are doing you aren't thinking of yourself as separate from the immediate activity. . . . You don't see yourself as separate from what you are doing."[3]

Aron Gurwitsch, who was both a student of Husserl's and a perceptive reader of Heidegger, gives in his interpretation of *Being and Time* an excellent account of the sort of self-less awareness which accompanies any masterful coping:

What is imposed on us to do is not determined by us as someone standing outside the situation simply looking on at it; what occurs and is imposed are rather prescribed by the situation and its own structure; and we do more and greater justice to it the more we let ourselves be guided by it, i.e., the less reserved we are in immersing ourselves in it and subordinating ourselves to it. We find ourselves in a situation and are interwoven with it, encompassed by it, indeed just "absorbed" into it.[4]

According to this philosophically unprejudiced description of everyday skillful coping, there is awareness but no self-awareness. That is, there is no self-referential experience of acting as this is understood by Searle (and would have been understood by Husserl), i.e., no experience of volition with the conditions of satisfaction that this experience of acting cause the action. As Heidegger puts it:

Self and world belong together in the single entity, Dasein. Self and world are not two entities, like subject and object . . . but self and world are the basic determination of Dasein itself in the unity of the structure of being-in-the-world. (BP, 297)

Or, even more directly, "Dasein . . . is nothing but . . . concerned absorption in the world." (HCT, 197)

We should try to impress on ourselves what a huge amount of our lives—dressing, working, getting around, talking, eating, etc.—is spent in this state, and what a small part is spent in the deliberate, effortful, subject/object mode, which is, of course, the mode we tend to notice, and which has therefore been studied in detail by philosophers. John Dewey introduced the distinction between knowing-how and knowing-that to make just this point:

We may . . . be said to know how by means of our habits. . . . We walk and read aloud, we get off and on street cars, we dress and undress, and do a thousand useful acts without thinking of them. We know something, namely, how to do them. . . . If we choose to call [this] knowledge . . . then other things also called knowledge, knowledge of and *about* things, knowledge *that* things are thus and so, knowledge that involves reflection and conscious appreciation, remains of a different sort.[5]

Lest it appear that Heidegger's account of everyday dealings and the circumspective taking account of the environment which makes them possible, denying as it does self-referential mental states, is committed to interpreting action as mindless, mechanical behavior, one needs to see that everyday *comportment*, while not deliberate *action*, differs in at least five ways from the mechanical *behavior* of a robot or an insect:

1. *Circumspection is a mode of awareness.* It is a form of experience, opening onto the world and the things in it. Heidegger actually uses the term experience (*Erfahrung*) in saying that "in the mode of everydayness... something has already been experienced ontically" (86) [59]. But this experience can be characterized only as openness. It is not mental, inner, first-person, private, subjective experience (*Erlebnis*, Husserl's term), separate from and directed towards nonmental objects.

2. *Comportment is adaptable and copes with the situation in a variety of ways.* Carpenters do not hammer like robots. Even in typing, which seems most reflex-like and automatic, the expert does not return to the home keys but strikes the next key from wherever the hand and fingers are at the time. In such coping one responds on the basis of a vast past experience of what has happened in previous situations, or, more exactly, one's comportment manifests dispositions that have been shaped by a vast amount of previous dealings, so that in most cases when we exercise these dispositions everything works the way it should.

3. *Comportment reveals entities under aspects.* Husserlian intentionality is sometimes called "aboutness," because mental content is directed toward an object under an aspect. Heidegger's more primordial intentionality is also appropriately called aboutness, but in this case it is not the mind which is directed but the person going about his or her business. This aboutness, like the kind described by Husserl, is directed towards things under aspects. I can be going about my business in such a way as to use my desk in order to write on or to read at or to keep things in. Thus depending on what I am about, i.e., upon what Heidegger calls the "towards-which" of my activity, I am directed towards and reveal things under different aspects.

4. *If something goes wrong, people and higher animals are startled.* Mechanisms and insects are never startled. People are startled because their activity is directed into the future even when they are

not pursuing conscious goals. Dasein is always ahead of itself (see chapter 11).

5. *If the going gets difficult, we must pay attention and so switch to deliberate subject/object intentionality.* Then one has the sense of effort described by James and Searle. One will also have expectations, and so one can be successful, or fail and be surprised.

II. Deliberate Action: Representational Intentionality and Its Objects

The above description of the skilled use of equipment enables Heidegger to introduce both a new kind of intentionality (absorbed coping) which is not that of a mind with content directed toward objects, and a new sort of entity encountered (transparent equipment) which is not a determinate, isolable substance. If this introduction of a more primordial level of phenomena is to be convincing, however, it cannot ignore the traditional account of subjects and objects but, rather, must show its limited legitimacy. We shall see that there are subjects and objects but that the tradition has introduced them too early in the analysis and, moreover, has mischaracterized them so as to give them a foundational function they cannot perform.

Digging out Heidegger's account of the emergence of thematizing mental states and their proper domain will require what may look like a forced reading of Heidegger's text, since in the published part of *Being and Time* Heidegger does not explicitly try to do justice to the traditional account of intentionality. That he intended eventually to face this issue, however, is shown by a comment on Dilthey on effort. "Within the same consciousness," Heidegger writes in explanation of Dilthey, "the will and its inhibition emerge." Heidegger then asks, "What kind of being belongs to this 'emerging'? What is the sense of the being of the 'within'? What relationship-of-being does consciousness bear to the real itself? All this must be determined ontologically" (253) [209]. But Heidegger puts off the promised discussion, and refers to it again only on the last page of *Being and Time* where he asks: "What *positive* structure does the being of 'consciousness' have . . .?" (487) [437] So it is never clear to what extent Heidegger would accept a Husserlian/Searlean account of deliberate action. I shall nonetheless try to reconstruct Heidegger's account of the stance which reveals subjects and objects, i.e., mental content and its referent, and his explanation of how a misinterpretation of the shift to this stance leads to the mistakes of traditional epistemology.

In *Being and Time* Heidegger gives a hint of how thematic consciousness and its objects emerge.

Being-in-the-world, according to our interpretation hitherto, amounts to a *nonthematic circumspective absorption* in references or assignments constitutive for the availableness of an equipmental whole. Any concern is already as it is, because of some familiarity with the world. In this familiarity Dasein can lose itself in what it encounters within the world. ... The occurrentness of beings is thrust to the fore by the possible breaks in that referential whole in which circumspection "operates"... (107, my italics) [76]

Thus Heidegger leaves open a place for traditional intentionality at the point where there is a breakdown. For example, if the doorknob sticks, we find ourselves deliberately *trying* to turn the doorknob, *desiring* that it turn, *expecting* the door to open, etc. (This, of course, does not imply that we were trying, desiring, expecting, etc. all along.) With disturbance, a new way of Daseining comes into being. Dewey had already pointed out the same phenomenon:

It is a commonplace that the more suavely efficient a habit the more unconsciously it operates. Only a hitch in its workings occasions emotion and provokes thought.[6]

Although he concentrates on the special case of breakdown, Heidegger's basic point should be that mental content arises whenever the situation requires deliberate attention. As Searle puts it when discussing the place of intentional content, "Intentionality rises to the level of skill." The switch to deliberation is evoked by any situation in which absorbed coping is no longer possible—any situation that, as Heidegger puts it, requires "a more precise kind of circumspection, such as 'inspecting,' checking up on what has been attained, [etc.]" (409) [358]. Deliberate attention and thus thematic intentional consciousness can also be present, for example, in curiosity, reading instruments, repairing equipment and in designing and testing new equipment. Heidegger, however, concentrates on the specific experience of breakdown, that is, on the experience we have when ongoing coping runs into trouble.

A. Three Kinds of Disturbance: The Unavailable

Once ongoing activity is held up, new modes of encountering emerge and new ways of being encountered are revealed. When something goes wrong with my hammer, for example, I am forced to attend to the hammer and the hammering. According to Heidegger three modes of disturbance—conspicuousness, obstinacy, and obtrusiveness—progressively bring out both Dasein as a thoughtful subject and occurrentness as the way of being of isolated, determinate substances.

The modes of conspicuousness, obtrusiveness, and obstinacy all have the function of bringing to the fore the characteristic of occurrentness in what is available. (104) [74]

Heidegger does not distinguish clearly the different functions of each of these three modes of breakdown. I shall reorder and selectively interpret what Heidegger says, however, to show that in line with his disagreement with Husserl and the traditional understanding of intentionality, as well as with his goal of showing the proper place of Husserlian subjectivity, we can see these three modes of breakdown as increasingly serious disturbances in which a conscious subject with self-referential mental states directed towards determinate objects with properties gradually emerges. (The role of breakdown in revealing *the world* will be discussed in chapter 5.)

This reading of the three modes of breakdown gives more importance to the unavailable than the immediate text warrants. Still, it is clear that two of Heidegger's three modes, which I shall call *temporary breakdown* and *total breakdown*, reveal two new modes of encountering entities and two new ways of being of entities—unavailableness and occurrentness—both of which play an important role in the overall structure of *Being and Time*. The other kind of breakdown, *malfunction*, provides a preview of these two. In laying out the steps that lead from the available to the unavailable and then on to the occurrent, I will selectively use the text to relate my detailed description to Heidegger's sketchier account.

1. Malfunction (Conspicuousness)

When equipment malfunctions, Heidegger says, we discover its unusability by the "circumspection of the dealings in which we use it," and the equipment thereby becomes "conspicuous." "*Conspicuousness* presents the available equipment as in a certain unavailableness" (102–103) [73]. But for most normal forms of malfunction we have ready ways of coping, so that after a moment of being startled, and seeing a meaningless object, we shift to a new way of coping and go on. "Pure occurrentness announces itself in such equipment, but only to withdraw to the availableness of something with which one concerns oneself" (103) [73].

Another response is to ask for help. Heidegger mentions this possibility in his later discussion of language. Coping with malfunction "may take some such form as [saying] 'The hammer is too heavy,' or rather just 'Too heavy!,' 'Hand me the other hammer!' . . . laying aside the unsuitable tool, or exchanging it, 'without wasting words'" (200) [157]. If I get help, transparent circumspective behavior can be so quickly and easily restored that no new stance on the part of Dasein is required.

2. Temporary Breakdown (Obstinacy): From Absorbed Coping to Deliberate Coping to Deliberation

Temporary breakdown, where something blocks ongoing activity, necessitates a shift into a mode in which what was previously transparent becomes explicitly manifest. Deprived of access to what we normally count on, we act *deliberately*, paying attention to what we are doing.

When equipment breaks down, its various references show up. When, for example, the hammer I am using to pound nails is too big or too heavy to perform the task and I cannot reach another hammer, "the constitutive assignment of the 'in-order-to' [this hammer is something one uses to pound nails] to a 'towards-this' [pounding the nails into the wall to hold these shelves in place] has been disturbed" (105, my gloss in brackets) [74]. Heidegger claims that when things are functioning smoothly, "the assignments themselves are not observed; they are rather 'there' and we concernfully submit ourselves to them. But when an assignment *has been disturbed*—when something is unusable for some purpose— then the assignment becomes explicit" (105) [74].

When there is a serious disturbance and even deliberate activity is blocked, Dasein is forced into still another stance, *deliberation*. This involves reflective planning. In deliberation one stops and considers what is going on and plans what to do, all in a context of involved activity. Here one finds the sort of reasoning the tradition formalized in the practical syllogism.

The scheme peculiar to [deliberating] is the "if-then"; if this or that, for instance, is to be produced, put to use, or averted, then some ways and means, circumstances, or opportunities will be needed. (410) [359]

Deliberation can be limited to the local situation or it can take account of what is not present. Heidegger calls such long-range planning "envisaging."

> Deliberation can be performed even when that which is brought close in it circumspectively is not palpably available and does not have presence within the closest range. . . . In envisaging, one's deliberation catches sight directly of that which is needed but which is unavailable. (410) [359]

Envisaging seems to have the kind of aboutness or directedness of something in the mind to something beyond the local situation, which Husserl calls *referring* to distinguish it from *indicating*.[7] Heidegger warns, however, that the tradition has not paused to describe this phenomenon carefully, and so has found itself caught in a famous pseudoproblem: How can a mental state be directed to an object that is not even present? The traditional account supposes that a subject is related to an object by means of some self-sufficient mental content. On this account of intentionality, mental representations are assumed to be special entities in the mind of the subject that can be described in complete independence of the world, while the objects of such representations are equally independent referents. In *Ideas* Husserl calls the entities which make intentionality possible, senses or *noemata*, and claims that the phenomenologist can study them by performing the phenomenological reduction, i.e., by bracketing the world and reflecting directly on these senses. Heidegger rejects any version of a mentalistic account of our ability to refer to objects. "Circumspection which envisages does not relate itself to 'mere representations'" (410) [359].

Heidegger substitutes for Husserl's reduction to the *noema* a shifting of attention from *a being*—a hammer, for example—to Dasein's *ways of understanding of,* i.e., ways of coping with, *being*—unreadiness-to-hand, for example.

> For *Husserl* the phenomenological reduction, which he worked out for the first time expressly in *Ideas Toward a Pure Phenomenology and Phenomenological Philosophy* (1913), is the method of leading phenomenological vision from the natural attitude of the human being whose life is involved in the world of things and persons back to the transcendental life of consciousness and its noetic-noematic experiences, in which objects are constituted as correlates of consciousness. For us phenomenological reduction means leading phenomenological vision back from the apprehension of a being, whatever may be the character of that apprehension, to the understanding of the being of this being. . . . (BP, 21)

Heidegger does not, however, want to deny that when skillful coping reaches its limit and requires deliberate attention, a subject conscious of objects emerges; he wants, rather, to describe this subject accurately, and interpret it anew.

For what is more obvious than that a "subject" is related to an "object" and vice versa? This "subject-object-relationship" must be presupposed. But while this presupposition is unimpeachable in its facticity, this makes it indeed a baleful one, if its ontological necessity and especially its onto-logical sense are left in the dark. (86) [59]

To what extent then are *representations* involved when we run into a disturbance? Some sort of mental *content* is surely involved, we do have beliefs and desires and experience effort—but these need not involve the sort of self-sufficient mental entities philosophers since Descartes have supposed. The essential characteristic of repre-sentations according to the tradition is that they are *purely* mental, i.e., that they can be analyzed *without reference to the world.* Mind and world, Husserl holds, are two totally independent realms of reality. Heidegger focuses on this claim concerning mental content:

This distinction between subject and object pervades all the problems of modern philosophy and even extends into the development of contem-porary phenomenology. In his *Ideas*, Husserl says: "The theory of cat-egories must begin absolutely from this most radical of all distinctions of being—being as consciousness [*res cogitans*] and being as being that 'manifests' itself in consciousness, 'transcendent' being [*res extensa*]. Between consciousness [*res cogitans*] and reality [*res extensa*] there yawns a veritable abyss of sense." (BP, 124–125, Heidegger's brackets)

Heidegger rejects this traditional interpretation of the mental. Even deliberation is not the pure detached theoretical reflection described by the tradition. Rather it must take place on the background of absorption in the world.

Holding back from the use of equipment is so far from sheer 'theory' that the kind of circumspection which tarries and "considers" remains wholly in the grip of the available equipment with which one is concerned. (409) [357–358]

Even when people have "mental representations," i.e., mental content, such as beliefs and desires, and make plans, and follow rules, etc., they do so against a background of involved activity. Since, as we shall see in chapter 5, Heidegger holds that deliberate action and even theoretical contemplation always take place on the background of the world, he can say:

If, in the ontology of Dasein, we 'take our departure' from a worldless "I" in order to provide this "I" with an object and an ontologically baseless relation to that object, then we have 'presupposed' not too much, but *too little.* (363) [315–316]

Heidegger's point can be best illustrated by looking at the role rules play in dealing with the unavailable. Take speech-act rules for example. When I am acting transparently—for example, making a promise—I do not need any rules at all. I have learned from imitation how to promise, and I am a master promiser. But if something goes wrong, I may have to invoke a rule—for example, the rule that one must keep one's promise. But the important thing to notice is that this is not a strict rule whose conditions of application are stated in the rule itself. It is a ceteris paribus rule. In the case of an unfulfilled promise there are allowable excuses, such as I was sick, or I saw that what I promised would hurt you. The rule "always keep your promise" applies "everything else being equal," and we do not, and could not, spell out what everything else is nor what counts as equal. Moreover, if we tried to define each exception, such as being sick, we would again have to bring in further ceteris paribus conditions. These ceteris paribus conditions never capture, but rather presuppose, our shared background practices. These practices are an aspect of our everyday transparent ways of coping. Thus, understanding is not in our *minds*, but in Dasein—in the skillful ways we are accustomed to comport ourselves. Thus even when mental content such as rules, beliefs, and desires arise on the unavailable level, they cannot be analyzed as *self-contained* representations as the tradition supposed. Deliberative activity remains dependent upon Dasein's involvement in a transparent background of coping skills.[8]

Traditional philosophers, then, were right in thinking that human beings have some sort of privileged role in revealing objects, but this role is played not by subjects, but by Dasein. Therefore Heidegger sometimes refers to Dasein as "the subject" (in quotes):

If, then, philosophical investigation from the beginning of antiquity . . . oriented itself toward reason, soul, mind, spirit, consciousness, self-consciousness, subjectivity, this is not an accident. . . . The trend toward the "subject"—not always uniformly unequivocal and clear—is based on the fact that philosophical inquiry somehow understood that the basis for every substantial philosophical problem could and had to be procured from an adequate elucidation of the "subject." (BP, 312)

This would require an elucidation of the "subject's" way of of being, existence. But traditional philosophy failed to make what Heidegger sees as this obvious next move:

It will be expected that ontology now takes the subject as exemplary entity and interprets the concept of being by looking to the mode of being of the subject—that henceforth the subject's *way of being* becomes an ontological problem. But that is precisely what does not happen. The motives for modern philosophy's primary orientation to the subject are not fundamental-ontological. The motive is not to know precisely *that* and *how* being and being's structure can be clarified in terms of Dasein itself. (BP, 123)

Heidegger adds:

Intentionality, self-relation to something, seemed at first sight to be something trivial. However, the phenomenon proved to be puzzling as soon as we recognized clearly that a correct understanding of the structure has to be on its guard against two common errors which are not yet overcome even in phenomenology (erroneous objectivizing, erroneous subjectivizing). Intentionality is not an occurrent relation between an occurrent subject and an occurrent object but is constitutive for the relational character of the subject's comportment as such.... Intentionality is neither something objective nor something subjective in the traditional sense. (BP, 313–314)

If we work out a phenomenological ontology of the "subject," we find that, contrary to the tradition, mental states are not basic. We have seen that, in dealing with the available, Dasein is transparently absorbed in equipment without experiencing its activity as caused by a "mental state." We have now added that temporary breakdown calls forth deliberate action and thus introduces "mental content," but only on the background of nonmental coping.

On the side of entities, there is no longer transparency either. Just as temporary breakdown reveals something like what the tradition has thought of as a "subject," it also reveals something like an "object," and just as the "subject" revealed is not the isolable, self-sufficient mind the tradition assumed, but is involved in the world, so the "object" revealed is not an isolable, self-sufficient, substance, but is defined by its failure to be available. In breakdown "the available is not thereby just *observed* and stared at as something occurrent; the occurrentness which makes itself known is still bound up in the availableness of equipment. Such equipment still does not veil itself in the guise of mere things" (104) [74].

This means that the unavailable necessarily shows up in a practical context:

When something cannot be used—when, for instance, a tool definitely refuses to work—it can be conspicuous only in and for dealings in which something is manipulated. Even by the sharpest and most persevering "perception" and "representation" of things, one can never discover anything like the damaging of a tool. (406) [354]

To see what Heidegger is getting at, consider a malfunctioning radio. To say that the radio does not work is to say that it has ceased to function with respect to Dasein's dealings. The electrons, however, continue to function perfectly; that is, they continue to obey the laws of nature. Mere careful listening cannot determine that the static coming out of the radio does not fit into Dasein's everyday activities.

Involved use, however, *can* reveal unavailable characteristics. Indeed, when equipment temporarily breaks down and circumspection becomes deliberate, involved users no longer encounter equipment as transparent, but as having specific characteristics that are different from those they counted on. For instance:

When we are using a tool circumspectively, we can say ... that the hammer is too heavy or too light. Even the proposition that the hammer is heavy can give expression to a concernful deliberation, and signify that the hammer is not an easy one—in other words, that it takes force to handle it, or that it will be hard to manipulate. (412) [360]

Thus a way of being of equipment is revealed which is more determinate than transparent functioning and yet whose way of being is not that of an isolated, determinate, occurrent thing with occurrent properties.

When the hammer I am using fails to work and I cannot immediately get another, I have to deal with it as too heavy, unbalanced, broken, etc. These characteristics belong to the hammer only as used by me in a specific situation. *Being too heavy* is certainly not a *property* of the hammer, and although the philosophical tradition has a great deal to say about properties and the predicates that denote them, it has nothing to say about such situational characteristics. There are one-place predicates, like heavy, and relational predicates, like heavier than, but no set of fixed logical relations captures situational characteristics like "too heavy for this job." Indeed, although we spend a great deal of our lives dealing with things in terms of the characteristics they reveal when there is a disturbance, there is no philosophical term for these characteristics. Heidegger, therefore, refers to them by putting the term property in quotation marks, as in its second occurrence below:

The term "property" is that of some definite character which it is possible for things to possess. Anything available is, at the worst, appropriate for some purposes and inappropriate for others; and its "properties" are, as it were, still bound up in these ways in which it is appropriate or inappropriate. (114–115) [83]

I shall call these situational characteristics overlooked by the tradition *aspects*, to distinguish them from the decontextualized *features* that Heidegger, following the tradition, calls properties.

(It is important to note an asymmetry here. Aspects illuminate something about the object in the situation which was already the case. The hammer was too heavy before I noticed it. But as we have just seen, when I start to deliberate, I do not just notice mental states that were already there; I start to have beliefs and desires. Thus, in a Heideggerian vein one might hold, and, indeed, Sartre in *Transcendence of the Ego* did hold, that the subject/object distinction characteristic of Cartesianism results when we treat deliberation and reflection on the same model as the noticing of aspects. Then we assume that the self-referential mental states that show up when we reflect on our deliberate activity have been on the periphery of our consciousness causing that activity all along.)

There are many kinds of aspects. Disturbance can, for example, lead us to notice the functional aspects of a piece of equipment. This, in turn, enables us to pick out its parts. One can pick out (Heidegger would say "free") the seat and back of a beanbag chair, to take an extreme example, only when one is already relating to it *as a chair*. Or, to take a purely perceptual example, if we are looking for something red, we may notice the woolly, warm red of a sweater, or the shiny, cold red of a fire engine. These aspects are not context-free properties expressible in predicates. The sweater and fire engine could, however, be seen as having identical properties by matching the warm, wooly red and the cold, metallic red to a color chart and discovering that both match the same context-free color patch. Heidegger hints at this when he speaks of the way a property "gets loosened, so to speak, from its unexpressed inclusion in the entity itself" (199) [157]. This brings us to the sort of isolated entities and their isolable properties that are the building blocks of scientific theory and traditional ontology.

3. Total Breakdown (Obtrusiveness): Transition from Involved Deliberation and Its Concerns to Theoretical Reflection and Its Objects

A situation in which a piece of equipment is missing can be the occasion for a transition from the unavailable to the occurrent. Heidegger points out that in such cases the elements in the situation that are not missing lose the character of availableness and reveal themselves in the mode of mere occurrence.

> The more urgently we need what is missing, and the more authentically it is encountered in its unavailableness, all the more obtrusive does that which is available become—so much so, indeed, that it seems to lose its character of availableness. It reveals itself as something just occurrent and no more ... (103) [73]

Once our work is permanently interrupted, we can either stare helplessly at the remaining objects or take a new detached theoretical stance towards things and try to explain their underlying causal properties. Only when absorbed, ongoing activity is interrupted is there room for such theoretical reflection.

> If knowing is to be possible as a way of determining the nature of the occurrent by observing it, then there must first be a *deficiency* in our having-to-do with the world concernfully. (88) [61]

This is what Heidegger usually means when he says that the theoretical attitude presupposes a withholding of the practical attitude. Heidegger, however, sometimes seems to say that the theoretical stance is merely what is left over after the cessation of practical activity. In this extreme view, the only stance that is left when we withhold our present concern and relinquish our immediate project is just staring at things.

> When concern holds back from any kind of producing, manipulating, and the like, it puts itself into what is now *the sole remaining mode of being-in*, the mode of just tarrying alongside. ... This kind of being towards the world is one which lets us encounter intraworldly entities purely in the way *they look*. .. (88, my italics) [61]

This account would equate theoretical knowing with mere staring. Heidegger retracts this implication in a marginal note: "Looking away from is not looking at. The latter has its own origin and has as a necessary result this looking away from. Observation has its own primordiality" {83}. That is, observing is not just staring. Once there is a break in our ongoing activity we *can* just stare at objects, but we can also engage in a new activity, theoretical reflection, which operates by "depriving the world of its worldliness in a definite way" (94) [65]. As we shall see, there are, according to Heidegger, two distinct modes of "just looking": gazing with curiosity for the sake of distraction, and observing with the wonder that leads to theory. The isolation of properties required by theory (looking away from their context) is independently motivated and requires its own kind of skill. For Heidegger, scientific theory is an *autonomous stance*. It is not mere curiosity, nor is it based on an interest in control. Science is *not* instrumental reason. Here Heidegger is more traditional than pragmatists such as Nietzsche, Peirce, or early Habermas.

Heidegger turns to the special character of the theoretical attitude later in *Being and Time* when he introduces his account of theoretical science.

When in the course of *existential ontological* analysis we ask how *theoretical* discovery "arises" out of circumspective concern, . . . we are asking which of those conditions implied in Dasein's being make-up are existentially necessary for the possibility of Dasein's existing in the way of scientific research. This formulation of the question is aimed at an *existential conception of science.* (408) [356–357]

To begin with, theory requires decontextualizing characteristics from the context of everyday practices. For example, we move from encountering the hammer's *aspect*, heaviness, to encountering what philosophers call the *property*, heaviness. Even though we may use the same words—"The hammer is heavy"—in both cases, in the case of properties,

this proposition can mean that the entity before us, which we already know circumspectively as a hammer, has a weight—that is to say, it has the "property" of heaviness: it exerts a pressure on what lies beneath it, and it falls if this is removed. When this kind of talk is so understood, it is no longer spoken within the horizon of . . . an equipmental whole and its involvement-relationships. (412) [360–361]

In the "physical" assertion that "the hammer is heavy" we overlook ... the tool-character of the entity we encounter ... (413)[361]

Here we find a new attitude that reveals a new way of being, occurrentness. Heidegger sums up this important changeover.

Why is it that what we are talking about—the heavy hammer—shows itself differently when our way of talking is thus modified? Not because we are keeping our distance from manipulation, nor because we are just looking *away* from the equipmental character of this entity, but rather because we are looking at the available thing which we encounter, and looking at it "in a new way" as something occurrent. *The understanding of being* by which our concernful dealings with intraworldly entities have been guided *has changed over.* (412)[361]

Once characteristics are no longer related to one another in a concrete, everyday, meaningful way, as aspects of a thing in a particular context, the isolated properties that remain can be quantified and related by scientific covering laws and thus taken as evidence for theoretical entities. "By reason of their being-just-occurrent-and-no-more . . . entities can have their 'properties' defined mathematically in 'functional concepts'" (122)[88]. For example, heaviness is related by the law of gravity to the attraction of the earth. Likewise, isolated properties with no contextual meaning can be combined according to the predicate calculus and used in formal models. Laws and formal models provide a new, essentially meaningless, context for occurrent properties.

Heidegger wants to stress three points. (1) It is necessary to get beyond our practical concerns in order to be able to encounter mere objects. (2) The "bare facts" related by scientific laws are isolated by a special activity of selective seeing rather than being simply found. (3) Scientifically relevant "facts" are not merely removed from their context by selective seeing; they are theory-laden, i.e., recontextualized in a new projection. In Newtonian theory, for example,

something constantly occurrent (matter) is uncovered beforehand, and the horizon is opened so that one may be guided by looking at those constitutive items . . . which are quantitatively determinable (motion, force, location, and time). Only "in the light" of a nature which has been projected in this fashion can anything like a "fact" be found and set up for an experiment regulated and delimited in terms of this projection. The "grounding" of "factual science" was possible only because the researchers understood that in principle there are no "bare facts." (414)[362]

(Note that Heidegger's account of theoretical projection here has nothing to do with the notion of projection introduced in chapter 11.)

It is important to note Heidegger's derivation of the theoretical attitude and the scientific entities and relationships it reveals, because it is often mistakenly said that he has no account of theoretical knowledge. In fact, Heidegger provides a sophisticated account of science which, like Kuhn's, emphasizes the role of scientific skills and theory in producing data, but, unlike Kuhn's, still leaves room for scientific realism. (See chapter 15.)

Theory requires a special attitude Heidegger calls *thematizing.*

The scientific projection of any entities which we have somehow encountered already lets their kind of being be understood explicitly. . . . The articulation of the understanding of being, the delimitation of an area of subject-matter . . . , and the sketching-out of the way of conceiving which is appropriate to such entities—all these belong to the totality of this projecting; and this totality is what we call "*thematizing.*" Its aim is to free the intraworldly entities we encounter, and to free them in such a way that they can "throw themselves against" a pure discovering—that is, that they can become "objects." Thematizing objectifies. (414) [363]

It might look as if Heidegger's account of thematizing as objectifying puts his whole project in jeopardy, in that his "thematic analysis of being-in" (169) [130] would have to objectify Dasein. Husserl actually made this objection when reading *Being and Time.* This criticism of philosophical reflection, however, though applicable to Plato or Descartes, radically misunderstands Heidegger's undertaking in *Being and Time.* We must be careful to distinguish *objectifying thematizing* from simply noticing something unavailable, which Heidegger calls *thematic consciousness.* Heidegger's method in *Being and Time* is a systematic version of everyday noticing and pointing out. Heidegger finds himself already having a way of being (existence) that he only dimly understands. He is trying, in a mode of concern, to detach himself from his local, practical context but nonetheless to clarify this understanding from within, by pointing out its various aspects.

But as we have just noted, the natural scientist too is concerned with his work and dwells in the world of his discipline. How, then, does his objectifying stance differ from Heidegger's hermeneutic stance? The answer is clear if we see that the scientist is detached from and so is able to thematize and objectify his object, nature, while the hermeneutic ontologist makes his theme precisely the shared background understanding in which he dwells and from which he cannot detach himself. (See chapter 11.) Indeed, Heidegger would probably claim that his hermeneutics is a special form of involved deliberate attention—an authentic response to anxiety, a special form of disturbance. (See chapter 10.) If this is so, then Heidegger must mean to distinguish his involved *thematic* analysis of existence, which reveals that in which we always already dwell, from the detached, objectifying thematization characteristic of any discipline from physics to factual history.[9]

III. Transition from Theoretical Reflection to Pure Contemplation

Although he is detached from the everyday practical context, the scientist is interested in his work and dwells in the "disciplinary matrix" that forms the basis of his skillful observing and theorizing. Another possible stance in the absence of involved activity, however, is pure, disinterested contemplation. This stance, "letting entities be encountered purely in the way they look"—unlike theory—*is* pure staring and can, indeed, be called a merely deficient mode of involvement.

Given the distinction between theoretical projection and mere contemplation Heidegger can distinguish the wonder, which motivates theoretical reflection to try to understand by finding new abstract relationships, from the curiosity that just stares at things.

In rest, concern does not disappear; circumspection, however, becomes free and is no longer bound to the world of work. . . . When curiosity has become free, however, it concerns itself with seeing, not in order to understand what is seen . . . but just in order to see. . . . Curiosity [thus] has nothing to do with observing entities and marvelling at *them* . . . (216, my italics) [172]

Heidegger claims that pure contemplation provides the basis for traditional ontology. "Being is that which shows itself in the pure perception which belongs to beholding, and only by such seeing does being get discovered. Primordial and genuine truth lies in pure beholding. This thesis has remained the foundation of Western philosophy" (215) [171]. Heidegger grants that this sort of stance is possible, but claims it does not have the foundational status traditional philosophy has supposed. As we shall see in chapter 6, Heidegger, in opposition to traditional philosophers from Plato to

Husserl, denies the philosophical relevance of what shows up to pure beholding.

IV. Philosophical Implications

A. Summary of Four Ways of Being of Entities Other than Dasein

Let us first review the four ways Dasein can cope with beings and the four ways of being of the entities thus revealed. (See Table 3 on pages 124–125.)

1. Dasein can simply cope. Or, if there is a problem, Dasein can just switch to some other mode of coping and keep on going. In both cases all that is revealed is the manipulability of the available, i.e., *availableness*.

2. Dasein can confront its equipment in context as somehow defective and try to fix or improve it and get going again. Dasein thus emerges as a "subject" with "mental content" directed at independent things with aspects whose way of being is *unavailableness*.

3. Dasein can decontextualize its object. Then it reveals context-free features or properties. These can be recontextualized in formal models and in scientific theories. The scientist is, however, still an involved skillful subject, not an autonomous, detached subject as in the traditional account of theory. What is revealed is *occurrentness*.

4. Dasein can just stare without recontextualizing. Such disinterested attention and the isolated entities it reveals gives rise to traditional ontology—a constantly renewed but unsuccessful attempt to account for everything in terms of some type of ultimate substances on the side of both subject and object. Thus we get the phenomenon mistakenly characterized by traditional philosophy of mind as an isolated, self-contained subject confronting an isolated, self contained, object—two examples of a fictive way of being Heidegger calls *pure occurrentness*.

One might wonder whether later Heidegger still held that availableness and occurrentness were the basic ways of being of entities other than Dasein. Already in *Being and Time* he did not think they were the only such ways of being (see the discussion of the primitive view of nature in chapter 6), and with his later discussion of things and works of art he introduced detailed accounts of several other ways. But he never gave up or historicized the two basic modes of being laid out in *Being and Time*. In his last published work, *On Time and Being*, he singles out availableness and occurrentness as "modes of presencing."[10]

B. The Question of Priority

We can now ask, what sort of priority does Heidegger claim for the level of everyday coping, and what sort of argument does he have to back up his claim? I have to speak for Heidegger here, since he does not directly address the issue. I think he would make two related claims concerning the inadequacy of the traditional epistemological account of occurrent subjects with mental contents directed towards occurrent objects.

1. Subjects with inner experience standing over against outer objects do not necessarily arise in Dasein's way of being. Dasein could simply be absorbed in the world. A simplified culture in an earthly paradise is conceivable in which the members' skills mesh with the world so well that one need never do anything deliberately or entertain explicit plans and goals.[11]

2. In our world subjects often need to relate to objects by way of deliberate action involving desires and goals, with their conditions of satisfaction. But even if Searle is right that this can be best described in terms of self-referential mental contents, all thematic intentionality must take place on a background of transparent coping. In order even to act deliberately we must orient ourselves in a familiar world.[12] (See chapter 5 for details.)

If one were determined to defend the epistemological tradition, and thus the priority of mental content, one could still argue, as Husserl did argue in *Crisis* (148–151), and as cognitive scientists argue today, that even in everyday transparent, skillful coping a person is following unconscious rules, and that our everyday background practices are generated by an unconscious or tacit belief system. Leibniz, for example, thinks of skills as theories we are not yet clear about. He says, "the most important observations and turns of skill in all sorts of trades and professions are as yet unwritten. . . . Of course, we can also write up this practice, since it is at bottom just another theory."[13] That is, the way we cope with the available is based on the application of occurrent rules to occurrent facts—all knowing-how is really knowing-that, only we are not clear about what we are really doing. Jürgen Habermas still holds this cognitivist view: "In goal-directed actions . . . an implicit knowledge is expressed; this know-how can in principle also be transformed into a know-that."[14] The work of Seymour Papert of the M.I.T. Artificial Intelligence Laboratory is an example of the cognitivist culmination of this tradition. Papert claims that even physical skills such as bike-riding and juggling are performed by following theories. One would be better able to learn bike-riding if one followed the steps of a bike-riding program. According to Papert, when one sees one's skills as programs "the reward is the ability to describe analytically something that until then was known in a global, perceptual-kinesthetic way."[15]

Against this claim Heidegger can give no knock-down argument, if an argument has to deduce conclusions from agreed upon premises; but Heidegger can and does claim to have given a concrete demonstration of his position, by showing that when we carefully describe everyday ongoing coping activity we do not find any mental states. Thus we must not take for granted, as Daniel Dennett for example does, that people going about daily tasks such as making a turkey sandwich are solving problems by forming beliefs about what will happen if the refrigerator door is opened and how well turkey sticks to bread.[16] Likewise, we cannot assume, as traditional philosophers from Aristotle to Davidson and Searle have done, that, simply because our concept of action requires that an action be explainable in terms of beliefs and desires, when we don't find conscious beliefs and desires causing our actions, we are justified in postulating them in our explanations.

The traditional approach to skills as theories has gained attention with the supposed success of expert systems. If expert systems based on rules elicited from experts were, indeed, successful in converting knowing-how into knowing-that, it would be a strong vindication of the philosophical tradition and a severe blow to Heidegger's contention that there is no evidence for the traditional claim that skills can be reconstructed in terms of knowledge. Happily for Heidegger, it turns out that no expert system can do as well as the experts whose supposed rules it is running with great speed and accuracy.[17] Thus the work on expert systems supports Heidegger's claim that the facts and rules "discovered" in the detached attitude do not capture the skills manifest in circumspective coping.

All this does not *prove* that mental states need not be involved in everyday activity, but it does shift the burden of proof to those who want to give priority to mental representations, since they are now in the unphenomenological, although rather typical, philosophical position of claiming that in order for their theories to be true, our way of being must be totally different from what it appears to be.

5

Worldliness

I. The Worldliness of the World

In chapter 3 we saw that Heidegger criticizes the idea of a self-contained subject directed toward an isolable object and proposes to redescribe intentionality as the ontic transcendence of a socially defined "subject" relating to a holistically defined "object," all on the background of a more originary transcendence. Then in chapter 4 we followed Heidegger's attempt to do justice to the insights of the epistemological tradition while avoiding its distortions by giving a detailed description of various modes of ontic transcendence from pure coping, to the thematically conscious practical subject, to the thematizing theoretical knower. We saw how Heidegger uses against traditional *epistemology* with its subject/object relation the *ontological* observation that our transparent everyday way of coping with the available can be carried on independently of the emergence of a thematically conscious subject with mental content, which must then be related to an object. With all this in mind we can finally turn to Heidegger's main concern in Chapter III—originary transcendence or the worldliness of the world.

In describing the phenomenon of world Heidegger seeks to get behind the kind of intentionality of subjects directed towards objects discussed and distorted by the tradition, and even behind the more basic intentionality of everyday coping, to the context or background, on the basis of which every kind of directedness takes place. Against traditional *ontology*, Heidegger will seek to show that all three ways of being we have considered—availableness, unavailableness, and occurrentness—presuppose the phenomenon of world (with its way of being, worldliness), which cannot be made intelligible in terms of any of these three. The description of the world as having a distinctive structure of its own that makes possible and calls forth Dasein's ontic comportment is the most important and original contribution of *Being and Time*. Indeed, since worldliness is another name for disclosedness or Dasein's understanding of being, worldliness is the guiding phenomenon behind Heidegger's thought in *Being and Time* and even in his later works.

Heidegger begins by distinguishing the traditional from the phenomenological sense of "world." These two senses of the term are generalizations of the categorial and existential senses of "in" discussed in chapter 3.

II. Four Senses of World

On page 93 [64–65 in the original] Heidegger lays out the categorial and existential ways in which the term world is used, distinguishing an ontical sense (which relates to entities) from an ontological sense (which relates to the way of being of those entities). Heidegger lists four senses of "world." We can lay them out more perspicuously as two senses of "universe" and two of "world."[1]

A. Inclusion

1. The Ontical-Categorial Sense (Heidegger's number 1)
"World" can be used to mean a *universe*, conceived of as a totality of objects of a certain kind. For example, the physical universe as the set of all physical objects, or a universe of discourse, such as mathematics, as the realm of all objects studied by mathematicians.

2. The Ontological-Categorial Sense (sense number 2)
A set of particulars specified in terms of the essential characteristics of the entities that make up the set. For example, what defines the "physical world," i.e., what *all* physical objects have in common. The same goes for the world of abstract entities. This is what Husserl called the *eidos* defining each region of being, and what Heidegger calls each region's way of being.

B. Involvement

3. The Ontical-Existentiell Sense (sense number 3)
The world is "that 'wherein' a factical Dasein as such can be said to 'live'" (93) [65].[2] This sense of world is reflected in such locutions as "the child's world," "the world of fashion," or "the business

world" (this, as opposed to one's place of business, is what one is "in" when one is in business). What Kuhn calls a "disciplinary matrix"—"the entire constellation of beliefs, values, techniques, and so on shared by the members of a given community"[3]—would be a world in this sense. Thus we can appropriately talk, for example, of the world of mathematics being shaken by Gödel's proof. It helps here to contrast the *physical world* (sense number 1)— as a set of objects—with *the world of physics*—a constellation of equipment, practices, and concerns in which physicists dwell. Another way to see the radical shift in senses is to note that we can speak of the sins of the world, but not the sins of the universe. Such worlds as the business world, the child's world, and the world of mathematics, are "modes" of the total system of equipment and practices that Heidegger calls *the* world. Their way of being given, Heidegger calls the "phenomenon of world" (119) [86].

Among the various possible modes of the world, Heidegger includes "the 'public' we-world, or one's 'own' closest (domestic) environment" (93) [65]. It is important to note that all such "special worlds," as he also calls them, are public. There is no such thing as *my* world, if this is taken as some private sphere of experience and meaning, which is self-sufficient and intelligible in itself, and so more fundamental than the shared public world and its local modes. Both Husserl and Sartre follow Descartes in beginning with *my* world and then trying to account for how an isolated subject can give meaning to other minds and to *the* shared intersubjective world. Heidegger, on the contrary, thinks that it belongs to the very idea of a world that it be shared, so *the* world is always prior to *my* world.

Dasein is with equal originality being-with others and being-amidst intraworldly beings. The world, within which these latter beings are encountered, is . . . always already world which one shares with the others. (BP, 297)

Our understanding of the world is preontological. We dwell in the equipment, practices, and concerns in some domain without noticing them or trying to spell them out.

The world as already unveiled in advance is such that we do not in fact specifically occupy ourselves with it, or apprehend it, but instead it is so self-evident, so much a matter of course, that we are completely oblivious of it. (BP, 165)

4. The Ontological-Existential Sense (sense number 4)
The worldliness of the world. This is the way of being common to our most general system of equipment and practices and to any of its subregions. (When we try to imagine another reality, as in science fiction, we can only imagine our world changed in certain details. Likewise, when we try to imagine what it is like to be a cat or a dolphin, we can only understand them as having a sort of impoverished version of our world. Thus Heidegger says, "The ontology of life is accomplished by way of a privative Interpretation" (75) [50].)

World in this existential sense has been passed over by the tradition.

The concept of world, or the phenomenon thus designated, is what has hitherto not yet been recognized in philosophy. (BP, 165)

So the general structure of the world must be laid out by Heidegger in his ontological investigation. Nonetheless, the structure of the world is not, strictly speaking, a structure that can be spelled out completely and abstracted from all instances, so as to be understandable to a rational being who does not inhabit our world, nor can this structure be shown to be *necessary* for any world as such. Thus we cannot achieve the a priori knowledge concerning the world traditionally claimed for propositions about essential structures. The structure of the world is "a priori" only in the weak sense that it is *given* as *already* structuring any subworld.[4] The best we can do is point out to those who dwell in the world with us certain prominent structural aspects of this actual world. If we can show a structure to be common to the world and each of its modes, we shall have found the structure of the world as such. (In Division II Heidegger will seek to show that this structure is isomorphic with the structure of temporality.)

III. The Structure of the World

A. Involvement
We have seen that equipment is *defined* by its function (in-order-to) in a referential whole. Heidegger now adds that, to actually *function*, equipment must fit into a context of meaningful activity. Heidegger calls this fitting in *involvement* (*Bewandtnis*). (The word could equally well be translated as "bearing upon" or "pertinence

to." "Involvement" has unfortunate associations, but it will do, as long as a chair's involvement in my activity of eating is not confused with the sort of existential in-volvement human beings have with each other and in their world, discussed in chapter 3.) The involvement whole is that in which particular involvements make sense.

Whenever something available has an involvement [is relevant] . . . , *what* involvement this is [how it is relevant], has in each case been outlined in advance in terms of the whole of such involvements [relevance relations]. In a workshop, for example, the whole of involvements which is constitutive for the available in its availableness, is "earlier" than any single item of equipment. (116, my gloss in brackets) [84]

Putting this important point more generally and relating it to world, we can say:

An involvement is itself discovered only on the basis of the prior discovery of an involvement-whole. So in any involvement that has been discovered . . . , the "worldly character" of the available has been discovered beforehand. (118) [85]

Hammers make sense by referring to nails, etc. But how does the activity of hammering make sense? Equipment makes sense only in the context of other equipment; our use of equipment makes sense because our activity has a point. Thus, besides the "in-order-to" that assigns equipment to an equipmental whole, already discussed, the use of equipment exhibits a "where-in" (or practical context), a "with-which" (or item of equipment), a "towards-which" (or goal), and a "for-the-sake-of-which" (or final point). To take a specific example: I write on the blackboard *in* a classroom, *with* a piece of chalk, *in order to* draw a chart, as a step *towards* explaining Heidegger, *for the sake of* my being a good teacher.[5]

We shall return in a moment to the for-the-sake-of-which but first we must pause to consider the "towards-which." It is a mistake to think of the toward-which as the goal of the activity, if one thinks of this goal intentionalistically as something that Dasein has in mind.

The awaiting of the "towards-which" is neither a considering of the "goal" nor an expectation of the impendent finishing of the work to be produced. It has by no means the character of getting something thematically into one's grasp. (405) [353]

Heidegger would object to traditional accounts of everyday activity such as those found in Aristotle's discussion of the practical syllogism and in contemporary philosophies of action such as Donald Davidson's, which hold that we must explain an action as caused by the desire to reach some goal. Heidegger, as we have seen, would also reject John Searle's claim that even where there is no desire, we must have in mind conditions of satisfaction, so that the experience of acting contains within itself a representation of the goal of the action. According to Heidegger, to explain everyday transparent coping we do not need to introduce a mental representation of a goal at all. Activity can be *purposive* without the actor having in mind a *purpose*.

Phenomenological examination confirms that in a wide variety of situations human beings relate to the world in an organized purposive manner without the constant accompaniment of representational states that specify what the action is aimed at accomplishing. This is evident in skilled activity such as playing the piano or skiing, habitual activity such as driving to the office or brushing one's teeth, unthinking activity such as rolling over in bed or making gestures while one is speaking, and spontaneous activity such as jumping up and pacing during a heated discussion or fidgeting and drumming one's fingers anxiously during a dull lecture. In general, it is possible to be without any representation of a near- or long-term goal of one's activity. Indeed, at times one is actually surprised when the task is accomplished, as when one's thoughts are interrupted by one's arrival at the office. Or take Boston Celtics basketball player Larry Bird's description of the experience of the complex purposive act of passing the ball in the midst of a game: "[A lot of the] things I do on the court are just reactions to situations . . . . I don't think about some of the things I'm trying to do. . . . A lot of times, I've passed the basketball and not realized I've passed it until a moment or so later."[6]

Such phenomena are not limited to muscular responses, but exist in all areas of skillful coping, including intellectual coping. Many instances of apparently complex problem solving which seem to implement a long-range strategy, as, for example, making a move in chess, may be best understood as direct responses to familiar perceptual gestalts. After years of seeing chess games unfold, a chess grandmaster can, simply by responding to the patterns on the chess board, play master level chess while his deliberate, analytic mind is absorbed in something else.[7] Such play, based as it is on previous attention to thousands of actual and book games, incorporates a tradition that determines the appropriate response to each situation and therefore makes possible long range, strategic, purposive play, without the player needing to have any plan or goal in mind.

Thus a description of nondeliberate action shows that we often experience ourselves as active yet are not aware of what we are trying to do. Such unthinking comportment seems to be at least as typical of the activities in a normal day as its opposite. In fact, it provides the nonsalient background that makes it possible deliberately to focus on what is unusual or important or difficult.

Yet, according to Heidegger, the tradition is right about something: Such skilled behavior is not an undifferentiated flow. One can make sense of it as having a direction and recognizable chunks. For example, I leave home, drive to the campus, park, enter my office building, open my door, enter my office, sit down at my desk and begin working. We make sense of our own comportment, or the comportment of others, in terms of such directedness towards long-range and proximal ends. But this should not mislead us into postulating mental intentions in action, since there is no evidence that this division into intelligible subsets of activity need be in the mind of the person who is absorbed in the activity any more than an athlete experiencing flow is purposefully trying to achieve a basket or a touchdown. The "towards-which" is Heidegger's nonintentionalistic term for the end points we use in making sense of a flow of directed activity.

Heidegger next spells out the end of the line of towards-whichs—that for the sake of which the activity is done:

The primary "towards-which" is a "for-the-sake-of-which." (116)[84]

With hammering, there is an involvement in making something fast; with making something fast there is an involvement in protection against bad weather; and this protection "is" for the sake of [*um willen*] providing shelter for Dasein—that is to say, for the sake of a possibility of Dasein's being. (116)[84]

The "for-the-sake-of" always pertains to the being of *Dasein*, for which, in its being, that very being is essentially an *issue*. (116–117)[84]

Making a shelter, however, is an unfortunate example of a for-the-sake-of-which, since it suggests an instinctual necessity built into the organism by nature, rather than a possible way in which

Dasein's being is an issue for it. In Heidegger's defense we should note that he speaks of providing a shelter as a *possibility* of Dasein's *being*. The idea may be that people are not caused to build houses the way birds are caused by their instincts to build nests. Being a homemaker is a possible way for Dasein to be. In some cultures one can, for example, interpret oneself as being a hermit and live outdoors on a mountainside.

Heidegger's uses the term "the for-the-sake-of-which" to call attention to the way human activity makes long-term sense, thus avoiding any intimation of a final goal. A for-the-sake-of-which, like *being* a father or *being* a professor, is not to be thought of as a goal I have in mind and can achieve. Indeed, it is not a goal at all, but rather a self-interpretation that informs and orders all my activities.

As a first approximation, we can think of the for-the-sake-of-whichs to which Dasein "assigns itself" as social "roles" and "goals," but Heidegger never uses the terms "roles" and "goals." When I am successfully coping, my activity can be seen to have a point, but I need not have any *goal*, let alone a long-range life *plan* as AI researchers like Roger Schank[8] suppose.

"Role" is not quite right either. Role talk is the end-stage of a movement from transparent coping to thematization. If I run into trouble in the way my life hangs together, my for-the-sake-of-whichs can show up intentionalistically as unavailable goals I am striving to reach. I can shift my stance to deliberating about aspects of my life such as my *relationships* (student, lover, father, etc.), and I can think about my *occupation* and whether I should change it for another. As a parent or a teacher, I must conform to a whole set of norms concerning my responsibilities, which can be laid out in ceteris paribus rules if, for example, ongoing interactions break down and I have to go to court. Only at the occurrent level, however, does one observe, from outside (so to speak), *roles*. These are context-free features of people's lives corresponding to function predicates describing objective features of equipment, and just as function predicates, as we shall soon see, cannot capture the holistic character of equipment, role predicates cannot capture what one simply knows how to do and be when one is socialized into some of the for-the-sake-of-whichs available in one's culture.

Remember, however, that strictly speaking we should not speak of *Dasein*'s being socialized. Human organisms do not have Dasein in them until they *are* socialized. Dasein needs "for-the-sake-of-whichs" and the whole involvement structure in order to take a stand on itself, i.e., in order to *be* itself. That is why Heidegger says

Dasein has *always already* assigned itself to an in-order-to in terms of a for-the-sake-of-which.

Dasein has assigned itself to an "in-order-to," and it has done so in terms of an ability to be for the sake of which it itself is—one which it may have seized upon either explicitly or tacitly. (119)[86]

As "tacitly" suggests, for-the-sake-of-whichs need not be intentional at all. I pick up my most basic life-organizing self-interpretations by socialization, not by choosing them. For example, one behaves as an older brother or a mama's girl without having chosen these organizing self-interpretations, and without having them in mind as specific purposes. These ways of being lead one to certain organized activities such as being a teacher, nurse, victim, etc. Each such "role" is an integrated set of practices: one might say "a practice," as in the practice of medicine. And each practice is connected with a lot of equipment for practicing it. Dasein inhabits or dwells in these practices and their appropriate equipment; in fact Dasein takes a stand on its being by being a more or less integrated subpattern of social practices.[9]

Dasein finds "itself" primarily in what it does, uses, expects, avoids—in the environmentally available with which it is primarily concerned. (155)[119]

B. The Interdependence of Dasein and World
The idea that Dasein has a preontological understanding of the world or involvement whole allows us to understand a particularly dense passage. Bear in mind that, in dealing with equipment, "letting something be" or "freeing something" means using it. This is ontical. Ontologically such letting be requires *already knowing how* the thing fits into the involvement whole, and in this sense "previously freeing" it for all particular ontical uses:

Ontically, "letting something be involved" signifies that within our factical concern we let something available *be* so-and-so *as* it is already [e.g., be a hammer by hammering with it] . . . . The way we take this ontical sense of "letting be" is, fundamentally, ontological. And therewith we Interpret the meaning of previously freeing what is proximally available within-the-world. Previously letting something "be" does not mean that we must first bring it into its being and produce it; it means rather that something which is already an "entity" must be discovered in its availableness, and that we must thus let the entity which has this being encounter us [i.e., show itself]. This "*a priori*" letting-something-be-involved [i.e., knowing how to use it and how it fits in with other equipment and purposes] is the condition for the possibility of anything available showing up for us, so that Dasein, in its ontical dealings with the entity thus showing up, can thereby let it be involved [use it] in the ontical sense. (117, my gloss in brackets) [84–85][10]

Heidegger thus equates the involvement whole—the "wherein" of the available—with the world, and the structure of the "wherein" with the being of the world:

The "wherein" of an understanding which assigns or refers itself, is that on the basis of which one lets entities be encountered in the kind of being that belongs to involvements; this "wherein" is the phenomenon of the world. And the structure of that on the basis of which Dasein assigns itself is what makes up the worldliness of the world. (119) [86][11]

In laying out world, Heidegger seems to shift without explanation from speaking of the workshop, to the referential whole (*Verweisungsganzheit*), to the equipmental whole (*Zeugganzes*), to the involvement whole (*Bewandtnisganzheit*), to the phenomenon of world, to worldliness. The *equipmental whole*, I take it, describes the interrelated equipment; the *referential whole* its interrelations; and the *involvement whole* adds human purposiveness. The workshop is a specific example of all these wholes; the *phenomenon of world* is the special way the world manifests itself; and *worldliness* is the way of being of the world and of all its subworlds.

Heidegger next introduces the notion of significance:

The "for-the-sake-of-which" signifies an "in-order-to"; this in turn, a "towards-this"; the latter, an "in-which" of letting something be involved; and that in turn, the "with-which" of an involvement. These relationships are bound up with one another as a primordial whole; they are what they are as this signifying in which Dasein gives itself beforehand its being-in-the-world as something to be understood. The relational whole of this signifying we call "*significance.*" This is what makes up the structure of the world—the structure of that wherein Dasein as such already is. (120) [87]

Significance is the background upon which entities can make sense and activities can have a point.

Significance is that on the basis of which the world is disclosed as such. To say that the "for-the-sake-of-which" and significance are both disclosed in Dasein, means that Dasein is the entity which, as being-in-the-world, is an issue for itself. (182) [143]

"Subject" and "object," Dasein and world, are ultimately so intimately intertwined that one cannot separate the world from Daseining. "With equal primordiality the understanding projects Dasein's being both upon its "for-the-sake-of-which" and upon significance, as the worldliness of its current world" (185) [145]. As Heidegger later says of this discussion:

The upshot of that analysis was that the referential whole of significance (which as such is constitutive for worldliness) has been "tied up" with a "for-the-sake-of-which." The fact that this referential whole of the manifold relations of the "in-order-to" has been bound up with that which is an issue for Dasein, does not signify that a "world" of objects which is occurrent has been welded together with a subject. It is rather the phenomenal expression of the fact that the basic makeup of Dasein . . . is primordially a whole. (236) [192]

To understand the above passage, we must remember that any given piece of equipment, e.g., a hammer, is what it is in a referential whole which connects it with other equipment, and any use of equipment, e.g., hammering, takes place in an involvement whole that connects it with many ways of being human. The involvement whole and Dasein's life are both organized by the same for-the-sake-of-whichs. It helps to distinguish something like an "objective" and a "subjective" side of this phenomenon only to see that in the end they cannot be distinguished. On the "objective" side we would have equipment defined by its in-order-to, which in turn gets its point in terms of for-the-sake-of-whichs. On the "subjective" side we would have Dasein's self-interpretation which is accomplished by "assigning itself" to for-the-sake-of-whichs. But obviously this separation will not work. On the one hand, Dasein needs the referential whole and the involvement whole to be itself. On the other hand, the "objective" or equipment side is organized in terms of for-the-sake-of-whichs that are ways of being Dasein. The referential whole only makes sense because it all "hangs," so to speak, from for-the-sake-of-whichs that are Dasein's ways of taking a stand on itself, and Dasein exists and makes sense only because it takes over the for-the-sake-of-whichs that are built into and organize the involvement whole.

The shared familiar world, then, is what makes individual human beings possible.

Dasein itself, ultimately the beings which we call men, are possible in their being only because there is a world. . . . Dasein exhibits itself as a being *which is in its world but at the same time is by virtue of the world in which it is.* Here we find a peculiar union of being in the world with the being of Dasein which itself can be made comprehensible only insofar as that which here stands in this union, Dasein itself with its world, has been made clear in its basic structures. (HCT, 202)

This is not to deny that the world also depends on Dasein's way of being. Rather it shows that Dasein is nothing like what philosophers have thought of as a "subject." In his course the year after *Being and Time*, Heidegger addresses the question directly:

There is world only insofar as Dasein exists. But then is world not something "subjective"? In fact it is! Only one may not at this point reintroduce a common, subjectivistic concept of "subject." Instead, the task is to see that being-in-the-world, . . . fundamentally transforms the concept of subjectivity and of the subjective. (MFL, 195)

IV. Two Ways in Which the Phenomenon of World Is Revealed

A. Disturbance

The world, i.e., the interlocking practices, equipment, and skills for using them, which provides the basis for using specific items of equipment, is hidden. It is not disguised, but it is undiscovered. So, like the available, the world has to be revealed by a special technique.[12] Since we ineluctably dwell in the world, we can get at the world only by shifting our attention to it while at the same time staying involved in it. Luckily for the phenomenologist, there are special situations in which the phenomenon of world is forced upon our awareness:

To the everydayness of being-in-the-world there belong certain modes of concern. These permit the beings with which we concern ourselves to be encountered in such a way that the worldly character of what is intraworldly comes to the fore. (102)[73]

The discovery that a piece of equipment is missing, on Heidegger's account, reveals the workshop as a mode of the world. The disturbance makes us aware of the function of equipment and the way it fits into a practical context.

When an assignment to some particular "towards-this" has been . . . circumspectively aroused, we catch sight of the "towards-this" itself, and along with it everything connected with the work—the whole "workshop"—as that wherein concern always dwells. The nexus of equipment is lit up, not as something never seen before, but as a whole constantly sighted beforehand in circumspection [i.e., as already taken account of in our transparent everyday coping]. With this whole, however, the world announces itself. (105, my gloss in brackets) [74–75]

If we can't get back to work, we are left helpless, and in asking if we can abandon our project, the point of our activity becomes apparent to us.

Our circumspection comes up against emptiness, and now sees for the first time *what* the missing article was available *with*, and *what* it was available *for*. (105) [75]

B. Signs

Can we become aware of the relational whole of significance that makes up the world, without a disturbance? Can we be simultaneously absorbed in the successful functioning of things *and* notice the context in which they function?

Heidegger's answer is that there are, indeed, functioning entities whose function it is to show their practical context. Such entities are called signs. All equipment is *serviceable*, only signs *indicate*. Heidegger discusses signs at some length partly because he is rejecting Husserl's account of indication in *Logical Investigations*, i.e., that the indication relation of signs to what they are signs of is a causal relation based on some sort of spatial proximity. Also Heidegger wants to reject the semiotic view that signifying is an ontologically basic relation. But Heidegger is mainly interested in signs as illuminating the way equipment is what it is only in a context and only when it is actually taken up and used.

Signs are a type of equipment that in their functioning reveal their way of being and the context into which they fit.

A sign is something ontically available, which functions both as this definite equipment and as something indicative of the ontological structure of availableness, of referential wholes, and of worldliness. (114) [82]

Signs always function against a practical background that they presuppose and to which they direct our attention. Heidegger uses as example an automobile's turning signal:

This sign is an item of equipment which is available for the driver in his concern with driving, and not for him alone: those who are not traveling with him—and they in particular—also make use of it, either by giving way on the proper side or by stopping. This sign is available within-the-world in the whole equipment-nexus of vehicles and traffic regulations. (109)[78]

Although Heidegger does not say so, it would be in keeping with his account of circumspection to note that we can cope with signs without becoming thematically aware of them. We often act appropriately with respect to the turning signal of the car in front of us without being any more thematically aware of it than we are of the doorknob which we turn in order to enter the room. Still, Heidegger's point is that to cope with such signs is to cope not just with *them*, but with the whole interconnected pattern of activity into which they are integrated. If they are to function as signs for us we certainly cannot just stare at them, and we cannot use them in isolation. "The sign is *not* authentically 'grasped' if we just stare at it and identify it as an indicator-thing which occurs" (110)[79]. Moreover the sign does not simply point to other objects occurrent in the situation—e.g., the street or the direction the car will take— it lights up the situation itself.

Even if we turn our glance in the direction which the direction signal indicates, and look at something occurrent in the region indicated, even then the sign is not authentically encountered . . . . (110)[79] Such a sign addresses itself to the circumspection of our concernful dealings, and it does so in such a way that the circumspection which goes along with it, following where it points, brings into an explicit "survey" whatever aroundness the environment may have at the time. (110)[79]

Thus signs point out the context of shared practical activity, i.e., the world.

A sign is not a thing which stands to another thing in the relationship of indicating; it is rather an item of equipment which explicitly raises an equipmental whole into our circumspection so that together with it the worldly character of the available announces itself. (110)[80]

It follows that a sign cannot be understood as a mere *relation* of one thing to another. This is Heidegger's implicit critique of semiotics.

Being-a-sign-for can itself be formalized as a *universal kind of relation*, so that the sign-structure itself provides an ontological clue for "characterizing" any entity whatsoever. . . . [But] if we are to investigate such phenomena as references, signs, or even significations, nothing is to be gained by characterizing them as relations. Indeed we shall eventually have to show that "relations" themselves, *because of* their formally general character, have their ontological source in reference. (107–108) [77]

Signs can do their job only because we already know our way about in the world.

Signs always indicate primarily "wherein" one lives, where one's concern dwells, what sort of involvement there is with something. (111) [80]

A sign's signifying must take place *in a context*, and it signifies, i.e., it can *be* a sign, only for those who *dwell* in that context.

V. Disclosing and Discovering

Disclosing and discovering are two modes of revealing. *Disclosedness* of the world is required for what Heidegger calls Dasein's *discovering* of entities.

[The environment] is itself inaccessible to circumspection, so far as circumspection is always directed towards entities; but in each case it has already been disclosed for circumspection. "Disclose" and "disclosedness" will be used as technical terms in the passages that follow, and shall signify "to lay open" and "the character of having been laid open." (105) [75]

The basic idea is that for a particular person to be directed toward a particular piece of equipment, whether using it, perceiving it, or whatever, there must be a correlation between that person's general skills for coping and the interconnected equipmental whole in which the thing has a place. On the side of Dasein, originary transcendence (*disclosing*) is the condition of the possibility of ontic transcendence (*discovering*), and on the side of the world, *disclosedness* is the condition of the possibility of anything being *discovered.*

We are now in a position to understand (1) what sort of activity disclosing is and (2) how it is related to discovering.

A. Disclosing as Being-in-the-World

The clue to (1) is found in what we have said about the comportment in which Dasein uses the available. A particular piece of equipment can be used only in a referential whole. In his lectures, Heidegger calls Dasein's understanding of the referential whole *familiarity.* He explains:

My encounter with the room is not such that I first take in one thing after another and put together a manifold of things in order then to see a room. Rather, I primarily see a referential whole . . . from which the individual piece of furniture and what is in the room stand out. Such an environment of the nature of a closed referential whole is at the same time distinguished by a specific *familiarity*. The . . . referential whole is grounded precisely in familiarity, and this familiarity implies that the referential relations are *well-known*. (HCT 187)

This is a very important passage. Notice first that Heidegger is rejecting the Kantian idea that in order to see the whole room I have to synthesize a "manifold" of things, perspectives, sense data, or whatever. I just take in the whole room. I do it by being ready to deal with familiar rooms and the things in them. My "set" or "readiness" to cope with chairs by avoiding them or by sitting on them, for example, is "activated" when I enter the room. My readiness is, of course, not a set of beliefs or rules for dealing with rooms and chairs; it is a sense of how rooms normally show up, a skill for dealing with them, that I have developed by crawling and walking around many rooms.

Thus the sort of background familiarity that functions when I take in a room full of furniture as a whole and deal with it is neither a specific action like sitting in a chair, nor is it merely a capacity in the body or brain for carrying out specific actions. It is neither subjective intentionality nor objective muscle machinery (Searle's two alternatives). It is being ready in particular circumstances to respond appropriately to whatever might normally come along. Heidegger describes this background readiness as "the background of . . . primary familiarity, which itself is not conscious and intended but is rather present in [an] unprominent way" (HCT, 189). In *Being and Time* Heidegger speaks of "that familiarity in accordance with which Dasein . . . 'knows its way about' [*sich 'auskennt'*] in its public environment" (405)[354].

Of course, we do not activate this most general skill on only certain occasions; it is active all the time. In *Basic Problems* Heidegger calls it the "sight of practical circumspection . . . , our practical everyday orientation" (BP, 163).[13] We are masters of our world, constantly effortlessly ready to do what is appropriate.

Circumspection oriented to the presence of what is of concern provides each setting-to-work, procuring, and performing with the way to work it out, the means to carry it out, the right occasion, and the appropriate time. This sight of circumspection is the skilled possibility of concerned discovery. (HCT, 274)

On analogy with the way our eyes are constantly accommodating to the light, we might call the way we are constantly adapting to our situation "accommodation." But Heidegger needs no specific term for this most basic activity. It is so pervasive and constant that he simply calls it *being-in-the-world.*

Any concern is already as it is, because of some familiarity with the world. . . . Being-in-the-world . . . amounts to a *nonthematic circumspective absorption* in the references or assignments that make up the availableness of an equipmental whole. (107, my italics) [76]

It is this holistic background coping (disclosing) that makes possible appropriate dealings in particular circumstances (discovering). Only because, on entering the workshop, we are able to avoid chairs, locate and approach the workbench, pick out and grasp something as an instrument, etc., can we use a specific hammer to hit a specific nail, find the hammer too light or too heavy, etc.

  In his lectures Heidegger extends this account of Dasein's being-in-the-world to a phenomenological theory of perception that implicitly criticizes Husserl (and Searle).

Why can I let a pure thing of the world show up at all in bodily presence? Only because the world is already there in thus letting it show up, *because letting-it-show-up is but a particular mode of my being-in-the-world* and because world means nothing other than what is always already present for the entity in it. I can see a natural thing in its bodily presence only on the basis of this being-in-the-world. . . . (HCT, 196, my italics)

In then referring to absorbed being-in-the-world or background coping as the "founding steps" of perception, Heidegger uses the Husserlian intentionalist terminology he is criticizing in order to replace it.

I can at any time perceive natural things in their bodily presence directly, that is, without running through the founding steps beforehand, because it belongs to the sense of being-in-the-world to be in these founding steps constantly and primarily. I have no need to go through them because Dasein, which founds perceiving, is nothing but the way of being of these very founding steps, as concerned absorption in the world. (HCT, 197)

In response, then, to Husserl and Searle and their exclusive concern with subject/object intentionality, Heidegger points out that in order to reveal beings by using or contemplating them, we must simultaneously be exercising a general skilled grasp of our circumstances. Even if there were an experience of effort or acting accompanying specific acts of hammering (which Heidegger does not find in his experience) there would seem to be no place for an experience of acting with its conditions of satisfaction accompanying the background orienting, balancing, etc., which, as being-in-the-world, makes using specific things possible. It is hard to make sense of what a Husserlian/Searlean intentionalistic account of being-in-the-world would be. Searle would seem to have to make the implausible claim that one's being-in-the-world, which is "not conscious and intended" (HCT, 189), is still somehow caused and guided by intentions in action. To avoid this claim, Searle thinks of the background not as constant coping, but merely as a *capacity*. But the notion of a capacity leaves out the *activity of disclosing*—precisely what leads Heidegger to think of the background as an originary kind of intentionality.

Dasein's background coping, although not itself accompanied by a feeling of willing or effort, does make possible the experience of acting on those occasions when it occurs. But then, this experience cannot be the only kind of intentionality, but presupposes background intentionality.

Willing and wishing are rooted with ontological necessity in Dasein as care; they are not just ontologically undifferentiated experiences (*Erlebnisse*) occurring in a "stream" which is completely indefinite with regard to the sense of its being. (238)[194]

Precisely because the care-structure, which we shall later see is the structure of disclosedness, stays in the background, philosophers like Husserl and Searle overlook it in their account of mental states.

Care is ontologically "earlier" than the phenomena we have just mentioned, which admittedly can, within certain limits, always be "described" appropriately without our needing to have the full ontological horizon visible, or even to be familiar with it at all. (238)[194]

We are now in a position to understand how Dasein's activity of disclosing is related to the world as disclosedness. Just as in specific cases of coping with the available Dasein is absorbed in its activity in such a way that its experience does not have any self-referential intentional content, so, in general, Dasein is absorbed in the background coping that discloses the world as familiar in such a way that there is no separation between Dasein's disclosing comportment and the world disclosed. "We define [concerned being-in-the-world] as absorption in the world, being drawn in by it"(HCT, 196). Just as "dealings with equipment subordinate themselves to the manifold assignments of the 'in-order-to'" (98) [69], so "Dasein, in so far as it is, has always submitted itself already to a 'world'*[14] which shows up for it, and this submission belongs essentially to its being" (120–121) [87] [15]

B. The Identity and Difference of Disclosing and Discovering

Heidegger stresses the interconnection between Dasein's disclosing and discovering comportments. On the one hand, disclosing as skillful dealing with ways of being of entities in whole situations is more basic than discovering:

We must now manage to exhibit more precisely the interconnection between the discoveredness of a being and the disclosedness of its being and to show how the disclosedness . . . of being founds, that is to say, gives the ground, the foundation, for the possibility of the discoveredness of entities. (BP, 72)

In *Being and Time* the related passage reads, "'A priori' letting-something-be-involved is the condition for the possibility of encountering anything available" (117) [85].[16] Disclosing as letting something be involved is originary transcendence. Heidegger speaks of such transcendence in a passage that needs a lot of interpreting (my gloss is in brackets):

We must hold that the intentional structure of comportments is not something which is immanent to the so-called subject and which would first of all be in need of transcendence; rather, the intentional constitution of Dasein's comportments [disclosing, originary transcendence] is precisely the ontological condition of the possibility of every and any [discovering, ontic] transcendence. [Ontic] transcendence, transcending, belongs to the essential nature of the being that exists (on the basis of [originary] transcendence) as intentional, that is, exists in the manner of dwelling among the [available and the] occurrent. (BP, 65)

But, on the other hand, originary transcendence (being-in-the-world, disclosure) is not something radically different from ontic transcending (transparent coping with specific things, discovering); rather, it is *the same sort of coping* functioning as the holistic background for all purposive comportment. "The intentional constitution of Dasein's comportment is precisely the *ontological condition of the possibility of every and any transcendence*" (BP, 65). One needs to be finding one's way about in the world in order to use equipment, but finding one's way about is just more coping. Any specific activity of coping takes place on the background of more general coping. Being-in-the-world is, indeed, ontologically prior—in Heidegger's special sense, *a priori*—as the ontological condition of the possibility of specific activities, yet being-in-the-world is just more skilled activity.

> The previous disclosure of that on the basis of which what shows up within-the-world is subsequently freed, amounts to nothing else than understanding the world—that world towards which Dasein . . . always comports itself. (118) [85–86]

Our general background coping, then, our familiarity with the world, is our understanding of being.

> That wherein Dasein already understands itself . . . is always something with which it is primordially familiar. This familiarity with the world . . . goes to make up Dasein's understanding of being. (119) [86]

Thus Heidegger conceptualizes the difference between specific coping (ontic transcendence) and world-disclosing background coping (originary transcendence) as the difference between our relation to beings and our understanding of being. This is presumably the original version of the famous *ontological difference*, which, according to the later Heidegger, the tradition sought mistakenly to capture in its various accounts of the being of beings.

6

Heidegger's Critique of Recent Versions of Cartesianism

Now that we have described the world, rather than passing it over as the tradition has done, what implications do our results have for how we deal with traditional philosophical questions? So far we have seen the relevance of Heidegger's phenomenological description of coping with the available to the Cartesian *epistemological* account of a subject (*res cogitans*) contemplating objects (*res extensa*). Now we shall see the relevance of an account of worldliness to the other tradition that stems from Descartes: the *ontological* project of explaining everything in terms of some type of occurrent entity that is taken to be directly intelligible.

In Descartes's ontology the ultimate building blocks of the universe are the elements of nature (*naturas simplices*) understood by natural science. But one could also try to account for everything in terms of sense data, monads, or, as in Husserl, relations among the "predicate senses" corresponding to relations among the primitive features of the world to which these basic elements purport to refer. Heidegger presumably has this last stage of the atomistic, rationalist tradition in mind when he speaks of understanding the world in terms of "a system of relations" "first posited in 'an act of thinking'" (122) [88]. This Husserlian project culminates in recent attempts to understand the world and the objects in it as a complex combination of features, and the mind as containing symbolic representations of these features and rules or programs representing their relationships.[1]

Traditional ontology succeeds only if it can account for *all* modes of being, including Dasein's practical activity and the equipmental whole in which Dasein is absorbed, in terms of the law-like or rule-like combinations of occurrent elements. If it can be shown that the world is irreducible to occurrent elements, be they bits of matter, atomic facts, sense data, or bits of information, then an ontology based on the occurrent fails. Heidegger focuses on Descartes's attempt to understand everything in terms of nature. To follow Heidegger's critique, we must first understand Descartes's account of the relation of nature and world.

I. The Ontological Status of Nature

In his critique of naturalistic ontology, Heidegger does not want to deny that nature underlies and explains the functioning of equipment. We can hammer with iron and wood but not with rubber and ice. But the ontological significance of this seeming priority of nature turns out to be a complicated question.

To begin with, Heidegger distinguishes at least four different ways nature can be encountered. Heidegger tells us, "Nature is itself an entity which shows up within the world and which can be discovered in various ways and at various stages" (92) [63]. Nature shows up as available, unavailable, occurrent, and also, strangely, in some other way, which is none of the above. Let us now lay out these ways of being, noting at each stage the kind of concern involved. Our questions at this stage are: (1) Can Heidegger achieve his fundamental ontology, demonstrating that all modes of being, even the being of nature, can be made intelligible only in terms of Dasein's mode of being, and not vice versa? (2) Can he still leave a place for ontic, causal, scientific explanation?

A. Nature as Available

The entity which Descartes is trying to grasp ontologically . . . with his "extensio," is . . . such as to become discoverable first of all by going through an intraworldly entity which is proximally available—nature. (128) [95]

1. Natural Materials
Considered as the stuff out of which the available is made—the "whereof" of equipment—nature is "picked out" as raw material, and thus is "freed" or made intelligible in terms of the function it serves in supporting equipment.

In the environment certain entities become accessible which are always available, but which, in themselves, do not need to be produced. Hammer, tongs, and needle, refer in themselves to steel, iron, metal, mineral, wood, in that they consist of these. In equipment that is used, "nature" is discovered along with it by that use—the "nature" we find in natural products. (100) [70]

The properties of iron—its malleability, ductibility, hardness, etc.—make it moldable and able to withstand violent contact. Dasein, therefore, appropriates iron into its referential whole. It can be used in hammer heads, nails, anvils, chairs, statues, etc. Yet, of course, nature cannot be used in any way whatsoever. Occurrent nature sets limits as to what can be done with equipment. Given iron's causal powers and determinate properties, it cannot be used for fuel or a nourishing meal.

It seems that Dasein's self-interpreting everyday activity and nature codetermine what can be available for what. If Dasein insists upon using equipment in a particular way, regardless of the properties of what it is made of, it will break. When something thus becomes unavailable, its recalcitrant properties or aspects "announce themselves," as does nature's contribution to the equipment's serviceability.

Anything available is, at the worst, appropriate for some purposes and inappropriate for others; and its "properties" are, as it were, still bound up in these ways in which it is appropriate or inappropriate, just as occurrentness, as a possible kind of being for something available, is bound up in availableness. (115) [83]

2. Natural Regularities

In *Being and Time* Heidegger subscribes to the instrumental understanding of nature: "The wood is a forest of timber, the mountain a quarry of rock; the river is water-power, the wind is wind 'in the sails'" (100) [70]. Later he criticizes this stance for treating nature as "a gigantic filling station."[2]

Environing nature can also be useful to us without being used as raw material. For example:

When we look at the clock, we tacitly make use of the "sun's position," in accordance with which the measurement of time gets regulated in the official astronomical manner. When we make use of the clock-equipment, which is primarily and inconspicuously available, the environing nature is available along with it. (101) [71]

3. Nature Taken up into History

We contend that what is *primarily* historical is Dasein. That which is *secondarily* historical, however, is what we encounter within-the-world—not only available equipment, in the widest sense, but also the environing *nature* as "the very soil of history." (433) [381] Nature is historical as a countryside, as an area that has been colonized or exploited, as a battlefield, or as the site of a cult. (440) [388–389]

B. Nature as Unavailable: Natural Forces

We also encounter nature as not available but rather as a threat to our equipmental nexus. Here nature shows up and makes sense in terms of what it disturbs and how we protect ourselves against it.

In roads, streets, bridges, buildings, our concern discovers nature as having some definite direction. A covered railway platform takes account of bad weather; an installation for public lighting takes account of the darkness, or rather of specific changes in the presence or absence of daylight. (100) [71]

C. Nature as Occurrent

Nature can appear in several different ways to disinterested contemplation.

1. Pure Occurrentness

We have already seen that if nature as available and unavailable is disregarded, nature can appear in the privative mode of pure occurrence. "If its kind of being as available is disregarded, this 'nature' itself can be discovered and defined simply in its pure occurrence" (100) [70]. When recontextualized in a theory, this is the nature studied by natural science.

2. Natural Science

We have seen in chapter 4 that nature as studied by science is not revealed in passive contemplation but rather in a specific mode of concern, i.e., by "depriving the world of its worldliness in a definite way" (94) [65]—a way that makes possible recontextualization in a theory. Scientific observation can thus reveal a universe unrelated to human for-the-sake-of-whichs. This is the nature whose causal powers underlie equipment and even Dasein itself insofar as it has a body. We shall come back to this topic in chapter 15.

D. The Nature of Primitive Peoples and the Romantic Poets

"But when [science studies nature] the nature which 'stirs and strives,' which assails us and enthralls us as landscape, remains hidden" (100) [70]. In the case of poets, nature is not to be understood as that which is just occurrent, nor as the power of nature. . . . The botanist's plants are not the flowers of the hedgerow; the "source" which the geographer establishes for a river is not the "springhead in the dale." (100) [70]

Heidegger therefore notes:

Perhaps even availability and equipment have nothing to contribute as ontological clues in Interpreting the primitive world; and certainly the ontology of thinghood does even less. (113) [82]

Still, in *Being and Time*, Heidegger claims that "even the phenomenon of 'nature,' as it is conceived, for instance, in romanticism, can be grasped ontologically in terms of the concept of the world—that is to say, in terms of the analytic of Dasein" (94) [65]. In his later essays, however, Heidegger tries to show that this fourth way of being of nature, which the Greeks experienced as *physis* and which we still sometimes experience in a noninstrumental and yet noncontemplative relation to things, has been neglected by our tradition and *cannot* be understood by reference to Dasein's concerns.[3]

II. Heidegger's Critique of Scientific Reductionism

All of this has shown that nature does, indeed, show up as having each of the ways of being Heidegger has distinguished, but it has not answered the question: Which is ontologically more basic, equipment or the material in nature whose causal powers enable equipment to function?

This question must be taken seriously. At several points Heidegger calls attention to the phenomena that support the traditional naturalistic view. When our practical activity is disrupted, Heidegger points out, we then see that the occurrent has been there all along.

Conspicuousness presents the available equipment as in a certain unavailableness . . . . It shows itself as an equipmental thing which looks so and so, and which, in its availableness as looking that way, has constantly been occurrent too. (102–103) [73]

It is presumably the underlying constant occurrent material that accounts for the equipment's reliability,[4] or conversely, for its failure to function properly.

The occurrent *in* the available makes possible its availability. Heidegger grants that "only by reason of something occurrent, 'is there' anything available." But he immediately asks, "Does it follow, however, granting this thesis for the nonce, that availableness is *ontologically founded* upon occurrence?" (101, my italics) [71] It is contrary to Heidegger's main thesis to hold that occurrent properties are *ontologically* prior to available equipment and its aspects. Yet, in his lectures prior to *Being and Time* Heidegger goes out of his way to show the plausibility of the view he opposes:

The work-world bears within itself references to an entity which in the end makes it clear that it—the work-world, what is of concern—is not the primary entity after all. Precisely when we are led from an analysis of the work-world, in following its references to the world of nature, finally to recognize and to define the world of nature as the fundamental stratum of the real, we see that it is not . . . care which is the primary worldly presence, but rather the reality of nature. This conclusion, it seems, cannot be avoided. (HCT, 199)

It is important to realize, however, that ontology, as the science of everything that is, must make a stronger claim than natural science. Natural science tells us how hammers work but not what hammers *are*. It does not have to account for the being of equipment such as hammers, but only for the causal powers of the natural kinds of material such as iron and wood out of which hammers are made. Heidegger contends that nature can explain only *why* the available works; it cannot make intelligible availableness as a *way of being* because nature cannot explain worldliness.

Even if [traditional] ontology should itself succeed in explicating the being of nature in the very purest manner, in conformity with the basic assertions about this entity which the mathematical natural sciences provide, it will never reach the phenomenon that is the "world."* (92) [63]

Heidegger will argue for two theses. (1) Worldliness cannot be understood in terms of nature.

A glance at previous ontology shows that if one fails to see being-in-the-world as the make-up of Dasein, the phenomenon of world likewise gets *passed over*. One tries instead to Interpret the world in terms of the being of those beings which are occurrent within-the-world . . . namely, in terms of nature. . . . "Nature," as the categorial aggregate of those structures of being which a definite being encountered within-the-world may possess, can never make worldliness intelligible. (93–94) [65]

(2) Nature can be made intelligible only on the basis of worldliness.

The sense of worldliness *cannot* be read off from mere nature. The environmental references, in which nature is present primarily in a worldly way, tell us rather the reverse: nature as reality can only be understood on the basis of worldliness. (HCT, 199)

Heidegger begins to make his case by reminding us that whatever shows up for us as intelligible shows up on the background of significance as either in the way, threatening, or as something that can somehow be put to use. Things are not encountered as isolated occurrent entities to which we attach isolated function predicates. Heidegger offers as example the farmer's use of the south wind. For the farmer to use the wind as equipment, the wind must already show up as fitting into the everyday world, not as the meteorologist's stream of occurrent air molecules.

If, for instance, the south wind "is accepted" by the farmer as a sign of rain, then this "acceptance"—or the "value" with which the entity is "invested"—is not a sort of bonus over and above what is already occurrent in itself—viz., the flow of air in a definite geographical direction. The south wind may be meteorologically accessible as something which just occurs; but it is *never* occurrent *primarily* in such a way as this, only occasionally taking over the function of a warning signal. On the contrary, only by the circumspection with which one takes account of things in farming is the south wind discovered in its being. (111–112) [80–81]

Heidegger anticipates the traditional ontologist's objection:

But, one will protest, *that which* gets taken as a sign must first have become accessible in itself and been apprehended *before* the sign gets established. (112) [81]

He answers:

Certainly it must in any case be such that in some way we can come across it. The question simply remains as to *how* entities are discovered in this previous encountering, whether as mere things which occur, or rather as equipment which has not been understood—as something available with which we have hitherto not known "how to begin," and which has accordingly kept itself veiled from the purview of circumspection. And here again, when the equipmental characters of the available are still circumspectively undiscovered, they are not to be interpreted as bare thinghood presented for an apprehension of what is just occurrent and no more. (112)[81]

The "argument" for the ontological priority of worldliness and significance so far hinges on this claim that nothing is intelligible to us unless it first shows up as already integrated into our world, fitting into our coping practices.

III. Heidegger's Critique of Cognitivism

Granted that what shows up in the world, even nature, gets its intelligibility from its place in the world, does this demonstrate that the occurrent can never make worldliness intelligible?

Heidegger begins his answer by pointing out that traditional ontology claims to explain all kinds of being in terms of one basic kind of being. Therefore such an ontology must be able to build up everything, including equipmentality, out of whatever basic elements it claims are the ultimate constituents of reality.

Descartes . . . laid the basis for characterizing ontologically that intraworldly entity upon which . . . every other entity is founded—material nature. This would be the fundamental stratum upon which all the other strata of intraworldly actuality are built up. (131)[98]

Nature by itself obviously cannot explain significance. Therefore, to account for the equipmental whole in terms of occurrent elements, traditional ontology, as developed by Descartes and still found in Husserlian phenomenology, information processing psychology, and Artificial Intelligence research, must supplement the bare things in nature that serve in the explanations provided by natural science, with function or value predicates.[5] This amounts to taking the *whole* that Heidegger has just described as significance, which is prior to its parts, equipment, and analyzing it as a *complex totality*, built up out of occurrent elements. Heidegger gives an ironic paraphrase of the approach—of which cognitivist theory is a special case—that seeks to base all ways of being on the supposedly self-evident and directly intelligible way of being of occurrent nature plus occurrent mental predicates:

The extended thing as such would . . . provide the footing for such specific qualities as "beautiful," "ugly," "in keeping," "not in keeping," "useful," "useless." If one is oriented primarily by thinghood, these latter qualities must be taken as nonquantifiable value-predicates [function predicates] by which what is in the first instance just a material thing, gets stamped as something good [for something]. . . . The Cartesian analysis of the "world" would thus enable us for the first time to build up securely the structure of what is primarily available; all it takes is to round out the thing of nature until it becomes a full-fledged thing of use, and this is easily done. (131–132, my additions in brackets) [98–99]

Heidegger criticizes this position by claiming that there is no reason to think that one can arrive at an understanding of the available by adding together occurrent function predicates. The basic intuition behind Heidegger's critique of cognitivism is that one "frees" occurrent properties precisely by stripping away significance. Therefore it is highly implausible that one can reconstruct a meaningful whole by adding further meaningless elements.

When we speak of material thinghood, have we not tacitly posited a kind of being—the constant occurrence of things—which is so far from having been rounded out ontologically by subsequently endowing entities with value-predicates, that these value-characters themselves are rather just ontical characteristics of those entities which have the kind of being possessed by things? Adding on value-predicates cannot tell us anything at all new about the being of goods [functions], *but would merely presuppose again that goods [functions] have pure occurrentness as their kind of being.* (132, my additions in brackets) [99]

The Cartesian ontologist, like the modern cognitivist, would answer that it is not enough just to *say*, as Heidegger does, that such an ontology must fail in the attempt to put the whole together out of elements because the being of a piece of equipment is its role in the whole nexus of references and significance. The cognitivist would hold that he has merely patiently to spell out the relation of each type of equipment to other types of equipment and thus gradually build up a representation of the equipmental whole. For example, one can begin crudely with chairs, lamps, tables, etc. as items of equipment, each in isolation, then add predicates describing their relation to each other, and finally their relation to human skills and purposes.

How can Heidegger *argue* against this claim? Since trying to explain our everyday understanding in terms of occurrent elements only seems plausible if one has a traditional account of the world as a set of objects and of daily activity as rule-governed, the first step, as we have seen, is to show that traditional ontology *passes over the world.* For traditional ontologists and current cognitivists "The Interpretation of the world begins . . . with some intraworldly entity, so that the phenomenon of the world in general no longer comes into view" (122) [89]. Once we get our phenomenology of being-in-the-world right, Heidegger would say, we see the impoverishment that occurs as we strip away significance to arrive at the pure occurrent and inhibit skilled coping to arrive at deliberation. Cognitivism then seems highly implausible. The burden of proof shifts to anyone who expects it to succeed.

Heidegger could spell out his implausibility claim in two ways. First, there is the argument from *holism.* Just adding to the representation of a table the fact that it is to eat at or sit at barely scratches the surface of its involvement with other equipment and for-the-sake-of-whichs that define what it is to be a table. Such function predicates would not be sufficient to enable a person from traditional Japan to cope with our kind of tables or even fully understand Western stories where tables played their normal part. All the propositions spelling out tableness would have ceteris paribus conditions, and so would those conditions, etc.

Second, there is a related argument from skills. Computers programmed as physical symbol systems, that is, using rules and features, do not have skills; they do not come into a situation with a readiness to deal with what normally shows up in that sort of situation. Such a computer can only process occurrent elements. So when we program it, we must feed it the data and the rules it needs in order to build up a model of the situation and deal with tables. Just as in Bourdieu's account (see page 258) the anthropologist must invent rules to try to capture the *savoir faire* involved in exchanging gifts—knowing how much delay and how much difference is appropriate—so the cognitivist would try to capture in rules our *savoir faire* concerning tables. These would of course be ceteris paribus rules depending on background circumstances for their application, and this would in turn lead the cognitivist to search for strict rules to capture these background conditions, which would only reveal more *savoir faire.* For AI researchers, as for Husserl, this promises to be an infinite task.[6] For Heidegger, who claims our commonsense understanding is a kind of knowing-how, not a propositional knowing-that, things look even more discouraging for cognitivism. Since our familiarity does not consist in a vast body of rules and facts, but rather consists of dispositions to respond to situations in appropriate ways, there is no body of commonsense knowledge to formalize. The task is not infinite but hopelessly misguided.

Both arguments implied in *Being and Time* can be put in the form of a dilemma. Facts and rules are, by themselves, meaningless. To capture what Heidegger calls significance or involvement, they must be *assigned relevance*. But the predicates that must be added to define relevance are just more meaningless facts; and paradoxically, the more facts the computer is given the harder it is for it to compute what is relevant to the current situation. To compute relevance in a specific situation a computer would have to search through all its facts following rules for finding those that could possibly be relevant, then apply further rules to determine which facts are usually relevant in this type of situation, and from all these facts deduce which facts were actually relevant in this particular situation. But in a large data-base such a search would be hopelessly difficult and *would get more difficult the more facts one added to guide the search.* The program would thus get more and more bogged down as it executed the program designed to determine which of its vast data-base of meaningless facts and rules were currently meaningful.

To use Heidegger's favorite example, to understand a hammer a computer should not follow out *all* pointers in the data-base to nails, walls, houses, people, wood, iron, doorbells, strength-testing machines in circuses, murder instruments, etc. It should access only facts possibly relevant in the current context. But how could the programmer define the current situation for a detached theoretical subject like a cognitivist mind or a digital computer? Since a computer is not *in* a situation, the AI researcher would have to try to represent being-in-a-situation by some artificial restriction on what pointers to other facts should be followed out. Terry Winograd once attempted to work out just such an approach for story understanding. He noted:

The results of human reasoning are *context dependent*, the structure of memory includes not only the long-term storage organization (what do I know?) but also a current context (what is in focus at the moment?). We believe that this is an important feature of human thought, not an inconvenient limitation.[7]

Winograd saw that "the problem is to find a formal way of talking about . . . current attention focus and goals."[8] His "solution" was to limit the time that the computer could use to search the data-base in all directions from a given starting point. The idea was that this would enable the computer to call up only what was relevant to its current goals.

But clearly one's current context is not defined by what one can think of, given a short time to think. What shows up as relevant in my current situation is determined by what I was just doing and what I am about to do. I move from being in one situation to being in the next by shifts in my readiness, which is itself shaped by years of experience with how situations typically evolve. Dasein is always already in a situation and is constantly moving into a new one with its past experience going before it organizing what will next show up as relevant. The computer, by contrast, keeps having to come into some surrogate of the current situations de novo. Search limitation is no substitute for being already in an unfolding series of situations.

As Heidegger's analysis would lead one to expect, Winograd's solution to the relevance problem did not work out. Winograd now recognizes "the difficulty of formalizing the commonsense background that determines which scripts, goals and strategies are relevant and how they interact."[9] He has subsequently abandoned the search-limitation approach and having "lost faith" in AI now teaches Heidegger in his Stanford Computer Sciences courses.[10]

Having to program computers keeps one honest. There is no room for the armchair rationalist's speculations. Thus AI research has called the Cartesian cognitivist's bluff. It is easy to say that to account for the equipmental nexus one need simply add more and more function predicates and rules describing what is to be done in typical situations, but actual difficulties in AI—its inability to make progress with what is called the commonsense knowledge problem, on the one hand, and its inability to define the current situation, sometimes called the frame problem,[11] on the other—suggest that Heidegger is right. It looks like one cannot build up the phenomenon of world out of meaningless elements.

In the light of these difficulties—the legacy of Cartesian ontological assumptions—we can better appreciate Heidegger's injunction that we return to the phenomena. We have to know what we are trying to explain and whether the elements we are using are rich enough to explain it.

If we are to reconstruct this thing of use, which supposedly comes to us in the first instance "with its skin off," does not this require that we previously take a positive look at the phenomenon whose whole such a reconstruction is to restore? (132)[99]

And once we describe the holistic nature of significance and of our familiarity with it, we are in a position to understand Heidegger's few explicit remarks concerning formal models. A formal model is an abstract structure, which must be fully specified independently of what it models and of dispositions for dealing with what is modeled. Heidegger holds that formal or abstract models therefore fail to capture the know-how in skills such as "hammering with" or "sitting at," as well as the involvement structures of worldliness— "relationships in which concernful circumspection as such already dwells" (122) [88].

Heidegger concludes:

The context of assignments or references, which, as significance, is constitutive for worldliness, can be taken formally in the sense of a system of relations. But one must note that in such formalizations the phenomena get leveled off so much that their real phenomenal content may [sic] be lost, especially in the case of such "simple" relations as those which lurk in significance. The phenomenal content of those "relations" and "relata"—the "in-order-to," the "for-the-sake-of," and the "with which" of an involvement—is such that they resist [sic] any sort of mathematical functionalization. (121–122) [88]

Heidegger's statement is accurate and cautious. He knows that he cannot *prove* that formal models of everyday understanding *must* fail to capture the phenomena he has described, but he also knows that once the phenomena are correctly described the cognitivist project looks highly implausible. A Heideggerian understanding of the tradition leads one to expect the optimism of the cognitive scientist; a Heideggerian description of the phenomenon leads one to expect just the impasse cognitivism faces today.

Heidegger can now put both modern natural science and Cartesian ontology in their proper places. Science has a legitimate place in explaining the equipmental whole. The switchover to theory disconnects the available from the referential whole and from the for-the-sake-of-whichs. It leaves meaningless elements— just the sort of elements that can be treated formally in covering laws and programs. When theory decontextualizes, it does not *construct* the occurrent, but, as Heidegger says, it *reveals* the occurrent which was already there in the available. For example, when we strip away a hammer's being too heavy for this job, we can reveal its weighing 500 grams. Science, then, can discover occurrent properties and the causal relations between these properties.

That is, it discovers the physical properties of nature by leaving out all relevance to human purposes. (See chapter 15.)

> The more the initially experienced world is *deprived of its worldliness* . . . , that is, the more the initially experienced world becomes mere nature, the more we discover in it its mere naturality, for example, in terms of the objectivity of physics. (HCT, 168)

But traditional ontology failed to distinguish ontic (causal) explanations from ontological (phenomenological) accounts of significance.

> If we consider the work of Descartes in relation to the constitution of the mathematical sciences of nature and to the elaboration of mathematical physics in particular, these considerations then naturally assume a fundamentally positive significance. But if they are regarded in the context of a general theory of the reality of the world, it then becomes apparent that from this point on the fateful constriction of the inquiry into reality sets in, which to the present day has not yet been overcome. (HCT, 184–185)

IV. Conclusion

The phenomenological account of how scientific facts are arrived at by leaving out significance shows why, once we have stripped away all meaningful context to get the elements of theory, theory cannot give back meaning. Science cannot reconstruct what has been left out in arriving at theory; it cannot explain significance. For this reason, even though natural science can explain the *causal basis* of the referential whole, "'Nature' . . . can never make *worldliness* intelligible" (94) [65].

At this point Heidegger writes in his copy of *Being and Time*, "but just the reverse" {88}. It is, therefore, important to see what for Heidegger the (ontological) priority of worldliness and the available amounts to and how this priority is compatible with an *explanatory* (ontic) priority of nature and the occurrent. Although the occurrent is necessary for explaining the functioning of the available, Heidegger holds that the equipmental whole is a necessary condition for there being anything available to explain. To pick out (or, as Heidegger would say, "free") anything as a piece of equipment, we must pick it out in terms of its purpose, in the contextual whole of equipment.[12] As we have seen, no combination of properties can be used to pick out a chair—not even if we add the predicate "for sitting on." But once we have picked out a chair, we can discover that it is made of wood or steel, etc. and that these natural kinds and their causal powers make possible the functioning of the chair. The same relationships are even clearer for lamps. There is no way a lamp has to look, no specific shape it must have, no specific materials it has to be made of, even no single job it must do to function as a lamp—it could be a night-light, a streetlight, a reading light, or a traffic light. Only *after* we have picked out a lamp on the basis of its role can we abstract from its significance and use the occurrent properties that are revealed plus the laws of science to explain how it gives out light. In this sense worldliness as significance has priority.

The world itself is not an intraworldly entity; and yet it is so determinative for such entities that only in so far as "there is" a world can they be encountered and show themselves, in their being, as entities which have been discovered. (102) [72]

Traditional ontology has always sought to understand the everyday world by finding something on the level of the occurrent, such as substance, sense data, or representations in transcendental consciousness, that is supposed to be intelligible without reference to anything else, and then sought to show how everything else can be seen to be intelligible because it is built up out of these self-sufficient elements. This would be to read Table 3 with an intelligibility arrow going from bottom to top. Heidegger has argued that the elements ontology starts with are too impoverished to explain worldliness, and therefore the attempt to draw the ontological arrow of intelligibility from the bottom to the top of Table 3 has never worked. There is no reason at all (except the success of theory in ontic scientific explanation, which is not a valid reason) to think that anything occurrent could make worldliness intelligible.

Phenomenology, on the contrary, seeks to show that the everyday world is as self-sufficient and self-intelligible as the objects of theory. It cannot and need not be made intelligible in terms of anything else; rather, it can account for the possibility and place of theory. The world is what we directly understand and in terms of which one can see how nature, equipment, persons, etc. fit together and make sense. Thus worldliness and Dasein's correlative understanding of being are the proper themes for ontology.

The description of world as revealed by Dasein's being-in-the-world and of the ways of being revealed by Dasein's coping,

Heidegger calls *fundamental ontology*. It is the only kind of foundationalism he defends. The kind of intelligibility arrived at by phenomenological investigation is not the same as the kind of intelligibility sought by traditional ontology, viz. building up the whole from elements, but Heidegger claims that it is the only kind of philosophical intelligibility we need and can hope to get.

Thus, instead of shifting the burden of proof, as he did in answering the epistemologist (see chapter 4), Heidegger shifts the question. Science can correctly explain the functioning of the available in terms of causal relations between occurrent elements. (This ontic founding reads Table 3 from bottom to top.) But this is not the ontological issue. The issue is *understanding*, not *explanation*—making sense of how things *are*, not explaining how they *work*. We understand a phenomenon when we see how it fits in with other phenomena. Since one cannot make availableness intelligible on the basis of some combination of occurrent elements, one must turn the question around and seek to account for occurrentness by showing that the occurrent is revealed by selectively leaving out the situational aspects of the unavailable. "Nature is a limiting case of the being of possible intraworldly entities" (94) [65]. In this way we can make sense of the three ways entities can be encountered by reading Table 3 from top to bottom. We can also see that the *pure* occurrent, which provides the basis of traditional ontology, is not intelligible in itself at all, but can be understood only as an illegitimate extrapolation of a legitimate series of transformations of the available, in which everyday intelligibility is progressively removed.

Still, this is not the end of the argument. As in the case of Heidegger's critique of the Cartesian notion of self-sufficient subjects with their inner representations, the traditional ontologist can here claim that, although attempts to construct holistic significance out of meaningless elements seem extremely unpromising, still some such construction must be possible, since what is ultimately real are some sort of elements, and everything must be accounted for in terms of some theory relating these elements or else remain unacceptably mysterious.

To undermine this ontological imperative that prevents us from accepting the phenomenon at face value, one must show how the demand for an ontology based on occurrentness arose. Thus, in the promised Part Two of *Being and Time* Heidegger was going ask:

Table 3
Modes of being of entities other than Dasein.

Mode of being	What happens	Dasein's stance
Availableness	Equipment functioning smoothly.	Transparent coping. Absorbed in practical activity. Manipulation.
Unavailableness	Equipment problem:	
	(1) Malfunction (conspicuous: hammer too heavy).	Get going again (pick up another hammer).
	(2) Temporary breakdown (obstinate: head comes off hammer).	Practical deliberation. Eliminating the disturbance.
	(3) Permanent breakdown (obtrusive: unable to find hammer).	Helpless standing before, but still concerned.
Occurrentness	Everyday practical activity stops.	Detached standing before, Theoretical reflection. (Wonder.)
		Skilled scientific activity. Observation and experimentation.
Pure occurrentness	Rest. Getting finished.	Pure contemplation. Just looking at something. (Curiosity.)

What is encountered	What does the encountering
Transparent functioning, availableness.	No subject. No thematic reflective awareness.
	Subject with mental content on a nonmental background.
Context-dependent aspects or characteristics of "objects" (hammer as "too heavy").	
Ceteris paribus rules. The interconnectedness of equipment. The toward-whichs.	
The worldly character of the workshop, including the for-the-sake-of-whichs.	
Just occurrent and no more. Isolable, determinate properties, and objects as collections of properties (hammer weighs 500 g). Recontextualized. The *universe* as a law-governed set of elements. Attempt to explain human action by strict rules.	Subject with mental content on a nonmental background.
Bare facts, sense data, *res extensa*	Self-sufficient subject.

Why was the phenomenon of the world passed over at the beginning of the ontological tradition which has been decisive for us (explicitly in the case of Parmenides), and why has this passing-over kept constantly recurring?[13] (133) [100]

Heidegger adds:

When our analytic of Dasein has given some perspicuousness to those main structures of Dasein which are of the most importance in the framework of this problematic, and when we have assigned to the concept of being in general the horizon within which its intelligibility becomes possible, so that availableness and occurrentness also become primordially intelligible ontologically for the first time, only then can our critique of the Cartesian ontology of the world (an ontology which, in principle, is still the usual one today) come philosophically into its own. (133) [100]

He promises:

In the answers to these questions a positive understanding of the problematic of the world will be reached for the first time, the sources of our failure to recognize it will be exhibited, and the ground for rejecting the traditional ontology of the world will have been demonstrated. (134) [100]

I take this to mean that phenomenological critique must be complemented by what Heidegger in *Basic Problems* calls "deconstruction" (BP, 22–23). He explains:

We understand this task as one in which by taking *the question of being as our clue*, we are to *destroy* the traditional content of ancient ontology until we arrive at those primordial experiences in which we achieved our first ways of determining the nature of being—the ways which have guided us ever since. (44) [22]

Only when we understand the sources of our ontological assumption that intelligibility is achieved by having a *theory* of all domains of reality, i.e., when we see this assumption as historically determined rather than philosophically necessary, will it lose its grip on us.

Of course, a traditional ontologist could still claim that Parmenides was simply the first to see what true intelligibility amounts to, and that a project does not become less sound simply by being shown to have arisen at some point in history. At that point one can only return to the phenomenon and argue that traditional ontology is prima facie implausible, and there is no *independent reason* to seek an ontology based on the constant presence of self-sufficient substances, or to think of such an ontology as an ahistorical necessity.

It is characteristic of early Heidegger, i.e., Heidegger in *Being and Time*, to want to go even further and make what he considers a stronger argument. He wants to show

that passing over the world and those entities which we primarily encounter is not accidental, not an oversight . . . but that it is grounded in a kind of being which belongs essentially to Dasein itself. (133) [100]

That is, as we shall see in the Appendix, Dasein not only needs to be absorbed in using objects to take a stand on itself but also interprets itself as having a fixed and self sufficient nature like the occurrent in order to hide "the inessentiality of the self" (MFL, 140), and this in turn gives rise to an ontology based on the occurrent. Thus in Division II of Part One, traditional ontology will be criticized as part of a systematic cover-up motivated by Dasein's intrinsic inability to face the truth about itself.

Later Heidegger rejects this hermeneutics of suspicion, as well he might, rehabilitates Parmenides, and concludes that soon after the time of Parmenides, it simply happened that worldliness, which had been taken for granted by the pre-Socratics, was passed over by Plato—as Heidegger later put it: with the pre-Socratics "the essence of truth . . . appears . . . and then immediately disappears again."[14] According to later Heidegger, there is no sense in looking for a cause of such profound "events" that determine what counts as being and intelligibility; one can only try to free oneself from them by recounting their history. That is one reason why later Heidegger turns from "transcendental hermeneutic phenomenology to thinking being historically."[15]

7

Spatiality and Space

We have seen that traditional ontology in its modern form begins when Descartes takes bits of objective space (*res extensa*) as the elements in terms of which to explain everything in the world. Heidegger now turns explicitly to showing the limits of this ontology and also to giving it its legitimate place.

There is some phenomenal justification for regarding the *extensio* as a basic characteristic of the "world," even if by recourse to this neither the spatiality of the world nor that of the beings we encounter in our environment . . . can be conceived ontologically. (134) [101]

One must note Heidegger's quotation convention here. He is saying that *extensio* is the basic stuff of the "world," i.e., the physical universe, but he will argue that it cannot explain the world (without quotation marks). In opposition to Descartes, Heidegger asserts:

The aroundness of the environment, the specific spatiality of beings encountered in the environment, is founded upon the worldliness of the world, while contrariwise the world, on its part, is not occurrent in space. (135) [101–102]

How do Dasein's concerns enable it to reveal spatiality and how is this existential spatiality related to physical space? One who is not yet convinced that the possibility of encountering every sort of entity, even rocks and sunsets, depends on Dasein's concernful dealings may be more inclined to believe it if Heidegger can demonstrate that everyday space and time are structured by Dasein's concerns while still preserving our conviction that physical space and time are independent of Dasein.

We have already seen that Dasein is not "in" the world in the same way that an occurrent thing is in physical space. This is not to say that Dasein has no spatiality. There is a spatiality of in-volvement:

Even if we deny that Dasein has any insideness in a spatial receptacle, this does not in principle exclude it from having any spatiality at all, but merely keeps open the way for seeing the kind of spatiality which is constitutive for Dasein. This must now be set forth. (134)[101]

Heidegger does not argue that space and time are synthesized from a here-now stream of inner experiences by the individual ego's meaning-giving activity as Husserl does, but rather that the structure of public space and time presupposes the structure of existence, the way of being of the being whose being is an issue for it. In his discussion of space, Heidegger (1) shows that public space is a function of concern, (2) describes the type of spatiality peculiar to existence, and (3) shows that physical (disinterested) space can be understood as a privative, i.e., deworlded, mode of the space of everyday involvement.

The discussion of spatiality is one of the most difficult in *Being and Time*, not because it is deeper than any other discussion but because it is fundamentally confused. Heidegger himself later came to realize that he had not clearly distinguished *public* space in which entities show up for human beings, from the centered spatiality of each *individual* human being. In the course of explicating the text I shall try to sort out this confusion.

I. Public Spatiality

In chapter 3 I distinguished two senses of in: in-clusion and in-volvement. These two ways of being in can now be related to the distinction between available equipment and occurrent objects. To begin with, equipment has its place.

This must be distinguished in principle from just occurring at random in some spatial position. When equipment for something or other has its place, this place defines itself as the place of this equipment—as one place out of a whole totality of places ... belonging to the nexus of equipment that is environmentally available. (136)[102]

For example, each tool has a specific *place* in a workshop. Here again the whole determines what counts as the parts. The workshop as a *region* makes possible places for the saw, the lathe, the work bench, etc.

Something like a region *must first be discovered* if there is to be any possibility of allotting or coming across places for an equipmental whole that is circumspectively at one's disposal. (136, my italics)[103]

Moreover, places are public and thus independent of the location of particular people.

The regional orientation of the multiplicity of places belonging to the available goes to make up the aroundness—the "round-about-*us*"—of those entities which *we* encounter as closest environmentally. . . . The "above" is what is "on the ceiling"; the "below" is what is "on the floor"; the "behind" is what is "at the door"; all "wheres" are discovered and circumspectively interpreted as *we* go *our* ways in everyday dealings. (136–137, my italics) [103]

Regions, in turn, are laid out in terms of Dasein's concerns, and so ultimately this aspect of spatiality refers back to the being whose being is an issue for it. (As we shall see, this is as near as Heidegger comes to successfully grounding spatiality in care.)

Dasein, in its very being, has this being as an issue; and its concern discovers beforehand those regions in which some involvement is decisive. This discovery of regions beforehand is codetermined by the involvement whole for which the available, as something encountered, is freed. (137) [104]

II. Spatiality as a Function of Existential Concern

The spatiality of Dasein's encountering the available depends on Dasein's concernful being-in-the-world.

To encounter the available in its environmental space remains ontically possible only because Dasein itself is "spatial" with regard to its being-in-the-world. . . . Dasein . . . is "in" the world in the sense that it deals with beings encountered within-the-world, and does so concernfully and with familiarity. So if spatiality belongs to it in any way, that is possible only because of this being-in. (138) [104]

To explain the role of Dasein's concern in the spatial way equipment shows up, Heidegger introduces the notion of what our translators call "de-severance" (*Ent-fernung*). The literal translation of *Entfernung* is "remoteness" or "distance," but Heidegger uses the word with a hyphen which, given the negative sense of *ent*, would literally mean the *abolishing* of distance. He uses it this way to mean *the establishing and overcoming of distance*, that is, the opening up of a space in which things can be near and far. I will try to capture the word-play by playing on the negative sense of "dis" and thus translating *Ent-fernung* as *dis-stance*. Dasein brings things close in the sense of bringing them within the range of its concern, so that they can be experienced as near to or remote from a particular Dasein.

Dis-stance . . . is an existentiale; . . . Only to the extent that beings are revealed for Dasein in their dis-stancedness, do "remotenesses" and distances with regard to other things become accessible in intraworldly beings themselves. (139) [105]

We must distinguish dis-stance from distance. *Dis-stance* has no degrees, but makes it possible to encounter degrees of nearness and remoteness, accessibility and inaccessibility. Once an object has been brought into the referential nexus, dis-stanced, it can be more or less available, i.e., more or less distant from particular individuals, more or less integrated into each individual's activities. The degree of availability is the nearness of concern. (Here Heidegger actually uses the idea of being "at hand" in the German term *Zuhandenheit*, which we translate as *availableness*.)

What is available in our everyday dealings has the character of *nearness*. To be exact, this nearness of equipment has already been intimated in the term "availableness" (*Zuhandenheit*), which expresses the being of equipment. Every entity that is "to hand" (*zur Hand*) has a different nearness, which is not to be ascertained by measuring distances. This nearness regulates itself in terms of circumspectively "calculative" manipulating and using. (135) [102]

In keeping with the difference between dis-stance and distance, in describing space Heidegger has two separate tasks. (1) To show how a way of being called existence opens up a shared world in which things can be encountered as present, and therefore capable of being either near or far. (2) To explain how things can be experienced as near to or far from a particular Dasein. We must therefore be careful to distinguish the role of concern in opening up the *possibility* of nearness and remoteness, from the nearness and remoteness of a *specific* piece of equipment vis-à-vis a particular Dasein.

Heidegger, however, blurs this distinction in passages such as the following:

"Dis-stancing" amounts to making the farness vanish—that is, making the remoteness of something disappear, bringing it near. Dasein is essentially dis-stancial: it lets any being be encountered nearby as the being which it is. (139) [105]

Here Heidegger fails to distinguish the general opening up of space as the field of presence (dis-stance) that is the condition for things being near and far, from Dasein's pragmatic bringing things near by taking them up and using them. Such pragmatic bringing near as Heidegger uses the term can only be near to *me*, it is not a dimension of public space. Heidegger takes note of the mistake in the passage just quoted in a marginal comment: "Nearness and *presence*, not the magnitude of separation, is what is essential"{140}. That is to say, if one wants to understand how things show up for Dasein as spatial, what is essential is how they show up as present at all. Dis-stance as an existential is prior to a particular Dasein's distance from particular objects. How far away an object is in each case must be understood on the basis of presence. For example, a table can be present in a classroom without its having to be present to (and therefore near or far from) any particular person.[1] Only because it thus shows up as present can such a table serve my purposes by supporting my papers and thus be near, i.e., available to, me. We can now understand why next to the passage "In Dasein there lies an essential tendency to nearness" (140) [105], Heidegger writes in the margin: "How much and why? Being as constant presence has priority, making present" {141}.

To make Heidegger's chapter consistent, one would have to stick to the priority of the presence of equipment in public, workshop space—which Dasein is always in and which has its regions, its places, and its accessibility to anyone—over the nearness or farness of specific equipment from a particular Dasein. Only then could Heidegger avoid the Cartesian/Husserlian traditional move of giving priority to *my* world of closeness and farness over *the* world with its public regions and places, and only then could Heidegger derive the occurrent "world" space by progressive decontextualization of the public space of the world.

But in *Being and Time* to give an ontological account of presence means to show how presence is grounded in Dasein as the being whose being is an issue for it. This is what misleads Heidegger into giving priority to the nearness and farness of things as defined by the degree of concernful coping with them. This amounts to giving priority to the spatiality of the individual Dasein. Heidegger tries to get out of this difficulty by arguing in Section 70 that space is grounded in temporality, and so only indirectly grounded in Dasein's being an issue for itself. But he later admits that this move does not work.[2] Later Heidegger accepts that spatiality cannot be grounded directly or indirectly in the individual Dasein's concern about its own being. The problems of this chapter can be seen as the sort of difficulties that led Heidegger to abandon the project of a fundamental ontology, i.e., an ontology that grounds all ways of being in Dasein's way of being.

III. Dasein's Location

Heidegger stresses that in understanding distance from a particular individual, Dasein must be thought of as pure concern, not as a physical body located at a certain point in objective space.

If Dasein, in its concern, brings something nearby, this does not signify that it fixes something at a spatial position with a minimal distance from some point of the body. . . . Bringing-near is not oriented towards the I-thing encumbered with a body, but towards concernful being-in-the-world. (142)[107]

If distance from Dasein is not to be defined with respect to the location of Dasein's body, how is distance from Dasein to be thought of? Heidegger answers: "Circumspective concern decides as to the nearness and farness of what is primarily available environmentally. Whatever this concern dwells with beforehand is what is nearest" (142)[107]. Things in the world show up as having a certain accessibility—that is, a certain nearness or farness—according to my ability to "grasp" or "procure" them.

That which is presumably "nearest" is by no means that which is at the smallest distance "from us." It lies in that which is distanced to an average extent when we reach for it, grasp it, or look at it. (141)[106–107]

A thing is near to me when I am able to get a maximal grip on it. "When something is nearby, this means that it is within the range of what is primarily available for circumspection" (142)[107]. So nearness is correlated with a different physical distance, for example, in the case of a picture on the wall and a postage stamp.
Another determining characteristic of nearness is interest.

One feels the touch of [the street] at every step as one walks; it is seemingly the nearest and realest of all that is available, and it slides itself, as it were, along certain portions of one's body—the soles of one's feet. And yet it is farther remote than the acquaintance whom one encounters "on the street" at a "remoteness" of twenty paces when one is taking such a walk. (141–142)[107]

It seems that for Heidegger for something to be near it must be *both* something I am coping with and something absorbing my attention. It cannot be just the street under my feet, nor can it be a friend far away in Paris no matter how intense my concern. *What is near is that with which I am currently absorbedly coping.*

An individual Dasein is located in the referential whole of equipment by occupying a position from which some equipment is easily available and some is out of reach.

The "here" of [Dasein's] current factical situation never signifies a position in space, but signifies rather the leeway of the range of that equipmental whole with which it is most closely concerned . . . (420) [369]

The degree of accessibility of all things yonder defines my centered, lived space—my here.

Dasein, in accordance with its spatiality, is primarily never here but yonder; from this "yonder" it comes back to its "here"; and it comes back to its "here" only in the way in which it interprets its concernful being-towards in terms of what is available yonder. (142) [107-108]

Because the equipment "yonder" is public, the "here" is public too. "The boundary between my own environing world and a public one can be defined by modes of a varied disposability" (HCT, 192). Thus Heidegger can do justice to the fact that each Dasein has its own here without his account falling prey to the Cartesian/ Husserlian claim that each Dasein has or is a private perspective on the world. The idea that my consciousness contains a stream of perspectival experiences (*Erlebnisse*), as if my mind were a movie camera or a moving geometrical point, is a distortion of everyday coping experience (*Erfahrung*). It is a possible description of my experience when I am no longer engaged in coping but reflect on myself and my relation to the occurrent, but that interpretation should not be read back into my experience of coping with the available. Painters did not paint the world from a perspectival viewpoint until the fourteenth century. Before then, they painted larger what was more important—what they were involved with. Heidegger revives this naive experience of absorbed openness, but he gives it a modern, pragmatic twist by adding that each Dasein is involved in coping with things more or less accessible, and that the systematically shifting accessibility of things is their changing existential nearness and farness.

But here again Heidegger confuses dis-stance as an existential structure with the nearness and farness of things from a particular Dasein. This leads to an especially murky passage:

> As being-in-the-world, Dasein maintains itself essentially in a dis-stance. This dis-stance—the farness of the available from Dasein itself—is something that Dasein can never cross over. . . . So little has Dasein crossed over its dis-stance that it has rather taken it along with it and keeps doing so constantly. (142) [108]

So far Heidegger seems to be saying that the public presence of accessible things is a constant characteristic of everyday experience. But he goes on:

> [Dasein] cannot wander about within the current range of its dis-stances; it can never do more than *change them.* (143, my italics) [108]

Heidegger here fails to distinguish ontic distance (which constantly changes) from ontological dis-stance (which does not). Thus dis-stance is confused with the shifting distance of specific things from an individual Dasein. But if each Dasein had its own dis-stance which it took with it, and this dis-stance were *both* the ontological opening up of presence *and* the changing accessibility of things from a center, there could be no public space. We would have a number of *monads* each with its own centered experience of presence, and public space would be a *construct.* Heidegger, of course, wants to resist this Husserlian and Sartrean subjectivist treatment of space.

> Space is not to be found in the subject, nor does the subject observe the world "as if" that world were in a space; but the "subject" (Dasein), if well understood ontologically, is spatial. (146) [111]

But the above murky passage can be saved from a subject-centered account of spatiality only if we distinguish, as Heidegger later admits he has not, the way Dasein in general opens public dis-stance and a particular Dasein "takes with it" this opening of presence, on the one hand, from the way particular Daseins take their centered range of pragmatic activity with them as they deal with equipment, on the other.

To avoid subjectivism Heidegger should have stressed that my centered space depends on and is located in a public field of presence, that my here does not mean a private, subjective perspective but is located vis-à-vis public equipment in a public world. Thus, my pragmatic perspective is not private. The equipment directly accessible to me is what anyone would have accessible if he or she were in my place. In this way Heidegger could have done justice to the fact that each Dasein carries with it the center of its activity and yet have avoided seeming to make public space depend upon a plurality of individual perspectives.

IV. Orientation

Spatiality is not only organized into places and regions but it has directions—right/left, front/back and up/down. Dasein orients itself in terms of these directions. Heidegger discusses only right/left orientation and his discussion is rather obscure. He acknowledges that

Both orientation and dis-stance, as modes of being-in-the-world, are guided beforehand by the circumspection of concern. Out of this orientation arise the fixed directions of right and left. Dasein constantly takes these directions along with it, just as it does its dis-stances. (143) [108]

Dasein takes its orientation with it in the sense that its coping skills are correlated with equipment that is to the right or to the left.

Left and right are not something "subjective" for which the subject has a feeling; they are directions of one's directedness into a world that is available already. (143) [109]

When I am familiar with a room, I am already set to reach for some things on my right and some on my left. If the position of all the objects in the room were systematically reversed, my readiness would no longer mesh with the referential whole and I would immediately sense something was wrong. Heidegger presumably has this in mind when he criticizes as half right but still too subjective Kant's argument against Leibniz that right/left directionality cannot be analyzed merely in terms of relations among objects but requires *memories* of where things were.

Suppose I step into a room which is familiar to me but dark, and which has been rearranged during my absence so that everything which used to be at my right is now at my left. If I am to orient myself, the "mere feeling of the difference" between my two sides will be of no help at all as long as I fail to apprehend some definite object "whose position," as Kant remarks casually, "I have in mind." But what does this signify except that whenever this happens, I necessarily orient myself both in and from my being already amidst a world which is "familiar". . . . The psychological interpretation according to which the "I" has something "in memory" is at bottom a way of alluding to the existential make-up of being-in-the-world. (144) [109–110]

Right and left would seem to depend upon having a body. But Heidegger again holds that the body is not essential. He mentions it only in parentheses: "(This bodily nature [of Dasein] hides a whole problematic of its own, though we shall not treat it here.)" (143) [108] Heidegger must therefore separate the issue of Dasein's embodiment from the issue of orientation. He seems to hold that orientation is a result of the fact that not all equipment is accessible at the same time. I can turn to one thing or another but not both at once. These incompatible fields of action group simultaneously accessible things together in opposed regions called right/left, and also front/back. But still without the body there could be no account of why there are just these regions. We would not be able to understand, for example, why the accessibility of right and left is not symmetrical, or why we must always "face" things in order to cope with them. On Heidegger's account these would just remain unexplained asymmetries in the practical field. This is not inconsistent, but it is unsatisfying.[3]

V. The Derivation of Physical Space from Existential Spatiality

Heidegger has now shown that in our interested dealings in the world we disclose pragmatic spatiality; but our familiarity with this spatiality has not yet disclosed physical space.

The space which is thus disclosed with the worldliness of the world still lacks the pure multiplicity of the three dimensions. In this disclosedness which is closest to us, space, as the pure "wherein" in which positions are ordered by measurement and the situations of things are determined, still remains hidden. (145) [110]

In Heidegger's "derivation" of physical space from existential spatiality, we will notice some close parallels to his "derivation" of the occurrent from the available. The derivation consists again in a move from everyday coping, to practical deliberation, followed by a move to theoretical reflection. Heidegger describes these moves with surprising brevity, perhaps because they should be familiar from the previous derivation. Let us follow his steps carefully. They are summarized in Table 4.

To begin with, places and regions are noticed only when there is some sort of disturbance and they become unavailable:

The availableness which belongs to any . . . region beforehand has the *character of inconspicuous familiarity*, and it has it in an even more primordial sense than does the being of the available. The region itself becomes visible in a conspicuous manner only when one discovers the available . . . in the deficient modes of concern. (137–138) [104]

Likewise, practical distances between me and accessible things, if they become problematic, are noticed and a thing's accessibility assessed. Difficulty reveals "aspects" such as nearness and remoteness:

A pathway which is long "objectively" can be much shorter than one which is "objectively" shorter still but which is perhaps "hard going" and comes before us as interminably long . . . The objective distances of occurrent things do not coincide with the remoteness and nearness of what is available within-the-world. (140–141) [106]

As in the case of the functionality of equipment, Heidegger here claims that pragmatic estimates reveal space as it is *in itself*. He continues:

When one is oriented beforehand towards "nature" and "objectively" measured distances of things, one is inclined to pass off such estimates and interpretations of dis-tance as "subjective." Yet this "subjectivity" perhaps uncovers the "reality" of the world at its most real; it has nothing to do with "subjective" arbitrariness or subjectivistic "ways of taking" an entity which "in itself" is otherwise. The circumspective dis-stancing of Dasein's everydayness reveals the being-in-itself of the "true world" . . . (141) [106–107]

Normally, we do not notice that things are accessible; we just transparently use them, or notice the difficulty of access to them, but go on anyway. But if there is an obstacle I may have to stop and think about how to reach my goal. In designing something or in a dispute, I may have to measure distances. But even then, as in dealing with the unavailable, I do so on a transparent background of places and accessibilities. Still such a move begins to reveal occurrent space underlying the spatiality of the available.

Table 4

Physical space	Existential spatiality
Geometrical space, the space of the occurrent.	Lived space, the space of the available.
Homogeneous, no center.	Personal: centered in each of us.
Pure extension.	Orientation (up/down, right/left).
Three-dimensional multiplicity of positions.	Remoteness/nearness of objects.
	Public: has regions and, in these, places.
Measurements of distance.	Degree of availability.

The spatiality of what we proximally encounter in circumspection can become a theme for circumspection itself, as well as a task for calculation and measurement, as in building and surveying. Such thematization of the spatiality of the environment is still predominantly an act of circumspection by which space in itself already comes into view in a certain way. (146)[111–112]

Now comes the move to reflection and theory—from unavailable *spatiality* to occurrent *space*. In special cases I can leave out my interest altogether. I can ignore the accessibility of things, and even the context of places and directions.

When space is discovered noncircumspectively by just looking at it, the environmental regions get neutralized to pure dimensions. Places—and indeed the whole circumspectively oriented whole of places belonging to available equipment—get reduced to a multiplicity of positions for random things. . . . The "world,"* as a whole of available equipment, becomes spatialized to a nexus of extended things which are just occurrent and no more. The homogeneous space of nature shows itself only when the entities we encounter are discovered in such a way that the worldly character of the available gets specifically deprived of its worldliness. (147)[112]

Heidegger spells out this "de-worlding" later in the book in his phenomenological derivation of the way of being of the entities revealed by science.

In the "physical" assertion that "the hammer is heavy" we *overlook* not only the tool-character of the entity we encounter, but also something that belongs to any available equipment: its place. Its place becomes a matter of indifference. This does not mean that what is occurrent loses its "location" altogether. But its place becomes a spatiotemporal position, a "world-point," which is in no way distinguished from any other . . . The multiplicity of places of available equipment within the confines of the environment becomes modified to a pure multiplicity of positions. (413) [361–362]

Thus occurrent space is revealed as having been there all along. One can see this from Heidegger's remark: "A three-dimensional multiplicity of possible positions which gets filled up with things occurrent is never primarily given. This dimensionality of space *is still veiled* in the spatiality of the available" (136, my italics) [103].

The physical space revealed by theory plays a legitimate and important role in explanatory natural science. It should again be clear, however, that Heidegger is no physicalist. Once we see that everyday spatiality with its places and regions must be "overlooked" to reveal objective space, we see that we cannot hope to understand the everyday world of places and regions in terms of pure extension, and that therefore, as far as intelligibility is concerned, Dasein's pragmatic spatiality is ontologically primary.

The "Who" of Everyday Dasein

I. Being-in-the-World as Being-With

We have seen that "Dasein, in its familiarity with significance, is the ontical condition for the possibility of discovering entities" (120), i.e., that all entities can show up directly or indirectly by virtue of an entity's, i.e., Dasein's, readiness to cope with them. This is clearly a rejection of Husserl's attempt to ground all forms of intentionality in the meaning-giving activity of a detached transcendental subject, but it still has a decidedly Husserlian ring. It is as if Heidegger has substituted one absolute source for another, replacing the constituting activity of detached transcendental consciousness with the constituting activity of involved existential Dasein.

The magnitude of such a move should not be underestimated. For Husserl the intentional content of individual transcendental consciousness was self-sufficient, intelligible, immediately and indubitably given to phenomenological reflection, and could be made completely explicit. The skills of Dasein, on the other hand, have been shown to be neither self-sufficient (since they are not analyzable in terms of intentional content), nor intelligible apart from the world (which is not directly given but necessarily stays in the background), nor explicitable (since they do not involve conscious or unconscious beliefs and rules). So the phenomenological description of coping skills has freed us from the idea of a self-contained, occurrent subject à la Husserl and even from the universality of the mind/world representational relation defended by Searle.

Still, someone like the Sartre of *Being and Nothingness* could stay half within the tradition by holding that the individual, through his practical activities, first gives practical meaning to the human organisms in his own world and through them gives meaning to the shared public world. Heidegger makes a much more radical departure from Husserl. He rejects the Husserlian and Sartrean claim that philosophy must start with a separate sphere of ownness, a self-contained source of intentionality that first gives meaning to transcendental intersubjectivity and finally to a common world. On the contrary, Heidegger seeks to show that while there are a plurality of centered disclosing activities, these activities *presuppose* the disclosure of one shared world. As Heidegger says in his earlier lectures:

In order to give a more accurate portrayal of the phenomenal structure of the world as it shows itself in everyday dealings, it must be noted that what matters in these dealings with the world is not so much anyone's own particular world, but that right in our natural dealings with the world we are moving in a common environmental whole. (HCT, 188)

If Heidegger can show that the source of meaning does not reside in each particular Dasein, he will have taken the last step toward overcoming the "illusion" fostered by the Cartesian tradition.

This . . . illusion is maximally reinforced by philosophy through the latter's setting up the dogma that the single and separate human being is single and separate in his own eyes and that the single and separate I is, with its first-personal domain, that which is initially and most certainly given to him. Thereby, the opinion is philosophically sanctioned that would make being-with-one-another something that had originally to be created out of this solipsistic isolation.[1]

Frederick Olafson, in his helpful account of the project of *Being and Time*, sees that Heidegger was trying to avoid a Husserlian account which started with *my* world and then moved to *the* world. He even finds striking formulations of Heidegger's view on this matter. For example:

Insofar as a human being exists, he is transposed into other human beings. . . . The ability to transpose oneself into other human beings, understood as a going-with them and with the Dasein in them, has always already occurred on the basis of the Dasein in man. . . . For Dasein means: being-with others and this in the mode of Dasein, that is, of existence.[2]

But Olafson thinks that, despite such descriptions, Heidegger has no basis for his claim that he has avoided the transcendental solipsism Husserl embraced.

Although it is understood that it is an essential feature of Dasein that the entities it uncovers are, at least in principle, the same entities in the same world that other like entities uncover . . . there is no real account of the way in which *my* uncovering an entity depends on someone else's doing so as well. As a result, the uncovering of entities as entities by one Dasein comes to seem quite distinct from their uncovering by others, even though it is stipulated that each such Dasein understands that its uncovering is not unique and that the entities uncovered are the same from one case to another. At no point is there any definite indication of why uncovering *must* be joint and convergent.[3]

If Heidegger cannot make this case his whole project fails, so we must now turn to Heidegger's Chapter IV, where he introduces the missing piece of his phenomenological account. Olafson is clear about what Heidegger should have held:

If a theory that does justice to . . . *Mitsein* [being-with] were to be developed, it would have to take into account such facts as that what I uncover as a hammer, say, has been previously used (and thus uncovered) as a hammer by others, and that it is normally from these others that I have learned what a hammer is and how to use one.[4]

But Olafson does not realize that, as I shall now marshal texts to show, Heidegger holds precisely this position.

That careful readers like Olafson and Sartre have missed Heidegger's point here is mostly his own fault. In many ways Heidegger's chapter on what the translation calls *the They*, and what I, for reasons to be given in a moment, prefer to call *the one*, is not only one of the most basic in the book, it is also the most confused. Heidegger is influenced by Kierkegaard and Dilthey, both of whom had a great deal to say about the importance of the social world. But, whereas Dilthey emphasized the positive function of social phenomena, which he called the "objectifications of life," Kierkegaard focused on the negative effects of the conformism and banality of what he called "the public." Heidegger takes up and extends the Diltheyan insight that intelligibility and truth arise only in the context of public, historical practices, but he is also deeply influenced by the Kierkegaardian view that "the truth is never in the crowd." If Heidegger had explicitly distinguished these opposed views and then integrated them, this could have been a rich and coherent chapter. Indeed, he does distinguish them in an earlier lecture by separating two questions:

The structure of Dasein must now be displayed in terms of how such a being-with-one-another determined by the world and the common understanding given with it are constituted in Dasein. The question is, who is it really who first of all understands himself in . . . being-with-one-another? . . . Upon this basis we can then ask a further question. . . . How is it that Dasein does not come to a genuine understanding precisely because there is always already an understanding of one another? (HCT, 243–244)

But unfortunately, in *Being and Time* Heidegger does not distinguish these two issues but jumps back and forth between them, sometimes even in the same paragraph. This is not only confusing; it prevents the chapter from having the centrality it should have in an understanding of *Being and Time.*

As it stands, Heidegger's Chapter IV seems just a short chapter on the problem of other minds and the evils of conformism, whereas, it is in fact, the last nail in the coffin of the Cartesian tradition. Indeed, the discussion of the way public norms are established makes this in many ways the pivotal chapter of the book. In laying out the chapter, I shall try to sort out and integrate the two strains in Heidegger's thought, highlighting the line of thought that leads from Hegel's notion of ethical practice or *Sittlichkeit,* to Dilthey on the objectifications of life, to Heidegger, and on to the later Wittgenstein's forms of life. Up to this point in my commentary, my Wittgensteinian interpretation of being-in-the-world in terms of shared background practices may seem an alien imposition on Heidegger. In this chapter, however, my interpretation and Heidegger's statements converge.

A. The Existential Interpretation of the Who: Human Being as Shared Social Activity

Heidegger will now draw out the implications of what he has already shown, viz. that Dasein's familiarity with significance depends on Dasein's taking over for-the-sake-of-whichs provided by society. Heidegger's basic point is that the background familiarity that underlies all coping and all intentional states is not a plurality of subjective belief systems including mutual beliefs about each others' beliefs, but rather an agreement in ways of acting and judging into which human beings, by the time they have Dasein in them, are "always already" socialized. Such agreement is not conscious thematic agreement but is prior to and presupposed by the intentionalistic sort of agreement arrived at between subjects.

On Heidegger's account, then, a plurality of Daseins each with its own background skills and for-the-sake-of-whichs *must* uncover a single shared world because background familiarity and ways of being Dasein are not a matter of private experiences but are acquired from society. Heidegger does not usually speak of Dasein genetically, but at one illuminating point in his lectures he remarks:

This common world, which is there primarily and into which every maturing Dasein first grows, as the public world governs every interpretation of the world and of Dasein. (HCT, 246)

This is a good first approximation, but talk about Dasein growing into a common world could be misleading. One cannot ask: At what age does Dasein get socialized? *Babies* get socialized, but they do not Dasein [verb] until they are *already* socialized. Public skills and for-the-sake-of-whichs must be taken over (presumably by imitation) before there can be any Dasein with thoughts and activities at all. Society is the ontological source of the familiarity and readiness that makes the ontical discovering of entities, of others, and even of myself possible.

Heidegger sets out to answer objections like Olafson's by demonstrating his case. He begins by reminding us of our starting point:

The answer to the question of who Dasein is, is one that was seemingly given in Section 9, where we indicated formally the basic characteristics of Dasein. Dasein is an entity which is in each case I myself; its being is in each case mine. (150)[114]

But whatever mineness means, we can already be sure it does not mean what Husserl called "the sphere of ownness"—the private world of each person's inner experiences. Rather it must mean that each Dasein is owned the way comportment is owned. I can speak of your comportment and my comportment, and the understanding of being in your activities and in my activities, but that should not lead me to think that your comportment is in your world and my comportment is in my world, or that you have your understanding of being and I have mine. So we should not be surprised when Heidegger undercuts the seemingly subjectivist implications of Dasein's mineness.

The assertion that it is I who in each case Dasein is, is ontically obvious; but this must not mislead us into supposing that the route for an ontological Interpretation of what is "given" in this way has thus been unmistakably prescribed. . . . It could be that the "who" of everyday Dasein is not the "I myself." (150) [115]

Heidegger proposes an existential approach to the question:

If the "I" is an essential characteristic of Dasein, then it is one which must be Interpreted existentially. In that case the "Who?" is to be answered only by exhibiting phenomenally a definite kind of being which Dasein possesses. (152) [117]

But to the tradition the answer is obvious. Descartes started with the givenness of the "I," and Husserl posited transcendental subjectivity. Heidegger, like Wittgenstein, imagines a traditional interlocutor who defends the self-evidence of this private starting point.

What is more indubitable than the givenness of the "I"? And does not this givenness tell us that if we aim to work this out primordially, we must disregard everything else that is "given"—not only a "world"* that is, but even the being of other "I"s? (151) [115]

Heidegger, however, questions whether such a procedure can disclose Dasein in its everydayness—or at all: "What if the afore-mentioned approach, starting with the givenness of the "I" to Dasein itself, and with a rather patent self-interpretation of Dasein, should lead the existential analytic, as it were, into a pitfall?" (151) [116] The pitfall is, of course, once more succumbing to the traditional tendency to interpret all ways of being as modes of occurrentness.

Even if one rejects the "soul substance" and the thinghood of conscious-ness, or denies that a person is an object, ontologically one is still positing something whose being retains the meaning of occurrentness, whether it does so explicitly or not. (150) [114]

The conception of Dasein as an occurrent subject isolates Dasein. It implies that each of us can know only our own experiences and leads us to ask skeptical questions concerning how I could ever know that others exist. But, as we have seen, Heidegger claims to have avoided this difficulty.

In clarifying being-in-the-world we have shown that a bare subject without a world never "is" firstly, nor is it ever given. And so in the end an isolated "I" without others is just as far from being firstly given. (152) [116]

In opposition to the interpretation of man as essentially a subject, Heidegger reminds us that as being-in-the-world Dasein must take a stand on itself and must be understood "in what it does, uses, expects, avoids—in the environmentally available with which it is primarily concerned" (155) [119]. In *Basic Problems*, Heidegger puts it more colloquially:

[Dasein] finds itself primarily and usually in things because, tending them, distressed by them, it always in some way or other rests in things. Each one of us is what he pursues and cares for. In everyday terms, we understand ourselves and our existence by way of the activities we pursue and the things we take care of. (BP, 159.)

Or to put it even more starkly, "'One *is*' what one does" (283) [239]. This can be viewed as a sort of behaviorism, the sort found in Wittgenstein, and perhaps in Gilbert Ryle, as long as one remembers that the behavior in question is not meaningless physical *movements* of some object, but the directed, significant, concernful *comportment* of human beings going about their business in a meaningful social world.

Still, a Cartesian interlocutor might say, even with this qualification, Heidegger's behaviorism has gone too far. A third-person description of behavior does not get at what is essential. What about Dasein's *consciousness* and its private mental states? "If the self is conceived 'only' as a way of being of this entity, this seems tantamount to volatilizing the real 'core' of Dasein" (153) [117]. It is important at this point to remember that Heidegger, like Wittgenstein, is not denying conscious experiences. Like Wittgenstein, he is trying to get rid of a certain picture of the self as containing a self-contained stream of experiences that are its essential content. What Heidegger denies is the foundational significance of mental states. He points out that what is "given" to reflection does not have the priority in everyday life that it has in Cartesian philosophy. As we have seen, Dasein encounters itself for the most part in the transparent coping that occupies most of its day, not in practical deliberation followed by purposive actions guided by self-referential intentions in action.

Even one's *own* Dasein becomes something that it can itself firstly "come across" only when it *looks away* from "experiences" [*Erlebnissen*] and the "center of its actions" [as a subject deliberately dealing with the unavailable], or does not as yet "see" them at all [as in pure coping with the available]. (155, my gloss in brackets) [119]

So, Heidegger is not saying there are no "contents of conscious-ness"; he is merely calling our attention to the fact that in our everyday activities inner experiences play a decidedly secondary role. Making them basic is a "perverse assumption" amounting to the claim that the subject is a self-sufficient substance.

Any apprehensiveness . . . which one may have about [ignoring the inner self] gets its nourishment from the perverse assumption that the entity in question has at bottom the kind of being which belongs to something occurrent, even if one is far from attributing to it the solidity of an occurrent corporeal thing. (153) [117]

Heidegger adds: "man's '*substance*' is not spirit as a synthesis of soul and body; it is rather *existence*" (153) [117]. That is, as Kierkegaard says in *Sickness Unto Death*, the self is not a synthesis of soul and body, inner and outer, experiences and movements; the self is the stand a certain way of being takes on itself. (See Appendix.) For Heidegger, moreover, this stand takes place in everyday activ-ity. Dasein is always interpreting its being in term of its for-the-sake-of-whichs, and since one's role, say that of being a professor, makes no sense without other roles, like that of being a student, as well as meshing with still other roles such as being a teaching assistant, librarian, advisor, registrar, etc. we cannot even make sense of a nonsocial Dasein.

B. Being-With

To appreciate Heidegger's account of our relation to others it helps to distinguish two views of shared intentionality. The Husserlian view, that begins with Descartes and is still carried on by Paul Grice and Stephen Schiffer, is that we must begin our analysis of meaning with our own individual intentional states and then derive shared public meaning from our beliefs that others have beliefs about our beliefs about their beliefs, etc. This "mutual knowledge," to use Schiffer's term, provides the basis of what Husserl calls "intersubjectivity." Heidegger, on the contrary, starts with our normal social way of being, which he calls being-with. Heidegger would not deny that in cases of breakdown we may form beliefs about others' beliefs, etc. This is the way being-with appears in the mode of unavailableness. Most of the time, however, Heidegger points out, we just work with and deal with others skillfully without having any beliefs about them or their beliefs at all.

By "others" we do not mean everyone else but me—those over against whom the "I" stands out. They are rather those from whom, for the most part, one does not distinguish oneself —those among whom one is too. This being-there-too with them does not have the ontological character of a being-occurrent-along-"with" them . . . . This "with" is something of the character of Dasein; the "too" means a sameness of being as circumspectively concernful being-in-the-world. "With" and "too" are to be understood *existentially*, not categorially. By reason of this *with-like* being-in-the-world, the world is always the one that I share with others. The world of Dasein is a *with-world*. Being-in is *being-with* others. (154– 155) [118]

Searle has recently come close to this conclusion. He has criticized mutual knowledge based on individual intentional states, arguing that such an analysis misses the phenomenon of "we intentionality."[5] Searle points out that my pushing a car as part of the activity of *our* pushing the car is a different activity than my pushing the car plus my believing that you are also pushing the car.

Heidegger focuses on the familiarity in our background practices that makes the "we intentionality" described by Searle possible. Whether there is any particular other there or not, when I perceive or use tools or speak, I'm always already involved in a shared world. According to Heidegger, "being-with" is a basic structure of Dasein's being, more basic than relating to particular others. Even when I am not encountering others nor using equipment, others are there for me. I have a readiness for dealing with them along with my readiness for dealing with equipment. Being-with would still be a structure of my Daseining even if all other Daseins had been wiped out.

The phenomenological assertion that "Dasein is essentially being-with" has an existential-ontological meaning. It does not seek to establish ontically that factically I am not occurrent alone, and that others of my kind occur. . . . Being-with is an existential characteristic of Dasein even when factically no other is occurrent or perceived. (156) [120]

Being-with is an aspect of being-in-the-world that makes possible all encountering of particular others whose way of being Heidegger calls Dasein-with.

We use the term "Dasein-with" to designate that being by virtue of which the others who are are freed within-the-world. (156) [120]

Thus familiarity with the world not only allows particular things to show up as available or occurrent, as being-with it also makes possible the encountering of others as Dasein-with.

C. Heidegger on Other Minds

Heidegger's existential analysis of the "who" has important implications for the traditional question: How can we know other minds? To begin with, Heidegger points out that normally "other minds" are directly accessible to us in our shared transparent activity of coping with equipment (concern) and coping with people (solicitude) in just the same way we are accessible to ourselves through our daily activity.

> Knowing oneself . . . operates primarily in accordance with the kind of being which is closest to us—being-in-the-world as being-with; and it does so by an acquaintance with that which Dasein, along with others, comes across in its environmental circumspection and concerns itself with . . . . Thus the other is primarily disclosed in concernful solicitude. (161) [124]

Others do not normally show up as minds, and we do not normally have beliefs about them. Heidegger must therefore account for how the problem of other minds can arise. His answer is that in special situations of breakdown we hold back, or disguise, our activities. Then, in effect, our relation to others becomes unavailable.

> When . . . one's knowing-oneself gets lost in such ways as aloofness, hiding oneself away, or putting on a disguise, being-with-one-another must follow special routes of its own in order to come close to others. (161) [124]

If this disturbance becomes too extreme it can lead to a detached attitude and the "theoretical problematic of understanding the 'psychical life of others'" (161) [124]. Then philosophers come up with explanations such as the theory of empathy (a variation of which was held by Scheler and by Husserl), which tries to account for how we get to know another person's conscious experiences "behind" his behavior. But, as usual, Heidegger argues that such problems, based on reflection and on private experiences, always presuppose the public world as background.

> "Empathy" does not first constitute being-with; only on the basis of being-with does "empathy" become possible: it gets its motivation from the unsociability of the dominant modes of being-with. (162) [125]

Thus the question of other minds, rather than remaining a basic philosophical problem, as it is for Descartes, Husserl, and Sartre, is "dissolved" by Heidegger, in a way familiar in Wittgenstein, by converting it into a question of determining in what *special derivative circumstances* our everyday familiarity breaks down and leads to the separation between psychic life and behavior, so that the problem of other minds can first arise.

The special hermeneutic of empathy will have to show how being-with-one-another and Dasein's knowing of itself are led astray and obstructed by the various possibilities of being which Dasein itself possesses, so that a genuine "understanding" gets suppressed, and Dasein takes refuge in substitutes . . . (163)[125]

Heidegger, like Wittgenstein, holds that the background of *shared* concerns and activities against which the special problem of knowing others arises is constitutive of worldliness and intelligibility. "Our analysis has shown that being-with is an existential constituent of being-in-the-world" (163)[125]. Therefore this background cannot be meaningfully called into question by these special cases. The traditional problem of other minds, then, is diagnosed as having arisen (1) by taking the self as an isolable occurrent entity rather than a pattern of public comportment, and (2) by generalizing a problem that arises in special cases into a problem about every case. This second move seems plausible only if one has overlooked the shared background practices, i.e., has passed over the phenomenon of world.

II. The One as Existentiale

A. The Public Character of Equipment
There are two important ways in which equipment is public. Equipment displays *generality* and obeys *norms*.

First, a piece of equipment is the equipment it is no matter who uses it. Hammers, typewriters, and buses are not just for me to use but for others too. Equipment is for "Anybody"—a general user.

Second, there is a normal (appropriate) way to use any piece of equipment. This norm is expressed by saying what "one" does, as in "one eats one's peas with a fork." To refer to the *normal* user, Heidegger coins the term *das Man*, which our translators call "the They." This translation is misleading, however, since it suggests that *I* am distinguished from *them*, whereas Heidegger's whole point is that the equipment and roles of a society are defined by norms that apply to *anyone*. But even, translating *das Man* by "we" or by "anyone" does not capture the normative character of the expression. *We* or *Anyone* might try to cheat the Internal Revenue Service, but still, *one* pays *one's* taxes. To preserve a feel for the appeal to normativity in statements about what one does and does not do, we must stay close to Heidegger's German and translate *das Man* by "the one." I shall retranslate all quotations accordingly.

It is important at the outset to be clear about this important and original insight of Heidegger's. Remember that one does not understand a chair by standing on it, but by knowing how to sit on it or by knowing that it is normally used for sitting. One sits on a chair. In this sense even equipment that only a single person can use, like prescription glasses and false teeth, are defined by the one (even if they cannot be used by just anybody). One uses glasses to help failing vision, etc. This use of "one" does not mean that glasses are *designed* for failing vision, although that is true. It tells us how glasses are normally or appropriately used. It is the same use of "one" as in "one pronounces 'Gloucester' with two syllables, even though it looks like it should have three," although the pronunciation of "Gloucester" is not designed for anything. Norms tell us right and wrong but do not require any justification. As Heidegger says, "The common sense of the one knows only the satisfying of . . . public norms and the failure to satisfy them" (334) [288].

The pronunciation example also enables us to distinguish social norms from both maxims of morality and prudence. The power of norms simply leads us to try to pronounce words correctly. Or better, we do not even try. If I pronounce a word or name incorrectly others will pronounce the word correctly with a subtle stress on what I have mispronounced, and often I shape up without even noticing. (We certainly do not notice how we are shaped into standing the distance from others one is supposed to stand.) Nor is our tendency to conform to the norm prudential. Up to a certain point I could be understood equally well even if I had deviant pronunciation. Still, I automatically conform. As Heidegger stresses:

None of these phenomena—this is characteristic precisely of the one— is in any way conscious or intentional. The obviousness, the matter-of-course way in which this movement of Dasein comes to pass also belongs to the manner of being of the one. (HCT, 282)

Only when there is some problem with the norms do I realize that I have all along been doing what one normally does.

If my deviation from the norm is explicitly pointed out, I feel I am in the wrong. Why this feeling of embarrassment when we fail to conform? It seems we just are norm-following creatures, and it makes us uneasy if our behavior is too distant from the norm.[6] "In one's concern with what one has taken hold of, whether with, for, or against, the others, there is constant care as to the way one differs from them" (163) [126]. Heidegger calls this concern with one's distance from the others "distantiality."

If we may express this existentially, such being-with-one-another has the character of *distantiality*. The more inconspicuous this kind of being is to everyday Dasein itself, all the more stubbornly and primordially does it work itself out. (164) [126]

Heidegger will later link this uneasiness with our deviation from norms to anxiety, and will interpret our eagerness to conform as a flight from our unsettledness—an attempt to get ourselves and everyone else to believe, or better, to act as if, there is a right way of doing each thing. (See Appendix.)

Heidegger calls the customary or normal comportment that we acquire along with our general familiarity with things and people, "averageness."

When beings are encountered, Dasein's world frees them for an involvement-whole with which the "one" is familiar, and within the limits which have been established with the "one's" averageness. (167) [129]

Averageness is not merely statistical. As we have seen, what Heidegger is getting at is the tendency to conform our behavior to a norm, even if that norm is frequently violated. To be told that 90 percent of the population does X, exerts pressure only on conformists, while norms gently influence everyone.

Norms and the averageness they sustain perform a crucial function. Without them the referential whole could not exist. In the West *one* eats with a knife and fork; in the Far East *one* eats with chopsticks. The important thing is that in each culture there are equipmental norms and thus an average way to do things. There *must be*, for without such averageness there could be no equipmental whole. It would not matter if each chimpanzee used a different stick in a different way to reach bananas, and, indeed, there is no "*right way*" to do it.

But for the functioning of the referential whole, everyone must (at least most of the time) eat the normal way. If some ate with forks, others with chopsticks, and still others used their right hands, the way food was cut up, and whether one got a washcloth with dinner, whether there was bread or rice, plates or bowls, etc. would be undecided and the whole equipmental nexus involved in cooking and eating a meal could not exist. For eating equipment to work, how *one* eats, when *one* eats, where *one* eats, what *one* eats, and what *one* eats with must be already determined. Thus the very functioning of equipment is dependent upon social norms. Indeed, norms define the in-order-tos that define the being of equipment, and also the for-the-sake-of-whichs that give equipment its significance.

B. The Positive and Negative Functions of the One

Now we can see how Heidegger would answer objections such as Olafson's. The one preserves averageness, which in turn is necessary for the functioning of the referential whole, and it is thanks to the one that there is a single shared public world rather than a plurality of individual worlds.

The one as that which forms everyday being-with-one-another . . . constitutes what we call *the public* in the strict sense of the word. It implies that the world is always already primarily given as the common world. It is not the case that on the one hand there are first individual subjects which at any given time have their own world; and that the task would then arise of putting together, by virtue of some sort of an arrangement, the various particular worlds of the individuals and of agreeing how one would have a common world. This is how philosophers imagine these things when they ask about the constitution of the intersubjective world. We say instead that the first thing that is given is the common world—the one. (HCT, 246)

Unfortunately Heidegger does not distinguish this constitutive *conformity* from the evils of *conformism.* Indeed, Heidegger, influenced by Kierkegaard's attack on the public in *The Present Age,* does everything he can to blur this important distinction. In order to appreciate what Heidegger is trying to say both about the importance of norms and the dangers of conformism, we must sort out on our own the positive and negative effects of the one.

1. The Positive Function of the One: Conformity as the Source of Intelligibility

On the positive side, Heidegger is clear that "the 'one' is an existentiale; and as an originary phenomenon, it belongs to Dasein's positive constitution" (167) [129].

Language provides the best example of the positive importance of averageness. "In the language which is spoken when one expresses oneself, there lies an average intelligibility" (212) [168]. This intelligibility, resulting from Dasein's tendency to fall in with public norms, is the basis of everyday understanding. "We have the *same thing* in view, because it is in *the same* averageness that we have a common understanding of what is said" (212) [168]. Indeed, as Wittgenstein stressed and we have already noted, in explaining most simple and basic things we finally have to say: "This is what one does." In this sense "Publicness primarily controls every way in which the world and Dasein get interpreted, and it is always right" (165) [127]. Wittgenstein answers an objector's question just as Heidegger would:

"So you are saying that human agreement decides what is true and what is false?"—It is what human beings say that is true and false; and they agree in the *language* they use. That is not agreement in opinions [intentional states] but in form of life [background practices].[7]

For both Heidegger and Wittgenstein, then, the source of the intelligibility of the world is the average public practices through which alone there can be any understanding at all. What is shared is not a conceptual scheme, i.e., not a belief system that can be made explicit and justified. Not that we share a belief system that is always implicit and arbitrary. That is just the Sartrean version of the same mistake. What we share is simply our average comportment. Once a practice has been explained by appealing to what one does, no more basic explanation is possible. As Wittgenstein puts it in *On Certainty*: "Giving grounds [must] come to an end sometime. But the end is not an ungrounded presupposition: it is an ungrounded way of acting."[8]

This view is entirely antithetical to the philosophical ideal of *total* clarity and *ultimate* intelligibility. Heidegger in *An Introduction to Metaphysics* suggests that there can be no such metaphysical grounding:

It remains to be seen whether the ground arrived at is really a ground, that is, whether it provides a foundation; whether it is an ultimate ground [*Ur-grund*]; or whether it fails to provide a foundation and is an abyss [*Ab-grund*]; or whether the ground is neither one nor the other but presents only a perhaps necessary appearance of foundation—in other words, it is a nonground [*Un-grund*].[9]

Philosophers seek an ultimate ground. When they discover there is none, even modern philosophers like Sartre and Derrida seem to think that they have fallen into an abyss—that the lack of an ultimate ground has catastrophic consequences for human activity. Whereas Wittgenstein, and Heidegger in Division I, see that the nonground is not an abyss. Counting on the shared agreement in our practices, we can do anything we want to do: understand the world, understand each other, have language, have families, have science, etc.

But Heidegger seeks some deeper understanding than that revealed in everydayness. Like Kierkegaard in *The Present Age* and unlike Wittgenstein, he holds that everyday intelligibility is a pseudoclarity achieved at the expense of a "genuine" clarity that is covered up. "By publicness everything gets obscured, and what has thus been covered up gets passed off as something familiar and accessible to everyone" (165) [127]. In Division II Heidegger's claim that in language there lies an "*average* intelligibility" comes to suggest that there could be an *above-average* intelligibility, if not of equipment then at least of Dasein and worldliness.

But why say that in everyday life intelligibility gets *obscured*, rather than that in public practice everything gets whatever intelligibility it has? Is there a higher intelligibility? Even in Division II Heidegger never denies that *all* significance and intelligibility is the product of the one; so what could this better intelligibility be? It cannot be the sort of higher intelligibility that the tradition claims to have found, which substitutes a different substantive account of the world and human beings for the one given in everyday understanding. Heidegger does not claim that all perception is confused (Descartes), or that in spite of appearances all everyday skills are really produced by unconscious theories (Leibniz), or that society is exclusively structured by class struggle (Marx), etc. This, according to Heidegger, is not the sort of truth or intelligibility that has been obscured, otherwise there would be no point in his constantly returning philosophical questions to the way Dasein and the world are given in everydayness.

There is, however, something that average everyday intelligibility obscures, viz., that it is *merely* average everyday intelligibility. It takes for granted that the everyday for-the-sake-of-whichs and the equipment that serves them are based upon God's goodness, human nature, or at least solid good sense. This is what Heidegger called "the perhaps necessary appearance of foundation." One cannot help thinking that the right (healthy, civilized, rational, natural, etc.) way to sit, for example, is on chairs, at tables, etc., not on the floor. Our way seems to make intrinsic sense—a sense not captured in saying, "This is what we in the West happen to do." What gets covered up in everyday understanding is not some deep intelligibility as the tradition has always held; it is that the ultimate "ground" of intelligibility is simply shared practices. There is no *right* interpretation. Average intelligibility is not inferior intelligibility; it simply obscures its own groundlessness. This is the last stage of the hermeneutics of suspicion. The only deep interpretation left is that there is no deep interpretation.

Even when Dasein becomes authentic, it does not arrive at totally unique ways of manifesting its self-interpretation. It must take over the average for-the-sake-of-whichs one has in one's culture just like everyone else; it just takes them over differently. This difference is described in the discussion of resoluteness in Division II. (See Appendix.) So Heidegger can conclude his discussion of "how understanding in general comes about" with the important statement that

Authentic self-being does not rest upon an extracted condition of a subject that has been detached from the "one"; *it is rather an existentiell modification of the "one"—of the "one" as an essential existentiale.* (168) [130]

2. The Negative Function of the "One": Conformism as Leveling

Heidegger's account of how "understanding . . . can be obstructed and misled"—how conformity degenerates into conformism— brings out an extremely subtle relationship between the averageness constitutive of intelligibility and the temptation to use norms to cover up the essential *un*intelligibility of Dasein itself. Averageness hides Dasein's unsettledness by suppressing all differences of depth or importance.

Averageness is an existential determination of the one; it is that around which everything turns for the one, what is essentially at issue for it. . . . This polished averageness of the everyday interpretation of Dasein, of the assessment of the world and the similar averageness of customs and manners watches over every exception which thrusts itself to the fore. Every exception is short-lived and quietly suppressed. (HCT, 246)

Like Kierkegaard, Heidegger calls this suppression of all meaningful differences "leveling."

Distantiality, averageness, and leveling down, as ways of being for the "one," constitute what we know as "publicness" . . . . By publicness everything gets obscured, and what has thus been covered up gets passed off as something familiar and accessible to everyone. (165) [127]

(I shall return to leveling in chapter 13 and in the Appendix.)

III. The One as the "Realest Subject" of Everydayness

We must now return to the question of the who of everyday Dasein and the final demonstration that the individual person is not the source of everyday significance. We shall now see that the one's way of being is existence; that the one takes the place of the individual subject as the source of significance; and that this blocks the Cartesian claim that meaning is grounded in the activity of an individual subject and thereby undermines the traditional claim that meaning is grounded in an absolute source.

A. The One as a Substitute Dasein

As we have already seen, the for-the-sake-of-whichs available to Dasein are not first created by you or me, but rather are public possibilities provided by society. They make no essential reference to you or me. Society, whatever its activity, is certainly not an occurrent subject, but then, according to Heidegger, neither is a human being. This raises the question: Is the social organization of "roles" and equipment a sort of activity at all, and if so, is it the sort of activity whose way of being is existence? It seems it must be, since we already know that existence is the way of being that makes possible the intelligibility of the world.

We have already seen that Dasein, besides being characterized as in each case mine, is also characterized as making an issue of its being, i.e., as existing. The public too behaves in a way that manifests a concern about its being. It embodies in its roles and norms a certain interpretation of what it is to be human, and it tends to preserve these norms by dealing with any deviation by inviting conformity or by cooptation.

The "one" has its own ways in which to be. That tendency of being-with which we have called "distantiality" is grounded in the fact that being-with-one-another concerns itself as such with averageness, which is an existential characteristic of the "one." *The "one," in its being, essentially makes an issue of this.* (164–165, my italics) [127]

Like a particular Dasein, the one in its being makes an issue of preserving a certain understanding of what it is to be a human being, and what it is to be in general.

B. The One as the Who of Everyday Dasein

We now have all the elements to answer the question: Who is everyday Dasein? We must first recall that Dasein is a way of being that is concerned about its own being, and yet must get its meaning by assigning itself to the occupations (including roles and equipment) provided by the one. "Dasein, in so far as it is, has always submitted itself already to a 'world'* which it encounters, and this submission belongs essentially to its being" (120–121)[87]. In Hegelian terminology, Dasein must objectify itself through its activities. But Heidegger avoids this way of talking because it implies that Dasein is first something immanent and subjective that needs to become public and objective. Dasein is always already outside. In fact, as it now turns out, Dasein just *is* a more or less coherent pattern of the comportment required by public "roles" and activities—an embodiment of the one. So Heidegger can conclude: "[The one] is the 'realest subject' of everydayness" (166)[128].

Each person grows up in norms that are already there. One takes over or develops a shared readiness to deal appropriately with things like rooms, tables, and chairs—the things one deals with in this culture—and with people as autonomous, gracious, suspicious, etc.—the ways people are in our world. One is what one takes over. There would be no norms without people, but there could be no people without norms.

It is as if, to use the metaphor of the selfish gene, patterns of norms use people as means to their perpetuation. Pierre Bourdieu makes this point forcibly from the side of anthropology, by means of his notion of *habitus*. (But, of course, Bourdieu's talk of objective structures, organisms, and dispositions would be too naturalistic for Heidegger.)

Habitus is the product of the work of inculcation and appropriation necessary in order for those products of collective history, the objective structures (e.g., of language, economy, etc.) to succeed in reproducing themselves more or less completely, in the form of durable dispositions, in the organisms (which one can, if one wishes, call individuals) lastingly subjected to the same conditionings.[10]

Bourdieu also sees the sense in which, thanks to the habitus, *the* world is prior to *my* world.

> Since the history of the individual is never anything other than a certain specification of the collective history of his group or class, *each individual system of dispositions* may be seen as a *structural variant* of all the other group or class habitus.[11]

So when we raise the question of Dasein's particularity existentially, i.e., in terms of its activities, we find that "the one is not nothing, but it is also not a worldly thing which I can see, grasp, and weigh. The more public this one is, the less comprehensible it is and the less it is nothing, so little that it really constitutes the who of one's own Dasein in each instance of everydayness" (HCT, 247).

> Primarily, it is not "I," in the sense of my own self, that "am," but rather the others, whose way is that of the "one." In terms of the "one," and as the "one," I am primarily "given" to "myself." Primarily Dasein is "one," and for the most part it remains so. (167) [129]

Thus:

> The "who" is not this one, not that one, not oneself, not some people, and not the sum of them all. The "who" is the neuter, *the "one."* (164) [126]

So Heidegger can conclude:

> The self of everyday Dasein is a *one's self.* . . . As a one's-self, the particular Dasein has been dispersed into the "one," and must first find itself. (167) [129]

This conclusion will seem strange to us unless we remember that Dasein is not an organism and not an ego containing a stream of private experiences, but rather is a mode of comportment.

We have now found the source of the "signifying in which Dasein gives itself beforehand its being-in-the-world as something to be understood" (120) [80]. Anonymous public practice has already decided on the roles, standards, norms, etc., for the sake of which Dasein engages in its everyday activities. Careful description of the way of being of Dasein shows that what is given in everydayness is not the meaning-giving activity of a plurality of transcendental subjects (as in Husserl), nor even active consciousness (as in Sartre)—entities that first give meaning to their own world and then to a shared world. We cannot even say that individuals take over everyday meanings by deciphering them and incorporating them into their belief systems. A particular Dasein can get its "role" and even its moods only by being socialized into the "stock" available in its society. Even an authentic Dasein must manifest its unsettledness through these everyday possibilities.

This need not mean, however, that the roles, norms, etc., available to Dasein are fixed once and for all. New technological and social developments are constantly changing specific ways for Dasein to be. Nor does it mean that there is no room for an individual or political group to develop new possibilities, which could then become available to the society. But it does mean that such "creativity" always takes place on a background of what *one* does—of *accepted* for-the-sake-of-whichs that cannot all be called into question at once because they are not presuppositions and in any case must remain in the background to lend intelligibility to criticism and change. Just as it is possible to find something occurrent and then give it a use, but only on the background of shared practical activities, so here too we have a case where *ontic* activity can create a new role or meaning, but only against an *ontological* background that is not subject to willed change. This sociocultural background too can change gradually, as does a language, but never all at once and never as the result of the conscious decision of groups or individuals.

C. The One as the Source of Significance and Intelligibility

As we have noted, the constant control the one exerts over each Dasein makes a coherent referential whole, shared for-the-sake-of-whichs, and thus, ultimately, significance and intelligibility possible. It is indicative of Heidegger's ambivalent attitude towards this original and important point that his crucial formulation of it occurs, as if in passing, in the middle of a paragraph.

Dasein is for the sake of the "one" in an everyday manner, [i.e., all for-the-sake-of-whichs are supplied by the one] and *the "one" itself articulates the referential nexus of significance.* (167, my italics and my gloss in brackets) [129]

There is certainly something unsettling about Heidegger's discovery. Traditionally all meanings have been traced back to some final self-intelligible, most real, occurrent source, e.g. the Good, God, or the transcendental ego. The one as ultimate reality—*"ens realissimum"* (166) [128], a philosophical version of God—cannot supply this sort of intelligibility. It can never be made completely explicit and justified. It contains an understanding of being and accounts for all intelligibility, yet it is no sort of intelligible thing at all.

The traditional response to this puzzling situation is to posit a source for the one, either in the activity of a preexistent Hegelian Spirit that expresses itself in the world or in the conscious meaning-giving activity of an individual subject. But the phenomena Heidegger has uncovered cannot be accounted for in terms of either of these alternatives. On the one hand, cultural norms are not given in such a way that their intelligibility can be traced back to lucid absolute consciousness. "The one is not something like a 'universal subject' which a plurality of subjects have hovering above them" (166)[128]. On the other hand, since a human being is socialized by other human beings—trained to comply with norms that are not fully available to consciousness—the result is misdescribed if we call it inter*subjectivity*.[12]

One may neither decree prematurely that this "one" is "really" nothing, nor profess the opinion that one can Interpret this phenomenon ontologically by somehow "explaining" it as what results from taking the being-occurrent-together of several subjects and then fitting them together. (166)[128]

That even the traditional logic fails us when confronted with these phenomena is not surprising. (166)[129]

Yet the one is surely *something*. As Heidegger says, "The more openly the 'one' behaves, the harder it is to grasp, and the slier it is, but the less is it nothing at all" (166)[128]. What could be more open yet more sly than the inculcation of the norms governing distance-standing practices, for example?

What is important is that, although norming activity depends on the existence of human beings, it does not depend on the existence of any particular human being but rather produces particular human beings. When faced with such strange phenomena all one can do is describe what is going on: "In working out concepts of being one must direct one's course by these phenomena, which cannot be pushed aside" (166)[128]. "Before words, before expressions, always the phenomena first, and then the concepts!" (HCT, 248) We can only describe the phenomena as they show themselves and show how they fit with the rest of human existence. This is precisely the job of hermeneutic phenomenology.[13]

The Three-Fold Structure of Being-In

Heidegger has told us from the start that Dasein is being-in-the-world. Chapters III and IV have laid out the structure of worldliness—the referential whole and significance—all as articulated by the one. But human beings are never directly in the world; we are always in the world by way of being in some specific circumstances. This situated way of being-in is the subject of Chapter V.

Heidegger calls the situation a *Lichtung*. The word *Lichtung* means literally a clearing in the forest. We can capture some of the sense of clearing by calling Dasein a *field* of disclosedness. For Heidegger this suggests an open space in which one can encounter objects. *Licht* also means light. Things show up *in the light of* our understanding of being. Heidegger thus relates Dasein's openness to the tradition which extends from Plato to the Enlightenment of equating intelligibility with illumination.

Heidegger reminds us that Dasein is not a subject related to an object, nor does it help to say, as Martin Buber does, that Dasein is "between" subject and object, since this still assumes there are entities between which Dasein is supposed to be. Rather Dasein, as being-in-the-world, is always already outside itself, formed by shared practices, and absorbed in active coping. But *current (jeweiliges)* Dasein, as Heidegger calls it, is only absorbed in *one* activity and so practices only a *few practices* at a time. (The term "current Dasein" would make no sense if Dasein were occurrent like a table; we have to remember Dasein is a way of acting, and think of current Dasein*ing*.) Current Dasein then is always in the world by way of being in a situation—dealing with something specific in a context of things and people, directed toward some specific end, doing what it does for the sake of being Dasein in some specific way.

Heidegger calls Dasein's activity of opening a clearing its being-cleared, its being-in or its being-its-there.

When we talk in an ontically figurative way of the *lumen naturale* [natural light] in man, we have in mind nothing other than the existential-ontological structure of this being, that it is in such a way as to be its "there." To say that it is "illuminated" means that *as* being-in-the-world it is cleared in itself, not through any other being, but in such a way that it *is* itself the clearing. (171)[133]

Note that Heidegger speaks of *its* there (*Da*) and of *the* clearing. Being-*its*-there is Dasein's opening onto *the* clearing.[1] "Da" in German means both "here" and "there" ("yonder"), or rather it doesn't distinguish these two meanings. It might help to think of our use of "there" in expressions such as "There I was, in trouble again." Heidegger uses "being-its-there" to express the centered way a particular Dasein is in the clearing. Thus "'here' and 'yonder' are possible only in a 'there'" (171)[132].

That the there (in the phrase "its there") is the existential version of an individual perspective on the shared situation or clearing can be seen from a careful reading of the following quotations. First Heidegger allows something like a spatial perspective:

In the term "Situation" . . . there is an overtone of a signification that is spatial. We shall not try to eliminate this from the existential conception, for such an overtone is also implied in the "there" of Dasein. (346)[299][2]

Then he reminds us that, as he showed in his discussion of spatiality, a spatial perspective is to be understood as a centered coping.

The "here" of [Dasein's] current factical situation never signifies a position in space, but signifies rather the leeway of the range of that equipmental whole with which [Dasein] is most closely concerned. (420)[369]

We have already been prepared in the spatiality discussion to understand that "Dasein brings its 'there' along with it" (171)[133]. That is, although Dasein's there is not a geometrical perspective, it is a moving center of pragmatic activity in the midst of a shared world. Since Dasein is not a mind but is absorbed in and defined by what it does, Heidegger can say that Dasein is its "there." "'Dasein *is* its disclosedness' means . . . that the being which is an issue for this entity in its very being is to be its 'there'" (171)[133].

A way to understand all these new terms, although this inter-pretation does not fit every passage, is as follows: first, as we have seen, *the world* is the whole of which all subworlds are elaborations. Now we add that subworlds are lived in by a particular Dasein by *being-in-a-situation.* Each Dasein's *there* is *the* situation as organized around *its* activity. The shared situation is called *the clearing*; being-in-the-clearing is *being-there.*

Dasein opens a clearing because its being is an issue for it. "That by which this entity is essentially cleared—in other words, that which makes it both 'open' for itself and 'bright' for itself—is what we have defined as 'care,' . . . . In care is grounded the full disclosedness of the 'there'" (401–402) [350]. Persons, if they are Daseining, are, in caring, performing an activity of clearing, both of themselves and of their situation. Yet, although each Dasein does its own caring and thus is its own "there," the result is one shared situation. We can thus distinguish *clearing* as an activity from *the clearing* that results from that activity. Think of a group of people all working together to clear a field in a forest. There is a plurality of activities of clearing, but all this activity results in only one cleared field. "The surrounding world is different in a certain way for each of us, and notwithstanding that we move about in a common world" (BP, 164). Thus Heidegger can say: "[Dasein] is cleared in itself . . . in such a way that it is itself the (sic) clearing" (171) [133]. Heidegger makes a similar point explicitly with respect to the now: "Although each one of us utters his own now, it is nevertheless the now for everyone" (BP, 264).

A way to see that several activities of clearing (verb) can produce one clearing (noun) is to think about the logic of being in a situation. Whereas it belongs to the essence of a mental state or experience (*Erlebniss*) to be private—I cannot share *your* headache since if I experience it, it becomes *my* headache—situations by their very nature can be shared. If I share your situation it becomes not my situation but *our* situation. As in-a-situation, "Dasein has always already *stepped out beyond itself,* ex-sistere, it is in a world. Consequently, it is never anything like a subjective inner sphere" (BP, 170). Indeed, "consciousness is only possible on the ground of the 'there,' as a derivative mode of it."[3] That Dasein's current situation can always in principle be shared with others is a consequence of the fact that its intelligibility depends upon *shared* practices. So each Dasein's "there" is a shareable grasp of an already shared world. "This entity carries in its ownmost being the character of not being closed off" (171) [132].

Heidegger stresses that the individual activity of being-in or clearing (verb) is correlative with the shared clearing (noun). "Dasein exhibits itself as an entity which is in its world but at the same time is by virtue of *the* world in which it is" (HCT, 202, my italics). An activity of clearing that is produced by the clearing (noun) it produces makes no sense for ontic activities, yet "an entity for which, as being-in-the-world, its being itself is an issue, has, ontologically, a circular structure" (195)[153]. This circular structure is not something logic can deal with, but it is nonetheless the structure of the unique ontological phenomenon called being-in-the-world.

Heidegger's interest in the contribution of individual activity to there being a world is his debt to Husserlian phenomenology. In his later work and in a marginal note in *Being and Time,* Heidegger reacts against this debt and stresses the *priority* of the clearing (noun) to individual, centered Daseins, as well as reemphasizing that Dasein's activity cannot be understood in terms of mental representations. Where the text speaks of Dasein's circular being, Heidegger later writes: "But this 'its being itself' is determined by the understanding of being, i.e., by standing in the clearing of presence. Moreover, neither the clearing as such nor presence as such becomes themes of representing" {204}.

Up to now in *Being and Time* Heidegger has been laying out the world side of Dasein's circular structure, with its in-order-tos, referential whole, significance, and for-the-sake-of-whichs, all organized by the one. Now we shift to the structure of the activity of being-in—Dasein's being-its-there. This is Heidegger's hardest phenomenological task, since being-in as the disclosive activity of the individual Dasein is what the tradition has always found easy to interpret as the activity of a monadic, transcendental subject—a "windowless" perspective that is precisely closed off. This activity has now to be reinterpreted as the activity of a being that presupposes and produces a shared clearing. As a situated activity, each Dasein has a three-fold structure.

When the "there" has been completely disclosed, its disclosedness is constituted by understanding, affectedness, and falling. (400)[349]

Each aspect of this structure is an existentiale, and no one is understandable without the others. As Heidegger puts it, all are equiprimordial. In the next three chapters I shall discuss in detail these three basic aspects of Dasein's involvement—understanding, affectedness, and falling—and show how they structure a Dasein's current situation.

10

Affectedness

Heidegger's term for the receptive aspect of Dasein's way of being, that it just *finds* things and ways of acting mattering to it, is *Befindlichkeit*. This is not a word in ordinary German, but is constructed from an everyday greeting, "*Wie befinden Sie sich?*," which literally asks "How do you find yourself?"—something like our greeting "How are you doing?" To translate this term we certainly cannot use the translators' term, "state-of-mind," which suggests, at least to philosophers, a *mental state*, a determinate condition of an isolable, occurrent subject. Heidegger is at pains to show that the sense we have of how things are going is precisely *not* a private mental state. And just as state-of-mind can be heard as too inner, another term I have tried, "disposition," because of its use by behaviorists as disposition to behave, can be heard as too outer. I also once tried "situatedness," but, as we have seen, situation is another name for the clearing.

Out of desperation I then turned to an expression as strange as Heidegger's *Befindlichkeit*, namely "where-you're-at-ness," but this leaves out the sensitivity to the situation. What one needs is an English word that conveys *being found in a situation where things and options already matter*. Since no word I know of conveys all this, I shall settle for "affectedness," which at least captures our being already affected by things, as in the following:

To be affected by the unserviceable, resistant, or threatening character of that which is available, becomes ontologically possible only in so far as being-in as such has been determined existentially beforehand in such a manner that what it encounters within-the-world can "*matter*" to it in this way. The fact that this sort of thing can "matter" to it is grounded in one's affectedness; and as affectedness it has already disclosed the world—as something by which it can be threatened, for instance. . . . Dasein's openness to the world is constituted existentially by the attunement of affectedness. (176) [137]

One also has to decide how to translate *Stimmung,* which is the normal German word for mood.

What we indicate ontologically by the term "affectedness" is *ontically* the most familiar and everyday sort of thing; our *Stimmung,* our being-at-tuned. (172)[134]

I shall stick to "mood," although for Heidegger, *Stimmung* has a broader range than "mood." Fear, for example, is a *Stimmung* for Heidegger, but it is clearly an affect not a mood. *Stimmung* seems to name any of the ways Dasein can be affected. Heidegger suggests that moods or attunements manifest the tone of being-there. As Heidegger uses the term, mood can refer to the *sensibility* of an age (such as romantic), the *culture* of a company (such as aggressive), the *temper* of the times (such as revolutionary), as well as the *mood* in a current situation (such as the eager mood in the classroom) and, of course, the mood of an individual. These are all ways of finding that things matter. Thus they are all ontic specifications of affectedness, the ontological existential condition that things always already matter.

Heidegger turns first to mood. This strategy has serious pedagogical drawbacks. Of the three aspects of being-in, affectedness, especially as manifested in individual moods, is the most dangerously close to Cartesianism. How can you and I be said to be open to the same situation if what each of us is in is threatening to me and exhilarating to you? At best our different moods seem to be subjective colorings projected onto a shared neutral scene. Worse, since the situation includes how it matters to me as one of its constitutive aspects, Heidegger runs the risk of making my personal situation, colored by my mood, into a private world cut off from and more fundamental than, the public world; just as by focusing on closeness rather than presence, he ran the risk of making my spatiality seem more primordial than public spatiality. But we are supposed to see that individual closeness and individual moods require a public clearing and that they reveal the situation and the things in it under some public aspect, i.e., an aspect available to others too.

If Heidegger had started his discussion of affectedness with cultural sensibility rather than individual mood, he could have avoided this possible Cartesian misunderstanding. Cultural sensibility is a mode of affectedness that is public and is prior to mood in that it governs the range of available moods. But Heidegger does not even mention cultural sensibility in *Being and Time*. He does, however, stress it in his lectures a few years later. There he says that the fundamental mood (*Grundstimmung*) at the Greek beginning of philosophy was wonder (*Erstaunen*), and the modern cultural mood is alarm (*Erschreckens*).[1] In his 1931 lectures Heidegger gives an important place to these cultural sensibilities. Indeed, they play a role in opening up a world parallel to that which familiarity plays in *Being and Time*.

It is only on the basis of a certain suppression and pushing aside of mood, . . . that one arrives at that which we call the simple representation of things. For representation is not primary, as if a world were to be constructed by layers by the heaping up of a bunch of represented objects. A world is never . . . stuck together from a multiplicity of perceived things collected after the fact, but it is what is the most primordially and the most properly manifest, within which we are able to encounter this or that thing. The movement of the opening of the world happens in the fundamental mood (*Grundstimmung*). . . . The fundamental mood determines for our Dasein the place and the time which are open to its being.[2]

Why does Heidegger not mention cultural sensibilities in *Being and Time?* Perhaps because by discussing it he would blur the point that, as he is introducing it here, affectedness is not a structure of the *world*, but rather a structure of the *there*—one of the three structural aspects of Dasein's way of disclosing a *current* situation. Moods vary with the current situation, but cultural sensibilities do not. What Heidegger should have done, I suggest, is distinguish three types of affectedness: a world type (cultural sensibility); a situation or current world type (mood); and the specific directedness mood makes possible (affect) (see Table 9 on page 240). (A similar architectonic problem arises when Heidegger deals with understanding, but in that case he does allow a world type, a situational type, and a personal, directed, intentional type; see chapter 11.)

I. Mood

A. Moods Are Public
Heidegger first recounts and rejects the traditional view that moods are private feelings that we project on the world and that we discover by reflecting on our experience.

While moods, of course, are ontically well known to us, they are not recognized in their primordial existential function. They are regarded as

fleeting experiences which "color" one's whole "psychical condition."
(390) [340]

But affectedness is very remote from anything like coming across a
psychical condition by the kind of apprehending which first turns round
and then back. Indeed it is so far from this, that only because the "there"
has already been disclosed in affectedness can immanent reflection come
across "experiences" at all. (175) [136]

Heidegger would no doubt appreciate the fact that we ordinarily
say we are *in* a mood, not that a mood is an experience *in* us.

If it seems difficult to divorce moods from *feelings* coloring my
world, it is helpful to recall, as Heidegger points out, that the public
too can have moods.

Publicness, as the kind of being which belongs to the one, not only has in
general its own way of having a mood, but needs moods and "makes" them
for itself. (178) [138]

Public moods would presumably include shock, frivolity, outrage,
mourning, etc.

Moods can also be social. Heidegger discusses social moods as
ways of being-with-one-another in his 1929 lectures.

A—as we say—well-disposed person brings a good mood to a group. In
this case does hc produce in himself a psychic experience, in order then
to transfer it to the others, like the way infectious germs wander from one
organism to others? . . . Or another person is in a group that in its manner
of being dampens and depresses everything; no one is outgoing. What do
we learn from this? Moods are *not accompanying phenomena*; rather, they
are the sort of thing that determines being-with-one-another in advance.
It seems as if, so to speak, a mood is in each case already there, like an
atmosphere, in which we are steeped and by which we are thoroughly
determined. It not only seems as if this were so, it is so; and in light of these
facts, it is necessary to dispense with the psychology of feelings and
experiences and consciousness.[3]

Moreover, if it were not for the way the *one* has moods, individuals
could not have moods at all.

The dominance of the public way in which things have been interpreted
has already been decisive even for the possibilities of having a mood—
that is, for the basic way in which Dasein lets the world "matter" to it.
(213) [169–170]

Shame over losing face, for example, is something one can feel only in Japan, while the exhilaration of romantic love was for a long time the exclusive property of the West.

Let us sum up the reasons why moods cannot be properly described as fleeting private feelings projected upon the world but must be understood as specifications of a dimension of existence, i.e., of affectedness as a way of being-in-the-world.

1. Cultures have longstanding sensibilities. In one culture things show up as occasions for celebrating the sacred, while in another everything shows up as a threat to survival.

2. Moods depend on the norms of the one. I can have only the sort of moods one can have in my culture; thus the public is the condition of the possibility of personal moods.

3. There are social moods.

4. My mood, while possibly at a given time mine alone, is not essentially private; another person in my culture could share the same mood.

But if a mood is not a first-person, *subjective state,* our Cartesian tradition has prepared us to think that it must then be some kind of third-person, *objective behavior.* The behaviorist approach which tries to reduce all psychological states to physical movements, however, is unable to account for the intentionality of moods. Gilbert Ryle and Ludwig Wittgenstein have therefore suggested a modified behaviorist approach. Wittgenstein points out that "expecting," for example, is neither a feeling, nor a set of objective movements. It is a certain unified style of activity in an appropriate situation. For example, when one is afraid, one does not merely *feel* fearful, nor is fear merely the *movement* of cringing; fear is cringing in an appropriate context. Heidegger seems to agree that moods cannot be inner states but are a kind of comportment when he says:

A mood is not related to the psychical . . . and is not itself an *inner condition* which then reaches forth in an enigmatical way and puts its mark on things and persons. . . . It comes neither from "outside" nor from "inside," but arises out of being-in-the-world, as a way of such being. (176, my italics) [137, 136]

But Heidegger would not endorse Wittgenstein's view, for, like crude behaviorism, it does not do justice to the phenomenon— moods determine not just what we *do* but *how things show up for us.*

How can we account for this basic function of mood as a kind of disclosing? As in the case of the one, we must simply describe the phenomenon of mood and resist all philosophical categories (both subjective and objective, inner and outer) that the tradition, and even its recent variations, presses upon us. When we stay with the phenomenon we find mood, as a kind of affectedness, is neither a feeling projected on the world nor merely a kind of comportment, but rather a unique component of the activity of clearing. "Existentially, affectedness implies a disclosive submission to the world, out of which we can encounter something that matters to us" (177) [137–138].

B. Mood Reveals Thrownness

Another important characteristic of mood is that it is pervasive—often so pervasive as to be transparent.

The most powerful moods are those that we do not at all attend to and examine even less, those moods that attune us as if there were no moods there at all.[4]

It is perhaps because of this pervasiveness that traditional philosophy has overlooked mood. Mood also contradicts the traditional assumption that one can always know something best by gaining a reflective and detached clarity about it. Moods reveal Dasein in a primordial way only when Dasein is *not* reflecting on them. Moreover, they cannot be placed fully before the mind even in reflection.

Ontologically mood is a primordial kind of being for Dasein, in which Dasein is disclosed to itself *prior* to all cognition and volition, and *beyond* their range of disclosure. (175) [136]

As Heidegger points out, we cannot get behind our moods; we cannot get clear *about* them, and we cannot get clear *of* them. "Dasein always has some mood" (173) [134]. I am always already surrounded by objects that matter in some specific way.

Dasein is thus always already given and then needs to take a stand on what it is. It is a self-interpreting foundness. Heidegger calls this foundness or givenness *thrownness*.

This characteristic of Dasein's being—this "that it is"—is veiled in its "whence" and "whither," yet disclosed in itself all the more unveiledly; we call it the "*thrownness*" of this entity into its "there" . . . . The expression "thrownness" is meant to suggest the *facticity of its being delivered over*. The "that it is and has to be" which is disclosed in Dasein's affectedness. (174) [135]

C. Mood as Originary Transcendence

Moods provide the background on the basis of which specific events can affect us. If I am in a frightened mood, every particular thing shows up as fearsome.[5] Mood colors the whole world and everything that comes into it, so that even what I remember, anticipate and imagine is bright or drab, reassuring or, in the above example, frightening, depending on my current mood. In this way moods are like the weather. On a sunny day not only are all present objects bright, but it is difficult to imagine a drab world, and, conversely on dull days everything that can show up is dull, and so is everything one can envisage. Indeed, far from being fleeting as the tradition has supposed, moods settle in like the weather and tend to perpetuate themselves. For example, when I am annoyed, new events, even those which when I am joyful show up as challenging or amusing, show up as grounds for further annoyance. As Heidegger puts the general point:

The "bare mood" discloses the "there" more primordially, but correspondingly it *closes it off* more stubbornly than any not-perceiving. (175) [136]

As the annoyance case makes clear, moods do not just let things show up as mattering; they also show you how things are going with you. One comes back from the yonder of annoying things and events to a realization that one is annoyed. This sort of reflection from the world, rather than introspection, is the way we find ourselves.

A being of the character of Dasein is its "there" in such a way that, whether explicitly or not, it finds itself in its thrownness. In affectedness Dasein is always brought before itself, and has always found itself, not in the sense of coming across itself by perceiving itself, but in the sense of finding itself in the mood that it has. (174) [135]

Heidegger wants as usual to stress that moods provide the background for intentionality, i.e., for the specific ways things and possibilities show up as mattering.

Mood has already disclosed, in every case, being-in-the-world as a whole, and makes it possible first of all to direct oneself towards something. (176) [137]

Things are always encountered in some specific way, as attractive, threatening, interesting, boring, frustrating, etc. Possible actions are always enticing, frightening, intriguing, etc. We care when a piece of equipment breaks down and whether or not we achieve our goals. Affectedness is the condition of the possibility of specific things showing up as mattering. Affectedness is therefore a dimension of Dasein's disclosing—an aspect of originary transcendence.

II. Affective Intentionality as Ontic Transcendence

Heidegger does not map out the various levels of intentionality that affectedness makes possible, but we can guess what he would say. Encountering something as threatening is a kind of intentionality, which, like coping with the available, requires no mental content. But if I find my situation disturbing, if for example something or someone shows up as both attractive and threatening, I may be led to reflect on my experience. Then I am on the level of the unavailable. Fear, for example, then shows up as an intentional state. Far from being transparent, it has distinguishable feeling and behavioral components. One feels palpitations and one cringes. Philosophers from Hobbes to Spinoza to John Searle have tried to define such affects in terms of subjective feelings, such as agitation, depression, etc., plus some intentional content. As usual such mentalistic philosophy begins one stage too late. It cannot take account of mood's role in opening up a world or of the transparent directedness of affects.

Finally, on the occurrent level, a behaviorist reduces moods to movements or a cognitivist like Paul Erkman decontextualizes affects and looks for objective defining features. He finds coding and decoding, display rules, appraisal mechanisms, etc. In these cases mattering is left out altogether and cannot be reconstructed from these impoverished elements no matter how complex or holistic their interrelations.

A. Fear and Anxiety

Heidegger works out a specific example of how affectedness, made concrete in a world-defining mood, makes intentional directedness towards entities possible. He also uses this occasion to contrast two basic modes of affectedness, fear and anxiety, and their respective objects.

1. Fear

Borrowing heavily from Kierkegaard's *Concept of Anxiety*, Heidegger develops a detailed description of fear in order to contrast it with anxiety. In the case of fear we can distinguish three aspects.

a. *The fearing as such.* This is the mood that lets something matter to us as fearsome.

b. *That which is feared.* Something specific coming at us, in some specific way, from some specific sector of the environment.

c. *That which is feared for.* Dasein itself as threatened in some specific respect. This need not be some part of the body. Fear can threaten Dasein's self-interpretation by threatening its projects. "Primarily and usually, Dasein is in terms of *what* it is concerned with. When this is endangered, being-amidst is threatened" (180–181)[141].

"Fear discloses Dasein predominantly in a privative way" (181)[141]. When Dasein is severely frightened it becomes paralyzed.

When concern is afraid, it leaps from next to next, because it forgets itself and therefore does not take hold of any definite possibility. . . . [A person's] "environment" does not disappear, but it is encountered without his knowing his way about in it any longer. (392)[342]

Note that panic parallels the breakdown caused by a missing tool. It makes the world obtrusive. "Fear closes off our endangered being-in, and yet at the same time lets us see it" (181)[141].

This description of fear as a mood in which one is afraid, an intentional directedness toward something fearsome, and Dasein's sense of being threatened prepares us for a discussion of anxiety as a "privileged way in which Dasein is disclosed" (228)[185].

2. Anxiety

Heidegger discusses anxiety at great length because, in order to do fundamental ontology, to trace back all modes of being to Dasein's mode of being, he needs to find a special method for revealing Dasein's total structure.

If the existential analytic of Dasein is to retain clarity in principle as to its function in fundamental ontology, then in order to master its provisional task of exhibiting Dasein's being, it must seek for one of the *most far-reaching* and *most primordial* possibilities of disclosure—one that lies in Dasein itself. . . . With what is thus disclosed, the structural whole of the being we seek must then come to light in an elemental way. (226)[182]

This would be Heidegger's existential equivalent of Husserl's transcendental reduction. Heidegger, in preparing this existential reduction, rejects the apparent self-evidence both of what Husserl calls the natural attitude and of private experiences.

Our everyday environmental experiencing [*Erfahren*], which remains directed both ontically and ontologically towards intraworldly entities, is not the sort of thing which can present Dasein in an ontically primordial manner for ontological analysis. Similarly our immanent perception of experiences [*Erlebnisse*] fails to provide a clue which is ontologically adequate. (226) [181–182]

To reveal Dasein simple and whole Heidegger chooses anxiety. Just as the breakdown of a piece of equipment reveals the nature both of equipmentality and of the referential whole, so anxiety serves as a breakdown that reveals the nature of Dasein and its world. But as one might expect, what is revealed in anxiety is precisely the opposite of what is revealed in Husserl's transcendental reduction. While both reductions isolate Dasein as a "solus ipse," and both reveal to the natural attitude that takes intelligibility for granted that intelligibility must be produced, Husserl's reduction reveals the transcendental ego as *the absolute source of all intelligibility*, while anxiety reveals Dasein as *dependent upon a public system of significances* that it did *not produce*.

Heidegger never makes this point explicitly but it seems to lie behind the following claim:

Anxiety individualizes Dasein and thus discloses it as "*solus ipse.*" But this existential "solipsism" is so far from the displacement of putting an isolated subject-thing into the innocuous emptiness of a worldless occurring, that in an extreme sense what it does is precisely to bring Dasein face to face with its world as world, and thus bring it face to face with itself as being-in-the-world. (233) [188]

Dasein has to define itself in terms of the public world. It has to accept the fact that in order to make sense of itself, it must already dwell in the meanings given by the one. "Dasein is not itself the basis of its being [in the sense that] this basis first arises from its own projection" (330–331) [285]. Dasein is alone in the sense that no meanings in the world refer to any individual Dasein or make a place for it qua individual, so no role—no way of being—has intrinsic meaning for it.

a. *What anxiety reveals*

Heidegger begins by contrasting anxiety and fear.

What is the difference phenomenally between that in the face of which anxiety is anxious and that in the face of which fear is afraid? That in the face of which one has anxiety is not an intraworldly entity. . . . This threatening does not have the character of a definite detrimentality which reaches what is threatened, and which reaches it with definite regard to a specific factical ability-to-be. That in the face of which one is anxious is completely indefinite. . . . Intraworldly entities are not "relevant" at all. (230–231)[186]

Since no for-the-sake-of-which is relevant either, significance disappears.

The involvement-whole of the available and the occurrent discovered within-the-world is, as such, of no consequence; it collapses into itself; the world has the character of completely lacking significance. (231)[186]

Yet worldliness obtrudes itself.

Intraworldly beings are of so little importance in themselves that on the basis of this *insignificance* of the intraworldly, the world in its worldliness is all that still obtrudes itself. (231)[187]

How can these remarks be reconciled? How can the world both lose significance and stand out? The clue is Heidegger's remark that worldliness *obtrudes*. This is the same term that described the way the referential whole stands out when a tool is missing. Remember:

When we notice what is unavailable, that which is available enters the mode of *obtrusiveness.* (103)[73]

When something available is found missing . . . circumspection comes up against emptiness, and now sees for the first time what the missing article was available *with*, and *what* it was available *for.* (105)[75]

In effect, the world has been like a tool for inauthentic Dasein. Dasein has taken up the equipment provided by the one, e.g., hammers for building houses to feel at home in, and for-the-sake-of-whichs like being a carpenter to know who one is—all this to turn away from its preontological sense of unsettledness.

When Dasein "understands" unsettledness in the everyday manner, it does so by turning away from it . . . in this turning-away, the "not-at-home" gets "dimmed down." (234) [189]

In anxiety, inauthentic Dasein experiences the world as an instrument that has failed to do its job.

Anxiety brings [Dasein] back from its absorption in the "world."*6 Everyday familiarity collapses. (233) [189]

The "world" can offer nothing more, and neither can Dasein-with others. Anxiety thus takes away from Dasein the possibility of understanding itself. . . in terms of the "world"* and the way things have been publicly interpreted. (232) [187]

Dasein's fundamental not-being-at-home breaks through.

In anxiety one feels "*unsettled.*" Here the peculiar indefiniteness of that amidst which Dasein finds itself in anxiety comes primarily to expression: the "nothing and nowhere." But here "unsettledness" (*Unheimlichkeit*) also means "not-being-at-home." (233) [188]

But unlike ordinary equipmental breakdown, anxiety is a *total* disturbance. Rather than revealing some part of the workshop world from the inside, it reveals the whole world as if from outside. It reveals the groundlessness of the world and of Dasein's being-in-the-world. "That in the face of which one has anxiety is being-in-the-world as such" (230) [186].

If this is the right way to understand what Heidegger is saying, then we must be clear that in revealing itself as insignificant the world does not cease to be a referential whole. (It does not collapse into an unstructured, viscous mass as it does for Roquentin in Sartre's *Nausea.* That could happen only if each individual Dasein gave the things in its own world their meaning and structure.) Rather the world collapses *away* from the anxious Dasein; it *withdraws.* No possibilities solicit Dasein. Instead of Dasein's transparently pressing into the future using some equipment towards some end, absorption simply ceases.

Anxiety is not conceptual. "Being-anxious discloses, primordially and directly, the world as world. . . . This does not signify, however, that in anxiety the worldliness of the world gets conceptualized" (232) [187]. One can, however, suggest a reflective reconstruction of it. When anxious Dasein is drawn away from the roles and equipment it has taken up, the for-the-sake-of-whichs provided by the one and the whole referential nexus appear as constructs—a cultural conspiracy to provide the illusion of some ultimate meaning-motivating action. Social action now appears as a game which there is no point in playing since it has no intrinsic meaning. Serious involvement is revealed as *illusio,* Bourdieu would say.[7] The anxious Dasein can still see that there is a whole system of roles and equipment *that can be used by anyone,* but, just for that very reason, this system has no essential relation to *it.* Equipment is still present with its in-order-tos, but Dasein no longer experiences itself as assigned to a for-the-sake-of-which and so lacks a reason for using it.

The threatening does not come from what is available or occurrent, but rather from the fact that neither of these "says" anything any longer. . . . The world in which I exist has sunk into insignificance; and the world which is thus disclosed is one in which beings can be freed only in the character of having no involvement. (393)[343]

In anxiety one knows, for example, that the telephone is for calling people, but instead of simply taking action one wonders why anyone would do that. If one stands back and looks for intrinsic reasons for one's actions, one discovers there are none.

Anxiety is thus the disclosure accompanying a Dasein's preontological sense that it is not the source of the meanings it uses to understand itself; that the public world makes no intrinsic sense for it and would go on whether that particular Dasein existed or not. In anxiety Dasein discovers that it has no meaning or content of its own; nothing individualizes it but its empty thrownness.

Anxiety is anxious about naked Dasein as something that has been thrown into unsettledness. It brings one back to the pure "that-it-is" of one's ownmost individualized thrownness. (393–394)[343]

In anxiety, as in fear, Dasein is "inhibited" and"bewildered" (395)[344]. At the limit Dasein is completely paralyzed. Indeed, at this limit, there is no Dasein at all, since Dasein is its concerns and activity. That is why, when he is consistent, Heidegger does not say "Dasein is anxious," but rather "anxiety is anxious."

Anxiety is not necessarily accompanied by sweating, crying, or wringing of the hands. Heidegger says in *What Is Metaphysics?* that anxiety can be serene. To get a feel for what Heidegger is trying to describe it helps to turn to Antonioni's movies, especially *The Eclipse* and *The Red Desert*. *The Red Desert* portrays the heroine as walking around in a perpetual fog, while in *The Eclipse*, which seems closer to Heidegger's account, objects are seen in stark clarity, with a kind of cold mysteriousness. They have lost their significance for the heroine who drifts past them unable to act, while other people go on busily using them.

In *The Eclipse* the heroine tries to get back in touch with the world of everydayness by getting involved with a man absorbed in the frantic activity of the stock market. In *The Red Desert* the first thing the woman does is grab a sandwich as if she were desperately hungry. She takes one bite, then drops it and forgets it. Heidegger says of anxiety:

Our concernful awaiting finds nothing in terms of which it might be able to understand itself; it clutches at the "nothing" of the world. (393) [343]

The Eclipse ends in an actual eclipse in which everything gradually becomes dark. The heroine seems more normal as the world becomes more strange. Heidegger notes that anxiety is like darkness, since in the dark one is surrounded by equipment with its in-order-to relations and yet is unable to use it.

In the dark there is emphatically "nothing" to see, though the very world itself is still "there," and "there" more obtrusively. (234) [189]

When an anxiety attack subsides inauthentic Dasein lets itself be absorbed back into making itself at home in the familiar world as if the anxiety had been nothing.

But that kind of being-in-the-world which is tranquillized and familiar is a mode of Dasein's unsettledness, not the reverse. From an existential-ontological point of view, the "not-at-home" must be conceived as the more primordial phenomenon. (234) [189]

b. *Fleeing anxiety*
Freud thought that anxiety arises from repressed fear and frustration. Heidegger reverses Freud: "Fear is anxiety, fallen into the 'world,'* inauthentic, and, as such, hidden from itself" (234) [189]. For example, rather than face anxiety, one can develop a phobia about taking plane trips and then take reassuring precautions to

avoid this specific danger. If fear is a way of avoiding anxiety, as Heidegger claims, it follows, as we shall see in the Appendix, that if one accepts anxiety, one becomes fearless. In general, accepting anxiety would be a positive version of an existential reduction, i.e., it would reveal Dasein and its world, not by breaking down Dasein's cover-up but by lighting up the world and Dasein in their full functioning while revealing their groundlessness. (See Table 5.)

But the average response to anxiety is to flee more actively. Rather than simply letting the cover-up in the one take me over, I can actively plunge into the world. I *identify* myself with those for-the-sake-of-whichs to which I am already assigned, and eagerly press into the possibilities that solicit me. I try to become so involved in what I am doing that I cannot stand back and ask myself why I am doing it. These strategies of *fleeing* suggest to Heidegger that the everyday world is organized precisely to provide Dasein with ways to cover-up its unsettledness. (For more on fleeing see Appendix.)

Table 5
Ways of relating to anxiety and their resultant disclosures.

	What happens	Dasein's stance	What shows itself
	Everydayness (behaving as "one does").	Absorption in things in the world, acting for the sake of the one.	Being-at-home, routine actions, routine choice.
	Anxiety hidden.	Fearful.	Particular things as threatening.
Negative existential reduction	Anxiety emerges.	Bewildered.	Not-being-at-home (unsettledness). The worldliness of the world as obtrusive, as not functioning for me. The necessity of "choosing" between facing up and fleeing.
Positive existential reduction	Accepting anxiety.	Resolute. Liberated from fear.	World as the product of the one, which I can nevertheless take over. Responding to the unique Situation.

11

Understanding

Affectedness and *understanding* are two correlative aspects of Dasein's disclosing of its current world—two aspects of Dasein's openness.

Affectedness is *one* of the existential structures in which the being of the "there" maintains itself. Equiprimordial with it in constituting this being is *understanding*. Affectedness always has its understanding. . . . Understanding is always attuned. (182)[142–143]

To get the right approach to understanding it is essential at the outset not to think of understanding as a cognitive phenomenon.

With the term "understanding" we have in mind a fundamental existentiale, which is neither a definite species of cognition distinguished, let us say, from explaining and conceiving, nor any cognition at all in the sense of grasping something thematically. (385)[336]

For Heidegger primordial understanding is know-how.

When we are talking ontically we sometimes use the expression "understanding something" with the signification of "being able to manage something," "being a match for it," "being competent to do something." (183)[143]

In ordinary language, we . . . say "He understands how to handle men," "He knows how to talk." Understanding here means "knowing how" [*können*], "being capable of." (HCT, 298)

To understand a hammer, for example, does not mean to know *that* hammers have such and such properties and *that* they are used for certain purposes—or that in order to hammer one follows a certain procedure, i.e., that one grasps the hammer in one's hand, etc. Rather, understanding a hammer at its most primordial means *knowing how* to hammer. Heidegger puts it even more clearly in *The*

Basic Problems of Phenomenology (with a little help from the translator):

> In German we say that someone can *vorstehen* something [literally, stand in front of or ahead of it, that is, stand at its head, administer, manage, preside over it]. This is equivalent to saying that he *versteht sich darauf* [understands in the sense of being skilled or expert at it, has the know-how of it]. The meaning of the term "understanding" . . . is intended to go back to this usage in ordinary language. (BP, 276, phrases in brackets added by translator)

This know-how that makes possible skillful coping is more basic than the distinction between thought and action. "It is the condition of possibility for all kinds of comportment, not only practical but also cognitive" (BP, 276).

We have a skilled, everyday mastery of equipment and of ourselves. We know how to hammer and the point of our hammering. More generally, each of us knows how to be that particular for-the-sake-of-which each of us is—father, professor, etc. We are skilled at existing. "In understanding, as an *existentiale*, that which we have such competence over is not a 'what,' but being as existing" (183)[143]. Moreover, we *are* such skills. "Dasein is not something occurrent which possesses its competence for something by way of an extra; it is primarily its ability to be. Dasein is in every case what it can be" (183)[143].

But skillful coping cannot be exactly what Heidegger wants to call attention to with the existentiale called understanding, since coping covers all aspects of our activity in the current situation. What Heidegger wants to distinguish as understanding is one out of *three aspects* of what makes the current activity of dealing with things possible. He has so far introduced *affectedness*: what I am doing *matters*. Now he adds *understanding*: I *know how* to go about what I am doing, I am able to do what is appropriate in each situation. And just as affectedness reveals things as threatening, or interesting, and possibilities as indifferent, attractive, etc.; understanding reveals some actions as doable, as making sense, and others as not, or, better, it does not reveal these other possibilities as possibilities at all. (In chapter 13 we shall see that *falling*, the third structural condition of my current activity, singles out my *absorption* in what I am doing.)

I. Three Levels of Understanding

We must now turn to specific coping activities and their conditions of possibility. Paralleling the way mood as atmosphere allows specific affects, we would expect the *background* to allow specific local coping. Thus what Heidegger calls "room for maneuver" (*Spielraum*) permits particular coping activities to show up as possible in the current world. (See Table 9 on page 240.) We would further expect an even more fundamental background (corresponding to sensibility) that makes the understanding aspect of the current world possible. This most fundamental understanding is the intelligibility provided by our familiarity with significance.

> The disclosedness of understanding, as the disclosedness of the "for-the-sake-of-which" and of significance equiprimordially, pertains to the entirety of being-in-the-world. (182) [143]

Heidegger is here referring back to his treatment of understanding in Section 18 (see chapter 5), where he said:

> In *understanding*, which we shall analyze more thoroughly later (compare Section 31), the relations [of Dasein's assigning itself] must have been previously disclosed; understanding holds them in this disclosedness. (120) [87]

> The "for-the-sake-of-which" signifies an "in-order-to"; this in turn, a "towards-this." . . . These relationships are bound up with one another as a primordial whole; they are what they are as this signifying in which Dasein gives itself beforehand its being-in-the-world as something to be understood. (120) [87]

In order to comprehend this chapter, then, we must distinguish each of the three levels of understanding or know-how just mentioned—directed coping, local background, and general background. Remember that each level makes the next more specific level possible but is also dependent on the more specific level. I shall start with the most local and specific.

A. Current Coping as Pressing into Possibilities

My understanding activity is directed toward bringing something about. Coping with the available proceeds by pressing into possibilities. Such coping always has a point. The way my coping is organized by a for-the-sake-of-which Heidegger calls *projection*:

Why does the understanding . . . always press forward into possibilities? It is because the understanding has in itself the existential structure which we call *"projection."* (184–185)[145]

A for-the-sake-of-which such as being a father as a way of understanding myself is not a *goal* I can strive to achieve, like having a child.

Projecting has nothing to do with comporting oneself towards a plan that has been thought out. . . . On the contrary, any Dasein has, as Dasein, already projected itself; and as long as it is, it is projecting. (185)[145]

The character of understanding as projection is such that the understanding does not grasp thematically that upon which it projects—that is to say, possibilities. (185)[145]

(Even my goals need not be aimed at. I have already noted, in discussing master-level chess in chapter 4, that in skilled activity planning is not necessary as long as everything is going in its customary way. In that case one simply responds to the solicitations of the situation, doing what worked last time—the brain can handle that without thought—and this sets up the next situation, which in turn only requires its appropriate response and so on. This *purposive* ongoing activity will look *purposeful*, i.e., it will bring about long-range results that can be described in terms of goals, but no conscious or unconscious goals need play any role in producing the activity.)

One might reasonably ask, how can Dasein have *always already* projected? Must it not begin sometime? By now, however, it should be clear what Heidegger's answer to this question would be. Of course the human organism must at some time begin to take a stand on itself by pressing into human possibilities. It cannot do this just by reflex action or even by animal directedness. Before it can humanly cope, the baby must be socialized into shared, ongoing activities by imitating people and accumulating the necessary experiences until it begins to do what one does for-the-sake-of whatever it is one is. As soon as the baby is seen as up to something, i.e., its activity can be seen as making sense, then it can be seen as Daseining, i.e., as *already* projecting on possibilities. We have seen the same argument, that Dasein is *always already* X-ing, applied to moods and to being with others, and we shall see it again when we come to falling and telling. Of course, the whole Dasein structure does not suddenly take over the baby. The organism starts Daseining gradually. As Wittgenstein says in a similar context concerning language: "Light dawns gradually over the whole." But to be said to have Dasein in it, the organism must already be pressing into social possibilities that matter to it.

It follows that one cannot give a genetic account of the development of *Dasein*, but Heidegger would not deny that one could give a genetic account of how Dasein comes into human organisms. It makes sense to ask, When and how do infants acquire language? When do they start to have moods, rather than just reflex crying and laughing? When does a baby's thrashing about start to be purposive? But before one begins such empirical investigations, one had better be clear what one is asking about. Therefore, as Heidegger would say, the existential analytic of Dasein is prior to any empirical investigation.

Heidegger further claims that the whole system of existentiales that structure the "there" are equiprimordial. They cannot come one at a time. This does not seem to be an empirical claim but a transcendental claim—similar to the claim Kant makes concerning the categories—that the existentiales are interdefined. Heidegger would argue that his claim is supported in Division II by the way the structure of the clearing maps onto the structure of temporality.

Returning to projection, I note that what I am currently doing makes sense in terms of my self-interpretation. I am thus defined not by my current projects or goals but by the possibility of being a father, teacher, etc. "As projecting, understanding is the kind of being of Dasein in which it *is* its possibilities as possibilities" (185) [145]. I am my for-the-sake-of-whichs. These organize and give sense to whatever specific possibilities I am pressing into. If I am currently building a house, understanding who I am requires understanding what is going on, which in turn brings in my towards-which (a finished house) and ultimately my for-the-sake-of-which (being a homemaker, let us say).

This means that Dasein can never be characterized essentially by a set of *factual* features, like its current goals and accomplishments. It is always taking a stand on its factual features in its activity, and it is the stand it takes. For example, masculine Dasein is defined by its interpretation of its maleness, not by the factual features of its anatomy. Yet Dasein is never more than it *factically* is, because factically it is precisely its stand on itself, as manifest in its unreflective current action.

Because of the kind of being which is constituted by the *existentiale* of projection, Dasein is constantly "more" than it *factually* is, supposing that one might want to make an inventory of it as something occurrent. . . . But Dasein is never more than it *factically* is, for to its facticity its ability-to-be belongs essentially. . . . [So] Dasein . . . *is* existentially that which, in its ability to be, it is *not yet.* (185–186, first two italics added) [145]

A factical self-interpretation, such as being a conscientious carpenter, is never understandable in terms of past and present achievements, but rather in terms of the possibilities opened by a Dasein as it takes a stand on itself by pressing into the future.

Since the for-the-sake-of-whichs that define who we are are not goals, they cannot be grasped explicitly.

Grasping [that upon which it projects] would take away from what is projected its very character as a possibility, and would reduce it to the given contents which we have in mind; whereas projection, in throwing, throws before itself the possibility as possibility, and lets it *be* as such. (185) [145]

Choosing one's self-interpretation and all one's "values" would be absurd. If there were no difference between *that which* we choose and *that on the basis of which* we choose, if *everything* were up for choice, there would be no basis left for choosing one thing rather than another, and free choice would amount to absurdity. Fortunately, since our self-interpretation is not a specific goal but has to be worked out as we go along, we cannot get it before our mind.

B. Room-for-Maneuver: The Range of Possibilities Available in the Current World

Dasein also projects its possibilities on the basis of the local background in terms of which particular actions make sense:

With equal primordiality, the understanding projects Dasein's being both upon its "for-the-sake-of-which" and upon significance, as the worldliness of its current world. . . . Projection is the existential being make-up by which [Dasein's] factical ability to be gets its *room for maneuver.* (185, my italics) [145]

Heidegger thus introduces the idea of a space of possibilities that constrains Dasein's range of possible actions without in any way determining what Dasein does. The clearing both limits and opens up what it makes sense to do. When Heidegger speaks of Dasein's possibilities, he might seem to be referring to physical possibilities such as being capable of swimming but not flying. What Heidegger is getting at here, however, is some subset of all the things that are logically or physically possible in a situation. He is interested in those activities that are *existentially* possible, i.e., that are actually open in a situation—what William James calls "live options."

This important idea of *existential* possibilities needs an illustration. If Heidegger's carpenter sees that it is lunch time, it is logically possible for him to eat rocks, and physically possible for him to eat acorns. He could also arbitrarily choose not to eat at all and go fishing. However, given his cultural background, his current mood of, let's say, professional seriousness ("By way of having a mood, Dasein 'sees' possibilities, in terms of which it is" (188) [148]), and his current involvement in his work, only a certain range of possibilities, say knackwurst or bratwurst, are actually available to him. Or, to take a case closer to home, if a student's paper is not ready on time, he can work all night or get an extension or get drunk or leave town, etc., but he cannot commit hara-kiri. For one thing, the idea would never occur to an American student; it is not something it makes sense for him to do. Moreover, given our world of equipment and norms, even if he plunged a knife into his guts with exactly the right motion, it still would not be hara-kiri.

The range of possibilities that Dasein "knows" without reflection, sets up *the room for maneuver* in the current situation. This is the commonsense background of circumspection—"the circumspection of concern is understanding as *common sense*" (187) [147]. Thus the existential possibilities open in any *specific* situation can be viewed as a subset of the *general* possibilities making up significance. They reveal what in a specific situation it makes sense to do.

Existential possibilities, then, show up within a room for maneuver, and differ from both the intentionalistic, first-person possibilities entertained by a subject and third-person, objective, logical and physical possibilities. First-person possibility comprises all the actions that, looked at from a detached perspective, I *could* initiate: Everything I can *think* of doing. The carpenter could in principle step back and freely choose to eat anything from chocolate covered ants to sauerkraut. But "possibility, as an *existentiale*, does not signify a free-floating ability-to-be in the sense of the 'liberty of indifference' (*libertas indifferentiae*)" (183) [144].

From an objective, third-person point of view, possibility includes what is logically possible, and what, contingently, is physically possible. But "the being-possible which Dasein is existentially in every case, is to be sharply distinguished both from empty logical possibility and from the contingency of something occurrent" (183) [143].

Correlatively, existential or *governing causality* does not make things happen in the way choosing to do something does, nor in the way physical causality does. It does not determine anything. It in no way interferes with first-person choice or with physical causation. But where involved active beings are concerned, existential causality crucially both enables and constrains action.

In a later work Heidegger calls the unnoticed way that the clearing *governs* activity, its "unobtrusive governance (*Waltens*)."[1] If one wants to understand human actions, one has to take into account this governing causality as well as intentional (subjective) and physical (objective) causality. Michel Foucault devoted *The Order of Things* to describing the space of possibilities governing serious thought in each age, and Pierre Bourdieu's concept of the social field highlights the way social practices govern which actions show up as possible, i.e., as making sense to do.

Room for maneuver is the condition of the possibility of specific occasions of noncognitive intentionality, of specific pressings into possibilities. "The phenomenal basis for seeing [existential possibilities] is provided by the understanding as a disclosive ability-to-be" (183) [144]. It is not some specific skill but rather the readiness to cope correlative with the whole current situation. Thus the room for maneuver is a version of originary transcendence.

To sum up: Just as the sensibility of a culture allows only certain moods, so the for-the-sake-of-whichs, the norms, and the equipmental whole in which I am always already involved, i.e., *understanding as significance*, allows in any specific situation an open-ended but limited range of possible activities to show up as sensible. This is *understanding as room for maneuver*. And just as a mood makes possible specific ways things can show up as mattering, thanks to this understanding I can press into specific ways of acting, i.e., *understanding as pressing into possibilities*. Moreover, just as mood, not sensibility, is treated in the section on affectedness because the subject of discussion is being-in, so, in this section on understanding, room for maneuver refers to the range of possible actions available *in this current situation*, not to the full range of possibilities available in the culture, which, as significance, has already been discussed under worldliness.

C. Significance, Worldliness, and the Background Understanding of Being

We have seen that the existential possibilities that make sense to someone involved in the current situation must be distinguished from the whole range of possibilities opened by the world—*all* the ways of acting that make sense. But as the hara-kiri example shows, understanding at the world level, like sensibility at the world level, must be limited to the possibilities that make sense in a particular culture. Early Heidegger, however, is not interested in this cultural, historical level of analysis. He is interested only in the ahistorical structure of being-in-the-world, which in *Being and Time* he equates with Dasein's taking a stand on itself and significance. Dasein's consequent familiarity with the three basic ways of being—existence, availableness, and occurrentness—he equates with Dasein's understanding of being in general.

In the way in which [Dasein's] being is projected both upon the "for-the-sake-of-which" and upon significance (the world), there lies the disclosedness of being in general. Understanding of being has already been taken for granted in projecting upon possibilities. . . . An entity whose kind of being is the essential projection of being-in-the-world has understanding of being, and has this as constitutive for its being. (187–188) [147]

II. Authentic and Inauthentic Understanding

In understanding the world, being-in is always also understood, while understanding of existence as such is always an understanding of the world. (186) [146]

In understanding, a particular Dasein takes a stand on itself in a *local situation* by appropriating a for-the-sake-of-which and some in-order-tos from *the world*—the nexus of equipment organized by the one. In a difficult paragraph Heidegger relates this two-sided character of understanding to authenticity and to inauthenticity. It may seem as if Dasein can understand itself either in terms of the public world or in terms of its own individual situation.

Dasein can, primarily and usually, understand itself in terms of its world. Or else understanding throws itself primarily into the "for-the-sake-of-which"; that is, Dasein exists as itself. (186) [146]

But these are not separable. To be *genuine*, a Dasein's activity must express being-in-the-world as a whole:

The "in-" of "inauthentic" does not mean that Dasein cuts itself off from its self and understands "only" the world. The world belongs to being-one's-self as being-in-the-world. Likewise, authentic understanding, no less than that which is inauthentic, *can* be either genuine or not genuine. (186) [146]

That is, even authentic Dasein can manifest its whole structure in its activity or it can omit some aspect of what it is. This distinction between genuine and nongenuine understanding suggests Heidegger is working with a *five-fold* classification of existential understanding.

A. *Inauthentic*

1. *Nongenuine*

(a) *By way of being lost in the world*
One can try to embrace the world by treating everything, even other cultures, as something to be taken over and integrated into a syncretic world view.

The opinion may . . . arise that understanding the most alien cultures and "synthesizing" them with one's own may lead to Dasein's becoming for the first time thoroughly and genuinely enlightened about itself. Versatile curiosity and restlessly "knowing it all" masquerade as a universal understanding of Dasein. (222) [178]

Thus nongenuine inauthentic existence can take the form of a "spiritual" trying-to-be-saved-in-every-possible-way by, for example, practicing yoga, transcendental meditation, Greek body-building, and Christian love all at once.

(b) *By way of being lost in the self*

This alienation drives [Dasein] into a kind of being which borders on the most exaggerated "self-dissection," tempting itself with all possibilities of explanation, so that the very "characterologies" and "typologies" which it has brought about are themselves already becoming something that cannot be surveyed at a glance. (222) [178]

Examples of getting lost in the self might include Jungians (whom Heidegger seems to be referring to with his talk of typologies), but also the human potential movement's idea of getting in touch with your feelings, or trying, through Freudian therapy, to find the deep truth hidden in your desires.

2. *Genuine*
Being-in-the-world by manifesting one's-self in an everyday occupation is the normal, positive, and thus genuine way both undifferentiated and inauthentic Dasein goes about making itself at home in the world.

This inauthentic self-understanding ... by no means signifies an ungenuine self-understanding. On the contrary, this everyday having of self within our factical, existent, passionate merging into things can surely be genuine, whereas all extravagant grubbing about in one's soul can be in the highest degree counterfeit or even pathologically eccentric. Dasein's inauthentic understanding of itself via things is neither ungenuine nor illusory, as though what is understood by it is not the self but something else. (BP, 160)

B. Authentic

1. *Nongenuine*
It is hard to think of a way that authentic Dasein's self-understanding could be nongenuine, since authenticity is, precisely, owning up to what Dasein essentially is. Perhaps the best candidate for nongenuine authenticity is holding onto anxiety and thus being totally without a world and unable to act. (See Appendix.)

2. *Genuine*
This is the self-understanding of resolute Dasein, acting in the world for the sake of its ownmost possibility (death). (See Appendix.) This activity is *perspicuous* in Heidegger's (and Kierkegaard's) technical sense that the activity manifests fully what it is to be Dasein.

The sight which is related primarily and on the whole to existence we call *"perspicuity."* We choose this term to designate "knowledge of the self" ... so as to indicate that here it is not a matter of perceptually tracking down and inspecting a point called the "Self," but rather one of seizing upon the full disclosedness of being-in-the-world throughout all the constitutive items which are essential to it, and doing so with understanding. (186–187) [146]

Such perspicuity is a style of absorbed activity. It is the furthest thing from lucid, reflective self-awareness.

III. Three Types of Understanding: Coping, Interpreting, Asserting

Following the basic method of *Being and Time*, we would expect Heidegger to "derive" the two basic types of understanding distinguished by contemporary philosophers—understanding as *interpreting* in the human sciences, and understanding as *explaining* in the natural sciences—as transformations of the understanding of everyday coping. This is just what he proposes to do.

> If we Interpret understanding as a fundamental *existentiale*, this indicates that this phenomenon is conceived as a basic mode of Dasein's *being*. On the other hand, "understanding" in the sense of *one* possible kind of cognizing among others (as distinguished, for instance, from "explaining"), must, like explaining, be interpreted as an existential *derivative* of that primary understanding which is one of the constituents of the being of the "there" in general. (182, last italics added) [143]

The derivation implicitly follows the now familiar steps from the available, to the unavailable, to the occurrent. Briefly: Understanding, i.e., unreflective, everyday, projective activity such as hammering, becomes explicit in the practical deliberation necessitated when a skill fails to suffice, and what thus becomes thematic can be expressed in speech acts such as "This hammer is too heavy." That which is laid out as the unavailable, in what Heidegger calls "interpretation" (*Auslegung*), can then be privatively (selectively) thematized as occurrent by means of assertions stating propositions assigning predicates to subjects, such as "This hammer weighs one pound." (Laying-out is a literal rendition of the German *Auslegung*, translated as *interpretation* with a lower-case *i*. The German term *Interpretation*—translated as *Interpretation* with an upper-case *I*—refers to academic interpreting of texts and to the theory of interpretation itself, as in *Being and Time*.)

Interpretation (*Auslegung* and its subtype, hermeneutics) is a *derivative* but not a *deficient* mode of understanding. Rather it enriches our understanding by "working-out... possibilities projected in understanding" (189) [148]. "In interpretation, understanding does not become something different. It becomes itself" (188) [148]. But propositional assertions, which the tradition misunderstands as expressing a passive registering of the way things present themselves to pure intuition, and mistakenly supposes get at the objective, explanatory basis of everything, do express a deficient mode of understanding.

A. *Derivation of Interpretation*

Now to the first step of the derivation. When we are no longer able simply to cope, understanding may develop a new form.

> The projecting of the understanding has its own possibility—that of developing itself. This development of the understanding we call "interpretation." In it the understanding appropriates understandingly that which is understood by it. (188)[148]

> This means that interpretation as such does not actually disclose, for that is what understanding or Dasein itself takes care of. Interpretation always only takes care of *bringing out what is disclosed* as a cultivation of the possibilities inherent in an understanding. (HCT, 260)

When things are not functioning smoothly we have to pay attention to them and act deliberately.

> The "world"* which has already been understood comes to be interpreted [literally, "laid out"]. The available comes *explicitly* into the sight which understands. All preparing, putting to rights, repairing, improving, rounding-out, are accomplished in the following way: we take apart in its "in-order-to" that which is circumspectively available, and we concern ourselves with it in accordance with what becomes visible through this process. (189)[148–149]

> With such an interpretation, this thing only now actually enters the environing world as something present and understandable, even though only provisionally, for it is truly understood only when it is taken up into the referential relations it has with environmental things. (HCT, 261)

In attentively taking care we first notice things as having certain functions. For example, when deciding what kind of doorknob to install or when the doorknob sticks, circumspection discovers what the doorknob is for, although it only fully understands it in using it.

We have already been using something as something (using doorknobs for opening doors), but now we *see it* as something for something (see the doorknob *as* something for opening doors).

> The interpretation . . . brings to prominence "*as what*" the encountered thing can be taken, how it is to be understood. The primary form of all interpretation as the cultivation of understanding is the consideration of something in terms of its "as what," considering something as something. (HCT, 261)

That which has been circumspectively taken apart with regard to its "in-order-to" . . . —that which is *explicitly* understood—has the structure of *something* as *something*. The circumspective question as to what this particular thing that is available may be, receives the circumspectively interpretative answer that it is for such and such a purpose. (189)[149]

Heidegger does not make the mistake, criticized by Wittgenstein, of supposing that some *uninterpreted* matter is *used as* or *seen as* equipment. He asks rhetorically:

If such perception lets us circumspectively encounter something as something, does this not mean that in the first instance we have experienced something purely occurrent, and then taken it *as* a door, *as* a house? (190)[149–150]

And he answers that "This would be a misunderstanding of the specific way in which interpretation functions as disclosure" (190)[150]. Rather, "in the mere encountering of something, it is understood in terms of an involvement-whole" (189)[149]. Heidegger is clear that things are always already understood, although we only subsequently see them explicitly *as* something:

That which is disclosed in understanding—that which is understood—is *already* accessible in such a way that its "as which" can be made to stand out explicitly. The "as" makes up the structure of the explicitness of something that is understood. It constitutes the interpretation. (189, my italics)[149]

Seeing a "mere physical thing," which Husserl holds is basic (*Cartesian Meditations,* 78), is for Heidegger a privative form of seeing, which itself presupposes everyday coping, which in turn gets laid out in interpretation.

In interpreting, we do not, so to speak, throw a "signification" over some naked thing which is occurrent, we do not stick a value on it; but when something within-the-world shows up as such, the thing in question already has an involvement which is disclosed in our understanding of the world, and this involvement is one which gets laid out by the interpretation. (190–191)[150][2]

For Heidegger, in the final step of the derivation, the *bare object* is derived by leaving out the contextual meaning of everyday activity. Heidegger contrasts the everyday coping he ironically calls "mere seeing" and "mere understanding" with "merely staring" and its resultant privative seeing.

When we have to do with anything, the mere seeing of the things which are closest to us bears in itself the structure of interpretation, and in so primordial a manner that just to grasp something *free*, as it were, *of the "as,"* requires a certain readjustment. When we merely stare at something, our just-having-it-before-us lies before us *as a failure to understand it any more.* This grasping which is free of the "as," is a privation of the kind of seeing in which one *merely* understands. It is not more primordial than that kind of seeing, but is derived from it. (190) [149]

Such privative seeing can be caused by psychosis (in Sartre's *Nausea* Roquentin experiences a doorknob he is grasping as a round metal object sticking to the palm of his hand), drugs, constant repetition of a word, extreme fatigue, etc. It is always a breakdown of normal activity.

The three types of understanding we have been considering can be illuminated by a simple example. If one has the linguistic abilities of an average American plus a smattering of German, then one *understands* English (i.e., can use it transparently), one can *interpret* German (i.e., use it in a deliberate but still context-dependent way), but one must *decipher* Japanese (i.e., treat it as a meaningless code).

To do its job of letting thing show up as interpretable, the referential whole must remain in the *background.* Here Heidegger actually uses the term:

The available is always understood in terms of an involvement whole. This whole need not be grasped explicitly by a thematic interpretation. Even if it has undergone such an interpretation, it recedes into an understanding which does not stand out from the background. And this is the very mode in which it is the essential foundation for everyday circumspective interpretation. (191) [150]

B. The Three-Fold Structure of Interpretation
We have so far discussed everyday interpretation, i.e., laying out the as-structure in some local, practical context when there is some sort of problem. Heidegger now gives an account of the structure of interpretation that covers both the everyday way of laying things out in a specific context and the more general use of interpretation outside of some local practical context, as in the so-called hermeneutic versions of anthropology, sociology, and political science.

An interpretation always presupposes a shared understanding and so always has a three-fold structure which Heidegger calls the "fore-structure."

1. All interpretation must start with a *Vorhabe*—a fore-having—a taken-for-granted background.

> In every case . . . interpretation is grounded in *something we have in advance*—in a *fore-having*. As the appropriation of understanding, the interpretation operates in . . . an involvement whole which is already understood. (191)[150]

The background already circumscribes the domain in question and thus already determines possible ways of questioning.

2. There needs to be some sense of how to approach the problem, some perspective from which to undertake the interpretation.

> A point of view, which fixes that with regard to which what is understood is to be interpreted. In every case interpretation is grounded in *something we see in advance*—in a *fore-sight*. (191)[150]

3. The investigator already has expectations as to what he will find out.

> The interpretation has already decided for a definite way of conceiving [the entity to be interpreted], . . . either with finality or with reservations; it is grounded in *something we grasp in advance*—in a *fore-conception*. (191)[150]

Being and Time, as an ontological Interpretation, is a special case of the sort of interpretative approach Heidegger is describing, so we would expect it to exhibit the above fore-structure, and indeed it does. (a) To ask the question about the meaning of being presupposes a fore-having, viz. our preontological understanding of being. (b) Heidegger chooses, as his method of approaching the problem, asking about Dasein, the being whose way of being (existence) is to take a stand on its own being. "Originary existentiality is something we *see in advance*, and this assures us that we are coining the appropriate existential concepts" (364, my italics) [316]. This is not the only approach one could have, and in fact may be too close to the subjectivist tradition. Later Heidegger prefers to start with asking about things rather than people. (c) Heidegger tells us from the start that we can expect our answer to have something to do with time. His fore-conception is that one can make sense of the system of existentiales in terms of temporality.

When applied to hermeneutic disciplines, Heidegger's account of the fore-structure of interpretation raises the problem of the hermeneutic circle. If all interpreting takes place on a background understanding that it presupposes—a background, moreover, that conditions from the start what questions can be formulated and what counts as a satisfactory interpretation, yet that can never be made completely explicit and called into question—all interpreting is necessarily circular. Heidegger acknowledges this, but he insists that "if we see this circle as a vicious one and look out for ways of avoiding it, even if we just 'sense' it as an inevitable imperfection, then understanding has been misunderstood from the ground up" (194) [153].

How, then, one might ask, can there be a responsible investigation? Heidegger answers: "What is decisive is not to get out of the circle but to come into it in the right way" (195) [153]. Only much later, when he discusses the meaning of *primordial*, does it become a bit clearer what this might mean. Heidegger uses the term in two senses:

(a) *Primordial evidence.* As Heidegger uses the term, primordial evidence arises from our most direct or revealing kinds of encounters with entities. Thus hammering gives us the most primordial understanding we can have of what it is to be a hammer, and living in anxiety is the most primordial way of disclosing human being. This is what Heidegger has in mind when he says we must turn to "the things themselves," not to our everyday conceptions, let alone the philosophical tradition.

Our first, last, and constant task is never to allow our fore-having, fore-sight, and fore-conception to be presented to us by fancies and popular conceptions, but rather to make the scientific theme secure by working out these fore-structures in terms of the things themselves. (195) [153][3]

(b) *Primordial interpretation.* In this sense of primordial, one interpretation is more primordial than another if it is more complete, i.e., detailed, and more unified, i.e., all the aspects are interconnected. Thus, for example, the Interpretation of Dasein as temporality in Division II, which interconnects all the existentialia as aspects of temporality, is more primordial than the account in Division I.

In beginning an interpretation, one must start with the most immediate and comprehensive phenomenon available—primordial in both senses above. Thus in Interpreting Dasein, for example:

We must . . . endeavour to leap into the "circle," *primordially* and *wholly*, so that even at the start of the analysis of Dasein we make sure that we have a full view of Dasein's circular being. If, in the ontology of Dasein, we "take our departure" from a worldless "I" in order to provide this "I" with an object and an ontologically baseless relation to that object, then we have "presupposed" not too much, but *too little*. (363, my italics) [315–316]

But the talk of leaping into the circle in the right way, especially in connection with the interpretative approach of *Being and Time*, raises a new problem. If we are already *in* the hermeneutic circle thanks to our *fore-having*, why talk of leaping into it at all? Heidegger is none too clear about this, but the best way to make sense of what he is saying is to distinguish the circularity of *Being and Time*, where one is laying out the circular structure of Dasein from the inside so to speak, from the circularity of other types of interpretation of texts, epochs and cultures in which one does not already dwell. In the first case Heidegger tells us:

The "circle" in understanding belongs to the structure of sense, and the latter phenomenon is rooted in the existential make-up of Dasein—that is, in the understanding which interprets. A being for which, as being-in-the-world, its being is itself an issue, has, ontologically, a circular structure. (195) [153]

In the second case, one approaches the subject matter from outside so to speak and so one has to take up a perspective which will in turn determine what one finds. Here the problem is, indeed, one of leaping into this circle, i.e., into a fore-sight, in the right, i.e., primordial, way.

Of course, even in the second case one chooses one's approach on the basis of an already given background understanding (fore-having). It is precisely this necessity of dwelling in a background understanding that makes possible an account of interpretation that avoids the traditional opposition between the claim that interpretation is about facts, viz. intentional states (E. D. Hirsch), and the claim that interpretation is based on convention or arbitrary decision (Rorty). For Heidegger, like Wittgenstein, meaning is grounded neither in some mental reality nor in an arbitrary decision, but is based upon a form of life in which we necessarily dwell, and which, therefore, is neither immediately given nor merely a matter of choice. This is *the* essential character of interpretation.

C. Levels of Interpretation

Thus far the kinds of interpreting Heidegger has been discussing have been on the level of the unavailable, but all levels of understanding have some sort of *fore-structure.*

1. Everyday Coping with the Available

(a) Everyday coping with the available has its kind of *fore-having.* Fore-having is, in fact, a misleading term. Dasein dwells in its background familiarity with the available. Our skills *have us* rather than our having them. In a later marginal note Heidegger remarks, with regard to the passage where he speaks of Dasein *having* a world, that it would have been better to speak of a world being "given" to Dasein. "Dasein never 'has' a world" [78]. For the same reason it would have been more accurate to speak of our basic ontological skills as fore-*given.* (b) *Fore-sight* on this basic level would be what Dasein is pressing towards in the current situation (the towards-which), and (c) the basic *fore-conception* (*Vorgriff* can mean anticipation) would be the final point of Dasein's activity (the for-the-sake-of-which), as long as this is not thought of as an intentionalistic expectation of an outcome.

2. Theory of the Occurrent

(a) At the other extreme, even scientific theory has a kind of *fore-having.* Scientists need shared theoretical and technical assumptions, explicitly entertained as well as embodied in shared laboratory practices. Kuhn calls this the scientists' disciplinary matrix. (b) Scientists also need some plan or *fore-sight* to organize their research. Heidegger calls this the sciences' projection.

> Only "in the light" of a nature which has been projected . . . can anything like a "fact" be found and set up for an experiment regulated and delimited in terms of this projection. The "grounding" of "factual science" was possible only because the researchers understood that in principle there are no "bare facts." (414) [362]

(c) Finally, scientists do not collect random data; rather, they have a specific hypothesis or *fore-conception* they are trying to confirm or refute.

D. Interpretive Understanding versus Theoretical Explanation

If the hermeneutic circle merely meant, as interpreters from Schleiermacher to Føllesdal have held, that the meaning of the elements depends on the meaning of the whole and vice versa, one would not be able to distinguish the hermeneutic disciplines that study human beings from within the human world from the nonhermeneutic but holistic disciplines such as natural science that, as Thomas Nagel says, study nature as if from nowhere.

One must be clear that the *theoretical* fore-structures are not like the fore-structures of everyday coping, nor like the fore-structure of everyday interpretation, nor even like the fore-structures of interpretation in the social sciences. Natural science, like any mode of existence, cannot make entirely explicit its projections, i.e., the basic assumptions and practical background skills in which the scientists dwell. The disciplinary matrix, as Kuhn says, "cannot be rationalized," but rather is passed on through apprenticeship and shared exemplars. Still, Heidegger would hold, the background fore-having does not play the same role in the theory it makes possible in natural science as it does in the interpretations it makes possible in the human sciences.

To argue this controversial claim requires getting clearer about the difference between the fore-structure of interpretation (understanding) and the fore-structure of scientific theory (explanation). To understand getting into the circle in the right way in each case, we must be clear what sort of ontological understanding is appropriate to the way of being of each subject matter. We must show that studying human beings as self-interpreting beings requires interpretation within *the full hermeneutic circle* of shared significance, whereas to have a science of any object including human beings as objects requires only the circularity of working within a theoretical projection.

A striking example of what it would be like to study human beings as objects was given inadvertently by a psychologist who explained that his science had shown that, although people classify some people as talkative and others as not, and although there is general agreement among participants in the everyday world as to which people belong in each class, the concept of talkativeness is unfounded. If you count the number of words uttered by an individual in a day, the "scientist" explained, you find that there is no significant difference in the quantity of words uttered by so-called normal and by so-called talkative people. The objective psychologist could not allow himself to consider the possibility that what makes a person count as talkative may be the *meaning* of what is said and the *situation* in which it is said. Talkative people say little of importance and say it during other people's lectures, with their mouths full, at funerals, etc. The general agreement among participants in the everyday world as to who is talkative is no illusion. Rather, the *evidence* for being talkative presupposes the background understanding of what it is to be talkative. One would like to find some objective features that correlate with being talkative, but there is no reason to suppose that there are any such features. Thus the surprising conclusion that there is no such characteristic as being talkative.

What really follows, however, is that the sort of projection appropriate in the natural sciences, where one is studying objects emitting noises, is inappropriate in the study of human beings' understanding of themselves and other human beings. People making judgments such as who is talkative agree because they dwell in a shared background of meaningful practices. In the human sciences an interpreter, if he is to understand what is going on, must share the general human background understanding of the person or group being studied.[4] Everyday objectivity disappears as soon as the meaning of the situation is bracketed out in a mistaken attempt to attain the sort of objectivity appropriate to natural science.

This important thesis can be further illustrated by the sort of difficulties that, according to Pierre Bourdieu, confront Claude Lévi-Strauss's structuralist theory of gift exchange. In *Outline of a Theory of Practice*, Bourdieu argues that Lévi-Strauss's formal, reversible rules for the exchange of gifts—abstracted as they are from everyday gift-giving—cannot account for and predict actual exchanges. His point is not that theory leaves out the subjective, so-called phenomenological, qualities of gift exchange. That would not be a valid objection. The natural sciences legitimately abstract from subject-relative properties. Bourdieu's point is that Lévi-Strauss's abstraction of pure objects of exchange leaves out something essential—the tempo of the event that actually *determines what counts as a gift.*

In every society it may be observed that, if it is not to constitute an insult, the counter-gift must be deferred and different, because the immediate return of an exactly identical object clearly amounts to a refusal.[5]

Predictions based only on formal principles fail in those cases in which what formally counts as a gift in the theory is rejected because it is reciprocated too soon or too late to count as a gift in everyday practice.

It is all a question of style, which means in this case timing and choice of occasion, for the *same act*—giving, giving in return, offering one's services, paying a visit, etc.—can have completely different meanings at different times.[6]

Thus the sense of the situation plays an essential role in determining what counts as an object or event; yet it is precisely this contextual sense that theory must ignore.

John Searle, like Bourdieu, argues that formal and causal accounts in the social sciences must fail, but he, like Husserl, holds that the problem is that intentional mental states play a causal role in human behavior and so must be taken account of in any science of human beings.[7] But since, as Heidegger and Bourdieu emphasize, much of human behavior could and does take place as ongoing skillful coping without the need for mental states (i.e., beliefs, desires, intentions, etc.), intentional causation does not seem to be the right place to start to look for an essential limit on prediction in the human sciences. What is crucial is that, even when no intentional states are involved, what human beings pick out as specific sorts of objects depends on background skills that are not representable.

Up to the 1970s the human sciences were trying to imitate the natural sciences, and it was important for Heidegger to point out that they could not and should not. But recently it has become fashionable in some quarters to deny there is any important difference between the natural and human sciences, since both are holistic and thus circular.[8]

Heidegger, however, for good reasons, holds the now old-fashioned view that there *is* an essential difference between the *human* sciences and the *natural* sciences. He makes this point cryptically in his discussion of understanding. Natural science, he says, is "a subspecies [of understanding] which has strayed into the legitimate task of grasping the occurrent in its essential incomprehensibility" (194) [153]. He spells out in one of his lectures the sense in which nature as studied by natural science is incomprehensible.

Every explanation, when we speak of an explanation of nature, is distinguished by its involvement in the *incomprehensible* [*Unverständlich*].... Nature is what is in principle explainable and to be explained because it is in principle incomprehensible.... And it is incomprehensible because it is the *"deworlded" world*, insofar as we take nature ... as it is discovered in physics. (HCT, 217–218)

To say that *physical nature* is incomprehensible is to say that the nature studied by physics is abstracted from the everyday world, i.e., does not fit into the referential whole and connect up with our purposes and for-the-sake-of-whichs. It therefore has no significance in Heidegger's sense of the term.

Of course, *scientific theories* of nature are not incomprehensible since they do have a purpose and so fit into our world. Indeed Heidegger thinks that the purpose of theories is to arrive at truth—to discover the occurrent.

The kind of discovering which belongs to . . . science . . . awaits solely the discoveredness of the occurrent. . . . This projection is possible because being-in-the-truth makes up a definite way in which Dasein may exist. (415)[363]

Thus, unlike Nietzsche, Heidegger does not think of the pursuit of disinterested, objective truth as a self-deceptive activity arising from disguised psychological motivations. Disinterested inquiry is pursued for its own sake by the authentic theorist. "Science has its source in authentic existence" (415)[363].

Nature, because it is deworlded and thus incomprehensible, can, at least in principle, be described in theoretical terms, i.e., in terms of context-free features to which strict laws unambiguously apply. In another context Heidegger notes that "we look theoretically at what is just occurrent" (177)[138]. Scientific theory frees its pure objects by means of agreed-upon methods for matching meaningless data to explicit concepts defined in terms of meaningless formal marks and features.

Theoretical behaviour is just looking, without circumspection. But the fact that this looking is noncircumspective does not mean that it follows no rules: it constructs a canon for itself in the form of *method.* (99)[69]

Thus the pure objects of theory can be recognized without appeal to our everyday background understanding.

But Nancy Cartwright has pointed out that scientists must share background practices that enable them to pick out events in the everyday world that count as instances of the events and objects referred to in their theories, cases of force or of absorption, for example. Still there is an essential difference between the natural and the human sciences. What in everyday scientific practice counts as a force must be compatible with the way forces behave under ideal conditions such as weightlessness or in a vacuum. Since the everyday world can be transformed by degrees into an artificial world, the scientists can discover that they have been wrong about what in the everyday world they have been picking out as an instance of some theoretical entity such as a force. But the natives cannot be wrong about what, in the everyday world, is a gift, because a gift is *defined* by the practices of picking it out.

Still, as we have noted, scientists do not stop dwelling in everyday human practices, and they also dwell in special scientific practices (Kuhn's disciplinary matrices), which have their own history.

It is only on the basis of understandability that there is a possible access to something which is in principle incomprehensible, that is, to nature. Something like nature can be discovered only because there is history, because Dasein is itself the primarily historical being. And only because of this are there natural sciences. (HCT, 258)

So, then, it looks like Føllesdal and Rorty are right after all. The natural sciences are locked into their fore-having and so are caught in the hermeneutic circle just like the human sciences. How could there be any essential difference in the way the natural and the human scientists relate to their background practices?

Heidegger has already given his answer. In the natural sciences shared scientific background skills are necessary for deworlding nature and for testing theories, but these skills do not determine what is to count as the objects of the theory. The scientists' background skills function precisely to free the science's objects from dependence on *all* practices, including the practices that reveal them. They thus reveal incomprehensible nature.

Physics has, in the course of its development, progressively left behind our shared everyday understanding of space, time, objects and causality. There is no in principle limit to how far this deworlding can go. This is why we can make sense of the idea of an ideal natural science getting *the correct view* of natural kinds and their causal powers—a view a Martian could accept—but there is no equivalent idea of an ideal social science converging on *the context-free truth* about a practice like gift-giving or comportment like being talkative.

In short, since scientific theories state deworlded relations between deworlded data, the fact that such theories are arrived at by worldly practices is in principle irrelevant. Thus in spite of the fact that scientific practice like all practice is based on a fore-having in which the practitioner dwells, and in spite of the absence of bare facts in natural science, natural science is not subject to the sort of interpretive circularity definitive of the social and human sciences. In Heideggerian terms, one could say that the hermeneutic circle plays an essential and positive role in the human sciences, but that in the natural sciences it is, indeed, a sign of imperfection.

E. "Assertion": A Derivative Mode of Interpretation

Heidegger next offers his version of a phenomenological derivation of logic. In *Experience and Judgment*, Husserl had sought to derive logical functions such as negation, and logical forms such as subject and predicate, by showing how they were already implicitly in the propositional content of *perception*.[9] Heidegger, in opposition, derives logic by means of progressive abstraction from situated practical *activity* and seeks to show that Husserl's attempt to find a basis for logical form in passive perception is still caught in the tradition.

Heidegger begins with the practical function of language. Language is often used transparently in situations where there is no disturbance, such as when I say "See you at six." But Heidegger does not discuss this use of language. He begins at the level of interpretation with its thematizing assertions. "Assertion," as Heidegger uses the term, presupposes that there has been some sort of disturbance, and therefore that understanding has already been explicitly laid out. (The connectedness of things when made explicit is called by Heidegger *Articulation* with an upper-case *A* to distinguish it from everyday connectedness, which he calls *articulation*.) (See chapter 12.)

That which is understood gets Articulated when the entity to be understood is *brought close interpretatively* by taking as our clue the "something as something"; and this Articulation lies *before* our making any thematic assertion about it. In such an assertion the "as" does not turn up for the first time; it just gets expressed for the first time, and this is possible only in that it lies before us as something expressible. (190, my italics) [149]

To begin with, when local activity is disturbed it can be interpreted without using words at all.

Interpretation is carried out primordially... in an action of circumspective concern—laying aside the unsuitable tool, or exchanging it, "without wasting words." From the facts that words are absent, it may not be concluded that interpretation is absent. (200) [157]

In more difficult situations words may be used along with the tools.

> Interpreting . . . may take some such form as "The hammer is too heavy," or rather just "Too heavy!," "Hand me the other hammer!." (200) [p.157]

Heidegger discusses this use of language under the rather misleading rubric of "assertion" (in quotation marks) on pages 196 and 197 [154–155]. His point is that the *hermeneutic* assertion, since it is context-dependent, must be sharply distinguished from the privative *theoretical* assertion (assigning a predicate to a subject), which has been singled out by the tradition. Thus in my Table 6, "assertion" in quotes appears above the double line as a mode of the unavailable, while assertion without quotes appears below the double line as a deficient mode.

The move from interpretative "assertion" to theoretical assertion corresponds to the move from practical deliberation to theoretical reflection, i.e., from the unavailable to the occurrent. It also supplies the basis for the final move to propositions expressed in the predicate calculus. To begin with, however, we must study the interpretative use of language, or "assertion" in quotes.

Heidegger focuses on asserting as a speech act,[10] laying out three aspects of the unified structure of asserting. The important thing to bear in mind in the description of each of the three is that in "assertions" language functions as equipment, doing its job in a context of practical activity, although what is talked about can become more and more remote from the immediate context. The three aspects are ordered with respect to their increasing capacity to contribute to this remoteness.

1. *Pointing out.* If, in a shared context, something needs attention, language can be used to point out characteristics of the work in progress. Thus, while involved, I can point out, "The hammer is too heavy." Clearly, it is not too heavy in isolation, but it is too heavy for this specific job, and I point this out to someone on the job with me. What I let him/her see is the shared problem, not some representation or meaning I have in mind. The "assertion" is "apophantic" in the Greek, but not in the traditional, sense of the word; i.e., it makes something manifest.

> In telling (*apophansis*), so far as it is genuine, *what* is said is drawn *from* what the talk is about, so that telling communication, in what it says, makes manifest what it is talking about, and thus makes this accessible to the other party. This is the structure of *logos* as *apophansis*. (56) [32]

Table 6
Modes of understanding. (The double line indicates where "working-out" switches over to "leaving-out.")

Kind of entity	Kind of understanding	Result
Available	Primary understanding.	Everyday pressing into possibilities.
Unavailable	Interpretation (*Auslegung*). Existential hermeneutic-as.	Thematizing something *as* something.
	Interpretation (upper-case *i*) (*Interpretation*) of texts and text analogs such as Dasein.	Hermeneutic disciplines.
	"Assertion" (ordinary use).	Linguistic expression of interpretation. Calling attention to aspects.
Occurrent	Theoretical assertion. Traditional apophantic-as.	Attaching an isolated predicate to an isolated subject.
Purely occurrent	Pure intuition and abstract thinking; formal logic.	Contemplating essences and expressing their "logical form."

2. *Predication.* In pointing out the characteristic of the hammer that needs attention I can "take a step back" from the immediate activity and attribute a "predicate" ("too heavy") to the hammer as "subject." This singles out the hammer and selects the difficulty of the hammering from a lot of other characteristics, such as its being "too loud," thus narrowing our attention to this specific aspect of the total activity. (This is the fore-sight.) Here "predicate" in quotes is used in its grammatical sense but not yet as attributing an abstractable *property* to a subject.

When we give [the hammer] such a character, our seeing gets *restricted* to it . . . , so that by this explicit restriction of our view, that which is already manifest may be made *explicitly* manifest in its definite character. . . . We dim entities down to focus in on "that hammer there," so that by thus dimming them down we may let that which is manifest be seen in its own definite character as a character that can be determined. (197)[155]

3. *Communication.* Communication takes place in the course of shared activity. "That which is 'shared' is our *being towards* what has been pointed out—a being in which we see it in common" (197)[155]. It can also be "shared" with those who are not directly involved in the activity in question.

Others can "share" with the person making the assertion, even though the entity which he has pointed out and to which he has given a definite character is not close enough for them to grasp and see it. That which is put forward in the assertion is something which can be passed along in "further retelling." (197)[155]

This can have the positive function of giving others the information they need to contribute to the total job. "There is a widening of the range of that mutual sharing which sees" (197)[155]. However, it also makes possible the privative passing-the-word-along in the glibness of hearsay. "But at the same time, what has been pointed out may become veiled again in this further retelling" (197)[155].

To review section III thus far, we can sum up the levels of dependence of our three types of understanding as follows:

Addressing of something as something is possible only insofar as there is interpreting; interpretation in turn is only insofar as there is understanding, and understanding is only insofar as Dasein has the being make-up of discoveredness, which means that Dasein itself is defined as being-in-the-world. (HCT, 261)

F. Apophantic Assertion: A Deficient Mode of Hermeneutic "Assertion"

The familiar movement from primordial to positive to privative, in which an "assertion" is finally cut off from the context within which it refers, makes possible the move to the sort of assertion studied by traditional ontology. Heidegger first reminds us:

[Interpretative] assertion is not a free-floating kind of behaviour which, in its own right, might be capable of disclosing entities in general in a primary way: on the contrary it always maintains itself on the basis of being-in-the-world. (199)[156]

But this dependence of everyday asserting on the background is overlooked in the examples of assertion studied in logic, which concentrate on the "limiting case" (200)[157], in which our concern has switched over into theoretical reflection. Here the practical background is "ignored," as are aspects which depend upon the context. The remaining predicates can then be treated as properties. "The 'categorial statement'—for instance, 'The hammer is heavy' . . . is to be taken as: 'This thing—a hammer—has the *property* of heaviness'" (200)[157]. This is not wrong; it is merely partial, but it can be deceptive, suggesting that the predicate calculus is sufficient for describing the human world.

In summary Heidegger asks:

By what existential-ontological modifications does assertion arise from circumspective interpretation? (200)[157]

In his answer he first describes the move from the available to the unavailable.

The being which is held in our fore-having—for instance, the hammer— is primarily available as equipment. If this being becomes the "object" of an assertion . . . there is already a changeover in the fore-having. Something available *with which* we have to do or perform something, turns into something *"about which"* the assertion that points it out is made. Our fore-sight is aimed at something occurrent in what is available. (200)[157–158]

This sets up the possibility of a further step, from pointing out "aspects" of equipment to isolating "properties" of objects.

Within this discovering of occurrentness, which is at the same time a covering-up of availableness, something occurrent which we encounter is given a definite character in its being-occurrent-in-such-and-such-manner. Only now are we given any access to *properties* or the like. (200)[158]

The object and its aspects are thus cut off from their context (and the properties cut off from the object).

The as-structure of interpretation has undergone a modification. In its function of appropriating what is understood, the "as" no longer reaches out into an involvement-whole. As regards its possibilities for Articulating reference-relations, it has been cut off from that significance which, as such, constitutes environmentality. (200)[158]

Once the hammer is isolated, the use of the hammer in hammering can be construed only as a function predicate. However, as we saw in chapter 6, such function predicates cannot capture what it is to be a hammer.

Heidegger then completes his account of what has to be left out for there to be a predicate calculus. Once subject and predicate are isolated, the tradition since Aristotle assumes they must be bound together in a judgment. This leads to modern logic and makes possible computational formalization.

Binding and separating may be formalized still further to "relating." The judgment gets dissolved logistically into a system in which things are "coordinated" with one another; it becomes the object of a "calculus." (202)[159]

But modern logic lacks an ontological understanding of its foundation and, therefore, of the range of its appropriate application.[11] This leads to the current assumption that all discourse (and for some in Artificial Intelligence, such as John McCarthy, all aspects of human activity) can be formalized in the predicate calculus.

Of course, Heidegger would not claim that his derivation of the predicate calculus shows that one *cannot* represent everyday intelligibility in this or some other calculus. What he would claim is that once one sees that symbolic logic is the result of the progressive decontextualization and impoverishment of our everyday language for pointing out equipment and its aspects, one will no longer be inclined to believe that logic, although a universal and unambiguous medium, is an appropriate form in which to express all meaning. Heidegger's analysis, in effect, shifts the burden of proof to those who, like McCarthy, think that logic is the obvious form of representation for capturing human intelligence.

Finally, all this leads again to a critique of traditional ontology. "Assertion cannot disown its ontological origin from an interpretation which understands" (201) [158]. If it does "disown its origin," we arrive at the idea of mere uninterpretative looking as our access to truth. Indeed,

> this leveling of the primordial "as" of circumspective interpretation to the "as" with which occurrentness is given a definite character is the specialty of assertion. Only so does it obtain the possibility of exhibiting something in such a way that we just look at it. (201) [158]

This final stage of leaving out or covering up the practical context leads one to believe in the special kind of pure intuition of essences which has fascinated philosophers from Plato to Husserl. Heidegger suggests that if such passive, detached seeing reveals anything at all, it is because it is remotely related to practical activities which have already interpretively selected what is meaningful and relevant.

By showing how all sight is grounded primarily in understanding (the circumspection of concern is understanding as handiness), we have deprived pure intuition of its priority, which corresponds noetically to the priority of the occurrent in traditional ontology. "Intuition" and "thinking" are both derivatives of understanding, and already rather remote ones. Even the phenomenological "intuition of essences" is grounded in existential understanding. (187) [147]

12

Telling and Sense

I. Telling as an Existentiale

Rede ordinarily means talk, but for Heidegger *Rede* is not necessarily linguistic, i.e., made up of words. So I shall translate *Rede* by "telling," keeping in mind the sense of telling as in being able to tell the time, or tell the difference between kinds of nails.

We can make sense of Heidegger's use of both a linguistic and a nonlinguistic sense of telling if we first see that both require a prior structural articulation. To be articulated can simply mean having natural joints. Heidegger's word for this is *Gliederung*, articulation (with lower-case *a*). In this sense a skeleton is articulated, and so is the referential whole. The joints in this structure are significations. They signify or refer to other joints, hammers to nails, etc.

One manifests the already articulated structure of the referential whole in the most basic way simply by telling things apart in using them. Heidegger calls this *Articulation*. "Telling is the Articulation of intelligibility" (203–204)[161]. Thus, when I pick up a hammer and hammer with it, I pick out or Articulate one of its significations, i.e., the fact that it is used to pound in nails; if I use it to pull nails, I Articulate another. This does not mean that the joints of a skill domain need have names. They usually do not. In complex domains one does not have words for the subtle actions one performs and the subtle significations one Articulates in performing them. A surgeon does not have words for all the ways he cuts, or a chess master for all the patterns he can tell apart and the types of moves he makes in response.

Articulation is *Logos* as that which "lets us see something from the very thing which the telling is about" (56)[32]. "Spoken Articulation can belong to the *logos*, but it does not have to" (BP, 207). Still, our most general skill for making manifest is our use of language.

Then

the intelligibility of being-in-the-world . . . expresses itself as telling. The significations-whole of intelligibility is put into words. (204) [161]

Factically . . . telling expresses itself for the most part in language, and speaks proximally in the way of addressing itself to the "environment" by talking about things concernfully. (400) [349]

When what is pointoutable is pointed out, and the sayable is actually said, then telling becomes concrete. "When fully concrete, telling . . . has the character of speaking—vocal proclamation in words" (56) [32].

Yet we must bear in mind that all picking out and pointing out is dependent upon structural articulation. The referential whole plus the for-the-sake-of-whichs (significance) as articulated can be used without any pointing out or speaking taking place, but there cannot be any pointing out without the articulated referential whole already being in place. Heidegger spells out this dependency relation as follows:

In significance itself, with which Dasein is always familiar, there lurks the ontological condition which makes it possible for Dasein, as something which understands and interprets, to disclose such things as "significations"; upon these, in turn, is founded the being of words and of language. (121) [87][1]

Or, perhaps a bit more clearly:

Language makes manifest. . . . It does not produce . . . discoveredness. Rather, discoveredness and its enactment of being—understanding as well as interpretation—being grounded in the basic make-up of being-in, are conditions of possibility for something becoming manifest. As conditions of being, they enter into the definition of the essence of language, since they are conditions of possibility for such manifestation. (HCT, 262; see Table 7)

The existential-ontological foundation of language is telling. (203) [160]

Heidegger often uses the term for "X" to name the condition of the possibility of "X." Here he is introducing an ontological sense of telling as what makes possible everyday telling. Just as primordial understanding is not cognitive but makes cognition possible, telling in the ontological sense is not linguistic but gives us some-

Table 7
Levels of dependence of types of telling.

1. Originary telling as the activity of articulating significations.

2. *Picking out* significations by using them.

3. *Pointing out* significations.

4. Telling as language. Articulation by attaching words to significations.

thing to point out and talk about and so makes language possible. *Ontological telling* refers to everyday coping as manifesting the articulations already in the referential whole which are by nature manifestable.

Ontological telling, i.e., the Articulation of the joints of the significance whole which in turn makes prelinguistic and linguistic telling possible, is equiprimordial with affectedness and understanding.

The fundamental existentialia which constitute the being of the "there," the disclosedness of being-in-the-world, are affectedness and understanding. . . . Telling is existentially equiprimordial with affectedness and understanding. (203) [160–161]

But telling is not on a par with the other two aspects of Dasein's openness. Rather, telling refers to the way the whole current situation is Articulated by coping so as to be linguistically expressible.

When the "there" has been completely disclosed, its disclosedness is constituted by understanding, affectedness, and falling; and this disclosedness becomes Articulated by telling. (400) [349]

II. Language

"The way in which telling gets expressed is language" (207) [161]. Language has all the ways of being Heidegger has discussed so far. Words are things that can be used as *available.* "Language is a totality of words . . . . As an intraworldly entity, this totality . . . becomes something which we may come across as available" (204) [161]. It can also be studied as *occurrent.* "Language can be broken up into word-things which are occurrent" (204) [161]. And since it reflects Dasein's self-interpreting being-in-the-world, language also has Dasein's way of being, *existence.*

Language is not identical with the sum total of all the words printed in a dictionary; instead . . . language is as Dasein is . . . it exists. (BP, 208)

A. *Language and Sense*

Throughout his discussion of telling, Heidegger opposes the traditional account of language found in both Husserl and Searle— that language consists of occurrent noises or marks that are *given meaning*, either by minds that are the source of what Searle calls intrinsic meaning or, as in Husserl, by being paired with abstract entities similar to Fregean senses. Heidegger would also oppose the idea that language can be rationally reconstructed as marks and noises given a holistic *interpretation* in relation to the speaker's behavior and the salient objects in the vicinity, as Davidson holds. According to Heidegger, all such accounts address a pseudoproblem because their starting point is ontologically inadequate. "The *logos* gets experienced as something occurrent and Interpreted as such" (203) [160].

Heidegger begins his own account with a description of hearing that parallels his discussion of "seeing as." Just as we do not see pure meaningless sense data which then must be interpreted, so we do not hear pure meaningless sounds.

What we "first" hear is never noises or complexes of sounds, but the creaking wagon, the motorcycle. . . . It requires a very artificial and complicated frame of mind to "hear" a "pure noise." The fact that motorcycles and wagons are what we proximally hear is the phenomenal evidence that in every case Dasein, as being-in-the-world, already dwells amidst what is available within-the-world; it certainly does not dwell primarily amidst "sensations." (207) [164]

In the case of language this suggests that we do not first hear meaningless noises—acoustic blasts, as Searle calls them—and then use internal phonetic, syntactic, and semantic rules to interpret these sounds as expressing the intentional states of others. One way to see this is to recite a word over and over to oneself until it becomes a senseless noise. Then one realizes that while one was using it normally and transparently in context it was something quite different from a noise that required interpretation. Heidegger points out that:

> When we are explicitly hearing the telling of another, we immediately understand what is said, or—to put it more exactly—we are already with him, in advance, among the entities which the telling is about. . . . What we primarily do not hear is the pronunciation of the sounds. (207)[164]

When we stop dwelling in it and listen to it as occurrent, language, indeed, appears to us as a stream of mere sounds. It is then practically impossible to reconstruct the meaning from these meaningless units. This does not mean that the brain does not process physical inputs, but rather that there is no reason to suppose that any analogue of the *mental* rules and representations that would be required if we heard only occurrent sounds and tried to make sense of them plays a role in such brain-processing.[2] Heidegger would not be surprised that the attempt to develop flexible rule-based speech recognition systems starting with mere sounds—work that started more than a decade ago—has proved much more difficult than was originally anticipated.

When it comes to meaning, if we remain faithful to the phenomenon we see that: "To significations, words accrue. But word-things do not get supplied with significations" (204)[161]. Language is used in a shared context that is already meaningful, and it gets its meaning by fitting into and contributing to a meaningful whole.

The transparent use of meaningful linguistic tokens is thus part of the general activity of making sense of things, and

> sense is an *existentiale* of Dasein, not a property attaching to entities, lying "behind" them, or floating somewhere as an "intermediate domain." (193)[151]

On Heidegger's phenomenological account words as used in everyday talking do not get their meaning *from* anywhere. Once one has been socialized into a community's practices, as long as one dwells in those practices rather than taking a detached point of view, words are simply heard and seen as meaningful.

Only dwelling in our linguistic practices reveals their sense. This source of meaning is just what is inaccessible to detached philosophical reflection, whether it be the Husserl/Searle first-person or the Quine/Davidson third-person approach. Each of these theories gains its plausibility by assuming there are only two possible ways to account for linguistic meaning and then showing the serious problems raised by the other theory. We can see Heidegger's existential approach as a third way, which if worked out would avoid the Cartesian subject/object antinomy. He does not claim, however, to have fully clarified his notion of dwelling as the source of linguistic meaning. Indeed, he acknowledges that philosophers have not yet understood language.

In the last resort, philosophical research must resolve to ask what kind of being goes with language in general. . . . We possess a science of language, and the being of entities which it has for its theme is obscure. Even the horizon for any investigative question about it is veiled. (209) [166]

Several of Heidegger's later works are devoted to the question of the being of language.

B. Communication

Telling points things out and so makes communication possible. Communication can be the conveying of information in assertions, but, Heidegger warns, "communication in which one makes assertions—giving information, for instance—is a special case" (205) [162]. Heidegger mentions several other sorts of speech acts that are also forms of communication.

Being-with-one-another is telling as assenting or refusing, as demanding or warning, as pronouncing, consulting, or interceding, as "making assertions," and as talking in the way of "giving a talk." (204) [162]

In his account of speech acts Heidegger is nearer John Austin than John Searle, whose theory of speech acts requires intentional states. For Searle, a speaker must have the intention to get the hearer to recognize his intention to use language to convey his intentional state. Given his phenomenology of skill, Heidegger would no doubt respond that in communication one can use language transparently. One can say "Give me a lighter hammer," and receive one, without having either an intentional state (a desire for a lighter hammer) or the intention to communicate that state by using words. Indeed, this is the way language normally works. When he speaks of language as expression, Heidegger is careful to point out that it is not a way of externalizing something inner.

In telling, Dasein expresses itself not because it has, in the first instance, been encapsulated as something "internal" over against something outside, but because as being-in-the-world it is already "outside" when it understands. What is expressed is precisely this being-outside. (205) [162]

That is, Dasein uses language as a tool to point out aspects of its shared world.

The idea that everyday linguistic communication consists in exchanging inner information is so pervasive, however, that even the otherwise scrupulously stereotype-free *Sesame Street* TV program indoctrinates children into it. One sees a child with a picture of a flower in her head; she then gives out the word "flower" and another child gets the picture of a flower in his head. Heidegger's important insight is that everyday communication cannot be understood on this Cartesian model of messages sent from one isolated mind to another. Heidegger would point out that such an account treats language as a context-free code. It leaves out the essential fact that linguistic communication is possible only on the background of a shared world and that what one communicates about is an aspect of that shared world. In communication something is explicitly shared on the background of an already shared affectedness and understanding.

Communication is never anything like a conveying of experiences . . . from the interior of one subject into the interior of another. Dasein-with is already essentially manifest in a co-affectedness and a co-understanding. In telling being-with becomes "explicitly" *shared*; that is to say, it *is* already, but it is unshared as something that has not been taken hold of and appropriated. (205) [162]

The shared background, not being representable, cannot be communicated. But that need not worry us since all members of the linguistic community are socialized into the same world. It matters to those who need to represent the background in order to get computers to show linguistic competence, however, and it explains why there has been so little progress in programming computers to understand natural language.

III. Sense: The Background of Intelligibility

Heidegger defines his notion of sense as follows:

[Sense] is that wherein the understandability of something maintains itself . . . . "Sense" signifies the on-the-basis-of-which of a primary projection in terms of which something can be understood in its possibility as that which it is. . . . All ontical experience of entities— both circumspective reckoning with the available, and positive scientific cognition of the occurrent—is based upon projections of the being of the corresponding entities . . . . But in these projections there lies hidden the that-on-the-basis-of-which of the projection; and on this, as it were, the understanding of being nourishes itself. (370–371) [324]

Sense, then, is that on the basis of which we can make sense of something. It is a name for our background familiarity with each domain of being—a familiarity that enables us to cope with beings in that domain. Thus our familiarity with equipment's way of being, availableness, allows us to make sense of and cope with equipment, to see what it means to be equipment, what is possible for equipment, what can be done with it. Likewise, our familiarity with the occurrent guides our contemplation and our development of theories.

Heidegger also uses sense as a more abstract concept: "The concept of sense embraces the formal existential framework of what necessarily belongs to that which an understanding interpretation Articulates" (193) [151]. In this connection Heidegger later tells us that care is the being of Dasein, and that temporality, as unifying the threefold structure of care, is the sense of care, i.e., enables us to make sense of it. (See chapter 14.) Sense, then, is the *formal structure* of the background practices in terms of which ontologists can make sense of the understanding of being itself.

When Heidegger calls sense a "formal framework," he does not mean a *formalizable* structure abstractable from any instances and from the world of human activity (like Husserl's *eidos* or his *noema*). Sense is precisely what is left out in all formalization. Sense, for Heidegger, in opposition to Husserl, is the structure of the general background that can never be fully objectified but can only be gradually and incompletely revealed by circular hermeneutic inquiry. Sense is "formal" only in that it is a *general* ontological structure of human activity that can be filled out in various ways.

Sense is always filled in in some specific way, in some specific situation.

Dasein only "has" sense, so far as the disclosedness of being-in-the-world can be "filled in" by the entities discoverable in that disclosedness. (193) [151]

A particular Dasein can make itself at home in the world and fill up its life, and express itself by taking over the available equipment, or it can become paralyzed in anxiety and thus only clutch at things.

Hence only Dasein can be senseful or senseless. That is to say, its own being and the entities disclosed with its being can be appropriated in understanding, or can remain relegated to nonunderstanding. (193)[151]

Sense, as the background, "nourishes" being—that on the basis of which entities are determined as entities. Thus, sense as the ungrounded practices that make possible all intelligibility replaces the traditional idea of being as ultimate ground. But, as the only ground we have, our shared practices seem to the traditional thinker to be an abyss. Heidegger makes the point in a cryptic passage.

The sense of being can never be contrasted with entities, or with being as the "ground" which gives entities support; for a "ground" becomes accessible only as sense, even if it is itself the abyss of senselessness. (193-194)[152]

IV. Summary of the Aspects of Intelligibility

We are now in a position to understand and expand a condensed and important passage relating sense, telling, significance, interpretation, and assertion.

The intelligibility of something has always been articulated, even before there is any appropriative interpretation of it. Telling is the Articulation of intelligibility. Therefore it underlies both interpretation and assertion. That which can be Articulated in interpretation, and thus even more primordially in telling, is what we have called "sense." That which gets articulated as such in telling Articulation, we call the "whole-of-significations." (203–204)[161]

1. *Sense* is the background practices *on the basis of which* all activities and objects are intelligible or make sense. It is also the name for the general structure of that background, *in terms of which* the ontologist makes sense of being.

2. *Significance*, as we saw in chapter 5, is the relational whole of in-order-tos and for-the-sake-of-whichs in which entities and activities which involve equipment have a point.

3. *Articulation* (with a lower-case *a*) refers to the fact that the nexus of equipment has joints. That is, the world is organized into distinguishable entities and actions which we can tell apart.

4. *Telling* is picking out the joints of the equipmental whole in the course of using equipment. This is *Articulation* with an upper-case *A*.

5. *Interpretation* (lower-case *i*) denotes any activity in which Dasein points out the "as structure" already manifest in everyday Articulation.

6. *Significations* are particular reference relations (e.g., cases of usability and serviceability) that are picked out in coping and pointed out in language when necessary. (Significations are the nearest thing in Heidegger to what have traditionally been called senses.)

7. *Assertions* (usually in quotation marks, i.e., speech acts, not statements) are what result when we put significances into words. By the use of assertions, things in a shared situation can be pointed out, purposes communicated, etc. Primordial telling becomes concrete as linguistic telling.

13

Falling

To understand Heidegger's complex and confusing discussion of falling, we must disentangle a structural from a psychological sense of the term. Although Heidegger does not thematize this distinction, I shall treat these two topics separately: structural falling in this chapter and psychological falling in the Appendix.

I. Falling as an Existential Structure

"Falling reveals an essential ontological structure of Dasein itself" (224) [179]. Indeed, falling is the third structural aspect of being-in and does a lot of work in *Being and Time.* Yet of all the existentiales, falling is the hardest to get a focus on. One thing is clear: "falling" as an existential structure is Heidegger's term for the way Dasein is by its very nature drawn away from its primordial sense of what it is. "*Falling-away* is a kind of falling constitutive of Dasein itself insofar as it is . . . being-in-the-world" (HCT, 282, my italics). But it seems there are at least three different versions of falling-*away*, tracing it to absorption in the world, to language, and to a sort of reflexivity. To capture the results of each of these three forms of falling-away, Heidegger speaks of fallen Dasein as lost, uprooted, and covered-up, respectively. Heidegger offers his account of these various ways of falling away at different places in *Being and Time* without ever showing how they are related or which is supposed to be the most basic.

As if that were not trouble enough, falling also includes the way Dasein allows falling-away to cause it to *turn-away* from a primordial relation to itself. "In falling, Dasein *turns away* from itself" (230, my italics) [185]. This raises the question, why does "*falling-away*" lead to *turning away?* To this crucial question Heidegger has not just one but two answers, one structural and one psychological. Both answers push the question back to the *fallenness* of the one in which Dasein grows up. The structural account, however, attributes the fallenness of the one to the basic structure of intelligibility, while the other— a psychological account influenced by Kierkegaard—blames fallenness on the social sedimentation of strategies of flight from anxiety. (Such flight is, of course, to be distinguished from that studied by empirical psychology, but, as Kierkegaard sees in calling his *Concept of Anxiety* a psychological study, it is psychological all the same.)

In Division I falling is taken up immediately after telling. This makes sense if one follows the structural approach. But if falling is a response to the unsettledness revealed by anxiety, it should be taken up immediately after the discussion of anxiety. And, indeed, this is where Heidegger places his discussion when he returns to falling amidst the more Kierkegaardian concerns with inauthenticity and resoluteness in Division II. The shifting place of falling in the overall architectonic of *Being and Time* is a sign of Heidegger's hesitation between a structural and a motivational account.

The best way to make sense of all this, I think, is to factor out these two accounts and treat them separately. Since the motivational account in terms of fleeing is a secularized version of Kierkegaard's account of sin, I shall postpone it to its appropriate place in the Appendix. In this chapter I shall try to isolate the three structural aspects of *falling-away* and the kind of *fallenness* of the one each gives rise to and presupposes. This can then be used to explain the way that undifferentiated Dasein is constantly pulled toward *closing itself off* from primordiality. (To help keep the three structures and their effects in mind as we take them up, see Table 8.)

A. Absorption and Being Lost

The structural phenomenon most frequently described as *falling-away* is Dasein's being absorbed in coping with things.

In falling, Dasein *itself* as factical being-in-the-world, is something *from* which it has already fallen-away.... [Dasein] has fallen into the *world*, which itself belongs to its being. (220) [176]

In the kind of handling and being-busy which is "absorbed in the thing one is handling" ... the essential structure of care—falling—makes itself known. (420) [369]

Table 8
Types of structural falling and their effects.

Ontological structure	Misuse of the structure	Aspect of Dasein that is closed off	Resultant being closed off
Absorption	Fascination	Existence	Being lost
Language	Curiosity Idle talk	Concrete situation	Being uprooted, cut off
Reflexivity	Self-interpretation in terms of world	Self	Being distorted, covered up

This falling-away is certainly a structural necessity since Dasein has to take a stand on itself by taking up the for-the-sake-of-whichs provided by the one and manifesting its self-interpretation in its everyday activity.

Absorption is, indeed, equiprimordial with affectedness and understanding and deserves to be regarded as an existential. Dasein is always absorbed in doing something. All other versions of falling that are associated with inauthenticity, and so would not characterize authentic Dasein, cannot qualify as existentials, but are only existentielle possibilities. Heidegger's confusion of an existential and an existentielle sense of falling parallels his confusion in the discussion of the one between *conformity* as the existential and *conformism* as the existentielle source of leveling.

Structural falling-away produces a tendency or pull (*Zug*) toward interpreting Dasein in terms of the world. If not resisted this pull leads Dasein to *turn away* from itself.

Dasein gets dragged along in thrownness; that is to say, as something which has been thrown into the world, it loses itself in the "world"* in its factical submission to that with which it is to concern itself. (400) [348]

Dasein which is in its essence delivered to the world gets *entangled* in its own concern. It can *yield* to this tendency of falling to such a degree that it thereby cuts itself off from the possibility of returning to itself. (HCT, 281, second italics added)

[Dasein] turns *away from* itself in accordance with its ownmost pull of falling. (229) [184]

Heidegger sums this up in his claim that "Falling is conceived ontologically as kind of motion" (224) [180].

But even the authentic self that is in touch with itself "must forget itself if, lost in the world of equipment, it is to be able 'actually' to go to work and manipulate something" (405) [354]. Heidegger, therefore, needs some way of distinguishing the general structure of absorption from the kind of absorption that yields to the general structure in such a way as to turn away from itself.[1] He calls succumbing to the pull and thereby being closed-off, *fascination.*

In . . . familiarity Dasein can lose itself in what it encounters within-the-world and be fascinated with it. (107) [76]

"Inauthenticity" . . . amounts . . . to a quite distinctive kind of being-in-the-world—the kind which is completely fascinated by the "world"* and by the Dasein-with of others in the one. (220) [176]

Authentic Dasein, as we shall see in the Appendix, must continue doing what one does and being absorbed, even to the extent of being lost in its everyday work, while *resisting* becoming so *fascinated* by or taken over by the everyday activities that it loses itself and its primordial relation to its situation.

On this structural account, the tendency toward fascination remains unaccounted for.[2] Whatever the account, however, Dasein's structural *tendency* to fall away from itself in absorption, and even its *failure to resist* this tendency, are strikingly different from Dasein's psychological *temptation* actively to embrace absorption in order to hide its unsettling nullity, i.e., in order to *flee* from anxiety. In order to motivate falling, however, Heidegger confusingly conflates the two.

The everyday interpretation of the self . . . has a *tendency* to understand itself in terms of the "world"* with which it is concerned. When Dasein has itself in view ontically, it *fails* to see itself in relation to the kind of being of that entity which it is itself. . . . What is the motive for this "fugitive" way of saying "I"? It is motivated by Dasein's falling; for as falling, it *flees* in the face of itself into the "one." (368, first italics added) [321–322]

Heidegger thus collapses the distinction between *falling* and *fleeing.* Indeed, he conflates the structural and the psychological: "Dasein's falling into the one and the 'world'* of its concern, is what we have called a 'fleeing' in the face of itself" (230) [185]. "Fleeing [is] a basic disposition of Dasein which is constitutive of the being of

Dasein qua care, and for this very reason is the most radically concealed" (HCT, 283).

This mistaken conflation of structural falling with psychological fleeing leads to an even more unfortunate move. Although one side of Heidegger presents falling-away simply as a consequence of being-in-the-world, another side of Heidegger wants to *derive* falling-away from motivated flight. That is, he wants to *explain* the essential ontological structure of falling-away as a *consequence* of Dasein's *need* to deny its unsettled way of being. For example:

If Dasein itself, in idle talk and in the way things have been publicly interpreted, presents to itself the possibility of losing itself in the "one" and falling into groundlessness, this tells us that Dasein prepares for itself a constant temptation towards falling. Being-in-the-world is in itself *tempting*. (221)[177]

Dasein's absorption in the one and its absorption in the "world"* of its concern, make manifest something like a *fleeing* of Dasein in the face of itself—of itself as an authentic ability-to-be-its-self. (229)[184]

[Dasein is] always . . . absorbed in the world of its concern. In this falling being-amidst . . . fleeing in the face of unsettledness . . . announces itself. (237)[192]

As the above quotations show, fleeing is a repeated theme in *Being and Time*, yet if Heidegger derives falling as absorption from falling as fleeing, he makes authenticity impossible. Dasein is structurally absorbed in the world. If Dasein's absorption is a result of fleeing its unsettledness, Dasein's *structural tendency* to *fall away* is identified with giving in to the *temptation* to *cover up*. Falling as an existential structure would then entail that Dasein cannot own up to being the kind of entity it is. That would make Dasein *essentially* inauthentic. (As we shall see in the Appendix, a motivational story is perfectly plausible in the context of Kierkegaard's account of original sin, but it is incompatible with Heidegger's structural account of falling.)

B. Language as Uprooting

Language by its very structure leads Dasein away from a primordial relation to being and to its own being, thus making possible Dasein's slide from primordiality to groundlessness. The resulting movement is described in Heidegger's discussion of idle talk and again in his account of how Dasein is essentially in the untruth.

Dasein in making its activity intelligible to itself and others must lose its immediate relation to the world and to itself. It may then yield to this structural necessity in order to uproot its understanding of itself and its world.

In preparing to describe idle talk Heidegger hastens to assure us that "The expression 'idle talk' is not to be used here in a 'disparaging' signification. Terminologically, it signifies a positive phenomenon which constitutes the kind of being of everyday Dasein's understanding and interpreting" (211)[167]. Yet Heidegger immediately stresses that idle talk cuts Dasein off from primordiality.

When Dasein maintains itself in idle talk, it is . . . *cut off* from its primary and primordially genuine relationships-of-being towards the world, towards Dasein-with, and towards its very being-in. (214, my italics)[170]

We shall now follow Heidegger's introduction of falling-away and being closed off into his discussion of idle talk. However, before we can expound Heidegger's account of the tendency towards falling-away built into the structure of language, we must make explicit a three-fold distinction implicit in Heidegger's analysis of equipment. Our understanding of a specific piece of equipment can be:

1. *Primordial:* We actually *use* the equipment. "The more we seize hold of it and use it, the more primordial does our relationship to [the hammer] become" (98)[69].

2. *Positive:* In a great many cases we understand equipment we have not actually used. Most of us have not flown a jet, wielded a scalpel, or been pushed in a wheelchair. But luckily for everyday understanding and communication, we do not have to *use* each piece of equipment ourselves in order to understand it. As long as we know what counts as normal use by a normal user, and our activity takes appropriate account of this, we grasp equipment with an average intelligibility. We can then talk about it appropriately, call for it if we need it, etc.

In accordance with this intelligibility the telling which is communicated can be understood to a considerable extent, even if the hearer does not bring himself into such a kind of being towards what the telling is about as to have a primordial understanding of it. . . . But what the talk is about is understood only approximately and superficially. (212)[168]

Such secondhand understanding is necessary if there is to be the diversity and specialization characteristic of the equipmental whole. Yet, this secondhand understanding introduces a generality that tends towards banality. "We have *the same thing* in view, because it is in *the same averageness* that we have a common understanding of what is said" (212) [168].

3. *Privative.* Once one leaves primordial understanding behind, one can use the structure of language to cover up primordiality altogether:

Because this telling has lost its primary relationship-of-being towards the entity talked about . . . it does not communicate in such a way as to let this entity be appropriated in a primordial manner, but communicates rather by following the route of *gossiping* and *passing the word along.* . . . Idle talk is constituted by just such gossiping and passing the word along—a process by which its initial lack of grounds to stand on becomes aggravated to complete groundlessness. (212) [168]

The fact that something has been said groundlessly, and then gets passed along in further retelling, amounts to perverting the act of disclosing into an act of closing off. (213) [169]

We thus arrive at the kind of fallenness called uprootedness:

Idle talk, which *closes things off* in the way we have designated, is the kind of being which belongs to Dasein's understanding when that understanding has been *uprooted.* (214, my italics) [170]

Note that in the above quotation "idle talk" *is* being used in a "disparaging signification" and no longer "signifies a positive phenomenon which constitutes the kind of being of everyday Dasein's understanding." Idle talk *closes off* genuine and even average understanding.

One must then ask, what leads Dasein to make the move from the positive generality necessary for average intelligibility to the privative use of language to close off understanding? Heidegger's name for this movement seems to be curiosity. When he is being carefully structural, he holds that curiosity as he understands it is a *tendency* not a *temptation* and thus not a psychological state.

As a free-floating seeing . . . relaxed tarrying *eo ipso* tends not to tarry in what is nearest. This *tendency* is the care for the discovery and the bringing-near of what is not yet experienced or of what is not an everyday experience, the care of being "away from" the constantly and immediately available things. . . . This means that it does not dwell on something definitely and thematically grasped, but prefers characteristically to jump from one thing to another, a feature which is constitutive of *curiosity*. (HCT, 276, my italics)

In short,

Curiosity is characterized by a specific way of not tarrying amidst what is closest. (216) [172]

Not tarrying and distraction belong to the *structure* of the being of curiosity thus characterized. (HCT, 277, my italics)

The result is just the sort of uprooting we have been following:

Curiosity is everywhere and nowhere. This mode of being-in-the-world reveals a new kind of being of everyday Dasein—a kind in which Dasein is constantly *uprooting* itself. (217, my italics) [173]

C. Reflexivity and Distortion

The third way Dasein's structure leads Dasein to close itself off is its tendency to read back onto itself the being of the entities with which it deals.

The kind of being which belongs to Dasein is . . . such that, in understanding its own being, it has a *tendency* to do so in terms of that entity towards which it comports itself primarily and in a way which is essentially constant—in terms of the "world."* (36, my italics) [15]

Our being amidst the things with which we concern ourselves most closely in the "world"*—a being which is falling—guides the everyday way in which Dasein is interpreted, and *covers up*³ ontically Dasein's authentic being, so that the ontology which is directed towards this entity is denied an appropriate basis. (359, my italics) [311]

This structure and the distortion it fosters has no one name in *Being and Time*, but it is alluded to at crucial moments in the text to explain how Dasein could misunderstand its own way of being and how this misunderstanding could give rise to the traditional notion of human beings as self-contained, occurrent subjects.

But how is this distortion based on the necessary structure of Dasein as self-interpreting? Heidegger never answers this question in so many words, but in Division II he points out that Dasein is essentially a kind of nothingness—("a null basis of a nullity"—see Appendix). Nonetheless, Dasein must make itself intelligible. But the only source of intelligibility is the referential whole and its modifications, so Dasein's only recourse is to make sense of everything, including itself, in terms of availableness and occurrence.

> Dasein understands itself primarily and usually in terms of that with which it concerns itself . . . Everydayness takes Dasein as something *available* to be concerned with—that is, something that gets managed and reckoned up. (335–336, my italics) [289]

A structural account is also sufficient to explain how ontological reflection passes over transparent coping and its background and focuses on the occurrent.

> Where the issue is . . . one of ontological understanding, the interpretation of being takes its orientation in the first instance from the being of intraworldly entities. . . . Thereby the being of what is primarily available gets passed over, and entities are first conceived as a context of things which are occurrent. (245) [201]

> [Ontology] thus calls the ego, the subject, a res, a substantia, a subjectum. What appears here in a theoretical field of developed ontology is a general determination of Dasein itself, namely, that it has the *tendency* to understand itself primarily by way of things. (BP, 271–272, my italics)

Unfortunately Heidegger asks for a motive for this reflexive distortion, and brings in fleeing to explain Dasein's treating itself in terms of things in the world.

> What is at stake in the flight from unsettledness is precisely a cultivation of Dasein itself as being-in-the-world, so much so that it lets itself be determined primarily from the world. (HCT, 293)

II. Fallenness

In the Appendix I shall return to the move from structural *tendency* to psychological *temptation* and the connected idea of motivated flight. Meanwhile, there is a further aspect of falling that needs to be taken up. If we are to avoid the psychological account of falling based on motivated flight, we need a structural account of why Dasein *yields* to the pull of the world it is absorbed in and the seduction of language as the source of average intelligibility, so as to let itself be *turned away from* what is primordial in the world and in itself. Part of such an account is provided by Heidegger's description of the *fallenness* of the one. The idea is that average intelligibility, belonging to the structure of the one, is out of touch with the primordial. Dasein, then, does not choose to fall away; it is simply socialized into this lack of primordiality. Thus Heidegger would not need any independent psychological account of why Dasein succumbs to the tendency to fall away from itself. As a one-self, it has always already fallen.

The norms needed for intelligibility have an essential effect which Heidegger, following Kierkegaard, calls leveling.

> This essential averageness of the one is ... grounded in an original mode of being of the one. This mode is given in its absorption in the world, in what can be called the *leveling* of being-with-one-another, the leveling of all differences. (HCT, 246)

The standard is an essential structure of intelligibility.

> As something factical, Dasein's projection of itself understandingly is in each case already amidst a world that has been discovered. From this world [Dasein] takes its possibilities, and it does so first in accordance with the way things have been interpreted by the "one." This interpretation has already restricted the possible options of choice to what lies within the range of the familiar, the attainable, the respectable—that which is fitting and proper. (239) [193–194]

> Everything that is primordial gets glossed over as something that has long been well known. Everything gained by a struggle becomes just something to be manipulated.... This care of averageness reveals ... an *essential tendency* of Dasein which we call the "leveling down" of all possibilities of being. (165, my italics) [127]

Such leveling is an aspect of the structure of the one which Heidegger, again following Kierkegaard, calls *publicness*.

> Averageness and leveling down ... constitute what we know as "public-ness." Publicness proximally controls every way in which the world and Dasein get interpreted. (165) [127]

> This public world ... is right in everything, not by virtue of a primordial relationship to the world and to Dasein itself, not because it might have a special and genuine knowledge of the world and of Dasein, but precisely by talking over everything while not going "into the matters" and by virtue of an insensitivity to all distinctions in level and genuineness. (HCT, 246)

Thus the one, in providing average intelligibility, opens up a standard world in which all distinctions between the unique and the general, the superior and the average, the important and the trivial have been leveled.

Furthermore, as I have mentioned and will show more fully in the discussion of guilt in the Appendix, the one offers its norms as guidelines that seem to follow from human nature, and its for-the-sake-of-whichs seem to offer an identity to the self. Thus the one offers both the groundlessness of idle talk, and the illusion of grounding; both distraction from unsettledness, and the illusion of being settled. In both cases, *falling in with* the public leads Dasein to *fall away from* itself.

In short, since norms are *shared* practices, the kind of life one lives and what one does at any given time will be just what anyone would do in that sort of situation. But why does Dasein *fall-for* this leveled account? Why is it pulled away from its primordial relation to itself and its situation? The answer is that in its *undifferentiated* mode Dasein has always already *fallen in with* publicness. Heidegger calls this state *fallenness*. ""Fallenness" into the 'world'* means an absorption in being-with-one-another, in so far as the latter is guided by idle talk, curiosity, and ambiguity" (220) [175]. "The self . . . is primarily and usually inauthentic,[4] the one-self. Being-in-the-world is always fallen" (225) [181].

Heidegger gives a structural, i.e., nonpsychological, account of fallenness.

[Since] covering up installs itself in opposition to every express intention, manifest in it and in the *tendency* toward it is a *structure* of Dasein's being which is given with Dasein itself. . . . Like discoveredness, being-with and being-in, falling refers to a *constitutive structure* of the being of Dasein, in particular a specific phenomenon of being-in, in which Dasein first constantly has its being. . . . This being's dwelling in the one and in idle talk is in an uprooted state . . . . (HCT, 274, my italics)

Simply by being socialized Dasein takes over the fallenness of the one.

Primarily and usually the self is lost in the one. It understands itself in terms of those possibilities of existence which "circulate" in the "average" public way of interpreting Dasein today. (435) [383]

Dasein is "thrown proximally right into the publicness of the one" (210) [167], so that "to be closed off and covered up belongs to Dasein's *facticity*" (265) [222].

There is, of course, the possibility of an authentic way of being absorbed that is not closed off—"'Absorption in . . .' has *mostly* the character of being-lost in the publicness of the one" (220, my italics) [175]—but each individual grows up in average intelligibility, so that even in Dasein's undifferentiated mode, leveling, and with it fascination, etc., is *always already* taken over. "Dasein has in every case already gone astray and failed to recognize itself" (184) [144]. *Falling-for* the nonprimordiality of the one, then, is not a positive act; it just happens to one like falling in a gravitational field. Thus undifferentiated Dasein literally has no choice, it has always already yielded to the pull away from primordiality. As Heidegger puts it, it is as if the one has already done the choosing.

With Dasein's lostness in the one, that factical ability-to-be which is closest to it (the tasks, rules, and standards, the urgency and extent, of concernful and solicitous being-in-the-world) has already been decided upon. . . . So Dasein makes no choices, gets carried along by the nobody. (312) [268]

As we shall see, even when Dasein acts authentically, it must do what makes sense according to public norms and use public equipment, so there is a constant pull away from primordiality in everything it does. Resisting falling requires constant effort.

The traditional philosophical interpretation of Dasein as occurrent can now be traced back to falling prey to the one. Indeed, one of the key passages concerning the traditional account of Dasein as occurrent is found at the end of the section on the one.

From the kind of being which belongs to the one—the kind which is closest—everyday Dasein draws its preontological way of interpreting its being. . . . Ontological Interpretation follows the tendency to interpret it this way: it understands Dasein in terms of the world and comes across it as an intraworldly entity. But that is not all: even that sense of being in terms of which these "subject" entities get understood, is one which that ontology of Dasein which is "closest" to us lets itself present in terms of the "world."* But because the phenomenon of the world itself gets passed over in this absorption in the world, its place gets taken by what is occurrent within-the-world, namely, things. (168) [130]

So far we have discussed (1) the three structural forms of *falling away*, a necessary structure even of authentic Dasein, and (2) the *fallenness* of the one that makes *having turned away* a necessary starting point for undifferentiated Dasein, and turning away a constant tendency even for authentic Dasein. We have postponed to the Appendix Heidegger's reliance upon a Kierkegaardian account of how public fallenness arises from *fleeing* and how a Dasein's way of being changes from *undifferentiated* to *inauthentic* when it gives in to the *temptation* to indulge in an *active cover-up* of its unsettledness.

The Care-Structure

I. Care as the Being of Dasein

Care unifies the various structural aspects of Dasein's way of being. Heidegger sums up the care structure and its relations to the structure of being-in as follows:

> Dasein exists as a being for which, in its being, that being is itself an *issue*. Essentially ahead of itself, it has projected itself upon its ability to be before going on to any mere consideration of itself. In its projection it reveals itself as something which has been thrown. It has been thrownly abandoned to the "world,"* and falls into it concernfully. As care—that is, as existing in the unity of the projection which has been fallingly thrown—this entity has been disclosed as a "there." (458) [406]

Caring, understood ontologically, is "making itself an issue," and we now know that making itself an issue can take many forms, from the most involved use of equipment to sheer disinterested staring.

> Care, as a primordial structural totality, lies "before" every factical "attitude" and "situation" of Dasein, and it does so existentially *a priori*; this means that it always lies *in* them. So this phenomenon by no means expresses a priority of the "practical" attitude over the theoretical. When we ascertain something occurrent by merely beholding it, this activity has the character of care just as much as does a "political action" or taking a rest and enjoying oneself. "Theory" and "practice" are possibilities of being for an entity whose being must be defined as "care." (238) [193]

This is not an ontic, psychological claim. Heidegger earlier remarks:

> [Care] is to be taken as an ontological structural concept. It has nothing to do with "tribulation," "melancholy," or the "cares of life," though ontically one can come across these in every Dasein. These—like their

opposites, "gaiety" and "freedom from care"—are ontically possible only because Dasein, when understood *ontologically*, is care. (84) [57]

Heidegger thus tries to ward off an understanding of care as worry or even simply pragmatic concern—the connotations of the term *Sorge*, which in German means care as in "the cares of the world." In a conversation with Heidegger I pointed out that "care" in English has connotations of love and caring. He responded that that was fortunate since with the term "care" he wanted to name the very general fact that "*Sein geht mich an*," roughly, that being gets to me. Thus all ontic senses of caring are to be included as modes of ontological caring:

Because being-in-the-world is essentially care (*Sorge*), being-amidst the available could be taken in our previous analyses as *concern* (*Besorgen*), and being with the Dasein-with of others as we encounter it within-the-world could be taken as *solicitude* (*Fürsorge*). (237) [193]

Care, then, is the "formal existential totality of Dasein's ontological structural whole" (237) [192]. (Here again "formal" has the meaning we have already seen in discussing "sense"; it is a very general structure that is always filled out in some specific way.) "The transcendental 'generality' of the phenomenon of care and of all fundamental *existentialia* is . . . broad enough to present a basis on which *every* interpretation of Dasein which is ontical and belongs to a world-view must move" (244) [199–200]. This is Heidegger's answer to total cultural relativism. There is a common structure to all ways of being human. Every culture is a different self-interpretation, but *any* self-interpreting way of being has the disclosedness-structure called care. (See Table 9.)

II. The Self

This seems a reasonable place to pull together Heidegger's dispersed discussion of Dasein as a self, which is explicitly addressed in Section 64 on Care and Selfhood.

A. A Problem of Priority

To begin with, there seems to be an inconsistency in Heidegger's account of the self. In his discussion of the relation between the one-self and the authentic self, it is not clear which is more basic. The contradiction comes out most clearly when one juxtaposes the following two quotations:

Table 9
Structure of disclosedness and disclosing: "Disclosedness . . . pertains equiprimordially to the world, to being-in, and to the self." (263)[220]

	Affectedness		Understanding
The world	(Sensibility.)	Articulation (lower-case *a*).	Significance.
Current world.	Mood.	Specific significations.	Room for maneuver.
The clearing (noun), the situation.	Things showing up as mattering.		Actions showing up as what it makes sense to do.
Being-in Current activity, being-my-there, clearing (verb).	Thrown. In a mood.	Falling. Absorbed in coping.	Projecting. Pressing into possibilities.
The self	How it's going with me.	Being what I am doing.	Ability-to-be me.
Care	Facticity. Being-already in.	Fallenness. Being-amidst.	Existence. Being-ahead-of- itself.
	Past.	Present.	Future.

Authentic self-being . . . is an existentiell modification . . . of the one as an essential existentiale. (168)[130]

The one-self . . . is an existentiell modification of the authentic self. (365)[317]

Which is a modification of which? To reconcile these two assertions, we must begin by distinguishing *three* ways in which Heidegger uses the term "self." First, Dasein as care, i.e., as making its own being an issue for it, is misleadingly called a self. "Care already harbors in itself the phenomenon of the self" (366)[318].

Second, since Dasein is always already socialized into public practices, Dasein is always already a one-self.

As an entity which has been delivered over to its being, it remains also delivered over to the fact that it must always have found itself—but found itself in a way of finding which arises not so much from a direct seeking as rather from a fleeing. (174)[135]

The question of the "*who*" of Dasein has been answered with the expression "self." . . . For the most part I myself am not the "who" of Dasein; the one-self is its "who." (312)[268]

Since Dasein must always find itself in public practices, Dasein begins as a one-self. This is what we earlier called Dasein in its undifferentiated mode.

Third, Dasein can become either inauthentic or authentic. Dasein can "choose the one for its hero," in which case it is inauthentic, or it can face up to anxiety and become an authentic self. (See Table 10.)

Authentic existence is not something which floats above falling everydayness; existentially, it is only a modified way in which such everydayness is seized upon. (224)[179]

When Dasein . . . brings itself back from the "one," the one-self is modified in an existentiell manner so that it becomes *authentic* self-being. (313)[268] (See the Appendix.)

This account of selfhood makes being an authentic self an existentiell modification of the one-self. Heidegger should have left it at this, but, as we have just noted, he also says that "the one-self is an existentiell modification of the authentic self." This is an unfortunate thing to say, but, as we shall see in the Appendix, Heidegger needs it in his discussion of the call of conscience. Conscience calls to the hidden authentic self over the head, so to speak, of the one-self.

And to what is one called when one is thus appealed to? To one's *own self.* Not to what Dasein counts for, can do, or concerns itself with in being with one another publicly, nor to what it has taken hold of, set about, or let itself be carried along with. . . . And because only the *self* of the one-self gets appealed to and brought to bear, the "*one*" collapses. (317)[273]

Of course, this deeper true self is not an isolated ego:

When the one-self is appealed to, it gets called to the self . . . not to that self which one has in mind when one gazes "analytically" at psychical conditions and what lies behind them. The appeal to the self in the one-

Table 10
Modes of disclosure of Dasein.

	Dasein's relation to norms	Dasein's understanding of itself	Dasein's mode of being
Primordial	Taking-over the one (while still owning-up-to itself).	Genuine understanding (reveals Dasein's being).	Authentic.
Positive	Falling-in-with the one (falling-away-from itself). Conformity.	Everyday understanding (lack of ground; closes off being).	Undifferentiated.
Privative	Falling-for the one (turning-away-from itself). Conformism.	Misunderstanding (complete groundlessness; covers up being).	Inauthentic.

self does not force it inwards upon itself, so that it can close itself off from the "external world." (318) [273]

But Dasein has not yet faced anxiety. How could the authentic self be already there to be appealed to? To make sense of this misleading claim, remember that since care describes Dasein's most basic structure as thrown into making its being an issue, Dasein is thrown into being a self. "In being its *self*, Dasein is, *as* a self, the entity that has been thrown" (330) [284–285]. Since this thrown care-structure is what is called to to become an authentic self, we could call it in a somewhat misleading way a potential authentic self. Heidegger comes close when he says:

Selfhood is to be discerned existentially only in [Dasein's] authentic ability-to-be a self—that is to say, in the authenticity of Dasein's being *as care.* (369) [322]

It would have been less misleading to call this basic "self" Dasein's ability-to-be-authentic rather than Dasein's authentic-ability-to-be.

B. The Problem of Solipsism

Another seeming contradiction emerges if one opposes the quotation already cited from the 1923 lectures—"Dasein as its own does not mean an isolating relativization to . . . the individual (*solus ipse*)"[1]—to the quotation from *Being and Time* in which Heidegger describes his view as "existential 'solipsism'" and says, "Anxiety individualizes Dasein and thus discloses it as '*solus ipse*'" (233) [188]. How are we to reconcile these two claims?

The Dasein revealed as *solus ipse* in anxiety cannot be the self of inauthentic or even of authentic Dasein, since these are defined as various ways of being-in-the-world. Rather, it must be what is left of Dasein when it is holding on to anxiety and standing out into nothing—when all that remains is anxiety being anxious. In this extreme condition of nongenuine authenticity, Dasein experiences itself not as a self but as a pure, thrown "that it is and has to be" (174) [135]. But this is an ultimate breakdown condition. It does not reveal what Dasein, as care, really is. Heidegger is no existential solipsist; that is why he puts solipsism in scare quotes in the passage just mentioned. The quotation on page 233 continues:

But this existential "solipsism" is so far from the displacement of putting an isolated subject-thing into the innocuous emptiness of a worldless occurring, that in an extreme sense what it does is precisely to bring Dasein face to face with its world as world, and thus bring it face to face with itself as being-in-the-world. (233) [188]

The same argument applies when in a later passage Heidegger speaks of being-unto-death as *unrelated*. (See Appendix.) This is presumably the breakdown condition caused by the anxiety of death, as opposed to the being-in-the-world-with-others that comes from resolutely facing death.

III. Temporality as Making Sense of Care

Just as care allows us to unify the various structural aspects of Dasein in the notion of a being that makes an issue of its being, so temporality enables us to make sense of the threefold structure of care.

When we inquire about the sense of care, we are asking what makes possible the totality of the articulated structural whole of care, in the unity of its articulation as we have unfolded it. (371) [324]

Heidegger defines care, which we should hear verbally as caring, as follows:

The being of Dasein means ahead-of-itself-being-already-in-(the-world) as being-amidst (entities encountered within-the-world). This being fills in the signification of the term "*care*," which is used in a purely ontologico-existential manner. (237)[192]

Dasein is thus *already in, ahead of itself,* and *amidst.* For this reason Heidegger speaks of *temporality* as the sense of care. "Temporality reveals itself as the sense of authentic care" (374)[326]. "The primordial unity of the structure of care lies in temporality" (375)[327].

The details of how temporality provides the ultimate horizon for understanding Dasein, world, and how they presuppose each other is the main contribution of Division II, and is beyond the scope of this commentary, but a rough idea can be gleaned from the following discussion. First Heidegger summarizes the basic phenomenological results of Division I and asks the most basic question:

Circumspective concern includes the understanding of an involvement-whole, and this understanding is based upon a prior understanding of the relationships of the "in-order-to," the "towards-which," the "towards-this," and the "for-the-sake-of-which." The interconnection of these relationships has been exhibited earlier as "significance." Their unity makes up what we call the "world."* *The question arises of how anything like the world in its unity with Dasein is ontologically possible.* In what way must the world *be,* if Dasein is to be able to exist as being-in-the-world? (415, my italics)[364]

Next Heidegger reviews the results of his existential analytic of everydayness. Dasein as thrown, falling, projecting, i.e., as being-already-in, being-amidst and being-ahead-of-itself, can now be seen to have what Heidegger calls an *ecstatic temporal structure,* i.e., the activity of clearing is *outside itself* in opening up the past, present, and future. Correlatively, equipment, as what is taken for granted as already a resource (the with-which), applied in present coping (the in-order-to), and directed toward some outcome (the towards-which), forms a clearing (noun) that has what Heidegger calls a *horizontal temporal structure.* If we then add that Dasein, as falling, must manifest itself through its absorption in the world, we see that the temporal *ecstasies* of Dasein's way of being must map onto the temporal *horizon* of the world of everyday activity. We then can finally understand at the most complete and satisfying level how and why each Dasein, through its there, its centered openness, is the world. Thus Heidegger concludes, "Dasein *is* its world existingly." (This is not an ideal formulation, but it must mean that Dasein is *the* world existing, since Dasein is being-in-*the*-world and the question in this section is: How is *the* world in its unity with Dasein ontologically possible?)

Heidegger lays out this final tour de force in two dense paragraphs.

We have defined Dasein's being as "care." The ontological sense of "care" is temporality. We have shown that temporality constitutes the disclosedness of the "there," and we have shown how it does so. In the disclosedness of the "there" the world is disclosed along with it. The unity of significance—that is, the ontological make-up of the world—must then likewise be grounded in temporality. The existential-temporal condition for the possibility of the world lies in the fact that temporality, as an ecstatical unity, has something like a horizon. . . . The horizon of temporality as a whole determines that on the basis of which factically existing entities are essentially disclosed. (416) [364–365]

In so far as Dasein exists factically, it understands itself in the way its "for-the-sake-of-itself" is connected with some current "in-order-to." That inside which existing Dasein understands itself, is "there" along with its factical existence. That inside which one primarily understands oneself has Dasein's kind of being. Dasein *is* its world existingly. (416) [364] [2]

15

Philosophical Implications of a Hermeneutics of Everydayness

I. Dasein, Worldliness, and Reality

Now we must investigate the epistemological and ontological implications of the phenomena we have been describing.

> We need to discuss the ontological interconnections of care, worldliness, availableness, and occurrentness. . . . This will lead to a more precise characterization of the concept of *reality* in the context of a discussion of the epistemological questions oriented by this idea which have been raised in realism and idealism. (228) [183]

Heidegger wants to reformulate and thereby dissolve the philosophical problems concerning the possibility of knowing an independent reality. These problems are connected with the question of the relation of human beings to things in themselves. The real is supposed to be independent of us and our practices. Heidegger's task is to show that the real must be *disclosed* on the basis of our being-in-the-world and yet it can *be* "in itself." Likewise, truth obviously relates to us since it is our assertions that are capable of being true, yet Heidegger needs to show how our assertions can be true of things independent of us. In both cases Heidegger wants to use his analysis of being-in-the-world to avoid traditional problems while saving what is phenomenologically defensible in common sense and in the philosophical tradition.

A. The Source of Traditional Ontology

Before introducing Heidegger's account of the relation of Dasein and reality, we must review Heidegger's account of curiosity and how he derives and criticizes the traditional ontological claim that ultimate reality is made up of context-free independent substances.

Concern may come to rest in the sense of one's interrupting [one's] performance and taking a rest . . . . In rest, concern does not disappear; circumspection, however, becomes free and is no longer bound to the world of work. . . . When circumspection has been set free, there is no longer anything available which we must concern ourselves with bringing close. . . . Dasein lets itself be carried along solely by the looks of the world; in this kind of being, it concerns itself with becoming rid of itself as being-in-the-world. (216) [172]

Traditional philosophy privileges this detached attitude:

Being is that which shows itself in the pure perception which belongs to beholding, and only by such seeing does being get discovered. Primordial and genuine truth lies in pure beholding. This thesis has remained the foundation of western philosophy ever since [Parmenides]. (215) [171]

In a later passage Heidegger adds to this account of the source of traditional ontology that traditional ontology understands all ways of being in terms of the way of being it finds when contemplating occurrent entities:

Our interpretation of understanding has shown that, in accordance with its falling kind of being, [Dasein] has, primarily and usually, diverted itself into an understanding of the "world." Even where the issue is not only one of ontical experience but also one of ontological understanding, the interpretation of being takes its orientation in the first instance from the being of intraworldly entities. Thereby the being of what is primarily available gets passed over, and entities are first conceived as a context of things (*res*) which are occurrent. "*Being*" acquires the meaning "*reality.*" Substantiality becomes the basic characteristic of being. . . . Like any other being, *Dasein* too *is occurrent as real.* . . . By this priority [of the occurrent] the route to a genuine existential analytic of Dasein gets diverted, and so too does our view of the being of what is primarily available within-the-world. (245) [201]

This derivation seems a bit facile. Indeed, at this point Husserl wrote in the margin of his copy of *Being and Time*: "Is all this an essential necessity?" Nonetheless, for better or worse, Heidegger's claim seems to be that, when Dasein rests, it then has time to reflect on what is revealed, and, forgetting the context in which it has been involved, it views the occurrent that contemplation reveals as the self-subsistent *pure*-occurrent of traditional ontology; and then seeks to explain everything else in terms of this ultimate reality.

[This] forces the general problematic of being into a direction that lies off course. The other modes of being become defined negatively and privatively with regard to reality [as pure-occurrentness]. (245) [201]

II. Reconsidering the Problem of Reality

If traditional, foundational ontology is basically perverted, a hermeneutic of everydayness will have to reconsider the traditional problems the old ontology raised and could not answer, in the hope of bypassing them.

A. The Epistemological Question of the Existence of the External World

It has long been held that the way to grasp the real is by that kind of knowing which is characterized by beholding. . . . In so far as reality has the character of something independent and "in itself," the question of the meaning of "reality" becomes linked with that of whether the real can be independent "of consciousness" or whether there can be a transcendence of consciousness into the "sphere" of the real. (246) [202]

Since Descartes, philosophers have tried to prove the existence of a world of objects outside the mind. Kant considered it a scandal that such a proof had never been successful. Heidegger holds that the scandal is that philosophers have sought such a proof. Part of the trouble is that the tradition does not distinguish between the "world" (universe) as a totality of objects and the world as the organized equipment and practices in which Dasein is involved, indeed, in terms of which Dasein defines itself. Rather than thinking of human beings as subjects standing over against a totality of objects, we need to realize that it is only on the background of already taken up practices and equipment that we can doubt the existence of particular objects, and even a whole domain of objects. To free ourselves from the traditional problems we must switch from epistemology to existential ontology:

Our discussion of the unexpressed presuppositions of attempts to solve the problem of reality in ways which are just "epistemological" shows that this problem must be taken back, as an ontological one, into the existential analytic of Dasein. (252) [208]

If the "*cogito sum*" is to serve as the point of departure for the existential analytic of Dasein, then it needs to be turned around, and furthermore its content needs new ontologico-phenomenal confirmation. The "*sum*" is then asserted first, and indeed in the sense that "I am in a world." As such an entity, "I am" the possibility of various ways of comporting myself (*cogitationes*) as ways of being amidst intraworldly beings. Descartes, on the contrary, says that *cogitationes* are occurrent, and that an *ego* is occurrent too as a worldless *res cogitans*. (254) [211]

It is only when we reflect philosophically on the structure of deliberative, representational intentionality that we get skepticism; coping practices, on the contrary, do not represent and so cannot misrepresent. Or more exactly, since even particular coping practices can "misrepresent" in the sense that we can take something as something it is not, and so fail to cope, what cannot fail is the background coping that makes the success or failure of all levels of specific coping possible. Once we understand Dasein as "being the world existingly," and the world as an organized pattern of practices and equipment that forms the background on the basis of which all activity and thought makes sense, we see that the world must be disclosed along with Dasein.

The question of whether there is a world at all and whether its being can be proved, makes no sense if it is raised by *Dasein* as being-in-the-world; and who else would raise it? (246–247) [202]

Since there can be no Dasein except as manifest in actual coping with equipment, etc.: "Along with Dasein as being-in-the-world, entities within-the-world have in each case already been disclosed" (251) [207].

The problem of the external world arises for those from Descartes to Husserl and Searle who believe that all our activity is mediated by internal representations, for then we can ask if our intentional contents correspond to reality, i.e., as Searle puts it, if their conditions of satisfaction are met. But if, in everyday Daseining, coping takes place without intentional content, the question of the satisfaction of intentional states cannot be raised.

Of course, when there is a disturbance we then have intentional states, and on reflection we can ask if *they* correspond to reality, i.e., we can question whether our *beliefs* are true, and whether our *visual experiences* are veridical. But intentional states make sense and determine conditions of satisfaction only on a background of coping not analyzable in terms of intentional content. Thus, while the question whether particular intentional states correspond to their objects can, in fact, be asked, there is no corresponding question to be asked about being-in-the-world.

Only when a philosopher like Husserl treats the background skills on the model of deliberation as a network of intentional states, i.e., a system of beliefs and rules, can one then ask if this whole network corresponds to reality, and again raise the skeptical question. But Heidegger has already argued that this move from intentional states that make sense on a background to the background as just more intentional states is illegitimate, since it results in an impoverished account of being-in from which one cannot reconstitute the original phenomenon under investigation.

Proving the existence of the external world, then, presents a problem only when we mistakenly take Dasein as an occurrent substance with experiences and meanings in it and the world as a set of occurrent entities external to the subject. Once we examine everydayness we see that the skeptical question, which Husserl was still asking, does not need to be answered and, moreover, that it violates the conditions for making sense.

The "problem of reality" in the sense of the question whether an external world is occurrent and whether such a world can be proved, turns out to be an impossible one, not because its consequences lead to inextricable impasses, but because the very entity which serves as its theme, is one which, as it were, repudiates any such formulation of the question. (250) [206]

All attempts such as Buber's, and on some readings Stanley Cavell's, to answer skepticism by arguing that a person's relation to the world is not one of knowing but rather of something else like an "I-Thou" relationship, or acknowledgment, or faith, miss the point.

To *have faith* in the reality of the "external world," whether rightly or wrongly; to "*prove*" this reality for it, whether adequately or inadequately; to *presuppose* it, whether explicitly or not—attempts such as these which have not mastered their own basis with full clarity, presuppose a subject which is proximally world*less* or unsure of its world, and which must, at bottom, first assure itself of a world. (250) [206]

Heidegger spells out this critique in a lecture:

Nothing exists in our relationship to the world which provides a basis for the phenomenon of belief in the world. I have not yet been able to find this phenomenon of belief. Rather, the peculiar thing is just that the world is "there" *before* all belief. . . . Inherent in the being of the world is that its existence needs no guarantee in regard to a subject. What is needed, if this question comes up at all, is that Dasein should experience itself in its most elementary being make-up as being-in-the-world. This eliminates the ground for any question of the reality of the world. (HCT, 215, 216)

In concluding this discussion, one cannot help noting that Heidegger never mentions dreams. This is natural in that Heidegger is reacting against the Husserl/Searle tradition in which it is the *self-sufficiency of intentional content,* not the *privacy of experiences,* that leads to skepticism. Thus one can only guess what Heidegger would say about dreams. Following upon the second before last quotation, one might suppose he would claim that, although we can understand what it is for an intentional state to be unsatisfied—for a belief to be false, for example—the idea that all our coping might be an inner state called a dream forgets that absorbed coping does not involve private intentional content or experiences at all. The traditional hypothesis that we might always be dreaming supposes from the start an isolated subject related to objects by way of inner experiences and thus distorts disclosedness.

Heidegger would perhaps admit that while dreams are not given as inner experiences, they are nonetheless experienced as a way of disclosing a world. Then if we dreamed we were coping with public objects and equipment, we would have to describe this not as having an inner stream of private dream experiences, but as an openness to a nonshared world. This does not answer the traditional question but does, as Heidegger would say, repudiate a certain formulation of it. Perhaps it would allow philosophers interested in the question of skepticism to come up with better ways of dealing with dreams.

B. The Ontological Problem of an Independent Reality

The status of the entities supposedly discovered by natural science, and the correlated question of the special authority of science in our culture—a question posed two decades ago by Thomas Kuhn's *The Structure of Scientific Revolutions*—has recently become a central issue of debate. Literary theorists, social scientists, and feminists, each for their own reasons, have found themselves allied with Kuhn in their attack on the special claim of the natural sciences to tell us the truth about objective reality. The literary theorists would like to one-up the sciences by showing that scientific theories are after all just interpretive texts and therefore fall into the domain of the humanities. Similarly, social scientists, by pointing out that scientific truth is a product of shared practices, seek to annex science to the domain of sociology and anthropology. Feminists would also like to undermine the authority of the scientific establishment, which they rightly regard as a bastion of male domination. All these groups would like to believe that natural science is just one more interpretive practice that has somehow conned our culture into thinking that it alone has access to the real. The stakes are high. As Evelyn Fox Keller puts it:

The question of whether scientific knowledge is objective or relative is at least in part a question about the claim of scientists to absolute authority. If there is only one truth, and scientists are privy to it... then the authority of science is unassailable. But if truth is relative, if science is divorced from nature and married instead to culture then the privileged status of that authority is fatally undermined.[1]

There is, indeed, something wrong with our culture's worship of natural science, as if what science tells us about the fundamental particles has fundamental importance for all aspects of life. The success of books like Fritjof Capra's *The Tao of Physics*, which tells us that we can breathe easier because science is no longer atomistic and materialistic but now is holistic and ethereal, shows that many people believe that science tells us the final truth about reality. But the attempt to limit science by denying that it discovers anything at all—as the title of a recent book, *Constructing Quarks*,[2] implies—is clearly an overreaction. It is a non sequitur to claim that because physical theories are developed by means of scientists' practices and the authority of science is constituted by way of other social practices, physics does not discover truths about nature and so has no legitimate authority. This approach only betrays the insecurity and resentment of the humanists, social scientists and feminists. If one wants to undermine the illegitimate authority of natural science, especially physics, in our culture, it would be sufficient to demonstrate that although natural science can tell us the truth about the causal powers of nature, it does not have a special access to ultimate reality. This is exactly what Heidegger attempts to show.

It might at first seem that Heidegger's way of answering skepticism, viz. that we have direct access to objects in our world because, as absorbed openness, we are the shared social world existingly, commits him to the view that we cannot have access to an independent reality—that we can never know the contents of the *universe.* It therefore seems to some interpreters that Heidegger must be an *internal* realist, i.e., that he must hold that there is no "in itself"— that "independent reality" exists only relative to our definition of it. And, indeed, as they would point out, he says:

Only because being is "in consciousness" [note the scare quotes]—that is to say, only because it is understandable in Dasein [i.e., in the activity of Daseining]—can Dasein also understand and conceptualize such characteristics of being as independence, the "in-itself," and reality in general. Only because of this are "independent" entities, as encountered within-the-world, accessible to circumspection. (251, my comments in brackets) [207]

Other interpreters understand Heidegger's phenomenology as a form of instrumentalism holding that scientific entities are social constructions essentially related to human purposes, or a form of operationalism equating scientific entities with their intraworldly effects or measurements. Such antirealists, as Arthur Fine puts it, "accept the behaviorist idea that the working practices of conceptual exchange exhaust the meaning of the exchange, giving it its significance and providing it with its content."[3] But Heidegger never concluded from the fact that our practices are necessary for *access* to theoretical entities that these entities must be *defined in terms of* our access practices.

I shall try to show that in *Being and Time* Heidegger is what one might call a minimal hermeneutic realist about nature and the objects of natural science, and that he remains such in his later work, even when he becomes severely critical of the understanding of being underlying scientific research and technology.

To begin with, Heidegger is not an instrumentalist. Unlike the pragmatists, Heidegger accepts the Greek view that human beings are capable of getting into a mood of pure equanimity and wonder in which they can form theories that do not have any necessary relation to their needs and purposes. In his course on Kant, contemporaneous with the publication of *Being and Time*, Heidegger offers the following description of scientific discipline (*Wissenschaft*):

Scientific knowing presupposes that existing Dasein takes as a freely chosen task the revealing of the entity it approaches *for the sake of revealing it*. . . . Thereby are discontinued all behavioral goals which aim at the application of the uncovered and known; and all those boundaries fall away that confine the investigation within planned technical purposes— the struggle is solely directed to the entity itself and solely in order to free it from its hiddenness and precisely thereby to help it into what is proper to it, i.e., to let it be the entity which it is in itself.[4]

Heidegger remained an anti-instrumentalist in this sense all his life. In 1954 he writes: "Even where, as in modern atomic physics, theory—for essential reasons—necessarily becomes the opposite of direct viewing, its aim is to make atoms exhibit themselves for sensory perception, even if this self-exhibiting of elementary particles happens only very indirectly and in a way that technically involves a multiplicity of intermediaries."[5]

To understand Heidegger's position, it helps to compare it to a view recently defended by Fine. Fine starts with the observation that the scientist "believes in the existence of those entities to which his theories refer."[6] He calls this the Natural Ontological Attitude (NOA). In this attitude, he tells us, one "accepts the evidence of one's senses [with regard to the existence and features of everyday objects] and . . . accept[s], *in the same way*, the confirmed results of science."[7] He then adds:

NOA helps us to see that realism differs from various antirealisms in this way: realism adds an *outer* direction to NOA, that is, the external world and the correspondence relation of approximate truth; antirealisms add an *inner* direction, that is, human-oriented reductions of truth, or concepts, or explanations. NOA suggests that the legitimate features of these additions are already contained in the presumed equal status of everyday truths with scientific ones, and in our accepting them both as *truths*. No other additions are legitimate, and none are required.[8]

Heidegger, like Fine, wants to remain true to the understanding in scientific background practices. Let us call this view hermeneutic realism. Hermeneutic realists hold that a science's background realism cannot be used to *justify* the claim that the objects of science exist independently of the activity of the scientists, nor can this understanding *dictate* what structure the science's objects must have. And as one would expect, Heidegger does not give arguments to convince us that science is converging on the truth about nature. Rather, he (1) spells out what everyday scientific practices take for granted, namely that there is a nature in itself, and that science can give us a better and better explanation of how that nature works, and (2) seeks to show that this self-understanding of modern science is both internally coherent and compatible with the ontological implications of our everyday practices.

According to the hermeneutic realist, natural science's background realism is compatible with neither metaphysical realism nor antirealism. Scientists work within social practices that neither they nor philosophers can transcend, and so science cannot justify a metaphysical realism claiming to have an *independent argument* that nature has the structure science finds and that science is converging on the one true account of this independent reality. Yet scientists suppose they *can* discover the truth about nature as it is, independent of scientific practices, and so antirealism in the form of metaphysical idealism or of instrumentalism is also unacceptable.

In *Basic Problems* Heidegger makes an ontological place for the realistic view that besides the way nature shows up in our world there is a way nature is in itself whether or not Dasein exists.

An example of an intraworldly entity is nature. It is indifferent in this connection how far nature is or is not scientifically uncovered, indifferent whether we think this being in a theoretical, physico-chemical way or think of it in the sense in which we speak of "nature out there," hill, woods, meadow . . . . Nonetheless, intraworldliness does not belong to nature's being. Rather, in commerce with this being, nature in the broadest sense, we understand that this being is as something occurrent . . . which on its own part always already is. It is, even if we do not uncover it, without our encountering it within our world. Being within the world *devolves upon* this being, nature, solely when it is *uncovered* as a being. (BP, 168–169)

Heidegger's hermeneutic realism concerning natural entities such as trees and dinosaurs, and presumably even quarks, is also evident in *Being and Time.*

Entities *are*, quite independently of the experience by which they are disclosed, the acquaintance in which they are discovered, and the grasping in which their nature is ascertained. (228)[183]

But this passage continues: "being 'is' only in the understanding of those entities to whose being something like an understanding of being belongs" (228)[183]. It seems that while natural entities are independent of us, *the being of nature* depends upon us.

It must be stated that the entity as an entity is "in itself" and independent of any apprehension of it; yet, the being of the entity is found only in encounter and can be explained, made understandable, only from the phenomenal exhibition and interpretation of the structure of encounter. (HCT, 217)

The basic point Heidegger wants to make—that nature *is* in itself and yet it is illegitimate to ask about "being" in itself—is summed up in two paradoxical propositions in a later lecture course:

(1) Beings are in themselves the kinds of entities they are, and in the way they are, even if . . . Dasein does not exist. (2) Being "is" not, but there is being, insofar as Dasein exists. (MFL, 153)

Getting this point sorted out requires getting clear about how Heidegger is using his terms. Only Dasein makes sense of things. So the intelligibility of each domain of things, or the understanding of the way of being of each, including that of natural things, depends upon Dasein. But nature as *a* being, or as a set of beings, does not depend on us, for one way Dasein can make sense of things—find them intelligible—is as occurrent, i.e., as not related to our everyday practices. As Heidegger says succinctly: "The cosmos can be without human beings inhabiting the earth, and the cosmos was long before human beings ever existed" (MFL, 169).

Occurrent beings are revealed when Dasein takes a detached attitude towards things and decontextualizes them—in Heidegger's terms, deworlds them. Then things show up as independent of human purposes and even of human existence. As we have seen, deworlding takes place in two stages. First we use skills and instruments to decontextualize things and their properties, which then appear as meaningless objects, colors, shapes, sounds, etc. Such data are independent of our for-the-sake-of-whichs but not independent of our senses. We then invent theories in which the occurrent data are taken as evidence for quasars and quarks and other entities we cannot directly experience. These theoretical entities need not conform at all to our everyday understanding of objects, space, time, and causality. Yet, our theory tells us that these entities belong to natural kinds—types of things in nature like water, gold, iron, etc.—and if correct, the theory describes the occurrent causal powers of these natural kinds. There is no way to stand outside current science and give it metaphysical support by arguing that there must be natural kinds or that these are what our science must be about. All that hermeneutic phenomenology can do is show the coherence of the natural scientist's background "assumption" that science can discover the way nature is in itself.

Of course, this understanding is achieved by human beings. If it were not for Dasein as a clearing in which entities could be encountered, the question of whether there could be entities independent of Dasein could not be asked, and more important, without Dasein's giving meaning to the occurrent way of being, the question would not even make sense. But since human beings do exist and have an understanding of occurrentness as a way of being, we can make sense of the questions, What was here *before we started to exist?* and even What would be left of nature *if Dasein ceased to exist?*

But of course we must ask these questions from within that understanding of being that alone gives sense to the questions. We cannot meaningfully ask, What would have been occurrent if Dasein *had never existed?* if by that we mean, What would have been the case if the above question made no sense? That would be to treat being—intelligibility—as if it were in itself. When Heidegger considers this move, he warns:

Of course only as long as Dasein is (that is, only as long as an understanding of being is ontically possible), "is there" being. When Dasein does not exist, "independence" "is" not either, nor "is" the "in-itself." (255) [212]

There is no intelligibility in itself. We cannot ask whether things were intelligible before we were around, or if they would go on being intelligible if we ceased to exist. Intelligibility is not a property of things; it is relative to Dasein. When Dasein does not exist, things are neither intelligible nor unintelligible. If Dasein does not exist, things are not revealed as anything, even as occurrent.

In such a case it cannot be said that entities are, nor can it be said that they are not. But *now*, as long as there is an understanding of being and therefore an understanding of occurrentness, it can indeed be said that *in this case* entities will still continue to be [i.e., to be occurrent]. (255) [212]

Since we do exist and make sense of entities as occurrent, we make sense of things as being independent of us, even though this mode of intelligibility, i.e., this way of being, like any other depends on us.

If we encountered entities only in using them, never in detachedly reflecting on them, so that availableness and unavailableness were the only ways of being we knew, we would not be able to make the notion of entities in themselves intelligible. But since we understand occurrentness, we can understand that occurrent entities would have been even if Dasein had never existed. Indeed, given our understanding of occurrentness, we must understand things this way. For example, what it is to be a hammer essentially depends upon Dasein and its cultural artifacts. As we have seen, to be a hammer is to be used to pound in nails for building houses, etc. For a culture that always tied things together, there could be no hammers because there would be nothing that it was to be a hammer. But there could, nonetheless, be pieces of wood with iron blobs on the end, since wood and iron are natural kinds and their being and causal powers make no essential reference to any in-order-tos or for-the-sake-of-whichs. Iron and wood are not here in order to do anything. Dasein can detach itself from its concerns and so can reveal entities that exist independently of us. In short, making sense of independent reality is something that we do, but what there really is does not depend on us:

> The fact that reality is ontologically grounded in the being of Dasein, does not signify that only when Dasein exists and as long as Dasein exists, can the real be as that which in itself it is. (255) [212]

In the years immediately following the publication of *Being and Time*, Heidegger made it clear that the "evidence" that there is a nature independent of us is provided not by natural science but by anxiety. Joseph Fell points out that in a footnote in *The Essence of Reasons*, Heidegger claims that "Nature is primordially manifest in Dasein because Dasein exists as attuned and affected in the midst of beings," and in *What Is Metaphysics?*, he adds that anxiety "discloses beings in their full but heretofore concealed strangeness as the pure other."[9]

Such pronouncements must have been taken to be reminiscent of Fichte, according to whom the ego *posits* nature as its pure other, so in his book on Schelling, Heidegger therefore feels called upon to repudiate the idea that pure otherness is a meaning given by Dasein.

> *Being and Time* has also among other things been equated with Fichte's basic position and interpreted by it, whereas if there is any possibility of comparison at all here, the most extreme opposition is dominant. But "opposition" is already false since the thinking in *Being and Time* is not just "realistic" in contrast to the unconditional "egoistic" idealism of Fichte. . . . According to Fichte, the ego throws forth the world . . . according to *Being and Time* . . . Dasein is the thrown.[10]

Dasein is presumably thrown into nature, but the nature Dasein is thrown into need not be thought of as an unstructured, viscous being-in-itself as in Sartre. Anxiety reveals nature as pure otherness, but this does not imply that nature has no ontic structure.

Still, there is a further problem that makes Heidegger seem to be, if not a Fichtian then at least a Kantian idealist. Since time, understood as a sequence of nows, before and after some present now, depends upon Dasein's temporality, it might seem to follow that nature cannot be in time. Heidegger seems to assert as much when he says, "There is no nature-time, since all time belongs essentially to Dasein" (BP, 262). And he repeats this claim as late as 1935:

Strictly speaking we cannot say: There was a time when man *was* not. At all *times* man was and is and will be, because time temporalizes itself only insofar as man is.[11]

This, however, still leaves open the possibility that, just as in the case of spatiality, "the homogeneous space of nature shows itself only when the entities we encounter are discovered in such a way that the worldly character of the available gets specifically deprived of its worldliness" (147) [112]; when temporality is detemporalized, a pure sequence of natural events would be revealed. In his discussion of space, Heidegger adds:

The fact that space essentially shows itself in a world is not yet decisive for the kind of being which it possesses. It need not have the kind of being characteristic of something which is itself spatially available or occurrent. (147) [112]

Likewise natural time need not even be occurrent, yet some sort of pure sequential ordering of events might well remain. Only this would allow us to make sense of what Heidegger calls the Cosmos and of a nature in itself revealed by science. Perhaps these unresolved tensions were troubling Heidegger when he said in a 1929 lecture:

The question of the extent to which one might conceive the interpretation of Dasein as temporality in a universal-ontological way is a question which I am myself not able to decide—one which is still completely unclear to me. (MFL, 210)

Whatever Heidegger's answer, it must not contradict his claim that natural kinds do not depend for their structure upon the world or upon human temporality. As Heidegger says in *Basic Problems*:

Occurrent things are . . . the kinds of things they are, even if they do not become intraworldly, even if world-entry does not happen to them and there is no occasion for it at all. Intraworldliness does not belong to the essence of the occurrent things as such, but it is only the transcendental condition, in the primordial sense, for the possibility of occurrent things being able to emerge as they are. (BP, 194)

After all, we do know substantive facts about nature. We know that dinosaurs existed, that they were animals, that some were vegetarians, etc. That is why Heidegger calls nature "the cosmos" and not "X" or the thing in itself.

If it allows a sequence of natural events, Heidegger's account is compatible with holding that science is converging on getting it right about natural kinds like iron and water and their causal powers. If these kinds of things turn out not to have the properties predicted and the natural kind terms referring to them have to be dropped from the lexicon of science like phlogiston was, then some other system of natural kind terms might, in principle, still be found that do refer to the natural kinds there really are, although, of course, we could never know for certain that we had the final account.

But even though Heidegger presumably thinks that physical science is progressing in its understanding of physical nature, he does not think that this shows that the scientific approach to reality is the only right one, or even that physical science has the only right approach to nature. In his lectures of 1928 he remarks:

Beings have stages of discoverability, diverse possibilities in which they manifest themselves in themselves. . . . One cannot say that, for example, physics has the genuine knowledge of the solar sphere, in contrast to our natural grasp of the sun.[12]

Thus, even if Heidegger's view is compatible with realism concerning the entities studied by science, he is not and could never be counted a physicalist, reductionist, or materialist. As we have seen, he argues at length in Sections 19, 20, and 21 that worldliness cannot be understood in terms of the occurrent, and that therefore the occurrent, even recontextualized in a successful science of nature, cannot provide the fundamental building blocks of reality. A theory of the physical causal powers of natural kinds tells us only what is *causally* real, it cannot account for Dasein's ability to deal with entities in various ways and so make intelligible various ways of being, thereby disclosing various beings including the entities described by physical science. Thus science cannot be a theory of *ultimate* reality. This is Heidegger's reason for rejecting *metaphysical* realism. "Realism tries to explain reality ontically by real connections of interaction between things that are real.... [But] being can never be explained by entities but is already that which is 'transcendental' for every entity" (251) [207–208]. Thus he can say:

If we consider the work of Descartes in relation to the constitution of the mathematical sciences of nature and to the elaboration of mathematical physics in particular, these considerations then naturally assume a fundamentally positive significance. But if they are regarded in the context of a general theory of the reality of the world, it then becomes apparent that from this point on the fateful constriction of the inquiry into reality sets in, which to the present day has not yet been overcome. (HCT, 184–185)

Heidegger further holds that modern scientific projection is not even the only way of understanding nature. If, like Aristotle, one wants to relate a wide variety of phenomena rather than to predict and control them, one may reveal final causes rather than the sort of causal powers discovered by modern physics. Thus there may be only one right answer to the search for *physical* causes, but many different projections can reveal nature as it is in itself.

What is represented by physics is indeed nature itself, but undeniably it is only nature as the object-area, whose objectness is first defined and determined through the refining that is characteristic of physics and is expressly set forth in that refining. Nature, in its objectness for modern physical science, is only *one* way in which what presences—which from of old has been named *physis*—reveals itself.[13]

Heidegger would thus deny that modern physics has found the right vocabulary for describing nature and that its vocabulary could be used for a foundational ontology. This, I presume, is the meaning of his Kuhn-like remark in 1938:

[We cannot] say that the Galilean doctrine of freely falling bodies is true and that Aristotle's teaching, that light bodies strive upward, is false; for the Greek understanding of the essence of body and place and of the relation between the two rests upon a different interpretation of entities and hence conditions a correspondingly different kind of seeing and questioning of natural events. No one would presume to maintain that Shakespeare's poetry is more advanced than that of Aeschylus. It is still more impossible to say that the modern understanding of whatever is, is more correct than that of the Greeks.[14]

Here Heidegger is obviously trying to counter the view that Galileo has refuted Aristotle. He is doing so not by holding that neither theory is true of nature (as Kuhn does), but rather by holding that both are true. This could be the innocuous claim that both are "illuminating," but in the context of the claim just quoted that "what is represented by physics is indeed nature itself," it must be the stronger claim that different theories can reveal different aspects of nature. Of course, if one thinks of Aristotle's theory of natural place as an account of physical causality meant to explain, for example, why rocks fall, in the same sense that modern physics claims to explain the same phenomenon, this position is untenable. In that case modern physics, as far as we know, would be right and Aristotle would simply be wrong. Heidegger, however, clearly holds that Aristotle and Galileo were asking *different kinds of questions*, and so could each be right about a different aspect of nature.

If one is interested neither in physical causality nor in final causes, but prefers to recontextualize the occurrent in a theory about the cosmic mind, that might be true too. It would not give one control of nature or a way of finding one's interests reflected in the cosmos, but it might give one enlightenment. Likewise, if one does not want to base one's account of ultimate reality on man's ability to decontextualize, but, like the Navajo, one is able to see the everyday world as sacred or full of gods (as long as these are not thought of as having physical powers), that might well allow sacred beings to show up.[15] Physics does not show Buddhism or the Navajo to be wrong, nor does it contradict Christianity. It can have no view on the ultimate meaning of reality. The ultimate *physical* power might well reside in quarks but the ultimate *saving* power, for example, might be the Christ. The physical powers of iron are essential for making effective hammers, but they are irrelevant when it comes to making powerful crucifixes.[16]

As noted in the introduction to this commentary, what counts as real for a culture depends upon the interpretation in its practices. We must now add that this does not make what is thus understood any less real. Where ultimate reality is concerned, later Heidegger could be called a *plural realist*. For a plural realist there is no point of view from which one can ask and answer the metaphysical question concerning the one true nature of ultimate reality. Given the dependence of the intelligibility of all ways of being on Dasein's being, and the dependence of what counts as elements of reality on our purposes the question makes no sense.[17] Indeed, since reality is relative to finite Dasein, there can be many true answers to the question, What is real? Heidegger looks like an idealist or a relativist only if one thinks that only one system of description could correspond to the way things really are. But for Heidegger different understandings of being reveal different sorts of entities, and since no one way of revealing is exclusively true, accepting one does not commit us to rejecting the others. There is a deep similarity between Heidegger and Donald Davidson on this point. Both would agree that we can make reality intelligible using various descriptions and that what our claims are true of under a given description has whatever properties it has even if these descriptions are not reducible to a single description, and whether we describers and our ways of describing things exist or not.[18]

Just as different cultural practices free different aspects of nature, so they free different sorts of cultural entities. Such historical entities have their own ontological status. Their way of being is not the deworlded being of the occurrent.

> There are entities . . . to whose being intraworldliness belongs in a certain way. Such entities are all those we call *historical* entities—historical in the broader sense of world-historical, all the things that the human being, who is historical and exists historically in the strict and proper sense, creates, shapes, cultivates: all his culture and works. Beings of this kind *are* only or, more exactly, arise only and come into being only *as* intraworldly. Culture *is* not in the way that nature is. (BP, 169)

Of course, not just any cultural interpretation will disclose entities. If, instead of encountering heroes or saints, a culture begins to develop practices for encountering aliens that are round and give out beams of light, it may well be that nothing at all will show up. But there are no clear limits as to what kinds of cultural entities can be encountered. In physical science, however, there seems to be one right answer as far as physical causality is concerned. Theoretical projections radically different from those proposed by modern physics would presumably not reveal physical causal powers. Heidegger notes this difference between a cultural interpretation and a scientific projection.

> The spiritual . . . offers less resistance than in the field of natural science, where nature immediately takes its revenge on a wrongheaded approach. (HCT, 203)

This sentence suggests how Heidegger would respond to scientific relativists like Rorty who scoff at the idea of a science's learning nature's own language. Granted that we can never completely decontextualize our data, and that therefore our scientific theories are always to some extent parasitical upon our cultural practices and language, still, once we discover that we have practices that can reveal meaningless occurrent data divorced from reference to our purposes, we can use recontextualization in theories to distance our scientific theories further and further from the everyday world. Our Newtonian theories seemed to reveal a universe similar to our everyday experience of occurrent space and time, but our interaction with nature has led us to replace these theories with relativistic and quantum indeterministic theories. It is as if nature *is* teaching the natural scientist, not *nature's own language*, since only a Platonist thinks that representations exist independently of meaningful practices, but rather nature is leading natural scientists to improve *their* language for representing her under one aspect.

In any case, once we have established what counts as real we must still find out what specific things there are. The Greeks stood in awe of the gods their practices revealed, and we have to *discover* the elementary particles—we do not construct them. Our understanding of being establishes what can count as a fact in whatever domain, but it does not determine what the facts are. As Heidegger says:

Being (not beings) is dependent upon the understanding of being; that is to say, reality (not the real) is dependent upon care [i.e., Dasein]. (255, my gloss in brackets) [212]

Heidegger thus holds a subtle and plausible position beyond metaphysical realism and antirealism. *Nature* is whatever it is and has whatever causal properties it has independently of us. Different questions, such as Aristotle's and Galileo's, reveal different natural kinds and different kinds of causal properties. Different cultural interpretations of reality reveal different aspects of the real too. But there is no right answer to the question, What is the ultimate reality in terms of which everything else becomes intelligible? The only answer to this metaphysical question is that Dasein, the being whose being is an issue for it, is the being in terms of whose practices all aspects of the real show up, because it is the source of sense, i.e., of the understanding of being and reality.

It is helpful to compare Heidegger and Rorty here, since they seem to be very close on this point. Both argue that the real can show up differently given different practices (vocabularies, Rorty would say) for giving meaning, and neither wants to allow that there is a way that ultimate reality is in itself—that there is a privileged description that founds all the others. Anyone who claims to have a description of ultimate reality claims a point of view outside of all particular, finite interpretations, and both Heidegger and Rorty think, given their understanding of understanding, that the very idea of such an interpretation-free understanding of what ultimately is does not make sense. But Rorty seems to think that this is an argument against minimal hermeneutic realism, whereas I (and Heidegger too, I have argued) would say, on the contrary, that one can reject the claim that there is *a* correct description of reality and still hold that there can be *many* correct descriptions, including a correct causal description of objectified physical nature.

III. Truth

The question of reality leads directly to the question of truth. Heidegger relates the two as follows:

Does it depend on the existence of Dasein whether there is or is not being? [As we have just seen, the answer is "yes."] [Even if] so, this does not . . . affirm that whether there are or are not beings, for example nature, depends on the existence of Dasein. The manner in which being is and can alone be given does not prejudice the case regarding whether and how beings are qua beings.

The problem becomes concentrated into the question, How is the existence of truth related to being and to the manner in which there is being? Are being and truth essentially related to each other? . . . Is it the case that a being, so far as it is, is independent of the truth about it, but that truth exists only when Dasein exists. . . ? (BP, 222–223, my gloss in brackets)

Heidegger's answer to the last question will be "yes." That is, Heidegger is once again prepared to make his basic move: just as, in the case of occurrentness, reality and being depend on Dasein's practices but the real and beings do not, so truth is dependent on Dasein but not what the truth is true of.

Truth has traditionally been thought of as the *correspondence* between the propositional content of either mental states or assertions, and facts in the world. This assumes that truth is simply a occurrent relation between two occurrent sorts of entities: between representations and facts. Heidegger will try to show what the traditional conception got right and what it got wrong. Roughly, truth can, indeed, be the *agreement* of an assertion with an occurrent state of affairs, but such an assertion is not occurrent and the relation between the assertion and the state of affairs is not occurrent either. Assertions and entities "correspond" only under a description, while making descriptions and using assertions presuppose our background familiarity.

A. Criticism of the Tradition

Heidegger first states the traditional view. There are two claims:

(1) that the "locus" of truth is assertion (judgment); (2) that the essence of truth lies in the "agreement" of the judgment with its object. (257) [214]

He then points out that this account is obscure. What is expressed in the assertion—a proposition? And how is such an "ideal content" supposed to relate to a fact?

This relationship pertains to a connection between an ideal content of judgment and the real thing as that which is judged about. . . . How are we to take ontologically the relation between an ideal entity and something that is real and occurrent? (259) [216]

Heidegger then uses his account of everyday coping to reformulate the question faced by those who, like Husserl, claim that the mind must relate to objects by means of intentional content, and that therefore truth must be the correspondence of propositional content and mind-independent object. If everyday coping with the available takes place without intentional content, the question becomes, how do my acts and words pick out things under aspects, and what is it for this directedness—this being-towards—to get things right? Heidegger turns to the phenomenon. We may suppose the carpenters have finished building a house, and the owners are making themselves at home. One of them asserts that the picture on the wall behind her is crooked. How does this assertion work? Not by way of the mediation of some intervening representation (propositional content, internal model, or *noema*).

To say that an assertion "is *true*" signifies that it uncovers the entity as it is in itself. Such an assertion asserts, points out, "lets" the entity "be seen" (*apophansis*) in its discoveredness. The *being-true* (*truth*) of the assertion must be understood as *being-discovering*. Thus truth has by no means the structure of an agreement between knowing and the object in the sense of a likening of one entity (the subject) to another (the object). (261) [218–219]

We must stick to the phenomena:

The asserting . . . is related . . . in that sense which is most its own, to the real picture on the wall. . . . Any Interpretation in which something else is here slipped in as what one supposedly has in mind . . . belies the phenomenal facts of the case. Asserting is a way of being toward the thing itself that is. (260) [217–218]

The assertion is a piece of equipment available for pointing out the picture as being a certain way, as having certain characteristics. If the assertion does its job of calling the other person's attention to the relevant aspect of the situation the assertion functions transparently.

What gets demonstrated is the being-discovering of the assertion. In carrying out such a demonstration, the knowing remains related solely to the entity itself. In this entity the confirmation, as it were, gets enacted. The entity itself which one is getting at shows itself *just as it is in itself*, that is to say, it shows that it, in its selfsameness, is just as it gets pointed out in the assertion as being—just as it gets discovered as being. (261) [218]

Thus Heidegger preserves the commonsense notion of agreement while rejecting the traditional account of this agreement as the correspondence of a subjective mental content with an objective state of affairs. His is a general characterization of truth whether we are pointing out perceived aspects of a hammer, aspects of a picture behind us that we do not currently perceive, or using the kind of pointing out appropriate to science to call attention to properties that show themselves indirectly in the way appropriate to theoretical entities.

How is such a characterization supposed to correct the tradition? The tradition begins by asking how assertions refer. It assumes that

the more exactly we pursue and explain in detail the relationship between noise, sound, word, meaning, thinking, and representing, the more scientific will be our explanation of what is generally called the correspondence of thinking with the object. (MFL, 125)

Husserl is again typical. In the *Logical Investigations* and in all his subsequent works, he held that for sounds or marks to refer to an object they must do so by being related to an ideal, mental entity, which he called a sense (*Sinn*) or *noema*. Heidegger again reverses Husserl's view in a fundamental way. He denies that representations (of conditions of satisfaction) as occurrent mental content can explain how language refers. He agrees with Husserl that for a judgment to relate to an object it must do so by way of sense (*Sinn*), but for Heidegger, in direct opposition to Husserl, sense is the structure of the background of shared practices on the basis of which actions and objects make sense. This is not a question, as Husserl thought, of isolated mental content vs. a holistic network of beliefs. When later Husserl admits that referring must take place on the background of a *network* of *noemata*, the problem of correspondence is merely displaced to the problem of how the whole occurrent network can correspond to the world.

Heidegger objects to the traditional account on three levels. First, he holds that language cannot be explained as meaningless sounds that are then given meaning. Second, he holds that meaningful assertions only have truth condition relative to a background. And third, he holds that referring itself is a social practice. As we shall see, these views lead him to conclude that

being-true as being-uncovering, is . . . ontologically possible only on the basis of being-in-the-world. This latter phenomenon, which we have known as a basic make-up of Dasein, is the foundation for the primordial phenomenon of truth. (261) [219]

Heidegger holds that there is no way to account for referring and truth starting with language as occurrent sounds coupled with occurrent representations. We saw in chapter 11 that Heidegger thinks that all sounds, from motorcycle roars to words, are directly experienced as meaningful. So if we stick close to the phenomenon we dissolve the Husserl/Searle problem of how to give meaning to mere noises, so that we can then refer by means of linguistic representations.

Does beginning with the phonetic articulation [what Searle calls the acoustic blast] . . . grasp what immediately presents itself to us? In no way. Suppose someone here in the classroom states the proposition "the board is black" and does so in an immediately given context. . . . To what do we then attend in understanding the statement? To the phonetic articulation? Or to the representation that carries out the making of the statement and for which then the sounds uttered are "signs"? No, rather we direct ourselves to the blackboard itself, here on the wall! In the perception of this board, in making present and thinking about the blackboard and nothing else, we participate in the performance of the statement. . . . The point of departure for every genuine clarification of a phenomenon lies in first grasping and holding onto what presents itself. (MFL, 125–126, my gloss in brackets)

But more is required than meaningful sounds to account for how meaningful utterances can refer. Only if we draw on the background familiarity that is not in the mind but in the shared practices can we understand how assertions can pick out objects.

A first consequence is that making statements . . . is not at all a primordial relation to entities but is itself only possible on the basis of our already-being-among-entities, be this a perceptual or some kind of practical comportment. We can say that making statements about X is only possible on the basis of *having to do with X.* (MFL, 126)

On this point Searle would agree with Heidegger. In his essay "Literal Meaning," Searle argues that even seemingly straightforward assertions such as "the cat is on the mat" do not have truth conditions in isolation.[19] What counts as the cat being on the mat would be different under conditions of weightlessness in space and even in certain situations on earth. The assertion can be true only once something can be described as the cat being on the mat, and that requires shared background practices. It follows that assertions do not determine truth conditions by virtue of their propositional content alone.

An assertion can finally be true, be adequate in propositional content to that about which the statement is made, only because the being it speaks of is already in some way disclosed. That is, a statement about X is only true because our dealing with that X has already a certain kind of truth. (MFL, 127)

Propositional truth is . . . rooted in already-being-amidst-things. The latter occurs "already," before making statements—since when? Always already! Always, that is, insofar as and as long as Dasein exists. Already being with things belongs to the existence of Dasein. (MLF, 127)

Only the shared background of common coping practices, not private entities in monadic minds, makes reference possible.

But this still does not tell us how assertions work. Is the referring relation one of correspondence, i.e., is the relation itself occurrent? Heidegger's answer is "no." Language is a complex piece of equipment, and assertions are like pointers:

The assertion expressed is something available, and indeed in such a way that, as something by which discoveredness is preserved, it has in itself a relation to the entities discovered. (267) [224]

Referring is a shared social skill, and Dasein is socialized into this practice of pointing. We can either stop with this claim and do empirical work in developmental psychology to find out how people get socialized into a practice, or we can attempt to lay out the general structure of the phenomenon. Heidegger, of course, chooses the latter approach.

B. Primordial Truth and Ordinary Truth

As we would expect, Heidegger takes up truth both on the level of originary transcendence or *primordial truth*—the clearing that makes truth claims possible—and on the level of the truth of particular acts of pointing out, *ontic transcendence.* In other words, he takes up truth as *disclosedness* and truth as *discoveredness,* i.e., as a way of being-towards. For Heidegger, each is a kind of truth because it is a step in bringing things out of concealment into the open—first by opening up a world and then by pointing out things in it. Thus Heidegger connects his conception of truth with the Greek term for truth, *aletheia,* which, he claims, means unforgetting (think of the river of forgetfulness, Lethe, and a negative prefix like the "a" in amoral). *Aletheia* means "taking entities out of their hiddenness and letting them be seen in their unhiddenness (their discoveredness)" (262) [219].

1. Primordial Truth as Disclosedness

Everyday discovery points out particular entities, but this nonrepresentational intentionality presupposes a more primordial intentionality.

Our analysis takes its departure from the traditional conception of truth, and attempts to lay bare the ontological foundations of that conception. . . . In terms of these foundations the primordial phenomenon of truth becomes visible. We can then exhibit the way in which the traditional conception of truth has been derived from this phenomenon. (257) [214]

As in his account of the traditional concepts of objects, space, understanding, assertion, and reality, Heidegger proposes to derive the traditional conception of truth from a more primordial, existential condition. And as we have seen, Heidegger often uses the term *"primordial* X" to name that which is *the condition of the possibility of X.* In Division II, Heidegger treats guilt and temporality in this way too. Indeed, in his discussion of primordial temporality he gives this move a name.

If . . . we demonstrate that the "time" which is accessible to Dasein's common sense is *not* primordial, but arises rather from authentic temporality, then, in accordance with the principle, "*a potiori fit denominatio,*" we are justified in designating as "*primordial time*" the *temporality* which we have now laid bare. (377) [329]

Here Heidegger makes the same move with respect to truth:

What makes this very discovery possible must necessarily be called "true" in a still more primordial sense. The most primordial phenomenon of truth is first shown by the existential-ontological foundations of discovering. . . . Being-true as being-discovering, is a way of being for Dasein. (263) [220]

Being-discovering is another name for Dasein's disclosing—the opening of a shared clearing, a local situation, a "there" in which objects can be encountered:

Our earlier analysis of the worldliness of the world and of intraworldly entities has shown . . . that the discoveredness of intraworldly entities is grounded in the world's disclosedness. But disclosedness is that basic character of Dasein according to which it is its "there." Disclosedness is constituted by affectedness, understanding, and telling, and pertains equiprimordially to the world, to being-in, and to the self. . . . Hence only with Dasein's disclosedness is the most primordial phenomenon of truth attained. (263) [220–221]

Things can be discovered because Dasein is fundamentally the activity of disclosing.

Assertion is not the primary "locus" of truth. On the contrary . . . assertion is grounded in Dasein's discovering, or rather in its disclosedness. The most primordial "truth" is the "locus" of assertion; it is *the ontological condition for the possibility* that assertions can be either true or false—that they may discover or cover things up. (269, my italics) [226]

Circumspective concern, or even that concern in which we tarry and look at something, discovers intraworldly entities. These entities become that which has been discovered. They are "true" in a second sense. What is primarily "true"—that is, discovering—is Dasein. (263) [220]

2. Derivation of Truth as Agreement of an Assertion with a State of Affairs

One now wants to know how Dasein legitimately moves step by step from context-dependent pointing out, where language functions as a pointer on the background of shared skills and a shared situation, to the theorist's use of theoretical assertions to point out decontextualized objects and events. That is, one wants a derivation of the possibility of agreement between theoretical assertions and objective states of affairs.

Our insight into these principles will not be complete until it can be shown: (1) that truth, understood as agreement, originates from disclosedness by way of a definite modification; (2) that the kind of being which belongs to disclosedness itself is such that its derivative modification . . . leads the way for the theoretical explication of the structure of truth. (265–266) [223]

Heidegger now takes up the decontextualizing of assertions and their objects:

The assertion is something available. The intraworldly entities to which it is related as something that discovers, are either available or occurrent. The relation itself presents itself thus, as one that is occurrent. (267) [224]

This leads to the misinterpretation of this relation by the tradition:

The relation itself now acquires the character of occurrentness by getting switched over to a relationship between things which are occurrent. The discoveredness of something becomes the occurrent conformity of one thing which is occurrent—the assertion expressed—*to* something else which is occurrent—the entity under discussion. (267) [224]

Thus arises the traditional theory that understands truth as the correspondence between self-sufficient propositions and uninterpreted facts. But such a correspondence is impossible for, as we have just seen, agreement presupposes shared practices for pointing out as well as the basic disclosedness that makes it possible for something to show up as something in the first place.

Assertion and its structure (namely, the apophantical "as") are founded upon interpretation and its structure (namely, the hermeneutical "as") and also upon understanding—upon Dasein's disclosedness. . . . Thus the roots of the truth of assertion reach back to the disclosedness of the understanding. (266) [223]

Once one sees that truth requires that things be disclosed and that practitioners share a skill for using assertions to point them out, there is nothing more that needs to be explained. But traditional ontology passes over the role of the shared background practices and starts with correspondence as an isolated relation.

That which is last in the order of the way things are connected in their foundations existentially and ontologically, is regarded ontically and factically as that which is first and closest to us. (268)[225]

When one thus ignores the background, one arrives at occurrent relata and an occurrent relation, and agreement becomes a philosophical *problem*. It looks like one needs a *theory* of the relation between representation and represented. The resulting correspondence theory, no matter what its details, is not legitimate in some domain but illegitimate in others, as one might expect Heidegger to hold on analogy with his account of science; rather, the correspondence theory is illuminating in one respect but distorted in another. That is, truth is, indeed, a matter of agreement between some sort of representing (even if it be pointing) and an object, and if the representing is done by a theoretical assertion, the assertion is, indeed, related to an occurrent object. But the relation itself can never be purely occurrent. It gets its meaning and its ability to refer by being embedded in a set of shared practices—practices that make meaning and reference possible as long as the practitioners dwell in them.

We can make scientific theories that point things out as they are in themselves, but we can do so only by dwelling in practices in a way that defies theory. Thus one does not need and cannot have a *theory* of truth. When Heidegger says: "In so far as Dasein *is* its disclosedness essentially, and discloses and discovers as something disclosed, to this extent it is essentially 'true.' *Dasein is 'in the truth.'*" (263)[221], he means that once the background practices are in place agreement is unproblematic, but one cannot give a detached, objective, theoretical account of our dwelling in the background practices.

C. Primordial Untruth

Now Heidegger turns to the problem of untruth. If we are in the truth, i.e., if we are socialized into practices that enable us to use assertions to point things out as they are in themselves, how is it that we sometimes make false assertions? What is the source of untruth?

Heidegger has a commonsense account of the possibility of ontic untruth and an existentialist account of the necessity of ontological untruth. Everyday untruth is possible because assertions are a special sort of equipment. They can be used to point not only to states of affairs that are right in front of us in the situation but to states of affairs behind us, like the picture's being crooked, and even to states of affairs that are somewhere else or have not yet occurred.

Dasein need not bring itself face to face with entities themselves in an "original" experience; but it nevertheless remains in a being-towards these beings. (266) [224]

But since pointing out is not an immediate access to the object pointed out, our assertions can always fail to agree with reality. In such cases we may use language to point toward something that is not the way we point it out, or not where we point, or even that does not exist at all. This makes untruth possible.

Existential untruth as the opposite of disclosedness would have to be some kind of concealment. Heidegger thinks that existential untruth is not just possible but inevitable. "In its full existential-ontological meaning, the proposition that 'Dasein is in the truth' states equiprimordially that 'Dasein is in untruth'" (265) [222]. Let us see why.

Primordial evidence is for Heidegger experiencing something present just as it is. If, however, we try to stabilize such evidence and preserve it in language beyond the time and place in which it occurs, we lose this primordial relation (see chapter 13). If we are simply interested in pointing out aspects of what is going on, the loss of primordiality poses no problem. But if we have the sort of insight that requires suffering or hard work to attain and that deviates from the general consensus, then, according to Heidegger, the loss of primordiality that comes with fixing the truth in assertions is exploited by the public to level the insight. In such cases the slide from truth to untruth is unavoidable.

The inevitability of leveling suggests an interesting account of originality. Dasein is in the untruth because Dasein normally falls into the world of idle talk—into the generality and banality of the one.

Average understanding . . . will never be able to decide what has been drawn from primordial sources with a struggle and how much is just gossip. The average understanding, moreover, will not want any such distinction, and does not need it, because, of course, it understands everything. (212) [169]

Occasionally, however, someone, by living in anxiety and thus facing his or her authentic condition, comes up with a new insight, a new way of looking at the world. To discover such a new truth, one must begin with conventional opinion, which presents averageness as if it were the whole story. One must, starting from this conventional account, break out of it.

The discovering of anything new is never done on the basis of having something completely hidden, but takes its departure rather from discoveredness in the mode of semblance. Entities look as if . . . That is, they have in a certain way, been discovered already, and yet they are still disguised. . . . Truth (discoveredness) is something that must always first be wrested from entities. (265, first ellipsis in original) [222]

In order to preserve and communicate an original insight, a person must then formulate it in the public language, in "assertions." These "assertions" can be used in a shared context.

This discoveredness is preserved in what is expressed. What is expressed becomes, as it were, something available within-the-world which can be taken up and spoken again. (266) [224]

But this common currency is easily devalued. Used by those who are not in the original situation and who have not undergone the necessary anxiety, the propositions become banalities that cover up rather than reveal the way things are.

Let us consider two examples of how existential truth is discovered and then covered up.

1. Kierkegaard
Kierkegaard, through his experience with Regine, and a great deal of anxious suffering, disclosed a way of seeing commitment implicit in the Bible but long disguised in the romantic view of love as two beautiful people being destined for each other.

Kierkegaard's concept of an "infinite passion" that gives a person his or her identity grew out of his intense personal suffering. It reveals the phenomenon of unconditional commitment in a new way by relating what had previously been considered disparate aspects of existence (temporality, anxiety, individuality, subjectivity, etc.). (See Appendix.)

But, of course, once Kierkegaard formulated his insight, it could be passed along outside his situation. It could, for example, be explained in class. Indeed, a perfect case of Heideggerian leveling to banality actually originated in my Kierkegaard course. I called Kierkegaard's infinite passion a defining relation. Stephen Weed, my teaching assistant, told the press that he had a Kierkegaardian defining relationship with Patty Hearst. The interview was printed and readers found themselves let in on important news, but in a purely privative relation to the phenomenon. They in turn could then pass the word along, ever further from Kierkegaard's original experience. As Heidegger puts it, "In a large measure discoveredness gets appropriated not by one's own discovering, but rather by hearsay of something that has been said" (266) [224].

2. Freud

Freud, in facing his own anxiety, was able to see that (as he put it) when two heterosexuals are in love, four people are involved: the man, his mother, the woman, and her father. He thus broadened our idea of love by uncovering relations among seemingly unconnected facts.

Such an interpretation, like Kierkegaard's, was intensely personal and unstable. When stabilized in assertions, it was at first resisted by the public. But it soon became banalized. In Kierkegaard's time everyone was a Christian. It was this banalization of the original insights of Christianity to which Kierkegaard reacted. Today everyone has an unconscious and makes Freudian slips. That *one* has a "defining relation" or an "Oedipus complex" seems to be simply a matter of asserting a truth that corresponds to the facts.

This slide from the truth of primordial pointing out to the untruth of mere correspondence is, of course, a danger to phenomenology itself.

Whenever a phenomenological concept is drawn from primordial sources, there is a possibility that it may degenerate if communicated in the form of an assertion. It gets understood in an empty way and is thus passed on, losing its indigenous character, and becoming a free-floating thesis. (60–61) [36]

As Heidegger in effect predicted, in the postwar years his existential phenomenology became sloganized into existentialism in just this way.

D. The Status of Truth

Just as reality depends on Dasein while the real does not, so *primordial truth* (disclosure) is a function of Dasein's practical activity in opening up a world, and pointing out particular truths (discovery) is also Dasein's doing, but what Dasein's assertions are true of does not depend on Dasein. Rather, how things are must be discovered in whatever way is appropriate given the practices in each particular domain. When states of affairs are discovered the assertions in which they are expressed point out objects as they are. We can thus make assertions even about remote scientific entities such as quarks and quasars which point out their properties. If Dasein did not exist, however, there would be no background activity, and so no disclosing and pointing out, and so no truth. Just as there is no being (intelligibility) without Dasein, so

"there is" truth only in so far as Dasein *is* and so long as Dasein *is*. Entities are discovered only when Dasein is; and only as long as Dasein is, are they disclosed. Newton's laws, the principle of contradiction, any truth whatever—these are true only as long as Dasein is. Before there was any Dasein, there was no truth; nor will there be any after Dasein is no more. For in such a case truth as disclosedness, discovering, and discoveredness cannot be. (269) [226]

But just as the absence of intelligibility before Dasein arrived on the scene does not mean that things were *un*intelligible, so in the case of truth:

Before Newton's laws were discovered, they were not "true"; it does not follow that they were false, or even that they would become false if ontically no discoveredness were any longer possible. (269) [226]

That is, it does not follow that if Dasein ceased to exist, the entities that our assertions are true of would cease to have the properties we have now discovered them to have. The dependence of truth on Dasein

cannot mean that the entity which is discovered with the unveiled laws was not previously in the way in which it showed itself after the discovering and now is as thus showing itself. Discoveredness, truth, unveils an entity precisely as that which it already was beforehand regardless of its discoveredness and nondiscoveredness. As a discovered being, it becomes intelligible as that which is just how it is and will be, regardless of every possible discoveredness of itself. For nature to be as it is, it does not need truth, unveiledness. (BP, 220)

Heidegger clearly is no Platonist. The agreement of assertions with states of affairs requires that the states of affairs be described or interpreted and requires the shared practices that make possible meaning and pointing out. Therefore truth cannot be an abstract, timeless relation of correspondence between propositions and facts:

Even the "universal validity" of truth is rooted solely in the fact that Dasein can discover entities in themselves and free them. (270) [227]

That there may be *eternal truths* will remain an arbitrary assumption and affirmation just so long as it is not demonstrated with absolute evidence that from all eternity and for all eternity something like a human Dasein exists, which can by its own ontological makeup unveil entities and appropriate them to itself as unveiled. (BP, 221, my italics)

But Heidegger is not a conventionalist either. The practices that make possible agreement between assertions and states of affairs under some description are not up to us—we are thrown into them. Moreover, what shows up depends on what entities there in fact are. Thus truth is not subjective:

If one Interprets "subjective" as "left to the subject's discretion," then [truth] certainly [is] not. For discovering, in the sense which is most its own, takes asserting out of the province of "subjective" discretion, and brings the discovering Dasein face to face with the entities themselves. (270) [227]

When Newton's laws become true, their content points out conditions in the universe totally independent of Dasein and its practices. And what they point out is as it is for all time and all places whether they point it out or not.

Through Newton the laws became true; and with them, entities became accessible in themselves to Dasein. Once entities have been discovered, they show themselves precisely as entities which beforehand already were. Such discovering is the kind of being which belongs to "truth." (269) [227]

Or, to take another example, "The content intended in the true proposition '2 times 2 = 4' can subsist through all eternity without there existing any truth about it" (BP, 220–221).

To sum up, as in the case of being (which depends on Dasein) and nature (which does not), truth as the revealing that results from using assertions to point things out depends on Dasein, while what an assertion is true of can be independent of Dasein.

Heidegger's emphasis on truth-determining practices is remarkably similar to Kuhn's in *The Structure of Scientific Revolutions*, but they draw opposed conclusions from their shared insights. For Kuhn, once one sees that the background practices determine what counts as true, since truth must be relative to current scientific practices, there can be no truth about how things are in themselves. Kuhn argues persuasively in his Sherman lectures that a given scientific lexicon of natural kind terms determines what can count as true, so that for Aristotle, for example, it was true that the sun was a planet and that there could not be a void, while for us Aristotle's assertions are neither true nor false because "planet" and "void" have different meanings in the lexicon of modern science. In general, the assertions picking out the sort of things taken to exist at each stage of a science can be true at that stage, but are neither true nor false at some other stage in some other system of terms. Kuhn concludes that assertions can never be true of things as they are in themselves.

Heidegger would, I think, agree with Kuhn's elegant argument that true statements in science can be made only relative to a lexicon. But the strong claim that no lexicon can be true or false of physical reality does not follow from the fact of incommensurate lexicons. Nor does it follow from the fact that our practices are a primordial form of truth that makes truth as agreement possible. Indeed, it conflicts with this view. It follows from Heidegger's account that several incompatible lexicons can be true, i.e., reveal how things are in themselves. Specifically, it follows from Heidegger's account that, although truth depends on Dasein's practices, among which is the linguistic practice of using incommensurate scientific lexicons, a *whole lexicon* can be true and another false depending upon whether a given set of natural kind terms actually picks out the sort of natural kinds it claims to pick out. As we learn more about the stars and the sun, sorting these bodies into the same category (star) makes more scientific sense—reveals more causal powers—than Aristotle's classification of the sun with the planets. Thus, insofar as it includes claims about physical causality, we should reject Aristotle's classification.

This is not to deny that, if we are looking for an all-embracing descriptive cosmology, we might find Aristotle's final causes more revealing. The kinds picked out by Aristotle's lexicon, like terminus ad quo and terminus ad quem, might be natural kinds too—kinds with final rather than physical causal properties. But in each case there is something the theory claims to be true of, and in each case the theory either points out or fails to point out its referent as it is in itself. As Heidegger notes, once we see that Newton's laws are true, we see that nature was already the way they reveal it to be even at the time of Aristotle. Conversely, if Aristotle's terms successfully picked out natural kinds (relative to final causes), his account is still true today. Again, instead of relativism, we get plural realism.

Heidegger seems to hold that there can be many systems of practices that support assertions that point out many different and incompatible realities. But (1) given any specific criterion of truth, i.e., any specific set of pointing-out practices, at most one system can be right. Since Aristotle's kind terms do not reveal physical causal powers, insofar as Aristotle's system cannot be purged of claims about physical causality, its truth claims do not point to anything real. And (2) even if a system does succeed in pointing things out as they are, that does not show that the kinds it discovers are the ultimate basis of reality. Reality can be revealed in many ways and none is metaphysically basic.

Why doesn't Kuhn share this conclusion? Perhaps because he implicitly accepts the traditional view that in principle only one lexicon can correspond to the kinds in nature, and, since he has discovered that relative to different lexicons incompatible theoretical assertions count as true, he concludes that none can correspond to things as they are in themselves. For Heidegger, on the contrary, as finite beings capable of disclosing, we work out many perspectives—many lexicons—and reveal things as they are from many perspectives. And just because we can get things right from many perspectives, no single perspective is *the* right one.

E. Conclusion

Dasein's preontological understanding of various ways of being opens a clearing in which particular entities can be encountered as entities to be used or as the referents of true assertions, etc. The disclosedness opened by Dasein's self-interpreting activity is called primordial truth. There would be no understanding of being without primordial disclosedness, and no disclosedness without this understanding of being, and both depend on Dasein. Thus:

Being (not entities) is something which "there is" only in so far as truth is. And truth is only in so far as and as long as Dasein is. Being and truth "are" equiprimordially. (272)[230]

If being and truth depend on Dasein, but entities and what is discovered about them do not, what are the implications for traditional philosophy? As we look back over the way we have traveled we see that for Heidegger the traditional account of substance (occurrentness), objective space and time, independent scientific reality, and truth as the agreement of assertions with states of affairs, have not been shown to be simply mistaken. Rather they all presuppose the primordial human practices within which the traditional account arises, and this dependence determines its legitimacy and limits. There are independent real things, objective space and time, and assertions can agree with the way things are in themselves—but these realities and the detached stance from which they are revealed cannot account for the meaningful practices in which we dwell. Yet these practices and our being-in them alone allow us access to what traditional philosophy has studied.

Appendix

Kierkegaard, Division II, and Later Heidegger
Hubert L. Dreyfus and Jane Rubin

I. Religiousness A

The Present Age is Søren Kiergegaard's analysis of modern nihilism. Kierkegaard defines nihilism—or, as he calls it, "leveling"—as a situation in which "qualitative distinctions are weakened by a gnawing reflection."[1] Qualitative distinctions are distinctions between the kinds of things that are worthwhile or significant and the kinds of things that are not. On Kierkegaard's analysis, these distinctions can be maintained only by commitment to the practices that embody them. For example, the distinction between serious literature and trivial literature can be maintained only by teachers who are committed to the practice of teaching serious literature. Kierkegaard refers to this kind of commitment as "the qualitative differentiating power of passion"[2] and contrasts it with the leveling reflection of the present age:

A disobedient youth is no longer in fear of his schoolmaster—the relation is rather one of indifference in which schoolmaster and pupil discuss how a good school should be run. To go to school no longer means to be in fear of the master, or merely to learn, but rather implies being interested in the problem of education.[3]

Kierkegaard's concern about the leveling of the distinctions between teachers and students, fathers and sons, kings and subjects, etc., is not an expression of social conservatism. As his favorable contrast of a revolutionary age with the present age makes clear, what bothers Kierkegaard about the present age is that it neither conserves nor destroys. Rather, "it leaves everything standing but cunningly empties it of significance."[4] Nor is Kierkegaard primarily concerned about leveling as a social problem. Rather he is concerned about leveling as a problem for individuals. That problem can be stated as follows: if the present age has leveled qualitative distinctions, how can I be committed to anything?

The problem of commitment is of particular importance to Kierkegaard because having a commitment and being a self are synonymous for him. Kierkegaard's[5] famous account of the self in *The Sickness Unto Death* defines the self in such a way that to be a self requires commitment:

> The human being is spirit. But what is spirit? Spirit is the self. But what is the self? The self is a relation which relates itself to itself. . . . A human being is a synthesis of the infinite and the finite, of possibility and necessity, of the eternal and the temporal. In short, a synthesis. A synthesis is a relation between two factors. Looked at in this way, a human being is not yet a self.[6]

As this passage indicates, Kierkegaard makes a distinction between a human being and a self. While a human being is a relation between infinite and finite, possibility and necessity, and the eternal and the temporal, a self is a relation that relates itself to itself. This distinction is crucial for Kierkegaard because he wants to claim that human freedom is the freedom of being self-defining. This means that infinite and finite, possibility and necessity, and the eternal and the temporal have no existence independently of my defining them by making a commitment. Kierkegaard calls the act of making such a commitment a "leap." He calls the forms of commitment that result from such leaps "spheres of existence."[7] There are four spheres of existence: the aesthetic, the ethical, Religiousness A, and Religiousness B. A person in the aesthetic sphere is committed to enjoyment. A person in the ethical sphere is committed to absolute choice. Religiousness A is the sphere for which "self-annihilation before God" is the object of commitment. In Religiousness B, a particular cause or project is the object of the individual's commitment. Thus, while every human being has the capacity to become a self, I become a self only by leaping into a sphere of existence and making a commitment that defines the factors.

There is one critical limitation on this freedom, however, a limitation expressed in Kierkegaard's definition of a human being as a "synthesis." When Kierkegaard defines a human being as a synthesis, he is asserting that I must define each pair of factors in such a way that the members of each pair reinforce rather than cancel each other. Each of the three lower spheres of existence collapses precisely because a person in each of these spheres defines the factors in such a way that they cancel each other out. According to Kierkegaard, the lower spheres define the factors in this way because they have the contradictory goal of wanting the benefits of commitment without the risks. Only Religiousness B, which accepts the risks of commitment, defines the factors in such a way that they reinforce each other.

What we need to understand at this point, then, is Kierkegaard's claim that commitment involves defining the infinite and finite, possibility and necessity and eternal and temporal factors. When Kierkegaard says that commitments are infinite, he means that they are world-defining. If I am committed to enjoyment, as in the aesthetic sphere of existence, everything in my world gets its significance or insignificance according to whether I enjoy it or not. If I am committed to choice, as in the ethical sphere, everything gets its significance or insignificance according to whether I choose to give it significance or not.

When Kierkegaard says that commitments are finite, he means that I cannot be committed to the world-defining in general. Rather, I have to be committed to something specific within my world. Thus, I cannot simply be committed to enjoyment. I have to be committed to some specific kinds of enjoyment. Similarly, I cannot simply be committed to choice. I have to be committed to specific choices.[8]

Kierkegaard's idea that commitments involve possibility suggests that it is up to me to determine what counts as satisfying my commitment. A commitment to enjoyment does not tell me what kinds of things to enjoy. A commitment to choice does not tell me what kinds of things to choose. It is up to me to determine what I am going to enjoy or choose.

His view that commitments involve necessity is meant to convey the idea that commitments give me my identity. While I do not have to commit myself to the enjoyment of skiing or to the choice of being a lawyer, once I have committed myself to these, I have become a skier or a lawyer. To lose the capacity to ski or practice law is therefore not only to lose the possibility of these commitments; it is to lose commitments that have become necessary to me.[9]

Finally, Kierkegaard's argument that commitments are eternal is an argument that they are not subject to retroactive reinterpretation and that they therefore establish continuity between my present, my past and my future. If I am in the aesthetic sphere, I know that it is settled that the significant times in my past were the times when I really enjoyed myself. Those times allow me to feel that there is a connection between who I am now and who I was in the past. I also know that my future will involve a commitment to enjoyment. Thus, I know that there is a connection between who I am now and who I shall be in the future. If I am in the ethical sphere, I know that the significant times in my past were the ones I chose to make significant. I know that my future will involve a commitment to choice. Thus, again, I know that there is a connection between who I am now, who I was, and who I shall be in the future.

Kierkegaard's argument that commitments are temporal holds that commitments change and that they therefore establish the distinction between my present, my past, and my future. While I am in the aesthetic sphere and committed to enjoyment, the particular kinds of things I enjoy can change. Though I once enjoyed skiing, I may now enjoy eating gourmet food, and in the future I may enjoy golf. These changes are significant changes because they are changes in my commitments. Similarly, though I once chose to make my relationship with my family significant and envisioned my future in terms of that commitment, I can now choose to see another aspect of my past as significant and can make that aspect important to me in the future.[10]

But with this definition of the self, we can also understand Kierkegaard's claim in *The Concept of Anxiety* that the psychological response to freedom is anxiety:

How does spirit relate itself to itself . . .? It relates itself as anxiety.[11]

Having defined anxiety as "a sympathetic antipathy and an antipathetic sympathy,"[12] Kierkegaard argues that the freedom of being self-defining is both attractive and repellent. It is attractive because it holds out the possibility of overcoming the leveling of the present age by taking a "qualitative leap" into a sphere of existence. It is repellent because I cannot know what it is like to be in any particular sphere until I am actually in it. The spheres of existence are incommensurable with the present age and with each other. As Kierkegaard describes it, the incommensurable is repellent because it presents itself as nothing:

The actuality of the spirit constantly shows itself as a form that tempts its possibility but disappears as soon as it seeks to grasp for it.[13]

What, then, is it? Nothing. But what effect does nothing have? It begets anxiety.[14]

According to Kierkegaard, the first response to anxiety is not a leap into a sphere of existence. Rather, human beings attempt to cover up their anxiety and to avoid the "decision in existence" by immersing themselves in the "spiritlessness" of the present age. In *The Sickness Unto Death*, Kierkegaard describes the way in which people in the present age cover up the possibility of the infinite/finite distinction by "[ascribing] infinite value to the indifferent" and "being altogether finitized, by instead of being a self, having become a cipher, one more person."[15] In a similar vein, he describes the way in which people in the present age cover-up the possibility of the distinction between possibility and necessity in probability.[16] And in *The Concept of Anxiety*, Kierkegaard describes the leveling of the eternal/temporal distinction as resulting in a situation in which one event simply follows another but none has any significance: "It really knows no distinction between the present, the past, the future, and the eternal. Its life and its history go on crabbedly like the writing in ancient manuscripts, without any punctuation marks, one word, one sentence after the other."[17]

If a human being chooses to face up to her anxiety rather than to cover it up, her first leap will be the leap into the aesthetic sphere of existence. There are two basic forms of the aesthetic sphere, the immediate and the reflective.[18] The immediate aesthetic sphere, as the name indicates, involves a commitment to immediate enjoyment. I let skiing or eating gourmet foods define my world and give me my identity. The problems with this position are fairly obvious. The immediate aesthetic is highly vulnerable. If I break my leg or develop food allergies, my commitment becomes unlivable and my world and my identity fall apart.[19]

The many stages of the reflective aesthetic attempt to overcome the vulnerability of the immediate aesthetic, while retaining the enjoyment, by making reflection about immediate experiences, rather than immediate experiences themselves, the source of enjoyment. While each of these stages has its own particular contradiction, the form of the contradiction is similar in each. This contradiction is illustrated in "Rotation of Crops" in Volume I of *Either/Or*.[20] In this stage I make reflection about past and future experiences the source of satisfaction. Thus, my imagination is the infinite factor and my particular fantasies are the finite factor.

The problem with this position is that, once all enjoyment is transferred to the realm of the imagination, it ceases to be enjoyment. When I aestheticize all of my experiences, the imagination of disaster is not qualitatively different from the imagination of a vacation on a tropical island, since my aestheticizing has taken away the possibility of actual disaster which made the difference. Thus, while the immediate aesthetic was enjoyable but vulnerable, the reflective aesthetic is invulnerable but indifferent. It has made itself safe at the price of failing to overcome the leveling of the present age.

One way to describe the despair of the reflective aesthetic is to say that it is the despair that nothing has any immediate significance. The ethical sphere responds to this despair by turning it into an opportunity. If nothing has any immediate significance, everything can have the significance I choose to give it. I can make particular desires and talents significant by choosing to express them through social roles such as work, marriage, and friendship. Thus, in the ethical sphere, a social role or a personal relationship is meaningful insofar as I choose to give it meaning. Choice resolves the problem of vulnerability because, while I can lose an object of choice, I cannot lose my capacity for choice. I shall always be able to choose another role or another relationship.

The problem with this position, on the other hand, is that, when choice is world-defining, it is impossible to have any standards for making particular choices, since these standards, too, must be objects of choice. Once it is up to me to give everything significance, the significance I give is completely arbitrary.

For Religiousness A, the third sphere, the contradictions of the aesthetic and ethical spheres conclusively demonstrate that the attempt to become a self will necessarily result in failure. Therefore, it is no surprise that the *Edifying Discourses* call Religiousness A "self-annihilation before God" and propose that a human being "arrives at the highest pitch of perfection when he becomes suited to God through becoming absolutely nothing in himself."[21]

In the discourse entitled "Man's Need of God Constitutes His Highest Perfection," Kierkegaard contrasts self-annihilation before God with the despairs of aesthetic enjoyment and ethical choice:

"Before this consolation can be yours, you must learn to understand that you are absolutely nothing in yourself. You must cut down the bridge of probabilities which seeks to connect the wish, the impatience, the desire, the expectation, with that which is wished, desired, and expected . . ." Or if some anxious soul had run riot in overmuch deliberation, and had become the prisoner of his many thoughts, so that he could not act because it seemed to him that the considerations on either side balanced each other exactly . . . [Religiousness A would] counsel him in these terms: "I know a way out of your difficulty which will give you full assurance of victory. Yield your wish and act; act in the conviction that even if the opposite of what you wish results from your action, you will nevertheless have conquered."[22]

Self-annihilation before God, however, does not mean a despairing return to the leveling of the present age. Rather, Religiousness A asserts that only once I give up trying to become a self can I overcome leveling. I do this by virtue of what the *Concluding Unscientific Postscript* calls "the simultaneous maintenance of an absolute relationship to the absolute 'telos' and a relative relationship to relative ends."[23] We can best understand what this means by understanding Religiousness A's definitions of each of the three sets of factors. Religiousness A defines the finite as my desires and the infinite as my absolute indifference to the satisfaction of my desires. To maintain an absolute relationship to the absolute "telos" and a relative relationship to relative ends, then, is to be absolutely indifferent to the satisfaction of my desires and thus to allow all of my desires to have only relative significance.

According to Religiousness A, the advantage of this definition of infinite and finite is that it overcomes the leveling of the present age by letting me act on my desires while making me invulnerable to situations in which my desires are not satisfied. On this analysis, people in the present age never fully commit themselves to the satisfaction of particular desires because they do not want to be vulnerable to situations in which their desires are not satisfied. According to Religiousness A, once I become absolutely indifferent to the satisfaction of my desires, I can commit myself to satisfying them because my world will not collapse if they are not satisfied. On the contrary, the experience of dissatisfaction will have its own particular significance. For example, I may have the desire to be a professional athlete. My commitment to the sports that satisfy this desire will give my life significance. But if I am injured tomorrow and cannot play again, it will make no difference to me, for I shall then have the very different, though no less significant, experience of going through rehabilitation, learning new job skills, and so on.

For Religiousness A, in other words, significance does not derive from the satisfaction of my desires but from having something that matters in my life, whether it brings enjoyment or misery. Kierkegaard makes this point in the discourse entitled "Every Good and Perfect Gift Is From Above":

And when the easy play of happiness beckoned you, have you thanked God? . . . And when you must deny yourself your wish, have you thanked God? And when men did you wrong and offended you, have you thanked God? We do not say that the wrong done you by men ceased to be a wrong, for that would be an untrue and foolish speech! Whether it was wrong, you must yourself decide; but have you referred the wrong and the offense to God, and by your thanksgiving received it from Him as a good and perfect gift? Have you done this? Then surely you have worthily interpreted the apostolic word to the honor of God, to your own salvation.[24]

To state the issue in another way, once I see that the point of Religiousness A is not the satisfaction of my desires—or, as Kierkegaard puts it, is "[not] the quality of the particular gifts"[25]— I can appreciate the significance of all of my experiences, whether satisfying or dissatisfying. Precisely because the athlete in our example is not concerned about the ultimate outcome, he can experience intensely the elation and depression that come with each successful and unsuccessful play. Thus, Religiousness A overcomes the despair of the ethical, because it is not a matter of choosing to give significance to some experiences and to withhold it from others but of accepting the significance that all of my experiences have when I am absolutely indifferent to the satisfaction of my desires:

Is it not true, my hearer, that you . . . were not perplexed as to what was a good and perfect gift, or whether it came from God? For, you said, every gift is good when it is received with thanksgiving from the hand of God, and from God comes every good and every perfect gift. You did not anxiously ask what it is which comes from God. You said gladly and confidently . . . I know it is that for which I thank God, and therefore I thank Him for it. You interpreted the apostolic word; as your heart developed, you did not ask to learn much from life; you wished to learn only one thing: that all things serve for good to those that love God.[26]

Religiousness A's definition of infinite and finite is a statement about the proper role of desire in an individual's life. Its definition of possibility and necessity is a statement about the proper role of need in an individual's life. Religiousness A defines necessity as my needs. It defines possibility as my absolute indifference to the satisfaction of my needs. According to Religiousness A, I shall always have some particular identity with some particular set of needs. However, none of these particular needs has to be satisfied. If I am an athlete, I need to be healthy, to have access to the proper equipment, and so on. If these needs are not satisfied, however, it will make no difference to me, for I shall then have a different identity with a different set of needs. I shall have the identity of a rehabilitating athlete who needs physical therapy, a job, and so on.

Religiousness A makes this point by asserting that my only real need is my need of God. My only real need, in other words, is to see all of my particular needs as relative:

> In the case of the earthly goods of life the principle obtains that man needs but little, and in proportion as he needs less and less he becomes more and more perfect. . . . But in the relation between a human being and God this principle is reversed: the more a man needs God the more perfect he is.[27]

There is, however, a crucial difference between desire and need. While no particular desire may ever be satisfied, as long as I am alive some particular needs will always be satisfied.

> He does not know from whence his needs are to be supplied. . . . Nevertheless, his wants are somehow supplied, the little that he needs in order to live.[28]

Finally, Religiousness A's definition of the eternal and temporal factors follows from its definitions of infinite and finite and possibility and necessity. For Religiousness A, my desires and needs are temporal while my absolute indifference to the satisfaction of my desires and needs is eternal.

To say that my desires and needs are temporal is to say that they are the condition of the possibility of significant change in my life. The fact that I have tried to satisfy a particular desire or need in the past does not mean that I have to try to satisfy it in the future. I can decide at any time to try to satisfy a different set of desires and needs than the ones I have tried to satisfy up to this point. Although I may have tried to satisfy my desire to be an athlete for most of my life, I can decide at any time to try to satisfy my desire to be an artist instead.

To say that my absolute indifference to the satisfaction of my desires and needs is eternal, on the other hand, is to say that it is unchanging. As such, it is the condition of the possibility of significant continuity in my life. I undoubtedly have had desires and needs that were not satisfied in the past. If I am absolutely indifferent to the satisfaction of my desires and needs, I can accept my past without wishing it had been different. Similarly, I undoubtedly have desires and needs which will not be satisfied in the future. If I am absolutely indifferent to the satisfaction of these desires and needs, I can anticipate my future without anxiety. In short, my absolute indifference to the satisfaction of my desires and needs allows me to live in a kind of eternal present in which I am not tempted to think that I would be happier now if things had worked out differently in the past or if I had the assurance that they would work out in the future. I have an eternal present because I accept my past and my future unconditionally.

Religiousness A spells out its definitions of the eternal and temporal with particular emphasis on my relationship to the future. The point of Religiousness A is to attempt to satisfy my desires and needs in the present while remaining absolutely indifferent to their being satisfied in the future. Religiousness A makes this point by saying that I should have an expectation that is not an expectation of anything in particular:

Not only does he not believe who expects absolutely nothing, but also he who expects some special thing, or he who bases his expectation on something special.[29]

Kierkegaard calls the expectation of nothing in particular an expectation of Victory but not victories. If I do not expect any particular desire or need to be satisfied, I can appreciate satisfaction and dissatisfaction equally:

It is true that he who expects something in particular may be disappointed; but this does not happen to the believer. When the world begins its sharp testing . . . when existence, which seems so loving and so gentle, transforms itself into a merciless proprietor who demands everything back . . . then the believer looks with sadness and pain at himself and at life, but he still says: "There is an expectation which all the world cannot take from me; it is the expectation of faith, and this is Victory. I am not deceived; for what the world seemed to promise me, that promise I still did not believe that it would keep; my expectation was not in the world, but in God. This expectation is not deceived; even in this moment I feel its victory more gloriously and more joyfully than all the pain of loss. If I lost this expectation, then would everything be lost. Now I have still conquered, conquered through my expectation, and my expectation is Victory.[30]

Religiousness A, then, seems to have realized the goal that the aesthetic and ethical spheres could not realize. It seems to have overcome leveling and achieved invulnerability by trying to satisfy particular desires and needs while remaining absolutely indifferent to their satisfaction. But when we examine Religiousness A more closely, we recognize that there is a basic contradiction in its definitions of each of the three sets of factors. This contradiction can be stated most briefly as follows: How can I be said to have particular desires and needs if I am absolutely indifferent to their satisfaction? To return to the example we have used throughout, can I really be said to have the desire to be an athlete if it makes absolutely no difference to me whether I am one or not? Can I be said to have the need to be in proper shape for competition if it makes absolutely no difference to me whether I am an athlete or not? Can I be said to have the desire to be an athlete and the need to be in proper shape if I am absolutely indifferent as to whether this desire and this need were ever satisfied in the past or will ever be satisfied in the future? Religiousness A's definitions of the factors are predicated upon the existence of desires and needs whose existence these definitions undercut at every point.

Religiousness A, in other words, falls prey to a contradiction parallel to the contradictions of the aesthetic and ethical spheres. Either I am absolutely indifferent to the satisfaction of my desires and needs, in which case I have no desires and needs and cannot overcome leveling, or I am not indifferent to the satisfaction of my desires and needs, in which case I am vulnerable to their not being satisfied.

In order to better appreciate this contradiction, it may be helpful to contrast Kierkegaard's Religiousness A with positions to which, at least on the surface, it appears to be quite similar. The idea that I should attempt to satisfy my desires and needs while remaining absolutely indifferent to their satisfaction brings to mind Buddhist exhortations to nonattachment to the objects of desire. Thus, if Religiousness A has irresolvable contradictions, Buddhism would seem to have them as well.

When we begin to make these comparisons, however, we see that Religiousness A's intention of overcoming the leveling of the present age by establishing qualitative distinctions makes it critically different from the Eastern traditions it seems to resemble. Buddhism is not trying to overcome leveling. It does not claim that I should be indifferent to the satisfaction of my particular desires in order to maintain a qualitatively differentiated world. On the contrary, Buddhism claims that to achieve absolute indifference to the satisfaction of my desires is to achieve a state of desirelessness, in Kierkegaard's terms, not to expect anything. Religiousness A, however, wants both the invulnerability of desirelessness and the desires that establish qualitative distinctions. Buddhism is a consistent position. Religiousness A is not.

Another way of making this same point is to say that what would be salvation for the Buddhist is despair for Religiousness A. This becomes clear when we examine Religiousness A's view of God. In the discourse "The Unchangeableness of God," Kierkegaard makes it clear that, for God, everything is leveled.

For God there is nothing significant and nothing insignificant . . . in a certain sense the significant is for Him insignificant, and in another sense even the least significant is for Him infinitely significant.[31]

To have an absolute relationship to the absolute means to see every object of desire as relative and therefore as of absolutely equal significance. But this is as much as to say that God—and, by extension, a human being who has an absolute relationship to God—is in despair. Kierkegaard describes this despair in terms of the relationship between the eternal and the temporal: "In a manner eternally unchanged, everything is for God eternally present, always equally before him."[32] And Kierkegaard concludes:

There is thus sheer fear and trembling in this thought of the unchangeableness of God, almost as if it were far, far beyond the power of any human being to sustain a relationship to such an unchangeable power; aye, as if this thought must drive a man to such unrest and anxiety of mind as to bring him to the verge of despair.[33]

This is the most direct statement of the despair of Religiousness A in the *Edifying Discourses*. However, this statement does not complete Kierkegaard's description of the sphere. When a person in one of the lower spheres of existence begins to become conscious of his despair, his first response is not to face up to his despair but to cover it up. This covering up of the despair of the sphere is essential to remaining in the sphere. Thus, it is essential to his remaining in the aesthetic sphere that A, the pseudonymous author of the first volume of *Either/Or*, tries to cover up the contradictions of the reflective aesthetic by claiming that no one can achieve being a reflective aesthete because no one can ever achieve the kind of total detachment the reflective aesthetic requires.[34] Similarly, it is essential to his remaining in the ethical sphere that Judge William, the pseudonymous author of the second volume of *Either/Or*, tries to cover up the contradictions of ethical choice by claiming that no one can ever be fully in the position of ethical choice because no one can ever get completely clear about himself.[35] No description of Religiousness A will be complete, then, until it has described the attempt of the person in Religiousness A to cover up his despair by redefining each of the three sets of factors.

We find the cover-up of the contradiction between infinite and finite in Religiousness A expressed mostly clearly in the edifying discourse entitled "The Joy In The Thought That It Is Not The Way Which Is Narrow, But The Narrowness Which Is The Way."[36] According to this discourse, I can never be absolutely indifferent to the satisfaction of my desires. Therefore, Religiousness A does not represent the achievement of this goal but the infinite task of attempting to achieve it. I must continually attempt to resist the temptation to care about the satisfaction of my desires. The discourse refers to this temptation as "affliction" and asserts that, for Religiousness A, "affliction is the way":

The way of perfection leads through tribulations; and the subject of this discourse is the joy for a sufferer in this thought. Hence the discourse is not this time the admonishing one of how one must walk on the way of affliction, but the joyful one for the sufferer, that the affliction is the how which indicates the way of perfection.[37]

Kierkegaard's puzzling assertion that the thought of affliction is joyful ceases to be puzzling when we recognize that it represents an attempt to save Religiousness A from its own despair. The upshot of this assertion is that I shall always have significance in my life because I shall always be tempted to care about satisfying some particular desire. The *Concluding Unscientific Postscript* refers to the task of continually attempting to overcome this temptation as "dying away from the life of immediacy."[38] The *Edifying Discourses* makes it clear that dying away from immediacy overcomes the reflection of the present age:

When affliction is the way, then is this the joy: *that it is hence IMMEDIATELY clear to the sufferer, and that he IMMEDIATELY knows definitely what the task is, so he does not need to use any time, or waste his strength, in reflecting whether the task should not be different.*[39]

By asserting that its goal is dying away from immediacy, then, Religiousness A covers up its despair. I can never have the despair of an absolute relationship to the absolute because this relationship can never be achieved.

Kierkegaard makes a similar move in relation to possibility and necessity in the discourse entitled "The Glory Of Our Common Humanity." Though the ostensible goal of Religiousness A is absolute indifference to the satisfaction of my needs, Kierkegaard asserts that this goal, too, can never be absolutely achieved. Rather, Religiousness A must face the fact that I have to satisfy some of my needs:

It is a perfection *to be able* to have a care for the necessities of life—in order to overcome this fear, in order to let faith and confidence drive out fear, so that one is in truth without a care for the necessities of life in the unconcern of faith.[40]

Or, as Kierkegaard states in another passage: "But then it is indeed a perfection to be able to be anxious about the necessities of life."[41]

Once again, a reversal that appears to destroy Religiousness A is actually intended to save it. If I always have to worry about satisfying some particular needs, I can never be in the position of not having any needs. I shall not be in the despair of having an absolute relationship to the absolute in which having no needs means having no qualitative differences and results in the failure to overcome the leveling of the present age.

Finally, in relation to the eternal and temporal factors, Kierkegaard asserts that I can never be absolutely indifferent to the future satisfaction of my desires and needs. "The Expectation of An Eternal Happiness" asserts that I cannot help being concerned about my future. Thus, dying away from this concern is an eternal task. Kierkegaard expresses this by saying that Religiousness A does not represent the achievement of eternal happiness but the concern for my eternal happiness:

If God held in His right hand eternal happiness, and in His left also the concern which had become your life's content, would not you yourself choose the left, even if you still became like one who chose the right?[42]

These attempts to save the position obviously destroy it. At this point we see that Religiousness A has exactly the same kinds of contradictions as did the aesthetic and ethical spheres whose contradictions it attempted to resolve. If I am absolutely indifferent to the satisfaction of my desires and needs, I have not overcome the leveling of the present age. But if I am not absolutely indifferent to the satisfaction of my desires and needs, I am just as vulnerable to their not being satisfied as is a person in the aesthetic or ethical spheres of existence.

Kierkegaard sees Religiousness A as the end of the line for attempts to overcome the leveling of the present age while achieving invulnerability. Like the aesthetic and ethical spheres, Religiousness A attempted to become invulnerable by making a formal capacity absolute. My capacity to be absolutely indifferent to the satisfaction of my desires and needs was invulnerable because it did not depend upon the satisfaction of any particular desires or needs. Similarly, my capacities for imagination or choice did not depend upon any particular objects of imagination or choice.

Religiousness B, in contrast, will propose that only a commitment to something concrete and specific, outside myself, can overcome leveling. Thus, if I am an athlete in Religiousness B, my particular sport—not fantasizing about sports, the choice of sports or indifference to the results of athletic activity—will be world-defining for me.

But how does a person get such a world-defining, concrete commitment in the first place? In *Training In Christianity*, Kierkegaard argues that Jesus is the model for Religiousness B and that a person becomes a self by imitating him:

> Christ's life here upon earth is the paradigm; it is in likeness to it that I along with every Christian must strive to construct my life."[43]

While Kierkegaard claims that Christ is the paradigm for becoming a self, the logic of his own arguments leads to the conclusion that anyone who has gone through the three lower spheres and who has a world-defining concrete commitment can be such a paradigm.[44] In *Sickness Unto Death*, Kierkegaard describes the difference between the lower spheres and Religiousness B as the difference between a self that relates itself to itself alone and a self that relates itself to something else:

> Such a relation, which relates to itself, a self, must either have established or have been established by something else.... Such a derived, established relation is the human self, a relation which relates itself to itself, and in relating to itself relates to something else.[45]

The "something else" is an individual in Religiousness B who serves as a model of what it is to have a world-defining commitment.

Given Kierkegaard's definition of Religiousness B, we can understand why someone in Religiousness B is vulnerable and why Kierkegaard sees the three lower spheres as refusals to face up to this vulnerability. If I am a Religiousness B tennis player and develop tendonitis, I cannot simply substitute another object of fantasy or choice and I cannot be indifferent. Rather, I experience the grief of having lost my world, my identity and the continuity of my life. A person in Religiousness A senses that she could have a differentiated world of her own only if she commits herself to something specific in such a way that everything in her world gets whatever significance it has by virtue of this specific commitment. But she also knows that the object of her commitment must be vulnerable. Although a differentiated world of my own is the ultimate attraction, the idea of exchanging the suffering of frustrated desires for the grief attendant upon the loss of the object of a total commitment seems like exchanging the miserable for the unbearable.

Accepting this risk is what Kierkegaard calls "faith." Life in Religiousness B manifests the famous absurdity of the Knight of Faith in *Fear and Trembling* who knows how "to live joyfully and happily . . . every moment on the strength of the absurd, every moment to see the sword hanging over the loved one's head and yet find, not repose in the pain of resignation, but joy on the strength of the absurd."[46] But the Knight of Faith achieves bliss only by accepting anguish. "Only one who knows anguish finds rest."[47]

For our present purposes, however, the details of Kierkegaard's solution to the despair of Religiousness A are less important than the convictions that lead him to it. As we have seen, Religiousness A collapses because it prevents me from making an individual commitment that according to Kierkegaard's Christianity is the only way to reintroduce meaningful differences in the face of the leveling of the present age. Suppose, however, that human beings did not need meaningful differences and so did not need an individual commitment in order to make life worth living? If such were the case, there might be a version of Religiousness A that had a way to avoid leveling because it simply got over seeking meaningful differences. We shall seek to show that Heidegger's account of authenticity describes such a way of life.

II. Authenticity

Kierkegaard insists that his claim that the self needs a world-defining individual commitment in order to be saved from despair is dogmatic.[48] In calling his claim Christian-dogmatic, Kierkegaard is emphasizing (1) that this is a cultural claim and (2) that it cannot be justified or grounded in any way, be it transcendental, empirical or phenomenological. Heidegger, on the other hand, seeks a phenomenological *demonstration* of those structures that are constitutive of *human being in general.* This repudiation of the Christian-dogmatic side of Kierkegaard's thought we call Heidegger's secularization of Kierkegaard. We shall argue that Heidegger, by correcting Kierkegaard's account of the relation between desire and action and by dropping the Christian-dogmatic account of the self as needing a world of its own, can propose a secularized version of Religiousness A that might actually work as a way of life. We shall also show how, in his account of an authentic life, Heidegger seeks to salvage as much of Religiousness B as makes sense without faith.

A. Heidegger and Kierkegaard on the Self

Heidegger takes over from Kierkegaard much more than he acknowledges. Not only does he build on Kierkegaard's understanding of the self as a set of factors that are defined by the stand this structure takes on itself, he also accepts Kierkegaard's account of the present age as an anxiety-motivated cover-up of the basic structure of the self.

We have seen in chapter 1 that "Dasein is an entity which does not just occur among other entities. Rather it is . . . distinguished by the fact that, in its very being, that being is an issue for it" (32)[12], and we have seen that this way of being, which Kierkegaard calls "spirit," Heidegger calls "existence." "Dasein always understands itself in terms of its existence—in terms of a possibility of itself: to be itself or not itself" (33)[12]. And just as spirit for Kierkegaard is not merely a "synthesis" of the factors but the way the relation relates itself to itself, so for Heidegger "man's 'substance' is not spirit as a synthesis of soul and body; it is rather *existence*" (153)[117].

Recall that Heidegger's existential analytic shows Dasein's existence to consist of two interrelated aspects, or, as he calls them, "existentials": thrownness and projection. *Thrownness* means that Dasein always finds itself already having some given content and concerns. "In thrownness is revealed that in each case Dasein, as my

Dasein and this Dasein, is already in a definite world and amidst a definite range of definite intraworldly entities" (264) [221]. This content constitutes Dasein's *facticity*.

On the basis of what it is already, its facticity, certain possible ways of being a self are opened up for Dasein and others are closed off. Since Dasein is what it does, it is always *projecting* on, i.e., acting on, some such possibility. Dasein's capacity for taking a stand on its current facticity by pressing into the future, Heidegger calls *transcendence*.[49] Although no footnote acknowledges Heidegger's source, one cannot help recognizing in the existential pairs, thrown/ projecting, facticity/transcendence—that which sets boundaries to possibilities and the possibilities themselves—versions of Kierkegaard's factors: necessity and possibility.

Facticity and transcendence require a middle term, which is the stand they take on themselves. Heidegger calls this *falling*. Falling is not a third factor but, as we saw in chapter 13, it is the everyday way the self takes a stand on itself, relating the two sets of factors in absorbed activity, normally so as to cover up or disown what being self-interpreting involves. We shall have more to say about falling later when we contrast it with Heidegger's account of *resoluteness*— a different way of acting in which the factors interpret themselves in a way that owns up to the self's peculiar nothingness.

For now it is important to note that not only does Heidegger take over from Kierkegaard the idea that the self is the stand a set of factors takes on itself, he also accepts that some stands define the factors so as to do justice to the structure of the self and some do not. Heidegger, however, does not agree with Kierkegaard that there is only one coherent way to fit the factors together. Thus he does not attempt to distinguish "better" from "worse" self-interpretations by finding out through living which ways of defining the factors cancel them out and lead to despair and which way reinforces them and leads to bliss. For Heidegger, as for Kierkegaard, there are nongenuine ways of living that do not do justice to both factors and a genuine way that does (see chapter 11), but in Heidegger's account these ways of life do not lead to despair and bliss respectively and are not what makes one way of existing superior to another. What makes one way of life superior to another for Heidegger is not whether the factors are concretely lived so as to reinforce each other rather than oppose each other, but instead a formal criterion, viz., whether a way of life does or does not own up to and manifest in action the implications of being a self-defining set of factors.

This deep difference as to what constitutes a superior way of life is related to another basic difference between Kierkegaard's and Heidegger's accounts of the relationship between self and world. Whereas Kierkegaard, in the name of Christianity, was trying to counter Hegel's overemphasis on the world spirit by emphasizing the individual, Heidegger is deliberately distancing himself from Husserl, who he thinks overemphasized individual subjectivity, by emphasizing being-in-the-shared-world. Thus, whereas Kierkegaard insists that to reach equilibrium the self must make a commitment that gives it its own individual world, Heidegger seeks to show that the shared public world is the only world there is or can be. Dasein cannot invent totally unique meanings and motivations. Rather each Dasein, as a particular "there," is a version of, or selection from, the moods, projects, and self-interpretations made available by the culture. Heidegger thus opposes any idea of a subject with a world of its own, whether this be Husserl's "sphere of ownness," a form of subjectivity prior to and intelligible independently of a public world to which it subsequently gives meaning, or Kierkegaard's totally different view that a human being begins dispersed in the public world but must finally acquire an individual world with its own differentiated content.

In chapter 4 we saw that Heidegger, in direct opposition to Husserl's account of intentionality and indirectly in opposition to Kierkegaard, emphasizes that ordinarily activity is simply ongoing coping. Heidegger points out further (see chapter 5) that Dasein is always in the process of using equipment *in-order-to* obtain some end *towards-which* the activity of Dasein is oriented, and that all this is *for-the-sake-of* some self-interpretation of Dasein. According to Heidegger, though, this activity need not be explicitly chosen and so need not involve any mental content such as intentions, desires, and goals. When everything is going smoothly I can, in keeping with my self-interpretation, such as my sense of myself as being a professor, head towards the desk in my office without having any goal and making any choices, indeed without having the future-directedness of my activity in any way dependent upon what is in my mind.

Thus, to sum up, for Heidegger (1) there can be no unique projects defining individual worlds, (2) human beings are not, except in cases of breakdown, subjects making choices as to how to satisfy their desires. Rather, being-there is doing something it makes sense to do given the public situation, and given already-taken-over public for-the-sake-of-whichs. The givenness of the public for-the-sake-of-whichs and situations gives the self its facticity. The power of the particular Dasein to press into some possibilities rather than others is its ontic freedom or transcendence. (Its ontological freedom consists in its ability to take part in the opening up of a world, but that does not concern us here.)

Once Heidegger rejects the traditional view that intentional states such as desires are necessary to motivate action, and also rejects the even more intellectualistic view that acting to satisfy one's desires requires a choice of purposes and goals, he is in a position to accept Kierkegaard's critique of the ethical, and at the same time to reject Kierkegaard's critique of Religiousness A.

Heidegger would see the contradictions in the ethical and Religiousness A as arising from Kierkegaard's overly intentionalistic account of the way the self is in the world. According to Heidegger, one can and does act most of the time without thematizing alternatives and selecting one of them. Normally, one simply lives out of one's culture's version of what it is to be normal and presses into what normally needs to be done. Only in cases of breakdown do I find myself having to choose my life plan and worrying about my desires and the risks involved in trying to satisfy them. However, as if in perpetual breakdown, the ethical person sees his *whole moral life* as cut off from everyday life. Thus, as Kierkegaard saw, he is in the paralyzing position of having to *choose* his way of life and each of his actions.

Heidegger's view that the ethical sphere's intentionalistic account of choice mistakes breakdown situations for normal ones, unintentionally makes Kierkegaard's point. As we argued above, Kierkegaard's spheres of existence are a response to the breakdown of modern culture. Precisely because the present age does not offer any nonleveled ethical possibilities to press into, the ethical individual must give his own meaning to his social roles. Thus Kierkegaard would presumably argue that we cannot escape the contradictions of the ethical sphere by adopting a view of intentionality as ongoing coping; nonleveled, ongoing, unreflective, ethical coping, is precisely what the reflective ethics of the present age destroys.[50]

According to Kierkegaard, both in the ethical sphere and in Religiousness A people make their lives unlivable by trying to live as if there were always a reason for action, whether it be stipulated by a moral choice or dictated by desires and needs. But while Heidegger would agree with Kierkegaard that there is no way out of the contradictions of the ethical sphere since it is based on a self-contradictory account of life as requiring constant and total responsible choice, Heidegger in effect argues that Religiousness A is not a despairing dead-end requiring a leap to Religiousness B. According to Kierkegaard, the person in Religiousness A thinks of *all* actions as motivated by desire and then tries to make himself secure by dying to all desires. This, indeed, generates a contradiction. But Heidegger points out that actions need not be and usually are not motivated by desires. For example, at Christmas time one sends out Christmas cards not because one *desires* to do so but simply because that is what one does. To avoid Kierkegaard's alleged contradiction in Religiousness A, Heidegger would hold, Dasein need only press into public possibilities, i.e., do what it makes sense to do in the current situation. There is no need to leap to yet another sphere in which an individual commitment creates a world that is uniquely mine.

Once he has rejected Kierkegaard's Christian claim that the self needs a world of its own, and that this need, combined with Religiousness A's version of desire, leads to the contradictory demand for both invulnerability and differentiated desires, Heidegger can embrace as a solution to the problem of the present age and, indeed, any age, a nonintentionalistic, nonindividualistic version of the way of life that Kierkegaard spells out in his *Edifying Discourses*.

Heidegger acknowledges his indebtedness to Kierkegaard in one of the three footnotes that make up the total references to Kierkegaard in *Being and Time*:

In the nineteenth century, Søren Kierkegaard explicitly seized upon the problem of existence as an existentiell problem, and thought it through in a penetrating fashion. But the existential problematic was so alien to him that, as regards his ontology, he remained completely dominated by Hegel and by ancient philosophy as Hegel saw it. Thus there is more to be learned philosophically from his "edifying" writings than from his theoretical ones—with the exception of his treatise on the concept of anxiety. (494) [235]

Although Heidegger is interested only in the *existential* structure of Dasein, and so dismisses Kierkegaard's Christian-dogmatic account as *existentiell*, he nonetheless needs an existentiell story himself since he admits that there is no way to approach the general structure of Dasein except by spelling out a specific way of life in which that basic structure is perspicuously revealed. Heidegger calls the way of life that provides existentiell access to Dasein's makeup "authenticity." It is a way of life that consists of Dasein's owning up to what it really is, rather than covering up or disowning the anxiety occasioned by its unsettledness.

We must now examine this authentic way of existing in detail. Our question is: Can Heidegger lay out a secularized interpretation of the self and authenticity that, by dropping Kierkegaard's Christian demand that each self have a world with its own differentiated meanings, shows the way of life sketched in the *Edifying Discourses* to be a workable answer to the indifference, leveling, conformism, and consequent dullness of everyday life?

B. Anxiety

Heidegger acknowledges in another brief footnote that his account of anxiety is a secular version of an explicitly Christian analysis developed by Kierkegaard: "The man who has gone farthest in analyzing the phenomenon of anxiety—and again in the theological context of a 'psychological' exposition of the problem of original sin—is Søren Kierkegaard" (492) [190]. Heidegger then proceeds to take up and incorporate the "antipathetic" half of Kierkegaard's account of anxiety as a "sympathetic antipathy."

According to Heidegger, in anxiety our taken-for-granted cultural ground drops away. "Everyday familiarity collapses" (233) [189]. Anxiety thus reveals that Dasein cannot have a meaningful life simply by taking over and acting on the concerns provided by society. "Anxiety discloses an insignificance of the world; and this insignificance reveals the nullity of that with which one can concern oneself" (393) [343]. Dasein's interpretation of itself in terms of that with which it is concerned is thereby undermined. "The world in which I exist has sunk into insignificance.... This implies ... that our concernful awaiting finds nothing in terms of which it might be able to understand itself" (393) [343]. In the face of anxiety the self is annihilated. There is only anxiousness. Adapting Kierkegaard's description of anxiety in *The Concept of Anxiety*, Heidegger says: "Anxiety is anxious in the face of the 'nothing' of the world" (393) [343].

Anxiety reveals that the self has no possibilities of its own, and so Dasein's response to anxiety cannot be to find some resource in *itself*. Heidegger shares with Kierkegaard the rejection of the Aristotelian and the medieval views of the self as aiming at self-realization. There is no human potential. But Heidegger does not accept Kierkegaard's substitution of the goal of creating one's identity *ex nihilo* through unconditional commitment. Heidegger holds that (1) all for-the-sake-of-whichs are provided by the culture and are for anyone and (2) Dasein can never take over these impersonal public possibilities in a way that would make them its own and so give it an identity.

C. Death and Guilt
Heidegger elucidates the two aspects of the nothingness revealed by anxiety—that Dasein has no possibilities of its own and that it can never acquire any—by relating them to the more familiar phenomena of guilt and death.

Before beginning his analysis, however, Heidegger points out that our ordinary understanding of these phenomena is distorted but nonetheless revealing.

All ontological investigations of such phenomena as guilt, conscience, and death, must start with what everyday Dasein "says" about them. [However,] because Dasein has falling as its kind of being, the way Dasein gets interpreted is for the most part *inauthentically* "oriented" and does not reach the "essence." . . . But whenever we see something wrongly, some injunction as to the primordial "idea" of the phenomenon is revealed along with it. (326) [281]

This is just what one should expect when dealing with everydayness that both manifests and covers up Dasein's unsettling way of being—indeed, which manifests it precisely *by* covering it up. Thus, in analyzing guilt and death we have to deal with perspicuous yet misleading phenomena that force us to get at the truth by going through semblance. As Heidegger puts it: "What has been discovered earlier may still be visible, though only as a semblance. Yet so much semblance, so much 'being'" (60) [36].

Although Heidegger deals with death before guilt, we take them up in what seems to us a more logical order of exposition—birth before death, as it were.

1. Guilt and the Breakdown of the Ethical
In Chapter II of Division II, Heidegger offers an existential account of *Schuld*, which means guilt, indebtedness, and responsibility. He begins as promised by interpreting the ordinary account of having a guilty conscience as a distorted form of existential guilt, warning

at the same time that taking the ordinary phenomena at face value is necessarily misleading:

> We must first show how the only phenomena with which the ordinary interpretation has any familiarity point back to the primordial meaning of the call of conscience when they are understood in a way that is ontologically appropriate; we must then show that the ordinary interpretation springs from the limitations of the way Dasein interprets itself in falling. (341)[294]

Our ordinary existentiell understanding of guilt is structurally similar to existential guilt, but at the same time it is an interpretation of existential guilt designed to cover up its true meaning.

Everyday guilt arises because Dasein, to cover up its unsettledness, takes over the cultural mores as binding. This gives one the comforting impression that there are moral norms that guide action. Failure to live up to such norms leads to a sense of guilt or debt to society that one calls conscience. Conscience becomes a double cover-up when further interpretation disguises the fact that the ethical practices it enforces are merely a culture's practices, by speaking in terms of what is universally *right*.

> This interpretation of the conscience passes itself off as recognizing the call in the sense of a voice which is "universally" binding . . . But this "public conscience"—what else is it than the voice of the one? (323)[278]

Existential guilt, which the call of conscience confirms, is, on the contrary, an empty formal indebtedness, covered up by the sense of one's *existentiell* indebtedness to God, reason, or society. It is the condition of possibility for any ordinary sense of debt or responsibility.

> This essential being-guilty is . . . the existential condition for the possibility . . . for morality in general and for the possible forms which this may take factically. Primordial "being-guilty" cannot be defined by morality, since morality already presupposes it. (332)[286]

Existential guilt reveals not inauthentic Dasein's moral lapses, or its essential failure to choose; it reveals an essentially unsatisfactory structure definitive of even authentic Dasein. Even if Dasein has done nothing wrong there is something wrong with Dasein—its being is not under its own power.

We define the formal existential idea of the "Guilty!" as "being-the-basis for a being which has been defined by a 'not.'" . . . As being, Dasein is something that has been thrown; it has been brought into its "there," but *not* of its own accord. (329) [283–284]

A particular Dasein does not choose to be brought up to be masculine or feminine, for example. Moreover, what each of these roles involves is too pervasive for one ever to get clear about all it implies so as to be able to accept or reject it in toto: "In no case is a Dasein, untouched and unseduced by this way in which things have been interpreted, set before the open country of a 'world-in-itself'" (213) [169]. For this reason,

the self, which as such has to lay the basis for itself, can never get that basis into its power; and yet, as existing, it must take over being-a-basis. . . . "Being-a-basis" means *never* to have power over one's ownmost being from the ground up. This "*not*" belongs to the existential meaning of "thrownness." [Dasein] itself, being a basis, *is* a nullity of itself. (330) [284]

The idea that what is wrong with Dasein is that it can never choose itself from the ground up is an unacknowledged borrowing from Kierkegaard. When an individual in the ethical sphere begins to recognize that the absolute choice which the ethical requires results in leveling, he attempts to cover up his despair by claiming that no one can ever make such a choice because no one can ever become completely clear about himself.[51] This attempt to turn the despair of the position into something positive receives its strongest expression in the sermon that concludes the second volume of *Either/Or.* The "ultimatum," whose major refrain is "Before God you are always in the wrong."[52]

This nullity leads to another. Since Dasein must act and choose, it must annihilate some possibilities while actualizing others.

The nullity we have in mind belongs to Dasein's being-free for its existentiell possibilities. Freedom, however, is only in the choice of one possibility—that is, in tolerating not having chosen the others and not being able to choose them. (331) [285]

When I lucidly understand my existential guilt, I see that, even when my choice involves matters of life and death, I have to choose one alternative, and do so without justifying principles to fall back on. Rather, I must choose on the basis of taken-for-granted practices that I can never fully grasp, yet for whose consequences I am fully responsible.

To sum up: Dasein's structural indebtedness to the culture for an understanding of itself that it can never clearly choose, yet out of which it must act and for which it is fully responsible, is existential guilt. The existential meaning of conscience is the call, not to do this or that, but to stop fleeing into the everyday world of moral righteousness or of moral relativism and to face up to Dasein's basic guilt:

What does the conscience call to him to whom it appeals? Taken strictly, nothing.... "Nothing" gets called to this self, but it has been summoned to itself—that is, to its ownmost ability-to-be. (318) [273]

The call of conscience has the character of an appeal to Dasein by calling it to its ownmost ability-to-be-itself; and this is done by way of summoning it to its ownmost being-guilty. (314) [269]

To account for the call to leap out of the leveling of the present age Kierkegaard finds a latent despair in the present age and a Christian need to become an individual self. Heidegger, however, secularizing Kierkegaard, claims simply that since Dasein is the being whose being is an issue for it, it is called to face up to the kind of being it is. Dasein has to choose itself, not so as to become an individual (although as pulled out of conformism it does become an individual of sorts), but for the formal reason that as care its being is an issue for it. "Conscience manifests itself as the call of care" (322) [277]. "Authenticity . . . in care, is the object of care . . .—the authenticity of care itself" (348) [301]. This formal reason alone is sufficient to call Dasein out of the present age, even though the public world is presented by Heidegger as a seductive haven of flight in which, far from feeling despairing or homeless, inauthentic Dasein is fully at home with things and "can dwell in tranquillized familiarity" (234) [189].

Since anxiety is the revelation of Dasein's basic groundlessness and meaninglessness, we would expect existential guilt to be associated with anxiety. And, indeed, Heidegger tells us that in the call of conscience Dasein is called to anxiety:

The caller is definable in a "worldly" way by *nothing* at all. The caller is Dasein in its unsettledness: primordial, thrown being-in-the-world as the "not-at-home"—the bare "that-it-is" in the "nothing" of the world. (321) [276–277]

The fact of the anxiety of conscience gives us phenomenal confirmation that in understanding the call Dasein is brought face to face with its own unsettledness. Wanting-to-have-a-conscience becomes a readiness for anxiety. (342)[296]

Heidegger brings guilt and death together as revealing two forms of the nullity of care:

Care itself, in its very essence, is permeated with nullity through and through. (331)[285]

Dasein, as care, is the thrown (that is, null) basis for its death. The nullity by which Dasein's being is dominated primordially through and through, is revealed to Dasein itself in authentic being-towards-death. . . . Care harbors in itself both death and guilt equiprimordially. (354)[306]

Dasein is, then, a null basis of a nullity. "Dasein's being means, as thrown projection, being-the-basis of a nullity (and this being-the-basis is itself null)" (331)[285]. So far we have seen the null basis; now we turn to the nullity.

2. Death and Dying to All Immediacy
Heidegger begins his discussion of death, as he did his discussion of guilt, by focusing on the existentiell phenomenon he intends to discuss. All living things *perish*, but only Dasein is capable of *demise*.

The ending of that which lives we [call] "perishing." Dasein too "has" its death of the kind appropriate to anything that lives . . . . In so far as this is the case, Dasein too can end without authentically dying, though on the other hand, qua Dasein, it does not simply perish. We designate this intermediate phenomenon as its *"demise."* (291)[247]

Heidegger does not explain the distinction between perishing and demise, but it is surely another example of the difference between factuality and facticity. It is a fact about all organisms that they perish, but each culture gives that fact a different meaning, and this always already interpreted facticity is what Heidegger calls demise. However, thinking of death as demise—the event of annihilation that has not yet happened but will happen *sometime in the future*—like thinking of conscience as the source of specific moral imperatives—is an existentiell way of fleeing and covering up the structural nullity that Dasein at every moment is. Just as guilt, existentially interpreted, reveals that Dasein as thrown *has* no possibilities of its own, *death*, understood existentially, illustrates in a perspicuous but misleading way that Dasein as transcendence *can never make* any possibilities its own.

We have seen that Dasein's everyday dealings make sense in terms of for-the-sake-of-whichs taken over from the one, and that in anxiety these ultimate possibilities for being Dasein are revealed as for anyone. They would be there whether I existed or not, and so they have no intrinsic meaning for *me*. Heidegger now adds that, moreover, no possibilities can be given meaning by becoming my defining possibilities as in Kierkegaard's Religiousness B. Thus Dasein can have no concrete possibilities of its own on which to project; it can have no fixed identity; indeed, its only essential or ownmost possibility is nothingness. Heidegger calls this the "inessentiality of the self" (MFL, 140). He attempts to illuminate this ultimate structural nullity definitive of Dasein, viz. the impossibility of Dasein's existence as an individual with an identity of its own, by bringing it into relation with the possibility of death, to which it has obvious formal similarities.

Death, as the end of Dasein, is Dasein's ownmost possibility.... The more unveiledly this possibility gets understood, the more purely does the understanding penetrate into it as the possibility of the impossibility of any existence at all. (303, 307) [258, 262]

Heidegger is careful to point out that death as he is using the term, in contrast to the way death is understood by the public so as to cover up Dasein's structural nothingness, is not demise. But Heidegger leans so heavily on the similarity between Dasein's structural lack of possibilities of its own and the annihilation of all possibilities at life's end that it may seem that when he talks of the existential possibility of having no possibilities he is simply calling attention to the existentiell possibility of demise. This is the usual way of reading Heidegger on death.[53] But if existential nullity cannot be understood in terms of demise, but is rather covered up by thinking of death as something that has not yet happened, then it seems natural to suppose that the *possibility* of demise as an event later in life would be a cover-up too. Moreover, this common interpretation of the text would contradict Heidegger's explicit assertion of the formal, ontological character of his analysis.

Methodologically, the existential analysis is superordinate to the questions of a biology, psychology, theodicy, or theology of death. . . . The results of the analysis show the peculiar *formality* and emptiness of any ontological characterization. (292)[248]

But the usual interpretation seems hard to avoid. When Heidegger speaks of existential death as the "ultimate possibility," and the "possibility of the impossibility of any existence at all" (307)[262], what can this mean but the possibility of just plain dying? The answer, however, must do justice to Heidegger's assertion that death is an existential structure that defines what Dasein is; it cannot be some event that is possible but not yet actual, or even the possibility of that event. The event of death when it comes must manifest what Dasein *has been all along*, which is not at all the same as saying that all along Dasein had been nothing more than the possibility of the event of death.

The only way dying, or the possibility of dying, could have existential meaning would be as what Kant calls an *analogon*. An analogon is a concrete example that stands for something else that cannot be represented. Death shows us in a specific case that Dasein can have no possibilities that define it and its world. "Death, as possibility, gives Dasein nothing to be 'actualized,' nothing which Dasein, as actual, could itself *be*" (307)[262]. Thus the anxiety at the moment of dying when I have no possibilities left, the world recedes, and everything is seen to be meaningless, can be an analogon for living lucidly in such a way that the world is constantly seen to be meaningless and I am constantly owning up to the fact that Dasein is not only a *null basis* as revealed in the anxiety of conscience but also is a *nullity* in that it can make no possibilities its own.

Anxiety is nothing other than the pure and simple experience of being in the sense of being-in-the-world. This experience can, though it does not have to . . . assume a distinctive sense in *death* or, more precisely, in *dying*. We then speak of the *anxiety of death*, which must be kept altogether distinct from the fear of death, for it is not fear in the face of death but anxiety as the affectedness of naked being-in-the-world of pure Dasein. There is thus the possibility, in the very moment of departing from the world, so to to speak, when the world has nothing more to say to us and every other has nothing more to say, that the world and our being-in-it show themselves purely and simply. (HCT, 291)

The cover-up consists in assuming that the anxiety of death is a response to the end of being alive or to the possibility of that end rather than to the true condition of Dasein.

But in saying that dying offers an experience of the true human condition, one has to be careful. Dasein is being-*with-others*-in-the-world; how can the *isolation* of death reveal Dasein as it truly is? Yet Heidegger does say "death ... is ... nonrelational" (303) [259]. This makes sense only if we see that death is a limit case in which Dasein is stripped of its genuine structure—a case of *nongenuine* authenticity. It is significant that in his final formulation of the comportment appropriate to being-towards-death—forerunning—Heidegger substitutes, as he should, passionate involvement for nonrelatedness. "Forerunning ... brings [Dasein] face to face with the possibility of being itself ... in an *impassioned* freedom towards death—a freedom which has been released from the illusions of the 'one' and which is factical, certain of itself, and anxious"[54] (311, our italics) [266].

The best way to understand Heidegger on death, then, is to see that the relation of being-unto-death to the event of dying is like the relation of the existential call of "Guilty!" to ordinary moral guilt. Ordinary death is a perspicuous but misleading illustration of Dasein's essential structural nullity, viz., that Dasein can have neither a nature nor an identity, that it is the constant impossibility of *being* anything specific. What Heidegger is getting at when he speaks of Dasein's constant and certain possibility of having no possibilities is the formal truth that Dasein has no possibilities of its own and that it can never have any.

Heidegger thus secularizes the "dying to *lower immediacy*"—to the satisfaction of desires and needs—definitive of Religiousness A. At the same time he excludes the possibility of faith and thus the possibility of a *higher immediacy*—a world-defining commitment to something outside the self.[55] For Heidegger being-unto-death, then, is dying to *all* immediacy.

Heidegger speaks at times of Dasein's becoming authentic by projecting upon "possibilit[ies] of its self," as if Dasein could have possibilities of its own:

Dasein "knows" what is up with itself, inasmuch as it has either projected itself upon possibilities of its self or has been so absorbed in the one that it has let its possibilities be presented to it by the way in which the one has publicly interpreted things. (315) [270]

But this talk of possibilities of its self cannot mean Dasein's "individual concrete content" or defining commitment; rather it must mean that authentic Dasein projects *public* possibilities in a way that reveals rather than covers up what it is to be a self. We shall see that this authentic way of acting *individuates* Dasein, but only in the negative sense that it takes it out of the anonymity and dispersion of the one and destroys its illusion of having an identity, not in the positive Kierkegaardian sense that it gives Dasein a self-definition in terms of something specific.

Heidegger equates the existential phenomenon of being-unto-death as individualizing in this negative sense with anxiety itself:

The affectedness which can hold open the utter and constant threat to itself arising from Dasein's ownmost individualized being, is anxiety. In this affectedness, Dasein finds itself face to face with the "nothing" of the possible impossibility of its existence.... Being-towards-death is essentially anxiety. (310) [265–266]

D. Falling, Fleeing, and Fallenness

We must now return to the discussion of anxiety and Dasein's response to it. We shall see that anxiety both motivates falling into inauthenticity—a cover-up of Dasein's true structure—and undermines this cover-up, thus making authenticity possible. But even more fundamentally, anxiety accounts for fallenness as the structure of the one. We saw in chapter 13 that *structurally* the one covers up primordiality, and that socialization into the one constantly pulls Dasein away from a primordial relation to itself and its situation. In Division II, we get a *motivational* account of this pull away from authenticity built into the one. It helps in understanding Heidegger here to realize that he can be read as again secularizing Kierkegaard, in this case Kierkegaard's interpretation of the Christian doctrine of the fall.[56]

Remember that, given the unavoidable risks connected with a total commitment, a Christian culture tends to accumulate, and everyone in a Christian culture tends to assimilate, practices that cover up the demands of a Christian life. Kierkegaard's analysis of the media in the present age is a most striking and prescient account of how cultural practices distract the individual from the Christian call to absolute commitment and its risks. Kierkegaard in his psychological account of the Fall calls the distraction and denial built into our everyday practices *sinfulness;* Heidegger, secularizing Kierkegaard, calls the cover-up that is always already in the one, *fallenness.* Interpreted as a *motivated cover-up,* the publicness of the one is no longer understood simply as the *structure of intelligibility.* The word "fallenness" and related terms come to have a *psychological* meaning. (See Table 11.)

Table 11
Ambiguous account of falling. (Bracketed terms are newly introduced; parenthesized terms are Kierkegaard's; all others are from *Being and Time*.)

Structural account	Heidegger's neutral terms	Psychological account
Turning away.	Falling-away, motion.	Fleeing.
Generality, banality.	Leveling, publicness, idle talk.	Diversion.
Closed off, uprooted.	Fallen.	Covered-up, buried. (Sinfulness.)
Tendency to get entangled.	Always already in the one. [Falling-in-with.]	Temptation to flee. (Original Sin.)
Yield to inertia.	[Falling-for.]	Plunge out of oneself. (Sinning.)
Undifferentiated mode.	Inauthenticity. Being dispersed into the one.	Inauthenticity. Choosing the one for one's hero.

According to Kierkegaard, sinfulness is a state of the culture into which we are born; *original sin* is the fact that we actively embrace this state. In Heidegger's secularized and de-intentionalized equivalent, the one preserves and perpetuates ways of covering up nothingness, and socialized Dasein drifts along in this motivated cover-up.

The obviousness, the matter-of-course way in which this movement of Dasein comes to pass also belongs to the manner of being of the one. Because the movements of being which Dasein so to speak makes in the one are a matter of course and are not conscious and intentional, this means simply that one does not discover them, since *the disclosedness which the one cultivates is in fact a covering up.* (HCT, 282, our italics)

That Heidegger is secularizing original sin is clear when he treats lostness in the one not as a structural *tendency* but as a psychological *temptation.*

If Dasein itself, in idle talk and in the way things have been publicly interpreted, presents to itself the possibility of losing itself in the one and falling into groundlessness, this tells us that Dasein prepares for itself a constant *temptation* towards falling. (221, our italics) [177]

Finally, according to Kierkegaard, human beings *sin* when they succumb to the temptation to flee anxiety by choosing "safe" spheres of existence. In Heidegger's account, sinning becomes choosing inauthenticity, i.e., disowning the self. After growing up in the social cover-up, Dasein can succumb to the temptation actively to embrace the distracting social practices of the public in order to flee anxiety. "Dasein plunges out of itself into itself, into the groundlessness and nullity of inauthentic everydayness" (223) [178].[57] That is, Dasein "[chooses] the one for its 'hero'" (422) [371]. Thereby Dasein becomes a one-self, which presumably means making oneself at home in the world and using the social for-the-sake-of-whichs to gain a pseudoidentity.[58] This passage from conformity to conformism is the secular version of sinning.

To sum up: In his account of *The Fall* Kierkegaard describes individual sin as a three-step flight from the anxiety produced by the risks imposed by the Christian demands on the self. The stages are: (1) the *sinfulness* of the public that denies the demand, (2) *original sin* as the way each individual actively takes over the condition of *sinfulness*, and (3) *sinning* as trying to achieve a risk-free life. In his account of falling, Heidegger presents a three-step, secularized story of Dasein's flight from anxiety understood as the experience of its nullity. (1) The one acquires practices of flight such as idle talk, curiosity, and ambiguity. This cover-up Heidegger calls *fallenness*. (2) Dasein in its undifferentiated mode takes over this flight simply by living and acting in the public world and so has always already *fallen*. (3) The one also offers a constant temptation to active covering up. In *choosing inauthenticity*, Dasein actively takes over the public practices of flight for-the-sake-of covering up its nullity.

E. Resoluteness

The alternative to fleeing anxiety is to hold onto it. Dasein lets itself become paralyzed by the revelation that all that it accepted as serious does not matter at all. Then "Dasein is taken all the way back to its naked strangeness and becomes dazed by it" (394) [344]. "Anxiety is *held on to* when one brings oneself back to one's ownmost thrownness" (394) [344].

But just facing anxiety does not enable Dasein to act. "Anxiety merely brings one into the mood for a *possible* resolution" (394) [344]. To be a self at all, Dasein must somehow get back into the public world, not by fleeing into distraction, or pseudoserious choice, but in some other way. Dasein must arrive at a way of dealing with things and people that incorporates the insight gained in anxiety that no possibilities have intrinsic significance—i.e., that they have no essential relation to the self, nor can they be given any—yet makes that insight the basis for an active life.

If such a stance could be found, it would amount to a secularized version of Religiousness A. But Kierkegaard has shown that a life that tries both to satisfy desires and to be absolutely indifferent to their satisfaction cannot be lived. Can Heidegger, by dropping the traditional account of desires as reasons for acting as well as the Christian demand for an individual differentiated world, offer a workable secular version of Religiousness A? Is there a way that accepting *the* world as offering no basis for rational choice and no basis on which to construct *my* world could make possible a differentiated and joyous life? Is there a consistent way for Dasein to interpret facticity and transcendence other than the fallen way the one normally interprets them? Can Dasein own up to its structural nothingness, groundlessness, meaninglessness, inessentiality, etc., in such a way as to gain a life that, if not just, fulfilling, holy, mature, or even satisfying—since these evaluative terms all reflect our culture's cowardly search for an ethical standard or ground—is nonetheless worth living? Heidegger's answer is yes. He claims that there is a joyful way of being in which Dasein "takes over authentically in its existence . . . the nullity by which Dasein's being is dominated primordially through and through" (354) [306].

But how could one get into such a sphere of existence? It might at first seem that since anxiety is a breakdown of the whole world, it presents Dasein with a total choice: to do nothing and so fall back into flight or else to resist the temptation to flee and instead hold onto anxiety. Such an authentic choice to face anxiety would be a response to the silent call of conscience that is always demanding of Dasein that it face up to its nullity. Heidegger does, like Kierkegaard's ethical judge, speak of inauthenticity as not choosing, and of authenticity as requiring one big responsible choice:

The one . . . hides the manner in which it has tacitly relieved Dasein of the burden of explicitly *choosing*. . . . When Dasein . . . brings itself back from the one, the one-self is modified in an existentiell manner so that it becomes *authentic* being its self. This must be accomplished by *making up for not choosing.* But "making up" for not choosing signifies *choosing to make this choice*—deciding for an ability-to-be, and making this decision from its own self." (312–313) [268]

The seeming similarity of this demand for lucid choice to Kierkegaard's ethical sphere, however, should make us suspicious. We have seen that Dasein's structural guilt means that it cannot get clear about its life so as to make an explicit total choice. Existential guilt, like the breakdown of the ethical, shows that total transformation cannot be deliberate. Rather, as in Religiousness A, the self must face the existential truth that for a being such as Dasein, total ethical choice is impossible. Moreover, the idea of total choice raises two tremendous difficulties: (1) Inauthentic Dasein fails to make the choice, and authentic Dasein is produced by the choice. Who then makes the choice? Some sort of noumenal self? (2) Does Dasein make this total choice again and again, or does it somehow make it in and for eternity?

As we might expect, the choice of authenticity is not a *choice* at all. Kierkegaard describes the leap into Religiousness A by saying that "a man must retire into himself so as to sink down into his own nothingness, making an absolute and unconditional surrender."[59] Heidegger, similarly, describes the "choice" of authenticity as "a way of letting the ownmost self take action in itself of its own accord" (342) [295].

Phenomenologically one can think of the transformation from inauthentic to authentic existence as a gestalt switch. Fleeing is inauthentic Dasein's response to its sense of its unsettled way of being. Its double nullity, experienced as something terribly wrong with it, shows up as a constant threat to its security—a threat that it cannot face. But this same nullity and the anxiety that reveals it could equally well reveal Dasein and its world as an exciting manifestation of Dasein's finitude. Death and guilt would then show up not as a threat or as something wrong with Dasein, but simply as revelations of the essential structure of Dasein's way of being. If Dasein accepted its nullity, the same structure that seemed to threaten all its secure projects and its very identity would be seen to be challenging and liberating. Anxiety then would not be paralyzing like fear but would make Dasein clear-sighted and fearless.

Heidegger has a special name for the result of this transformation: "Self-projection upon [Dasein's] ownmost being-guilty, in which it is ready for anxiety—we call 'resoluteness'" (343) [297].

"Resoluteness" signifies [Dasein's] letting itself be summoned out of its lostness in the one. (345) [299]

Resoluteness, *Entschlossenheit* in German, is an illuminating but potentially misleading pun. *Entschlossenheit* normally means determination or resolve, but, as we have already seen, understanding resoluteness as lucid, total choice leads to the despair of the ethical. Heard as *Ent-schlossenheit*, with a hyphen, however, as Heidegger sometimes writes it and always intends it, the term means unclosedness, i.e., "openness." As Heidegger explains in a 1953 lecture:

The essence of resoluteness (*Ent-schlossenheit*) lies in the opening (*Entborgenheit*) of human Dasein into the clearing of being, and not at all in a storing up of energy for "action." See *Sein und Zeit*, #44 and #60. Its relation to being is one of letting-be. The idea that all willing should be grounded in letting-be offends the understanding.[60]

Heidegger also felt he had to warn explicitly against any intentionalistic understanding of resoluteness as deliberate action:

The resoluteness intended in *Being and Time is* not the deliberate action of a subject, but the opening up of [Dasein], out of its captivity in that which is, to the openness of being.[61]

Ent-schlossenheit, then, is the openness that results from the acceptance of the breakdown of the ethical illusion of lucid total choice, and the realization that the self is impotent and empty. It is therefore misleading to call the change choosing to choose. Dasein does not choose at all. Rather, Dasein as a disclosing way of being accepts the *call* to acknowledge its essential empty openness.

The call comes from the soundlessness of unsettledness, and the Dasein which it summons is called back . . . as something that is to become still. Only in reticence, therefore, is this silent discourse understood appropriately. (343) [296]

Dasein's only choice, then, is whether to keep silent so as to hear the call or to try to drown it out by plunging into the noise of the everyday rat-race. This choice, as Dasein's letting itself be called, is receptive rather than willful.

When Dasein understandingly lets itself be called forth to this possibility, this includes its becoming free for the call . . . In understanding the call, Dasein is in thrall to its ownmost possibility of existence. It has chosen itself. (334) [287]

The ultimate "choice," then, is no choice at all. It is the experience of transformation that comes from Dasein's accepting its powerlessness:

Dasein understands itself in its own *superior power*, the power of its finite freedom, so that in this freedom, which "is" only in its having chosen to make such a choice, it can take over the *powerlessness* of abandonment to its having done so. (436) [384]

A serious problem remains, however. How could one live such an authentic life? On the reading of Heidegger we are advancing, anxiety reveals that there are no public projects worth choosing and, since Dasein has no possibilities of its own and cannot make any its own, authenticity cannot consist in a Kierkegaardian change from public projects to personal ones. How then can Dasein choose between projects if all projects are equally meaningless? Worse, how, in the face of anxiety, can Dasein choose any project at all? Why wouldn't the person who had seen the truth of the human condition, like the hero of Sartre's short story "The Wall" or John Barth's protagonist in *The End of the Road*, suddenly find himself paralyzed, unable to choose anything?

If human beings were ethical, autonomous subjects, choosing their life plans, or even Christians in Religiousness A, choosing their actions on the basis of reasons provided by their beliefs and desires, anxiety would, indeed, be the end of the road. But Heidegger does not hold that action normally requires choice, so he can avoid these traditional difficulties. Remember that, as Heidegger points out, Dasein normally does not make intentionalistic choices, but rather simply "press[es] forward into possibilities" (184) [145]. Indeed, even when Dasein is making conscious, intentionalistic choices of goals it is doing so on a background of for-the-sake-of-whichs, ways of being, that it has simply been socialized into and that are too basic and pervasive ever to be explicitly chosen.

When Heidegger does raise the question "But on what basis does Dasein disclose itself in resoluteness? On what is it to resolve?" (345) [298], he gives an answer that clearly denies any intentionalistic choosing, i.e., weighing alternatives and deciding among them.

Only the resolution itself can give the answer. One would completely misunderstand the phenomenon of resoluteness if one should want to suppose that this consists simply in taking up possibilities which have been proposed and recommended, and seizing hold of them. The resolution is precisely the disclosive projection and determination of what is factically possible at the time. (345) [298]

This should remind us of Kierkegaard's claim that the person in Religiousness A "immediately knows definitely what the task is." Precisely because resolute Dasein is clear that it can have no final meaning or settled identity, it is clear-sighted about what is actually possible.

Resolution does not withdraw itself from "actuality," but discovers first what is factically possible; and it does so by seizing upon it in whatever way is possible for it as its ownmost ability-to-be in the one. (346) [299]

In resoluteness Dasein becomes open to the "unique Situation" [*Situation* in German, translated as Situation with a capital *S*]. "The existential attributes of any possible resolute Dasein include the items constitutive for an existential phenomenon which we call a '*Situation*'" (346) [299]. Undifferentiated and inauthentic Daseins, on the contrary, have taken over the banality and leveling of the public and so are closed off to the demands of the unique Situation. They do what is proper and respectable, what typically makes sense, and thus respond only to the standard situation [*Lage*, translated as situation with a lower-case *s*] "For the one . . . the Situation is essentially something that has been closed off. The one knows only the 'general situation'" (346) [300].

As soon as Dasein hears the call and lets itself become resolute, i.e., open to the Situation, it finds itself already embarked upon a new, authentic way of life.

Resoluteness does not first take cognizance of a Situation and put the Situation before itself; it has put itself into that Situation already. As resolute, Dasein is already *taking action*. (347) [300]

According to Heidegger's nonintentionalistic account, authentic Dasein sees what needs to be done by finding itself pushed into doing it.

Resoluteness brings the self right into its current concernful being-amidst what is available, and pushes it into solicitous being with others. (344) [298]

The transformation to authentic action can be put in terms of the factors. *Falling*, as fleeing, is the stand the self takes on its self that gives the factors their *inauthentic* interpretation; *resoluteness* is the stand that produces the *authentic* self. In a resolute stand on the factors, anxiety has wiped out all intrinsic meaning and so all *reasons* for doing things. *Facticity* is then interpreted as what my situation demands, and *transcendence* as the self's capacity to do it. The result is not a determination to take responsibility for my deliberate choices (as in the ethical sphere), but neither is it some new content that defines me for all time (as in Religiousness B); rather (as in Religiousness A), it is an empty, open, spontaneous way of being-in-the-world.

The moment of transformation from falling to resoluteness Heidegger calls the *Augenblick*, literally the glance of an eye. This is Luther's term for what the King James Bible calls the "twinkling of an eye," in which "we shall be changed."[62] For Kierkegaard, the *Oieblik* is the moment that an unconditional commitment comes to define my world and redifferentiate the content of my past and future. For Heidegger, it is the moment of the total gestalt switch of Dasein's way of being-in-the-world from inauthenticity to authenticity. The translators of *Being and Time* translate the *Augenblick* as "the moment of vision," but it would be better translated "the moment of transformation." However, in fidelity to the German and to the standard translation of Kierkegaard, it is best translated simply as "the moment."

However one translates *Augenblick* in Kierkegaard, "moment" is bound to show up in the translation, and then one has a problem. For one thing is clear, a transformation, such as falling in love, or committing oneself to a cause, need not take place in a moment. Moreover, however long getting committed takes, the commitment is experienced as permanent—eternal, Kierkegaard would say. Indeed, for Kierkegaard, making an absolute commitment gives one "eternity in time." It is anything but momentary.

It helps here to note that in introducing the moment, Heidegger acknowledges his qualified debt to Kierkegaard for the third and last time and adds a critical comment:

Kierkegaard is probably the one who has seen the *existentiell* phenomenon of the *Augenblick* with the most penetration; but this does not signify that he has been correspondingly successful in interpreting it existentially. He clings to the ordinary conception of time, and defines the moment with the help of now and eternity. (497) [338]

Heidegger then secularizes and formalizes Kierkegaard's concept. In Heidegger's version, the moment is the form of the authentic present. This strange way of talking comes from trying to do justice to the very strange phenomenon which Kierkegaard was trying to express by saying that commitment is both an event in time and eternal. Heidegger wants to say that, viewed from the perspective of everyday temporality, Dasein's facing the truth about its being occurs at a certain datable time. But, since what Dasein discovers is what Dasein *is* (i.e., always has been and always will be), this truth, although not created at the moment of discovery as in Kierkegaard, crucially affects all Dasein's future acts as well as its interpretation of its past.

For Heidegger, the transformation to authenticity signals a transformation in the *form* of my everyday activity, leaving the *content* unchanged. I enact my authenticity in all my absorbed involved activity.

Authentic disclosedness modifies with equal primordiality both the way in which the "world"* is discovered . . . and the way in which the Dasein-with of others is disclosed. The "world"* which is available does not become another one "in its content," nor does the circle of others get exchanged for a new one; but both being towards the available understandingly and concernfully, and solicitous being with others, are now given a definite character in terms of their ownmost ability-to-be-themselves. (344)[297–298]

The transformation to owning up to Dasein's nullity is, of course, the same transformation we have already described as becoming open to the Situation.

When resolute, Dasein has brought itself back from falling, and has done so precisely in order to be more authentically "there" in the "moment" as regards the Situation which has been disclosed. (376)[328]

The "*moment*" . . . means the resolute [way] Dasein is carried away to whatever possibilities and circumstances are encountered in the Situation as possible objects of concern. (387)[338]

Thus, from the point of view of authentic temporality, the moment is the constant form of all present action.

F. Authenticity
The idea of undertaking all my specific projects in a style of openness that manifests my understanding that no specific project

can fulfill me or give my life meaning works the same way for Heidegger's authentic Dasein as expecting Victory works for the person in Kierkegaard's Religiousness A. Having "died to imme-diacy," the person in Religiousness A expects no finite fulfillment at all and so is not desperately concerned about everyday victories and defeats. Our authentic athlete does not expect his dedication to and success in sports to give his life intrinsic meaning because he lives in anxious certainty that no object of concern can give his life that. Giving up the hope for ultimate or intrinsic meaning lets him see and appreciate relative meaning, like the difference between making a brilliant basket and missing one. Similarly, if one does not insist that one has the final true interpretation of a text, one is open to see details that do not fit one's current account—details that may form the basis for another interpretation. This, incidentally, is why Heidegger thinks that a scientist must be authentic to break out of normal science.

Likewise, having faced its nothingness, authentic Dasein is ready for all specific disasters. Our authentic athlete can therefore pursue sports without worry, enjoy success without fear of being crushed by defeat, accept a broken leg without grief, and, indifferent to what one would normally do, he can find convalescing, if that is the immediate task the Situation imposes, as meaningful (i.e., meaningless) as winning a world championship. Indifferent to his desires and to making sense of convalescing as one normally does, e.g., as a reason to feel sorry for oneself or as an obstacle to getting back to pursuing one's life-goal, he can take up his new facticity in a nonnormal way as an exciting new opportunity. "The genuine individuation of the individual, determined by the moment . . . does not mean clinging obstinately to one's own private wishes but being free for the factical possibilities of current existence" (BP, 288). Once one stops demanding meaning and imposing stereo-types, one's facticity will always provide a Situation in which there are unique possibilities for action.

So far resoluteness sounds exactly like Religiousness A. But at this point Heidegger makes an original move that allows him to in-corporate an important aspect of Religiousness B into his description of authenticity. (See Table 12.) Under the influence of both Kierkegaard and the philosophical tradition, Heidegger holds that the self requires some sort of *continuity*. Kierkegaard's dogmatic Christian claim that the self must achieve eternity in time becomes in Heidegger's secularized version the claim that the authentic self must achieve "constancy." He thus tries to incorporate into his

Table 12
Ambiguous account of a life worth living. (Bracketed terms have been disassociated despite Heidegger's tendency to conjoin them.)

Secularized Religiousness A	Heidegger's neutral terms	Secularized Religiousness B
	Moment.	
Response to unique Situation.	Resoluteness. Readiness for anxiety. Authenticity.	Fate.
Selfsameness.	Constancy.	Steadfastness.
[Equanimity.]	Joy.	[Soberness.]

account of authenticity what he calls the *steadiness* and *steadfastness* of taking a stand. It is interesting to see how far he can go in claiming continuity for the life of authentic Dasein while rejecting faith, the ability to live in absurdity that makes possible the concrete continuity of unconditional commitment definitive of Religiousness B.

To show that "existentiality . . . provides the ontological makeup of Dasein's self-constancy" (370) [323], Heidegger begins by describing and rejecting the traditional view of the subject's connectedness through time typified by Husserl's account of internal time consciousness.[63]

What seems "simpler" than to characterize the "connectedness of life" between birth and death? It consists of a sequence of experiences (*Erlebnisse*) "in time." But if one makes a more penetrating study of this way of characterizing the "connectedness" in question, and especially of the ontological assumptions behind it, the remarkable upshot is that, in this sequence of experiences, what is "really" "actual" is, in each case, just that experience which is occurrent "in the current 'now,'" while those experiences which have passed away or are only coming along, either are no longer or are not yet "actual." Dasein . . . hops, as it were, through the sequence of "nows" of its own "time." (425) [373]

Heidegger then introduces his own proposal. Like Kierkegaard, he holds that Dasein is normally dispersed, so that achieving continuity requires *giving* constancy to one's otherwise dispersed life.

Everyday Dasein has been dispersed into the many kinds of things which daily "come to pass."... So if it wants to come to itself, it must first *pull itself together* from the *dispersion* and *disconnectedness* of the very things that have "come to pass." (441–442) [389–390]

This pulling together is the constancy achieved by taking a stand.

In terms of care the constancy of the self, as the supposed persistence of the subjectum, gets clarified. But the phenomenon of this authentic ability-to-be also opens our eyes for the constancy of the self in the sense of its having taken a stand. The constancy of the self, in the double sense of steadiness and steadfastness, is the authentic counter-possibility to the non-self-constancy which is characteristic of irresolute falling. (369) [322]

Resolute openness may sometimes require short-term, Zen-like spontaneity. (Of course, for authentic Dasein as for the Christian in Religiousness A, short-term actions are never undertaken merely for the sake of variety, as in Kierkegaard's aesthetic sphere.) In our culture, however, resolute openness normally finds that the Situation calls for the determined, steady pursuit of a long-term project. Since Dasein is thrown into a Christian culture in which life and death commitments are possible, it may find itself drawn into one. It may then in fact live a life that looks exactly like that of a Knight of Faith. Yet the anxiety of death as dying to *all* immediacy both lower and higher has shown that a long-term commitment can never be entered into in such a way as to define the self and its world, as in Religiousness B. And, of course, on Heidegger's account, unlike Kierkegaard's, such a commitment is not required to save the self from despair. Readiness for anxiety, i.e., accepting care as essentially a nullity, makes defining commitments both impossible and unnecessary. Rather than living in the absurd like Kierkegaard's Knight of Faith, accepting the risk of grief and thereby making higher immediacy possible, authentic Dasein, by soberly facing the impossibility of having any possibilities of its own, is insured against absolute commitments and their concomitant risk of grief. Thus authentic Dasein understands even long-range commitments as made only for as long as they happen to last, i.e., as long as the Situation keeps showing up as demanding that commitment. The openness of resoluteness assures that

[Dasein] simply cannot become rigid as regards the Situation, but must understand that the resolution, in accordance with its own meaning as a disclosure, must be held open and free for the current factical possibility.

The certainty of the resolution signifies that one holds oneself free for the possibility of *taking it back.* (355) [307–308]

Authentic Dasein, since it does not expect whatever project it is engaged in to give it an identity and a meaningful world, can follow a project tenaciously, yet let the project go without grief when the project becomes unrealistic, i.e., when it ceases to show up as being what needs to be done. Since the project never defines the self and its world there will always be something else in the world which becomes most important as soon as any particular project ceases to fill that role.

For Kierkegaard, steadiness and constancy come from an unconditional stand, an *absolute* commitment to *something specific.* But authentic Dasein, constantly facing its nothingness, cannot make unconditional commitments. So for Dasein the steadiness and steadfastness of a specific commitment cannot provide the continuity that Heidegger demands. Conditional commitments can provide some constancy, but on Heidegger's account only an empty *formal* constancy can be certain of spanning a whole life. The self must manifest its basic nothingness in each conditional commitment.

Resoluteness is freedom to give up some definite resolution, and to give it up in accordance with the demands of some possible Situation or other. The steadiness of existence is not interrupted thereby but confirmed. (443) [391]

To understand this claim, one must understand authentic temporality. Heidegger, like Kierkegaard, seeks to show that living as an authentic self amounts to a reinterpreting of each factor and that these reinterpreted factors fit together to produce a new temporal structure. The formal difference between irresoluteness and resoluteness in style but not in content—in the *how* not in the *what*, as Kierkegaard would put it—is reflected in a structural difference in the temporality of the inauthentic and authentic modes of existence.

Inauthentic Dasein either holds tenaciously to projects demanding unconditional meaning and drops them when they fail to provide it, or else it seeks meaning in each event that comes along, eagerly awaiting and then immediately forgetting each event. "Curiosity always holds by what is coming next, and has forgotten what has gone before" (398–399) [347]. In either case, inauthentic temporality has the form of *awaiting* and *forgetting*. Authentic Dasein, on the contrary, whether spontaneous or steadfast in its activity, does not *await* future events but *foreruns* its death, i.e., constantly expresses in the style of its activity the nothingness that it is:

Forerunning discloses to existence that its uttermost possibility lies in giving itself up, and thus it shatters all one's tenaciousness to whatever existence one has reached. (308) [264]

Likewise, when authentic Dasein keeps itself open to change it is constantly *repeating* (again a Kierkegaardian term) the basic nullity of its thrownness, whether or not it abandons its specific past projects.

The holding-for-true of resoluteness (as the truth of existence) by no means lets itself fall back into irresoluteness. On the contrary, this holding-for-true, as a resolute holding-free for taking back, is authentic resoluteness which resolves to keep repeating itself. (355) [308]

Thus when Dasein accepts anxiety the temporal structure of its life is transformed. While it still *expects* and *remembers* specific events, the temporal form of its relation to specific events changes from *awaiting* and *forgetting* to *forerunning* and *repetition*. Authentic Dasein in *forerunning, repeating, resoluteness,* lives out the temporality of Dasein in such a way as to give a *constant form* to its activity, no matter how its specific projects come and go.

This formal, structural approach, however, does not enable Heidegger to distinguish those public possibilities that promote an authentic life from those that promote an inauthentic one. *Any* possibility that makes sense given the culture can be taken up in a style in which anxiety is repressed. Then one responds to the general situation and either hangs onto possibilities too long or drops possibilities as soon as they fail to fulfill. Likewise, *any* possibility can provide a unique occasion on which to face anxiety and, having abandoned hope of "eternal" meaning or satisfaction, do whatever I do in the Situation impeccably and passionately simply because it demands to be done. Some for-the-sake-of-whichs, such as being a gossip columnist, might promote banality and flight whereas others, like counseling terminal cancer patients, might promote facing up, but any possibility could be realized in either style. There is no reason for Heidegger to draw back from the nihilistic conclusion that, given the leveling of the one and the meaning-undermining effect of anxiety, there can be no meaningful differences among projects, and that therefore we must base the distinction between authenticity and inauthenticity on the form or style of activity only, not upon its content. Yet, as we shall now see, Heidegger does draw back.

G. Historicality

In Chapter V, "Temporality and Historicality," Heidegger introduces a culture's history as source of *superior* possibilities. In discussing how Dasein takes over its past, Heidegger claims that in spite of the leveling power of the one there *are* possibilities in our past that can be taken up and repeated in such a way as to resist leveling. Heidegger first acknowledges that forerunning is only a *formal* criterion that does not produce any privileged possibilities:

We must ask whence, in general, Dasein can draw those possibilities upon which it factically projects itself. Forerunning projection on that possibility of existence which is not to be outstripped—on death—guarantees only the totality and authenticity of one's resoluteness. But those possibilities of existence which have been factically disclosed are not to be gathered from death. (434)[383]

He then tells us:

The resoluteness in which Dasein comes back to itself, discloses current factical possibilities of authentic existing, and discloses them *in terms of the heritage* which that resoluteness, as thrown, takes over. (435)[383]

To make sense of this notion of the heritage as well as to complete our understanding of falling, we need to make a three-fold distinction concerning the concealing and revealing possibilities of the practices of the one. It seems the one has three effects: banalizing, disguising, and preserving. We have already discussed the first two as kinds of leveling. To repeat: Most of what one does is done in the standard ways of coping with everyday things that make up what Heidegger calls "average intelligibility." This is a kind of leveling because it fosters generality and banality. We all tend to do things, understand things, and classify situations in the way that is typical in our culture. A second, more extreme and dangerous kind of leveling varies from period to period and culture to culture. This leveling results from the strategies of cover-up and escape that use the structural falling of Dasein to *disguise* its essential nullity. Heidegger, following Kierkegaard, seems to find such practices to be especially powerful in our current culture. He notes that "the extent to which [the one's] dominion becomes compelling and explicit may change in the course of history" (167) [129], and he sees in "all the ways in which we speed things up, as we are more or less compelled to do today" (140) [105], an increasing tendency to want to be present everywhere, which is a kind of leveling curiosity.

A third kind of possibilities found in society are *marginal practices* that have *resisted leveling.* These can be practices that were central in past epochs, like Christian caring in the early Christian communities and absolute commitment at the height of romantic chivalry, or Greek mentoring of adolescent boys. These practices were once central (and presumably therefore banalized) but have now become rare and therefore are no longer what one normally does. They therefore offer fresh ways of responding to the Situation.

Such alternative possibilities, precisely because they do not make good, average, everyday sense but rather seem old-fashioned, trivial, or meaningless, would neither be undermined by anxiety nor leveled by the public. They would therefore attract authentic individuals.

Resoluteness constitutes the loyalty of existence to its own self. As resoluteness which is ready for anxiety, this loyalty is at the same time a possible way of revering the sole authority which a free existing can have—of revering the repeatable possibilities of existence. (443) [391]

Marginal possibilities offer the loyal individual nonbanal ways of perceiving and responding to the Situation. Here *repetition* is not merely formal but acquires specific content.

An authentic individual could repeat the heritage unaware of its source, like a nurse taking up caring or a high school teacher taking up mentoring, even though these are not the normal things to do these days when one generally seeks status and high pay.

In [Dasein's] coming back resolutely to its thrownness, there is hidden a *handing down* to itself of the possibilities that have come down to it, but not necessarily *as* having thus come down. (435) [383]

It is not necessary that resoluteness should *explicitly* know the origin of the possibilities upon which it projects itself. (437) [385]

Or the individual could take up the heritage explicitly, as did Martin Luther King, Jr., when he took up the Christian role of the savior of the oppressed. Heidegger seems sometimes to want to reserve the term repetition, in the sense of retrieval, for this second type of case:

> The existentiell ability-to-be upon which it projects itself can be gleaned *explicitly* from the way in which Dasein has been traditionally understood. The resoluteness which comes back to itself and hands itself down, then becomes the *repetition* of a possibility of existence that has come down to us. (437) [385][64]

In either case Dasein's activity will be intelligible because it is doing what one does, but Dasein will not be doing what one *normally* does.

In order to act out of past possibilities, it is helpful, perhaps even necessary, to have a model so as to see what such a life would be like. One picks an exemplar such as Jesus, Florence Nightingale, or Mentor himself, sometimes without even knowing it. Heidegger calls this "the possibility that Dasein may choose its hero" (437) [385], although given the *receptiveness* of resoluteness, it might be more fitting to say that Dasein's hero chooses Dasein. Heidegger calls Dasein's letting itself be chosen by some possibility its accepting its fate.

> Once one has grasped the finitude of one's existence, it snatches one back from the endless multiplicity of possibilities which offer themselves as closest to one—those of comfortableness, shirking, and taking things lightly—and brings Dasein into the simplicity of its *fate.* This is how we designate Dasein's primordial historizing, which lies in authentic resoluteness and in which Dasein hands itself down to itself, free for death, in a possibility which it has inherited and yet has chosen. (435) [384]

In this connection Heidegger once again stresses Dasein's powerlessness in a way reminiscent of the self-annihilation of Religiousness A.

> Fate is that powerless superior power which puts itself in readiness for adversities—the power of projecting oneself upon one's own being-guilty, and of doing so reticently, with readiness for anxiety. (436) [385]

Of course, one cannot do in the present situation just what the exemplar from the past did, but if one is following an exemplar from the past one cannot do what one normally does either:

Arising, as it does, from a resolute self-projection, repetition does not let itself be persuaded of something by what is "past," just in order that this, as something which was formerly actual, may recur. Rather, the repetition makes a *reciprocative rejoinder* to the possibility of that existence which has-been-there. (437–438) [385–386]

The tension between the past hero and the current Situation eliminates both universal moral guidelines and reliance on the normal, making necessary a unique response.

Finally, Heidegger holds that at any given stage of history certain marginal practices will be especially relevant, so that in taking them up authentic Dasein can define the current issue for itself and its generation. "In repetition, fateful destiny can be disclosed explicitly as bound up with the heritage which has come down to us" (438) [386]. "Dasein's fateful destiny in and with its 'generation' goes to make up the full authentic historizing of Dasein" (436) [384–385].[65] Ecology, for example, might be the issue for our generation, requiring finding a hero such as John Muir and adapting past practices of preserving and respecting nature. (Such practices will, of course, subsequently be leveled to banality by the one.)

It is hard, however, to reconcile Heidegger's talk of the heritage and choosing superior possibilities with his account of anxiety. The heritage may escape *leveling* because such practices are too marginal to be taken seriously and banalized, but remember that resoluteness gives Dasein "a freedom which has been released from the illusions of the one, and which is factical, certain of itself, and *anxious*" (311) [266] and all differentiations are revealed by anxiety to be totally indifferent, and so all equally meaningless.

Heidegger would respond, presumably, that the *intrinsic meaning* of traditional meaningful practices that are now marginalized is, indeed, leveled by anxiety, but their *difference* from what is now generally done is still preserved. As long as these other practices from our past are still around they can show up for a Dasein for whom the one is no longer its hero as what needs to be done. Thus, granted that in the face of anxiety, no possibilities can have *intrinsic* or *enduring* meaning, the heritage is still available as a source of *meaningless* differences. These nonbanal, nonleveled possibilities can still serve as a source of unique possibilities as long as Dasein does not take them up with the pseudoseriousness of everyday conscience or the unconditional seriousness of Religiousness B.

Heidegger does not ask himself whether the culture might become so conformist and media-dominated that no unleveled heritage was left to repeat. As we have seen, this was Kierkegaard's main concern, which led him to propose the higher immediacy of Religiousness B. This fear perhaps grows on Heidegger and feeds into his preoccupation with nihilism after *Being and Time*. In *Being and Time*, however, Heidegger builds in a nihilistic response to the possibility of total leveling. The *form* of acting on *any* possibility is all that is absolutely essential for constancy, and constancy is all that is essential for authenticity.

> The self's resoluteness against the inconstancy of distraction, *is in itself* [i.e., regardless of content] a steadiness which has been stretched along— the steadiness with which Dasein as fate "incorporates" into its existence birth and death and their "between," and holds them as thus "incorporated." (442, our italics and our gloss in brackets) [390–391]

But how can anything matter to Dasein once it lives in anxiety, since, as we saw in chapter 10, anxiety makes all meaning and mattering slip away? Heidegger's answer is indirect and not totally convincing. It seems that on Heidegger's account what slips away in anxiety is only all *everyday mattering*—the *conventional seriousness* arising from fear, ambition, and conformism that generates the demands of the general situation. What then shows up as mattering to anxious authentic Dasein are the nonleveled possibilities of the heritage that generate the demands of the unique Situation.

Thanks to anxiety, an authentic Dasein is freed from the ambiguous pseudoseriousness of the one, which Kierkegaard first pointed out and which Heidegger calls *tranquilization*.

> The average everydayness of concern becomes blind to its possibilities, and tranquilizes itself with that which is merely "actual." This tranquilizing does not rule out a high degree of diligence in one's concern, but arouses it. In this case no positive new possibilities are willed, but that which is at one's disposal becomes tactically altered in such a way that there is a semblance of something happening. (239) [195]

All activity done while facing anxiety is, however, indifferent to this busy tranquilization.

> In using, manipulation, and producing . . . Dasein's authentic existence too maintains itself, even when for such existence this concern is "a matter of indifference." (403) [352]

It is precisely thanks to the "indifference" gained by facing anxiety that authentic Dasein overcomes the pseudoseriousness that permeates the one. Dasein is thus freed from the ambiguity, distraction, opportunism, and self-involvement, as well as the underlying dull banality and indifference of everyday human existence. Then authentic Dasein, Heidegger claims, finds its own kind of mattering. The hectic tranquillity bred of inauthenticity is replaced by an effortless *equanimity.*

[Inauthentic] indifference, which can go along with busying oneself head over heels, must be sharply distinguished from equanimity. This latter mood springs from resoluteness, which, in the moment, takes in those Situations which are possible in its ability-to-be-a-whole disclosed in forerunning to death. (396) [345]

In sum, banality is replaced by the demands of the unique Situation, and fearful business is replaced by anxious equanimity. The result of facing nothingness, then, is a life free from both the dullness of the public and the demands for Christian absolute commitment—a life that for these very reasons is definitely worth living:

Forerunning resoluteness [does not] stem from "idealistic" exactions soaring above existence and its possibilities; it springs from a sober understanding of what are factically the basic possibilities for Dasein. Along with the sober anxiety which brings us face to face with our individualized ability-to-be, there goes *an unshakable joy.* (358, our italics) [310]

H. A Remaining Problem
Authenticity seems to be a successfully secularized version of Religiousness A with all its benefits and none of its contradictions. Moreover, it has been expanded to include as much of Religiousness B as one can have without risk. But the very success of Heidegger's description of an authentic life makes his account of inauthenticity incoherent. This shows up in his confused account of falling as fleeing.

Remember that there are *two* versions of falling in *Being and Time.* One, as we saw in chapter 13, is the structural story that coping and intelligibility require absorption in equipment and conforming to the public norms of the one, and so tend to turn Dasein away from confronting itself. On this account, leveling comes along with practical intelligibility. Conscience calls for resistance but the self does not hear it. If one asks why not, one is, as we have seen, given a second account—the motivational story that Dasein *actively resists* hearing. On this Kierkegaard-influenced account, leveling is not basically *structural* but is a *motivated* form of cover-up. The absorption that closes off Dasein from the unique Situation and from its unsettledness is the result of Dasein's fleeing its nullity. Thus to explain the existence of everyday, public practices and Dasein's tendency to let them pull it away from facing its nullity and unsettledness, Heidegger moves from a structural account of fallenness as the result of *falling*-away to a psychological account of fallenness as the result of *running*-away.

This account makes sense in Kierkegaard's dogmatic Christian interpretation of The Fall where the individual and the public are trying to avoid risk, but it cannot be secularized. Heidegger's attempted secularization runs into a double contradiction; inauthenticity becomes both inevitable and incomprehensible. On the one hand, if one holds that falling as absorption is motivated by fleeing, i.e., that absorption is a way of covering up Dasein's nullity, then, since absorption is essential to Dasein as being-in-the-world, Dasein becomes essentially inauthentic. On the other hand, if facing the truth about itself leads Dasein to equanimity, appropriate action, and unshakable joy, resoluteness is so rewarding that, once one is authentic, falling back into inauthenticity becomes incomprehensible. Yet Heidegger tells us:

Dasein is already in irresoluteness, and soon, perhaps, will be in it again. The term "irresoluteness" merely expresses that phenomenon which we have Interpreted as a being-surrendered to the way in which things have been prevalently interpreted by the one. (345)[299]

As a constant possibility of Dasein, irresoluteness is *co-certain*. (356)[308]

But why is maintaining resoluteness difficult? Why does Dasein constantly fall back into irresoluteness? Why does resoluteness have to accept irresoluteness? Why does even authentic Dasein have a tendency to flee? *Why, in short, are we the kind of beings that can't face being the kind of beings we are?*

The obvious answer would seem to be that human beings seek secure meaning. The truth about Dasein's nothingness and meaninglessness as revealed in anxiety is, therefore, unbearable and one naturally wants to flee it. But the question returns: If anxiety reveals that Dasein is really a nullity, and if Dasein is called to manifest in its action what it is, why shouldn't Dasein seek to live in a way that manifests its nullity, rather than to try to hide its nullity in banality and pseudocontent? Anxiety might well be unbearable to a self brought up in a society that does not understand how to make meaninglessness the foundation of a life worth living, but once Dasein has seen in a moment of transformation that nullity is its truth and that the truth gives equanimity and joy, why should Dasein flee it? Granted that escape strategies are taken up from the culture with mothers' milk, and granted that it might take some time to overcome the habits and fears acquired by growing up in the everyday world, one would still expect authentic human beings to become more and more secure in their superior, fully human form of life. Yet, as we have noted, according to Heidegger, "Dasein prepares for itself a *constant temptation* towards falling" (221, our italics) [177]. In spite of his thoroughness and consistency in every other respect, Heidegger never raises these questions and, in fact, seems completely oblivious to the major inconsistency his account of falling as fleeing introduces into his otherwise successful secularization of Religiousness A.

The trouble goes back to Heidegger's incomplete secularization of Kierkegaard's concept of anxiety. As we saw above, Kierkegaard defines anxiety as a sympathetic antipathy. The Christian in Religiousness A sees that to get out of the despair of meaninglessness, he or she could make an absolute commitment. Thus the attraction of Religiousness B—the highest sphere of existence. But a person in Religiousness A cannot understand how anyone could be prepared to accept the anguish of risk and loss—thus the repulsion. But Heidegger does not have a Christian conception of the self as needing a meaningful world of its own and commitment as providing it, so the attraction of total commitment has no place in his account. However, having dropped the sympathy, he inexplicably holds onto the antipathy. Yet without the need for the meaningfulness of total commitment and the consequent risk of grief, Heidegger's secularized version of the antipathy of anxiety as repulsion in the face of meaninglessness makes no sense. If anxiety is the truth of Dasein's condition and the truth sets it free, why doesn't Dasein seek anxiety rather than flee it?

Heidegger's inability to account for Dasein's temptation to plunge into the one parallels Socrates' inability to explain why a person would choose evil when the good is more fulfilling. In *The Sickness Unto Death* Kierkegaard raises this traditional puzzle about incontinence and answers that only a Christian-dogmatic account of the self as requiring a differentiated world of its own, the risks attendant upon having such a world, and therefore the strategies of flight called sinfulness explains why anyone would be tempted to avoid what they most deeply require.[66] Heidegger might counter that traditional philosophy cannot solve the problem of incontinence, not because it lacks a notion of sin but because it has an overintellectualized conception of choice, whereas his account of how Dasein is socialized into doing what one does explains how, in the undifferentiated mode, Dasein is constantly taking over strategies for covering up anxiety without explicitly choosing to flee. But this only pushes the problem back a step. Why should fallenness, i.e., ways of covering up nullity, be built into every society?

In spite of his denial, and against his will, Heidegger seems to have taken over from Kierkegaard a dogmatic-Christian conception of society and of sinfulness. The difference between the two accounts, however, is that in Kierkegaard's version sinfulness as a constant temptation to flee "the call in existence" is supposed to characterize a *Christian* society with its built-in demand for commitment and risk of grief, and so makes sense, whereas Heidegger's attempt to formulate a secular, universal account of fallenness in terms of fleeing the call to face nullity does not. Perhaps this is why Heidegger drops all talk of fleeing in *Basic Problems* and thereafter.

I. *Beyond* Being and Time

Later Heidegger seems to have recognized this problem. He gives up his existential account of anxiety, and of falling as a motivated cover-up of Dasein's essential nullity and unsettledness. In his works after 1930, Heidegger distinguishes the specific understanding of what counts as real, which everyone brought up in the practices of a particular culture at a particular time shares, from the metaunderstanding of the thinker that this public understanding is nothing more nor less than an interpretation. It was this metaunderstanding—a preontological sense of unsettledness— that, in *Being and Time*, was supposed to be revealed to each human being in an ever-present but normally repressed sense of anxiety.

Heidegger elaborated his account of anxiety as a privileged revealing experience of man's essential nullity and rootlessness for the last time in his 1929 lecture "What is Metaphysics?" In a new introduction to that lecture in 1949, he presents anxiety quite differently. He still holds that anxiety as a revelation of unsettledness is no ordinary mood. It cannot, for example, be explained by sociology or removed by psychoanalysis. But anxiety is no longer interpreted as a source of insight into the true structure of Dasein, preontologically available to each human being, which hermeneutic phenomenology can uncover by violently wrenching away motivated disguises. It is now read as the experience of "the oblivion of being" uniquely characteristic of the modern age.[67]

On this interpretation, we moderns feel an "immeasurable need," and since it is painful, almost everyone flees it almost all of the time—but we do not flee because we grasp this pain's significance. Insofar as there is a shared interpretation of this shared distress in our practices, it is misleading and superficial—e.g., that anxiety is the result of urbanization, repression, overwork, etc. Heidegger, however, no longer attempts to uncover a preontological understanding shared by all human beings of what anxiety really means that this superficial understanding covers up. Anxiety can be seen as a special revealing mood only if it is *given* an interpretation. Heidegger the thinker (not the hermeneutic phenomenologist with a preontological understanding of the sense of being) interprets anxiety as a specific response to the rootlessness of the contemporary technological world.[68]

Anxiety is no longer interpreted, then, as a manifestation of the essential truth, accessible to all human beings, that, since reality is relative to human practices, and nothing can define the self, human beings can never find a foundation for their lives, and can never feel at home in the world. On the contrary, Heidegger becomes interested in how the pre-Socratic Greeks were free from modern anxiety and at home in their world. He even hopes to find hints in practices still left over from ancient times of how we can once again be at home in ours. Directly contradicting his early emphasis on man's essential experience of unsettledness, later Heidegger strives to give us "a vision of a new rootedness which someday might even be fit to recapture the old and now rapidly disappearing rootedness in a changed form."[69]

Thus later Heidegger never abandons the lasting contribution of *Being and Time,* namely the analysis of Dasein's understanding of being and the world it opens up; rather he historicizes world disclosing as Dasein's receiving of a succession of clearings. Starting with his reinterpretation of anxiety as occasioned by our modern understanding of being, Heidegger attempts to show that each specific epoch in the development of our historical culture is a metaphysical variation on the pre-Socratic interpretation of all reality as presencing. For the early Greeks, reality was that which opened itself and took man into its presence where he was "beheld by what is . . . included and maintained within its openness and in that way borne along by it, to be driven about by its oppositions and marked by its discord."[70] But for medieval Christians, reality was the presence of created things as finished products which were simply to be accepted, while for modern man, starting with Descartes, reality was made present to man by man himself and forced to live up to his standards of intelligibility.

Each of these understandings of being allows different sorts of beings to show up. The Greeks encountered *things* in their beauty and power, and people as poets, statesmen and heroes; the Christians encountered *creatures* to be catalogued and used appropriately and people as saints and sinners; and we moderns encounter *objects* to be controlled and organized by subjects in order to satisfy their desires. Or, most recently as we enter the final stage of technology, we experience everything including ourselves as resources to be enhanced, transformed, and ordered simply for the sake of greater and greater efficiency.[71] Anxiety is seen not as an existential structure but is reinterpreted as a sign, not yet read correctly in *Being and Time*, of the total nihilism of this last stage.

In his analysis of nihilism and how it might end, later Heidegger makes a clean break with an essentially Christian analysis of fallenness and turns to a reading of modern poets, especially Hölderlin on the Greeks. Kierkegaard is never mentioned except to portray his concept of existence as a stage in the nihilistic development of Western metaphysics.[72] Instead of concern with how a human being can become an individual living in a differentiated public world, Heidegger concerns himself exclusively with the leveling brought about by modern cultural practices. He offers a genealogical history of nihilism and calls attention to the saving power of what seems insignificant:

We are . . . summoned to hope in the growing light of the saving power. How can this happen? Here and now and in the humble things, that we may foster the saving power in its increase.[73]

One can see in Heidegger's concern for humble things a continuation of his interest in the heritage of marginal practices. He now sees them as possibilities that have saving power precisely because they have never been taken seriously by the metaphysical tradition. Such practices, which have not been singled out as important and so technologized, provide a basis for resisting the technological understanding of being. Heidegger also offers a cultural version of an exemplar or hero. Specific things, such as the Greek temple, have served as cultural exemplars or paradigms, which Heidegger calls gods, collecting together scattered practices and thereby setting up and stabilizing a differentiated meaningful world:

> It is the temple-work that first fits together and at the same time gathers around itself the unity of those paths and relations in which birth and death, disaster and blessing, victory and disgrace, endurance and decline acquire the shape of destiny for human being.[74]

Heidegger only occasionally considers how an individual in our nihilistic age should live while awaiting a nonnihilistic culture. When he does, what he proposes is not *Entschlossenheit*, with its misleading suggestions of willfulness and triumphant joy, or even *Ent-schlossenheit*, with its implication that openness to meaninglessness is an end in itself, but rather *Gelassenheit*, a serene openness to a possible change in our understanding of being. In this mood the thinker, while using technological devices, stands outside our nihilistic technological understanding of reality. He is thus open to other sorts of practices that still survive, and to a new understanding of reality, should one be given us by a new cultural paradigm. Like resoluteness, *Gelassenheit* is hard to arrive at and hard to maintain, but the unconvincing story that anxiety is unbearable and so resoluteness must constantly resist the temptation to flee it, has been replaced by the plausible account that since *Gelassenheit* requires a life outside the reigning technological understanding of being into which everyone is socialized, without as yet being able to turn to any other understanding, a struggle is necessary to achieve it, and it can be maintained only by constantly rethinking the history of our Western understanding of being.

To sum up, after Kierkegaard's profound but mostly unacknowledged influence on early Heidegger, we find Kierkegaard and the later Heidegger following separate but parallel paths. They agree that nihilism is the most crucial issue of our time, but they differ in their responses to that issue. Kierkegaard, as we have seen, is concerned with the way in which individuals can have commitments in a nihilistic culture. But he has nothing to say about how or whether our culture could be transformed from a nihilistic one to a nonnihilistic one. Given the structure of human beings which he has laid out, even a nonnihilistic culture would still require individual commitment in order for a human being to become a self. Thus, while Kierkegaard thinks that our culture poses special problems for human beings, his most fundamental concern is with the individual self and how it can be saved.

Later Heidegger, on the other hand, has little interest in how an individual can find life worth living even in a nihilistic culture. Instead, he is concerned with diagnosing the way philosophy propagates nihilism and with preserving those cultural practices that have not yet succumbed to the leveling of technology. The possibility of saving the culture as a whole, and not individuals, is the central concern of his later work.

The one thing upon which Kierkegaard and later Heidegger do agree is that only an incarnate god can save us. Kierkegaard's discussion of the God-man as a paradigm for individual commitment in *Training in Christianity* is his story about what individual salvation would look like. Heidegger's description of the Greek temple as a paradigm that defines what is important for a whole culture is his account of what cultural salvation would be. Like the rest of their work, Kierkegaard and Heidegger's descriptions of paradigms and how they function have both striking similarities and equally striking differences. Discussion of their complementary proposals for overcoming nihilism must await another occasion.

Notes

Works of Martin Heidegger cited in the notes

Basic Problems of Phenomenology (Bloomington: Indiana University Press, 1982); cited as BP in text

Basic Writings (New York: Harper & Row, 1977)

Being and Time (New York: Harper & Row, 1962)

Discourse on Thinking (New York: Harper & Row, 1959)

Early Greek Thinking (New York: Harper & Row, 1975)

The End of Philosophy (New York: Harper & Row, 1973)

The Essence of Reasons (Evanston: Northwestern University Press, 1969)

Gesamtausgabe, vols. 1, 2, 15, 25, 29/30, 39, 45, 61, 63 (Frankfurt: Klostermann, 1972–1988)

History of the Concept of Time (Bloomington: Indiana University Press, 1985); cited as HCT in text

Introduction to Metaphysics (New Haven: Yale University Press, 1959)

Kant and the Problem of Metaphysics (Bloomington: Indiana University Press, 1962)

Metaphysical Foundations of Logic (Bloomington: Indiana University Press, 1984); cited as MFL in text

Nietzsche, vol. 4: *Nihilism* (New York: Harper & Row, 1982)

On the Way to Language (New York: Harper & Row, 1982)

On Time and Being (New York: Harper Torchbooks, 1972)

Poetry, Language, Thought (New York, Harper & Row, 1971)

The Question Concerning Technology and Other Essays (New York: Harper & Row, 1977)

Schelling's Treatise on the Essence of Human Freedom (Athens: Ohio State University Press, 1985)

Zollikonner Seminare, Medard Boss, ed. (Frankfurt: Klostermann, 1987)

Introduction

1. Page references in parentheses are to to the English edition of *Being and Time*; page references in brackets refer to the original German edition.

2. Heidegger, "The Origin of the Work of Art," in *Poetry, Language, Thought*, 55.

3. Edmund Husserl, *Ideas Pertaining to a Pure Phenomenology and to a Phenomenological Philosophy* (The Hague: Nijhoff, 1982).

4. John Searle, *Intentionality: An Essay in the Philosophy of Mind* (Cambridge: Cambridge University Press, 1983). For a comparison of Husserl's and Searle's account of intentionality, see Hubert L. Dreyfus, ed., *Husserl, Intentionality, and Cognitive Science* (Cambridge: Bradford Books/MIT Press, 1982).

5. Edmund Husserl, *The Crisis of the European Sciences* (Evanston: Northwestern University Press, 1970), 237; henceforth cited as *Crisis*.

6. Peter Strawson, Review of *Martin Heidegger* by George Steiner, *New York Review of Books*, 19 April 1979; my italics.

7. Hans-Georg Gadamer suggested this to me. Heidegger thanks Lask for the insight that our categories correspond to functions that "stem from the use of expressions in living thought and knowing" (*Gesamtausgabe*, vol. 1, 227). He mentions pragmatism and supports its relativizing of knowledge structures to ways of life in his 1921 lectures (*Gesamtausgabe*, vol. 61, 135).

8. Ludwig Wittgenstein, *Remarks on the Philosophy of Psychology*, vol. 2, edited by G. H. von Wright and Heikki Nyman (Chicago: University of Chicago Press, 1980), 108, #629.

9. Ludwig Wittgenstein, *Remarks on the Philosophy of Psychology*, vol. 1, edited by G. E. M. Anscombe and G. H. von Wright (Chicago: University of Chicago Press, 1980), 97, #509.

10. Searle, *Intentionality*, 156–157.

11. Heidegger, *Basic Problems of Phenomenology*, henceforth cited as BP. This book is based on the lecture course Heidegger gave in 1927, the same year he published *Being and Time*. In all quotations I have changed the original translation to fit the conventions noted in the preface.

12. H. Dreyfus and M. Zimmerman, eds., *Applied Heidegger* (Evanston: Northwestern University Press, 1991).

13. Michel Foucault, "Final Interview," *Raritan*, Summer 1985, 8. "Le Retour de la Morale," interview conducted by Gilles Barbadette, *Les Nouvelles*, 28 June 1984.

14. Jürgen Habermas, "Work and Weltanschauung: The Heidegger Controversy from a German Perspective," in *The New Conservatism: Cultural Criticism and the Historians' Debate* (Cambridge: MIT Press, 1990).

Chapter 1

1. Recent editions of *Sein und Zeit* contain Heidegger's marginal notes from one of his own copies. I cite these comments where relevant, giving in curly brackets the page reference to *Sein und Zeit*, vol. 2 of Heidegger's *Gesamtausgabe*.

2. Joseph J. Kockelmans, *On the Truth of Being* (Bloomington: Indiana University Press, 1984), x.

3. That Heidegger equates the understanding of being with the background comes out clearly in a later seminar on Heraclitus published in *Gesamtausgabe*, vol. 15. Heidegger says:

Being is that which is not a being and does not belong to beings. . . . What is not accessible to direct representing and meaning: that is the genuine background. (125)

That this background consists of our everyday *skills* for dealing with things and people is hinted at in a later work on Anaximander in which Heidegger reads his account of the understanding of being in everyday practices back into the first philosopher. In his interpretation of a fragment from the work of Anaximander, Heidegger translates the Greek word *Creon* as a name for being and as meaning custom or usage (*der Brauch*). He goes on to comment that "usage is thought as essential presencing of being itself. . . . Usage enjoining order and so limiting what is present, distributes boundaries" (ibid., 53–54). Then, commenting on Heraclitus' use of *sophon* (wisdom), Heidegger relates skills and destiny so as to suggest a relation of skills to customs or practices that make up the destiny of the understanding of being in the West.

[When] it is appropriate (*schickliches*) . . . behavior becomes skillful (*geschickt*). When we want to say that someone is particularly skilled at something, we still employ such turns of speech as "he has a gift for that and is destined for it." In this fashion we hit upon the genuine meaning of *sophon*, which we translate as "fateful" ("*geschicklich*"). (Ibid., 68)

These ideas may also be related to the claim made in *On the Way to Language* that being needs (*braucht*) man. One natural way to read this remark is to see it as making the point, which I take to be basic to *Being and Time*, that intelligibility is correlative with those skills that make up human background practices or customs and thus being needs human beings.

4. Appendix to Edmund Husserl, *Phänomenologische Psychologie* (The Hague: Nijhoff, 1962), 601.

5. Martin Heidegger, "The Way Back Into the Ground of Metaphysics," in Walter Kaufmann, ed., *Existentialism from Dostoevsky to Sartre* (New York: Meridian Books, 1957), 270, 271.

6. John Haugeland, "Heidegger on Being a Person," *Noûs*, XVI, 1982.

7. Heidegger, "The Way Back," 272.

8. W. Caudill and H. Weinstein, "Maternal Care and Infant Behavior in Japan and in America," in C. S. Lavatelli and F. Stendler, eds., *Readings in Child Behavior and Development* (New York: Harcourt Brace, 1972), 78.

9. Pierre Bourdieu, *Outline of a Theory of Practice* (Cambridge: Cambridge University Press, 1977), 87.

10. Ibid., 94.

11. Ibid., 2.

12. Heidegger, *History of the Concept of Time* (henceforth cited as HCT), 246.

13. Just as Kant's categories tell us the general characteristics of an object, so Heidegger's existentiales tell us the general characteristics of Dasein. We must, however, be careful to avoid the temptation to think of the existentiales as the

general structure of *subjects,* analogous to the way that categories are the general structure of *objects.* Rather, since Dasein is essentially a self-interpreting being, existentiales give us the general structure of existence.

It is tempting to suppose that in *Being and Time* Heidegger is developing a transcendental (in Kant's sense of the term) analytic, in which Dasein is the *condition of the possibility* of the experience of objects, and Heidegger does sometimes use this Kantian language. But this is too traditional, for it implies that Dasein as the condition of *possibility* can be understood apart from the question of whether any objects *actually* exist, and that the categorial structure that makes possible the experience of objects can be made totally explicit as in Kant's transcendental deduction or Husserl's eidetic reduction. Therefore Heidegger calls his investigation an *existential* as opposed to a *transcendental* analytic. According to Heidegger's existential analytic, Dasein must exist factically—that is, Dasein (unlike the transcendental ego) is necessarily involved in, and dependent upon, the world it opens up, and can never get clear about the world it is in. Only thus is it the condition of anything showing up for us as anything.

14. For example, see Heidegger, *Kant and the Problem of Metaphysics,* 207.

15. In the transcendental idealism championed by Kant and Husserl, man is both too much a subject and too much an object—what Foucault calls a transcendental/empirical double. Man is both the idealist's transcendental source of all meanings and, at the same time, a constituted person with determinate objective natural and social properties.

Heidegger wants to do justice to both the idealist and naturalist positions without making the mistake of either. Dasein in its facticity is thus neither like Husserl's (self-constituting) transcendental ego nor like his (constituted) social person. Social Dasein is the source of interpretations and, as we shall see, is ultimately the source of what will count as a fact. Thus social Dasein, like the transcendental ego, is not factual. Still Dasein is always *factical*; it takes over interpretations always already provided by the culture. Thus social human being is the source of meaning for the world but is always already in the world to which it gives meaning.

16. Heidegger, *Ontologie (Hermeneutik der Faktizität),* in *Gesamtausgabe,* vol. 63, 7.

Chapter 2

1. Harold Garfinkel, *Studies in Ethnomethodology* (Englewood Cliffs, NJ: Prentice-Hall, 1967).

2. See especially Charles Taylor, "Interpretation and the Sciences of Man," in *Philosophical Papers,* vol. 2 (Cambridge: Cambridge University Press, 1985).

3. Clifford Geertz, *The Interpretation of Cultures* (New York: Harper & Row, 1973).

4. Thomas Kuhn, *The Essential Tension* (Chicago: University of Chicago Press, 1977).

5. Richard Rorty, *Philosophy and the Mirror of Nature* (Princeton: Princeton University Press, 1979).

6. Heidegger, *On the Way to Language,* 11.

7. Ibid.

8. Ludwig Wittgenstein, *Philosophical Investigations*, Part I (Oxford: Basil Blackwell, 1953), #129.

9. Paul Ricoeur blurs his classification by including Nietzsche, who, indeed, does not take our practices at face value, among those who practice the hermeneutics of suspicion. According to Michel Foucault's more illuminating classification, however, Nietzsche, while questioning our cultural self-interpretation, is not practicing a hermeneutics of suspicion because he does not assume that the distorted interpretation in our cultural practices is the result of a deliberate cover-up of an undistorted one. Nietzsche's *Genealogy of Morals*, for example, questions Western morality and metaphysics but it does not trace these practices back to a refusal to face a deep truth (as in Freud) or even the refusal to face the fact that there is no deep truth (as in Heidegger). Foucault points out that for Nietzsche our current self-interpretation is not in the service of a deliberate cover-up but rather is the result of many local power struggles. See: Michel Foucault, "Nietzsche, Genealogy, History," in Paul Rabinow, ed., *The Foucault Reader* (New York: Pantheon, 1984), and Hubert L. Dreyfus and Paul Rabinow, eds., *Michel Foucault: Beyond Structuralism and Hermeneutics* (Chicago: University of Chicago Press, 1982).

Chapter 3

1. See Mark Johnson, *The Body in the Mind* (Chicago: University of Chicago Press, 1987).

2. Michael Polanyi, *Personal Knowledge* (London: Routledge and Kegan Paul, 1962), chapter 4.

3. Thomas Kuhn, *The Structure of Scientific Revolutions* (Chicago: University of Chicago Press, 1970).

4. For a full discussion of this issue see chapter 15.

5. Edmund Husserl, *Cartesian Meditations* (The Hague: Nijhoff, 1960), 39.

6. Dagfinn Føllesdal, "Husserl and Heidegger on the Role of Actions in the Constitution of the World," in E. Saarinen et al., eds., *Essays in Honour of Jaakko Hintikka* (Dordrecht: Reidel, 1979), 371. A similar trivializing reduction of Heidegger's work to a practical variation on Husserl's is worked out in lucid and brilliant detail in Mark Okrent, *Heidegger's Pragmatism* (Ithaca: Cornell University Press, 1988). Okrent states bluntly: "As soon as one realizes that, for Heidegger, intentionality is always practical rather than cognitive and that the primary form of intending is doing something for a purpose rather than being conscious of something, the structural analogies between the argument strategies of Husserl and Heidegger become apparent" (10).

7. Ibid., 372.

8. Ibid., 376.

9. For an account of Husserl's phenomenological reduction, i.e., how Husserl and Searle are led by their theory of intentional content to what Jerry Fodor has called "methodological solipsism," see the introduction to Dreyfus, ed., *Husserl, Intentionality, and Cognitive Science*.

10. Paul Grice, "The Causal Theory of Perception," in Robert Swartz, ed., *Perceiving, Sensing, and Knowing* (New York: Anchor Books, 1965).

11. Searle, *Intentionality*, 107.

12. William James, "The Feeling of Effort," in *Collected Essays and Reviews* (New York: Longmans, Green and Co., 1920), 151–152.

13. Heidegger, *Zollikonner Seminare*, 284–285.

14. Friedrich Nietzsche, *The Gay Science* (New York: Random House, 1974), #354.

15. A nonmentalistic phenomenology of perception that parallels Heidegger's phenomenology of action in seeking a radical break with subject/object thinking is found in Maurice Merleau-Ponty's *Phenomenology of Perception* (London: Routledge & Kegan Paul, 1962). (Given that Merleau-Ponty attended Aron Gurwitsch's lectures in Paris explaining Heidegger's account of comportment in terms of gestalt perception, there may well be a direct line of influence here.) Merleau-Ponty develops the idea of perception as pure openness to the world:

The perception of other people and the intersubjective world are problematical only for adults. The child lives in a world which he unhesitatingly believes accessible to all around him. He has no awareness of himself or of others as private subjectivities, nor does he suspect that all of us, himself included, are limited to one specific point of view on the world. . . . He has no knowledge of points of view. For him men are empty heads turned towards one single, self-evident world where everything takes place . . . . Piaget brings the child to a mature outlook as if the thoughts of the adult were self-sufficient and disposed of all contradictions. But, in reality, it must be the case that the child's outlook is in some way vindicated against the adult's and against Piaget, and that the unsophisticated thinking of our earliest years remains as an indispensable acquisition underlying that of maturity, if there is to be for the adult one single intersubjective world. (355)

Chapter 4

1. The passage "das ist gegen Heidegger" can be found in original manuscript form under the signature B I 32, p. 30aff; the transcription is catalogued as B I 32 II, pp. 21ff. Quoted in Hubert Dreyfus and John Haugeland, "Husserl and Heidegger: Philosophy's Last Stand," in Michael Murray, ed., *Heidegger and Modern Philosophy* (New Haven: Yale University Press, 1978).

2. The term *circumspection* (*Umsicht*) is not used consistently by Heidegger. Here it clearly means nonthematic awareness of the environment, but in *Being and Time* Heidegger restricts *circumspection* to direct transparent coping and uses *disclosure* to name our nonthematic awareness of context:

It [the environment] is itself inaccessible to circumspection, so far as circumspection is always directed towards entities . . . (105) [75]

I shall use *circumspection* for both these forms of awareness, since the point is to contrast them with the thematic intentionality studied by Husserl and Searle.

3. Richard Mitchell, *Mountain Experience. The Psychology and Sociology of Adventure* (Chicago: University of Chicago Press, 1983).

4. Aron Gurwitsch, *Human Encounters in the Social World* (Pittsburgh: Duquesne University Press, 1979), 67.

5. John Dewey, *Human Nature and Conduct. An Introduction to Social Psychology* (London: George Allen and Unwin, 1922), 177–178. Dewey also remarks: "Knowledge . . . lives in the muscles, not in consciousness" (177). This can be spelled out concretely; see Jerome Wakefield and Hubert Dreyfus,"Intentionality and the Phenomenology of Action," in *John Searle and His Critics* (Oxford: Basil Blackwell, 1991).

6. Dewey, *Human Nature*, 178.

7. Husserl, *Logical Investigations*, vol. 1 (New York: Humanities Press, 1970), Investigation I, chapter 1.

8. Once one accepts that the mind/object relation first arises only on the level of the unavailable—a point Searle would, of course, dispute—Searle's theory of intentionality joins Heidegger's on this point. Both Searle and Heidegger agree that: (1) A mental state is not a relation to a representation (as Jerry Fodor, for example, holds) but can be a direct relation to an object. (2) Intentionality makes sense only on a background that cannot be analyzed in terms of more mental states; i.e., the background is not a belief system. For these reasons one can say that Searle, like Heidegger, rejects the traditional subject-object distinction, in which subjects are taken to be self-sufficient mental substances and representations are supposed to be self-sufficient entities in these subjects. The basic difference between Heidegger's and Searle's accounts of intentionality is that for Heidegger the relation of mental contents to objects (ontic transcendence) presupposes a mode of being (originary transcendence) that is not a relation at all, whereas Searle takes as basic the relation between mental content and things, holding that, in some sense, even the background, though not a belief system, is still mental. (See Searle, *Intentionality*, chapters 2 and 5.)

9. One might well wonder why there are just three forms of breakdown. Indeed, in Division I the list seems quite arbitrary. But in Division II Heidegger can perhaps be read as mapping the three forms of disturbance onto the three dimensions of time. *Conspicuousness* (malfunction) is associated with surprise as a failure of our pressing into the *future*.

When one is making present something available by *awaiting*, the possibility of one's *getting surprised* by something is based upon one's *not awaiting* something else which stands in a possible involvement nexus with what one awaits. (407) [355]

The *obstinacy* revealed in breakdown is associated with the *past*. Lacking the equipmental backup we were counting on in our project, we have to resign ourselves to doing what we are doing a harder way.

That which one has "not reckoned with" does not get forgotten; it gets retained, so that *in its very unsuitability* it remains available. (407) [356]

When something is missing it stops our ongoing absorption in our task. Things are revealed as *obtrusive*. This is a transformation of the *present*.

Such missing is by no means a not-making-present; it is rather a deficient mode of the present in the sense of the making-unpresent. (406–407) [355]

10. Heidegger, *On Time and Being*, 7.

11. Dewey makes a similar point and notes that it is lucky for us that our world is not perfectly attuned to our habits. We could think of consciousness, Dewey

notes, "as a kind of disease, since we have no consciousness of bodily or mental organs as long as they work at ease in perfect health." He adds, "The idea of disease, is, however, aside from the point, unless we are pessimistic enough to regard every slip in total adjustment of a person to his surroundings as something abnormal—a point of view which . . . would identify well-being with perfect automatism. The truth is that in every waking moment, the complete balance of the organism and its environment is constantly interfered with and as constantly restored" (*Human Nature*, 178–179).

12. Again Dewey would agree. After discussing the way things are constantly breaking down, he adds: "Normally, the environment remains sufficiently in harmony with the body of organized activities to sustain most of them in active function" (*Human Nature*, 179).

13. G. W. Leibniz, *Selections*, edited by Philip Wiener (New York: Scribners, 1951), 48.

14. Jürgen Habermas, *The Theory of Communicative Action*, vol. I (Boston: Beacon Press, 1981), 8.

15. Seymour Papert, *Mindstorms* (New York: Basic Books 1980), 99.

16. Daniel Dennett, "Cognitive Wheels: The Frame Problem of AI," in Zenon Pylyshyn, ed., *The Robot's Dilemma* (Norwood, NJ: Ablex, 1987), 46.

17. See H. and S. Dreyfus, *Mind Over Machine* (New York: Free Press, 1986).

Chapter 5

1. In *Basic Problems* Heidegger distinguishes the universe from the world as follows:

Nature—even if we take it in the sense of the whole cosmos as that which we also call, in ordinary discourse, the *universe* . . .—all these entities taken together, animals, plants, and humans, too, are not the world, viewed philosophically. (BP, 165, my italics)

2. Strictly speaking, according to Heidegger, organisms *live* in their *environment* which is not the same as a world or a universe. Dasein *dwells* in the *world*.

3. Kuhn, *Structure of Scientific Revolutions*, 175.

4. Heidegger introduces this sense of *a priori* in connection with space. "Here 'a priority' means the previousness with which space has been encountered (as a region) whenever the available is encountered environmentally" (146) [111].

5. The *intelligibility* of a piece of chalk is that it is used in order to write on blackboards; the *point* of writing on the board with a piece of chalk is tied into practices necessary for a self-interpretation, such as being a teacher. These must both be distinguished from *mattering*. On most days teaching and so also chalk matter greatly to me; on some days, however, they leave me indifferent. The fact that things can matter to Dasein in various ways and to varying degrees will be taken up in chapter 10.

6. Quoted in L. D. Levine, *Bird: The Making of an American Sports Legend* (New York: McGraw-Hill, 1988).

7. For a full discussion of the chess example, see Dreyfus and Dreyfus, *Mind Over Machine*.

8. See Roger Schank and Robert Abelson, *Scripts, Plans, Goals and Understanding* (Hillsdale, NJ: Erlbaum 1977). It is fascinating to see how Schank, as he tries to put enough understanding into a computer to enable it to understand stories, is led by the phenomenon to discover an objectified version of the structure of the world. Schank finds that in everyday activity there has got to be something one is trying to do; and that that activity makes sense only in a broader context in which there must be some goal; and finally all goals make sense or have a point in terms of some life theme.

9. Usually each human organism is one Dasein, one human being, because it has taken on one set of the available social ways of organizing its activities. In the case of Dr. Jekyll and Mr. Hyde, however, one organism alternates between two more or less integrated subpatterns of social practices. Other organisms, if catatonic or brain injured, can live on without Daseining, i.e., being human at all.

10. Heidegger again makes the basic point that our *general* coping skills allow *specific* things to show up for us in a difficult passage in *The Essence of Reasons*:

The *projection of world* makes a preliminary understanding of the being of beings possible and yet is not itself a relationship of Dasein to *beings*. Dasein, because of its *preoccupation* with beings, can find itself affected by and in the midst of beings, though indeed never without a disclosure of world. But its preoccupation is not a way of *comportment* toward beings. On the contrary, *both* Dasein's understanding of and its preoccupation with beings—in their unity as characterized above— make intentionality transcendentally possible. (113)

11. Translating *woraufhin* as *for which* in this and related passages completely obscures Heidegger's use of *woraufhin* to denote the background that allows particular things to show up and be intelligible. I shall translate *woraufhin* as *that on the basis of which*. The translators also insert "act of" before "understanding." To those sensitive to the issues, this is misleading because "mental *act*" is Husserl's name for the representational intentionality Heidegger's notion of understanding is designed to supplant.

Even today intentionality is taken simply as a structure of consciousness or of acts. . . . I point this out because we shall see how phenomenology, with this analysis of intentionality, calls for a more radical . . . development. (HCT, 46)

12. For Husserl, the *noema*, the intentional content that makes possible all relation to objects, is likewise hidden—we see right through it, so to speak, in directing ourselves toward objects. The transcendental phenomenologist makes the *noema* the object of a special act of reflection. Heidegger, however, holds that the world, the precondition for dealing with objects, is not itself a special sort of object (as Husserl claims the *noema* is) and cannot be discovered in detached reflection (as Husserl claims the *noema* can).

13. It will not be clear at this point why Heidegger speaks of *our* orientation. Why not say that it is *my* orientation and *my* readiness? Answer: Heidegger holds that being able to cope with public entities like rooms and chairs is a capacity that I share with everyone socialized into my culture. It is our skill. I may also have some more particular skills for coping with chairs if I am, say, a professional chair tester, and even some unique skills if I am a chair fetishist, but that is not relevant to Heidegger's concern here. This will become clear in chapter 8 on *shared* intelligibility.

14. Here as in many other places Heidegger uses misleading quotation marks around world; according to the convention established on page 93 of *Being and Time*, quotation marks are supposed to indicate the totality of objects (universe) rather than that in which Dasein dwells. Rather than noting each time Heidegger does this, I shall indicate with an asterisk when Heidegger does not observe his own convention.

15. At some later time Heidegger realized that speaking of "submitting itself" still sounds too intentionalistic. It could seem as if he had accepted the self-referential character of the experience of acting. So he wrote in the margin: "But not as an ego-like deed (*ichhafte Tathandlung*) of a subject" {117}.

16. Heidegger should be talking about the encountering of *any* entity, whether available or occurrent. He corrects himself in a marginal note: "Letting-be . . . completely broad for *every* entity" {113}.

Chapter 6

1. See Allen Newell and Herbert Simon, "The Physical Symbol System Hypothesis," in John Haugeland, ed., *Mind Design* (Cambridge: Bradford Books/MIT Press, 1981), and John Haugeland, *Artificial Intelligence: The Very Idea* (Cambridge: Bradford Books/MIT Press, 1985).

2. For more details see H. Dreyfus, "Between Techné and Technology: The Ambiguous Place of Equipment in *Being and Time*," in H. Dreyfus and H. Hall, eds., *Heidegger: A Critical Reader* (Oxford: Basil Blackwell, 1991).

3. See, for example, Heidegger, "The Thing," in *Poetry, Language, Thought.*

4. For more on reliability, see Heidegger, "The Origin of the Work of Art," in *Poetry, Language, Thought*, 34–35.

5. Husserl's version of this claim (*Cartesian Meditations*, 78), which obviously is aimed at Heidegger and his hammer, reads as follows:

Anything built by activity necessarily presupposes, as the lowest level, a passivity that gives something beforehand . . . The "ready-made" object that confronts us in life as an existent mere physical thing (when we disregard all the "spiritual" or "cultural" characteristics that make it knowable as, for example, a hammer . . .) is given, with the originality of the "it itself," in the synthesis of a passive experience. As such a thing, it is given beforehand to "spiritual" activities, which begin with active grasping.

6. See H. Dreyfus, "Husserl's Epiphenomenology," in H. R. Otto and J. A. Tuedio, eds., *Perspectives on Mind* (Dordrecht: Reidel, 1988).

7. Daniel G. Bobrow and Terry Winograd, "An Overview of KRL, A Knowledge Representation Language," *Cognitive Science*, vol. 1, no. 1, 1977: 32.

8. Terry Winograd, "Towards a Procedural Understanding of Semantics," *Revue Internationale de Philosophie* (Foundation Universitaire de Belgique), no. 117–118, 1976: 283.

9. T. Winograd, "Computer Software for Working with Language," *Scientific American*, September 1984: 142. For a discussion of my Heideggerian contribution to the debate, see *Scientific American*, January 1990, 33.

10. For Winograd's current Heideggerian approach to AI, see Terry Winograd and Fernando Flores, *Understanding Computers and Cognition: A New Foundation for Design* (Norwood, NJ: Ablex, 1986).

11. See H. and S. Dreyfus, "How to Stop Worrying about the Frame Problem Even Though It's Computationally Insoluble," in Zenon W. Pylyshyn ed., *The Robot's Dilemma* (Norwood, NJ: Ablex, 1987).

12. "Pick out" is more colloquial than "free," but like all attempts to replace Heidegger's special terminology it has its drawbacks. Picking something out, say a lamp, seems too intentionalistic. Heidegger wants to suggest that one can free objects in the process of transparent coping, e.g., just by turning on a lamp in the ongoing activity of entering a room. "Freeing," for Heidegger, is simply what happens to the object when we let it show up for us.

13. Later Heidegger reads Parmenides differently and shifts the source of our ontological tradition to Plato. See his *Early Greek Thinking*.

14. Martin Heidegger, *Nietzsche*, vol. 4: *Nihilism*, 211–212.

15. Heidegger, *The End of Philosophy*, 15.

Chapter 7

1. This is not to say that a table-shaped object is occurrent in the physical universe. That is true too, but Heidegger here is describing how the table as equipment shows up as present for use in the world, a world that does not depend on you or me but that, unlike the universe, would cease to exist if there were no Daseins at all.

2. "The attempt in *Being and Time*, Section 70, to derive human spatiality from temporality is untenable" (Heidegger, *On Time and Being*, 23).

3. For a more satisfying account, see Samuel Todes, *The Human Body as Material Subject of the World* (New York: Garland Press, 1990).

Chapter 8

1. Heidegger, *Der Grundbegriffe der Metaphysik: Welt-Endlichkeit-Einsamkeit*, in *Gesamtausgabe*, vol. 29/30, 301. Even Husserl admits that the very meaning of "Dasein" or "human person" already lies outside the sphere of ownness. But Husserl thinks that he can make sense of a source of meanings, viz. individual, transcendental consciousness, which does *not* make any intrinsic reference to others, while Heidegger, as we shall see, claims that such a private source of meanings makes no sense since meaning is itself a public phenomenon.

2. Heidegger, *Gesamtausgabe*, vol. 29/30, 301.

3. Frederick A. Olafson, *Heidegger and the Philosophy of Mind* (New Haven: Yale University Press, 1987), 146.

4. Ibid., 147.

5. John Searle, "Collective Intentions and Action," in P. R. Cohen, J. Morgan and M. E. Pollack, eds., *Intentions in Communication* (Cambridge: Bradford Books/ MIT Press, 1990), 401–415.

6. For a naturalistic account of this tendency to conform, see John Haugeland, "Heidegger on Being a Person," *Noûs*, vol. 16, no. 1: 15–28.

7. Wittgenstein, *Philosophical Investigations*, #241; my gloss in brackets.

8. Wittgenstein, *On Certainty* (New York: Harper & Row, 1969), #110, 17e.

9. Heidegger, *Introduction to Metaphysics*, 2–3.

10. Bourdieu, *Outline of a Theory of Practice*, 85.

11. Ibid., 86.

12. When the ultimate source of meaning is traced back to transcendental intersubjectivity as in Husserl, or to absolute spirit as in Hegel, the particular Daseins become "subjects" with a "universal subject" hovering over them. "The being of such 'subjects' is understood as having a character other than that of Dasein ... as cases of a genus of occurrents—cases which are factually occurrent" (166) [128]. Such "subjects" are really objects with *factual* properties. What is missing is the *facticity* of Dasein.

Heidegger faces this same problem. If he emphasizes the positive function of the one as the source of Dasein's for-the-sake-of-whichs, if the "who" of Dasein is the one, then Heidegger might seem to have saved the self-interpreting *factical* character of Dasein in general by reducing particular Daseins to *factual* social organisms passively constituted by society, as in the theory of Bourdieu.

Heidegger's answer to Husserl's, Hegel's, and Bourdieu's reduction of everyday men and women to passive social objects is to argue in Division II that *individual* Dasein is not passive, as the social person in the above accounts must be, but rather, as Kierkegaard claimed, that the individual self must *take over* the meanings provided by the one in such a way as to manifest rather than cover up its essential meaninglessness. Thus, a particular Dasein is both constituted (by the one) and self-constituting (as taking over significances from the one in such a way as to manifest Dasein's primordial way of being). This is Heidegger's (and Kierkegaard's) insight into the relation of the individual to the universal, a relation to which neither Hegel, with his exclusive emphasis on the universal and social, nor Husserl, with his exclusive emphasis on Cartesian individual subjectivity, could do justice. (See Appendix.)

13. The discovery of the crucial importance of the one is the final step in Heidegger's overcoming of Husserl's transcendental phenomenology. In Husserl, meaning-giving runs from the individual transcendental consciousness to the public world, whereas in Heidegger it is shown to run from the public world to the particular Dasein.

In response to reading *Being and Time*, Husserl attempted in *Cartesian Meditations* to incorporate Heidegger's insights. The impersonal, meaning-giving activity Heidegger attributes to the one Husserl attributes to *transcendental intersubjectivity*. According to Husserl, the individual transcendental ego first constitutes or makes sense of other minds. Then, on the basis of what it takes to be shared with other minds, it constitutes transcendental intersubjectivity, which, in turn, gives meaning to nature, the objective world, society, and finally "men" (Husserl's understanding of Dasein).

An Ego-community, which includes me, becomes constituted (in my sphere of ownness, naturally) as a community of Egos . . . which, moreover, (in its communalized intentionality) constitutes the *one identical world*. In this world all Egos again present themselves, but in an Objectivating apperception with the sense "men" or "psychophysical men as worldly Objects." (*Cartesian Meditations*, 107)

Thus, by equating transcendental intersubjectivity and the one, Husserl could agree with Heidegger that an anonymous social subject is the "'Realest subject' of everydayness" while still holding that individual transcendental subjectivity alone is fully intelligible, and thus is the ultimate ground of that anonymous subject and of everything else.

All these matters are governed by essential necessities; they conform to an essential style, which derives its necessity from the transcendental ego and then from the transcendental intersubjectivity which discloses itself in that ego. . . . If we succeed in uncovering these forms, the aforesaid a priori style acquires a rational clarification that has the highest dignity, the dignity of an ultimate, a transcendental intelligibility. (*Cartesian Meditations*, 136)

Husserl holds that, if for Heidegger Dasein is dependent upon the one in the same way as the social person is derived from transcendental intersubjectivity, then Heidegger is faced with a dilemma: either the activity of the public is taken as fundamental, in which case (as Husserl objects in his marginal notes to *Being and Time*) Heidegger must be doing sociology or anthropology instead of philosophy, or else Heidegger is doing philosophy, in which case the one itself must have some kind of self-intelligible transcendental source.

In *Being and Time* Heidegger's response to the dilemma is unclear. On the one hand he feels he must find some sort of transcendental source to answer Husserl, and in Division II he seems to suggest such a source for the everyday world and the self in originary temporality. Yet on the other hand his description of the phenomenon of everydayness in Division I affirms the one as *ens realissimum*— as the end of the line of explanations of intelligibility.

Chapter 9

1. The text never says Dasein is *its* clearing. "*The* there," as Heidegger occasionally uses the term, is usually the generic name for the particular theres; sometimes, however, Heidegger confusingly uses "the there" as synonymous with "the clearing."

2. We shall need to distinguish Situation (*Situation*) from situation (*Lage*) in the Appendix, but that distinction is not relevant here.

3. Heidegger, *Heraclitus Seminar (1951–1973)*, in *Gesamtausgabe*, vol. 15, 205.

Chapter 10

1. Heidegger, *Gesamtausgabe*, vol. 45, 197.

2. Heidegger, *Hölderlins Hymnen "Germanien" und "Der Rhein"* (1934/35), in *Gesamtausgabe*, vol. 39, 140–141.

3. Heidegger, *Der Grundbegriffe der Metaphysik* (1929/30), in *Gesamtausgabe*, vol. 29/30, 100.

4. Ibid., 101–102.

5. Of course, I can be frightened even when not in a fearful mood. This is because the capacity to be frightened belongs to my affectedness.

6. Misleading quotation marks again here and in the following quote. Dasein is not absorbed in the universe.

7. Pierre Bourdieu, *Leçon sur la leçon* (Paris: Les Editions de Minuit, 1982).

Chapter 11

1. Heidegger, "Letter on Humanism," in *Basic Writings*, 212.

2. Husserl's approach raises the traditional (pseudo) problem of how we get from our perception of mere objects to our understanding of equipment. The latest version of this problem crops up in Artificial Intelligence work on vision. David Marr has introduced the idea that the vision system produces a two-dimensional description of an object that must then be interpreted by higher processes as having some sort of significance. See David Marr, *Vision* (San Francisco: W. H. Freeman, 1982). But no one in AI has explained why the system must produce a *description* rather than an *image*, nor how such a description is *taken as* a description of something to use.

3. This is Heidegger's version of Husserl's notion of original evidence.

4. See Charles Taylor, "Interpretation and the Sciences of Man," in *Philosophical Papers*, vol. 2 (Cambridge: Cambridge University Press, 1985).

5. Bourdieu, *Outline of a Theory of Practice*, 5.

6. Ibid., 6.

7. John Searle, *Minds, Brains and Science* (Cambridge: Harvard University Press, 1984).

8. See Richard Rorty, *Philosophy and the Mirror of Nature* (Princeton: Princeton University Press, 1979), chapter 7.

9. Edmund Husserl, *Experience and Judgment* (Evanston: Northwestern University Press, 1973). See also the introduction to Dreyfus, ed., *Husserl, Intentionality, and Cognitive Science*.

10. See John Searle, *Speech Acts* (Cambridge: Cambridge University Press, 1969). Heidegger's unclear and inconsistent use of quotation marks to distinguish the act of *asserting* from what is asserted—the *assertion*—may come from the unnaturalness of expressing this distinction in German. When he wants to refer explicitly to the speech act of asserting, Heidegger is forced to use the locution "*aussagen machen*" (to make assertions) [161].

11. See Heidegger's review of Russell and Whitehead's *Principia Mathematica*, reprinted in his *Gesamtausgabe*, vol. 1.

Chapter 12

1. Later Heidegger finds this view one of the few serious mistakes in *Being and Time*. In the margin of his copy of the book, he writes: "Not true. Language is not tiered. Rather it is the primordial essence of truth as the there" {117}. This comment expresses later Heidegger's questionable view that language *makes possible* significance—not just that all significance is sayable, which is the more plausible view defended in *Being and Time*.

2. David Rumelhart and James McClelland have recently shown that a computer used to simulate a hypothetical model of brain-processing that makes no use of rules and features can learn to associate a simplified version of the phonetic representations of the infinitive of English verbs with the phonetic representation of their past tense. If given these verb pairs with the same frequency as that heard by children, the program even overgeneralizes at a certain stage of its learning and forms all past tenses by adding "ed," even though there are no rules such as "form the past tense by adding 'ed'" represented in the system. After more training, the system eventually gets both regular and irregular endings right. See David E. Rumelhart, James L. McClelland, and the PDP Research Group, *Parallel Distributed Processing: Explorations in the Microstructure of Cognition*, vol. 1 (Cambridge: Bradford Books/MIT Press, 1986).

Chapter 13

1. To be authentic, Dasein must accept the structural necessity of absorption without losing itself therein. This would be clear if it were not for an unfortunate passage where Heidegger tells us: "Dasein holds itself open for its *constant lostness* in the irresoluteness of the one" (356, my italics) [308]. But if Dasein were *constantly lost* in the one, there could be no authentic existence. Fortunately, this quotation is a mistranslation. Heidegger says only that there is a constant *possible* lostness.

2. One could try to fill out such a structural account, but Heidegger in *Being and Time* has recourse to a motivational account and so never faces the problem. Two years later in "What Is Metaphysics?" (in *Gesamtausgabe*, vol. 9), however, Heidegger proposes what may well be the missing structural story. He tells us that "In anxiety there lies a drawing back from . . . which is certainly not a fleeing." And he explains that "[The nothing] is essentially deflective" (114). "The nothing in its nothingness refers us directly to beings" (116). This seems to mean that Dasein *cannot* relate directly to the clearing, i.e., the nothing (no-thing), but only to things in the clearing. Therefore Dasein must turn *toward* what is disclosed—beings and public norms—and thus *turn away from* disclosedness and from itself as disclosing. This turn then accounts for Dasein's tendency to remain in publicness. "The more we turn to beings . . . the more we turn away from the nothing. So the more surely do we press into public superficiality" (116).

Merleau-Ponty proposes a similar structural account in *Phenomenology of Perception*. Human beings as being-towards-the-world naturally tend to become absorbed in things and so to overlook the process by which objects and their own selves are continually constituted. This tendency is hard to resist because treating things and people as finished, stable entities increases coping and control. Nietzsche has a similar idea; using categories like cause and substance falsifies the phenomenon but increases power.

3. Note that here *covers up* suggests a passive result of reflection not an act of covering up. The term suggests Dasein's being cut off from itself, rather than a motivated disguise.

4. Here "inauthentic" presumably means the same as "undifferentiated"; see Appendix, note 58.

Chapter 14

1. Heidegger, *Ontologie* (*Hermeneutik der Faktizität*), in *Gesamtausgabe*, vol. 63, 7.

2. For a subtle, original, and convincing unpacking of all this, see William David Blattner's Ph.D. dissertation, "Temporal Synthesis and Temporality in Kant and Heidegger," University of Pittsburgh, 1989.

Chapter 15

1. Evelyn Fox Keller, "The Gender/Science System: or, Is Sex to Gender as Nature is to Science?"*Hypatia*, vol. 2, no. 3, 1987: 45.

2. Andrew Pickering, *Constructing Quarks* (Chicago: University of Chicago Press, 1984).

3. Arthur Fine, *The Shaky Game: Einstein, Realism, and the Quantum Theory* (Chicago: University of Chicago Press, 1986), 140. See Joseph Rouse, *Knowledge and Power: Toward a Political Philosophy of Science* (Ithaca: Cornell University Press, 1987), and Mark Okrent, *Heidegger's Pragmatism: Understanding, Being, and the Critique of Metaphysics* (Ithaca: Cornell University Press, 1988). Both of these authors seem to think that Heidegger holds or should hold that the entities scientists discover are dependent upon the practices that disclose them.

4. Heidegger, *Phänomenological Interpretation von Kants Kritik der reinen Vernunft (1927/28)*, in *Gesamtausgabe*, vol. 25, 26.

5. Heidegger, "Science and Reflection," in *The Question Concerning Technology and Other Essays*, 173.

6. Fine, *The Shaky Game*, 130.

7. Ibid., 126ff.

8. Ibid., 133.

9. See Heidegger, *The Essence of Reasons*, 83, and "What Is Metaphysics?," in *Basic Writings*, 105, quoted by Joseph Fell in "The Familiar and the Strange: On the Limits of Praxis in the Early Heidegger," in Dreyfus and Hall, eds., *Heidegger: A Critical Reader*.

10. Heidegger, *Schelling's Treatise on the Essence of Human Freedom*, 187–188.

11. Heidegger, *Introduction to Metaphysics*, 71.

12. Heidegger, *Metaphysical Foundations of Logic*, 167.

13. Heidegger, "Science and Reflection," 173–174.

14. Heidegger, "The Age of the World Picture," in *The Question Concerning Technology and Other Essays*, 117.

15. The way of being of the sacred is neither the way of being of equipment defined by the equipmental totality nor the way of being of the occurrent defined by its nonrelation to cultural practices. Heidegger gestures in this direction when he notes, "perhaps even availableness and equipment have nothing to contribute as ontological clues in interpreting the primitive world; and certainly the ontology of thinghood does even less" (113)[82]. Later Heidegger develops this idea in his account of the way of being of works of art and of their role in revealing a world. (See Appendix.)

16. Alexander Nehamas, in *Nietzsche: Life as Literature* (Cambridge: Harvard University Press, 1985), claims to find what I take to be Heidegger's view of science already in Nietzsche: "[Nietzsche] does not object to science itself... but rather to an interpretation which refuses to acknowledge that science itself is an interpretation in the sense that it provides a revisable description of a part of the world which is no more [ultimately] real that any other. The problem has been that the methods of science have been assumed to be better than any others, and its objects have been considered to be more real or ultimate than anything else. Nietzsche attacks only this privileging of the methods and objects of science and not its methods or objects themselves" (65).

17. Wittgenstein makes a similar point in #46 of his *Philosophical Investigations*: "Both Russell's 'individuals' and my 'objects' (*Tractatus Logico-Philosophicus*) were [meant to be] primary elements. But what are the simple constituent parts of which reality is composed? ... It makes no sense at all to speak absolutely of the 'simple parts of a chair'" (21).

18. See Donald Davidson, "Mental Events," in *Essays on Action and Events* (Oxford: Oxford University Press, 1980).

19. John Searle, "Literal Meaning," in *Expression and Meaning* (Cambridge: Cambridge University Press, 1979).

Appendix

1. Søren Kierkegaard, *The Present Age* (New York: Harper & Row, 1962), 43.

2. Ibid., 43.

3. Ibid., 45.

4. Ibid., 42.

5. Kierkegaard does not claim authorship of the definition of the self. Rather, he attributes it to the pseudonym Anti-Climacus. While an understanding of the role of the pseudonyms is crucial for an understanding of Kierkegaard's work as a whole, for the present purposes we refer to Kierkegaard as the author of all of the works under consideration. For a discussion of Kierkegaard's use of pseudonyms, see Jane Rubin, "Too Much of Nothing: Modern Culture, The Self and Salvation in Kierkegaard's Thought," Ph.D. dissertation, University of California, Berkeley, 1984.

6. Søren Kierkegaard, *The Sickness Unto Death*, trans. Alasdair Hannay (London: Penguin Books, 1989), 43; trans. Walter Lowrie (Princeton: Princeton University Press, 1941), 146. We have made several changes in the text in order to clarify what we believe to be its meaning. First, we have substituted Walter Lowrie's term "factors" for Hannay's "terms" in the definition of the self, because it provides a convenient shorthand for describing the constituents of the synthesis. Second, we have changed the word "freedom" to "possibility." In other passages in *The Sickness Unto Death* and in *The Concept of Anxiety*, Kierkegaard uses the word "freedom" to refer to the self-defining nature of human beings. He uses the word "possibility" to refer to one factor of the synthesis that a human being defines. Though Kierkegaard is inconsistent in his use of terminology, the distinction between the two concepts is clear. Thus, we have changed the terminology in order to preserve the clear distinction between the two concepts. Finally, we have

reversed the order of the possibility/necessity and eternal/temporal factors, since Kierkegaard discusses them in this order in the remainder of *The Sickness Unto Death*, and we have changed the order of temporal/eternal to eternal/temporal in order to make it symmetrical with Kierkegaard's presentation of the other sets of factors.

7. This is not the place to defend the view that Kierkegaard's spheres of existence are a response to the leveling of the present age. Jane Rubin does so at length in "Too Much of Nothing."

8. For Kierkegaard's definitions of infinite and finite, see *The Sickness Unto Death*, 59–65.

9. For Kierkegaard's definitions of possibility and necessity see *The Sickness Unto Death*, 65–72.

10. For Kierkegaard's definitions of the eternal and the temporal see Søren Kierkegaard, *The Concept of Anxiety* (Princeton: Princeton University Press, 1980), 81–93.

11. Ibid., 44.

12. Ibid.

13. Ibid., 42.

14. Ibid., 41.

15. Kierkegaard, *The Sickness Unto Death*, 63.

16. Ibid., 71–72.

17. Kierkegaard, *The Concept of Anxiety*, 94. One extremely interesting aspect of Kierkegaard's analysis of the present age is his account of how the present age not only levels distinctions, but creates illusory versions of them. In the opening section of *The Present Age*, Kierkegaard describes the ways in which the present age creates the illusions of infinite and finite, possibility and necessity and the eternal and the temporal at the same time that it levels them. In a later section, Kierkegaard offers an extremely prescient analysis of the way in which the press—or, as we would say, the media—provides the illusion of the existence of four qualitative distinctions: public and private, form and content, revelation and concealment, and subjectivity and objectivity. By taking over these illusions, people cover up the leveling of the present age. See Kierkegaard, *The Present Age*, 33–41, 69–77. For an analysis of these sections of *The Present Age*, see Rubin, "Too Much of Nothing." This insight is reflected in Heidegger's account of ambiguity (*Being and Time*, Section 37).

18. We have borrowed the distinction between the immediate aesthetic and the reflective aesthetic from Mark C. Taylor, *Kierkegaard's Pseudonymous Authorship: A Study of Time and the Self* (Princeton: Princeton University Press, 1975), 128. While we accept the general distinction, we do not accept Taylor's specific categorizations of the stages of the aesthetic sphere.

19. For Kierkegaard's description of the immediate aesthetic sphere, see Søren Kierkegaard, *Either/Or*, vol. II (Princeton: Princeton University Press, 1987), 180–194. It is important to emphasize again that a sphere of existence is not a philosophical view but a way of acting. Thus, while it is easy to recognize the contradictions in the lower spheres when describing these spheres directly, a

person who is attempting to live in one of the lower spheres is constantly covering up its contradictions. Kierkegaard's use of indirect discourse in the lower spheres is a way of describing the spheres as they are actually lived. Our necessarily direct description of the spheres and their breakdowns cannot do justice to the plausibility of the lower spheres for those who are attempting to exist in them.

20. Kierkegaard, *Either/Or*, vol. I, 282–300.

21. Søren Kierkegaard, *Edifying Discourses*, edited by Paul L. Holmer (New York: Harper and Row, 1958), 155.

22. Ibid., 150–151.

23. Søren Kierkegaard, *Concluding Unscientific Postscript* (Princeton: Princeton University Press, 1941), 347.

24. Kierkegaard, *Edifying Discourses*, 42–43.

25. Ibid., 39.

26. Ibid., 41–42.

27. Ibid., 145.

28. Ibid., 139.

29. Ibid., 26.

30. Ibid., 22.

31. Ibid., 260.

32. Ibid., 262.

33. Ibid.

34. See Kierkegaard, *Either/Or*, vol. I, 17–43, 217–230.

35. See Kierkegaard, *Either/Or*, vol. II, 190. Kierkegaard's remarks on pages 329 and 332 that every human being is an exception to the universality of the ethical can be taken as a restatement of this point.

36. Readers familiar with Kierkegaard's use of pseudonyms and indirect discourse may object to the idea that the works Kierkegaard wrote in direct discourse under his own name could contain a cover-up of the despair of the position they claim to defend. For a defense of this position see Rubin, "Too Much of Nothing."

37. Kierkegaard, *Edifying Discourses*, 213.

38. Kierkegaard, *Concluding Unscientific Postscript*, 386.

39. Kierkegaard, *Edifying Discourses*, 214; the emphasis is Kierkegaard's.

40. Ibid., 244–245.

41. Ibid., 247.

42. Ibid., 134.

43. Søren Kierkegaard, *Training In Christianity* (Princeton: Princeton University Press, 1941), 109.

44. For a complete discussion of Kierkegaard's views about the role of paradigms in the constitution of the self and an argument that these views do not entail a commitment to Christianity, see Jane Rubin's forthcoming book.

45. Kierkegaard, *The Sickness Unto Death*, 44.

46. Søren Kierkegaard, *Fear and Trembling* (New York: Penguin Books, 1985), 79.

47. Ibid., 57.

48. It is hard to see the premodern Christian community as demanding any sort of individualism; it does seem plausible, however, to claim that Christianity has always demanded a world-defining, if not an individual, commitment.

49. In *Being and Time* Heidegger calls the existentiale that is the counterpart to facticity "existence." But this term is confusing, since, as we have seen, Heidegger stipulates that the whole way of being of Dasein in which its being is an issue for it is to be called "existence." So existence should be the way the whole relation relates to itself, not one aspect of it. In *The Basic Problems of Phenomenology* Heidegger calls Dasein's capacity for projecting, "transcendence." This Husserlian term suggests the mind's reaching out beyond itself, and so is also misleading; however, to avoid the double meaning of "existence" we use "transcendence" to name Dasein's pressing into possibilities.

50. For a Heideggerian account of an ethics based on care and a critique of reflective, cognitivist ethics, see Hubert Dreyfus and Stuart Dreyfus, "What Is Moral Maturity? A Phenomenological Account of the Development of Ethical Expertise," in David Rasmussen, ed., *Universalism vs. Communitarianism* (Cambridge: MIT Press, 1990).

51. Kierkegaard, *Either/Or*, 328–333.

52. Ibid., 335–354.

53. For a particularly convincing version of such a reading see Piotr Hoffman, *Doubt, Time, Violence* (Chicago: University of Chicago Press, 1986).

54. Heidegger rarely speaks of "passion." When he does, it describes the intensity of Dasein's absorption; e.g., "Dasein gives itself over . . . passionately to the world" (BP, 159).

55. Kierkegaard distinguishes the "lower immediacy" that characterizes the aesthetic, the ethical, and Religiousness A from the "higher immediacy" of Religiousness B. *Lower immediacy* consists of all the concrete content that an individual life simply has—the desires, talents, physical characteristics, and so forth of a person. *Higher immediacy* is the particular world-defining commitment that a person does not simply have but which he is given when he accepts a concrete world-defining commitment. In the logic of Kierkegaard's spheres, a person must definitively "die away from immediacy" in Religiousness A in order to be in a position to accept the higher immediacy of Religiousness B.

56. On this point Heidegger does not even include the usual reference to Kierkegaard as having seen an important phenomenon but only in a religious context. Not only does Heidegger fail to thank Kierkegaard in *Being and Time*, in his lectures he protests with strange vehemence against any idea that what he says about fallenness has religious or psychological associations:

It should be noted here that the explication of these structures of Dasein has nothing to do with any . . . theory of *original sin*. What is involved here is a pure consideration of structures, which *precedes* all such considerations. . . . It is possible, perhaps necessary, that all of these structures will recur in a theological anthropology. I am in no position to judge how, since I understand nothing of such things. (HCT, 283)

But Heidegger seems to allow that his view can be thought of as a secularized version of sinfulness by explicitly rejecting the idea of a prefallen state. He assures us we need not "take the fallenness of Dasein as a 'fall' from a purer and higher 'primal status'" (220)[176]. Kierkegaard also rejects the idea of a prefallen state in his account of sinfulness.

57. Note that psychological falling as actively plunging is quite different from structural falling, which is defined as yielding to a pull. (See chapter 13.)

58. As we saw in chapter 1, Heidegger does not always distinguish Dasein's undifferentiated mode from its inauthentic mode. Indeed, when he is opposing both to Dasein's authenticity, he often write as if Dasein came in only two modes. Yet sometimes he clearly entertains three possibilities:

We have defined the idea of existence as an ability-to-be—an ability which understands, and for which its own being is an issue. But this ability-to-be, as one which is in each case mine, is free either for authenticity or for inauthenticity or for a mode in which neither of these has been differentiated. (275)[232]

Heidegger's often leaving out the undifferentiated mode becomes somewhat more comprehensible, given his secularized version of sinfulness. On that Kierkegaardian interpretation, active flight from anxiety is built right into the one. The uncertain status of the undifferentiated mode in *Being and Time* reflects the sketchiness of Heidegger's structural account and the way it keeps being invaded by the secularized Kierkegaardian story.

59. Kierkegaard, *Either/Or*, 150.

60. Heidegger, *Introduction to Metaphysics*, 17.

61. Heidegger, "The Origin of the Work of Art," in *Poetry, Language, Thought*, 67.

62. "We shall all be changed, in a moment, in the twinkling of an eye." 1 Cor. 15:52.

63. See Edmund Husserl, *The Phenomenology of Internal Time-Consciousness*, edited by Martin Heidegger (Bloomington: Indiana University Press, 1966).

64. Since "repetition" seems to be used mostly to denote *explicitly* retrieving the heritage, rather than unreflectively taking it over, (not to mention the merely formal version of constantly manifesting thrownness), we can perhaps understand why Heidegger often uses the formula "resolute-forerunning" as if it were the whole of authentic temporality—e.g., "Temporality gets experienced in a phenomenally primordial way in Dasein's authentic being-a-whole, in the phenomenon of forerunning resoluteness" (351)[304]—but only once uses the formula that one would expect given the equal importance of death and guilt: "The moment of *forerunning repetition deprives* the "today" of its character as present, and weans one from the conventionalities of the one" (443–444)[391].

65. One can perhaps see here Heidegger's philosophical justification of his political engagement in support of the National Socialists in 1933. It is important to realize, however, that even if one believed that the issue for Heidegger's generation was whether or not to support the Nazis, nothing in *Being and Time* suggests that the Situation demanded a positive response. Of course, nothing suggests that it required a negative response either.

66. See *Sickness Unto Death*, chapter 2: The Socratic Definition of Sin.

67. Heidegger, "The Way Back into the Ground of Metaphysics," in Walter Kaufmann, ed., *Existentialism from Dostoevsky to Sartre* (New York: Meridian Books, 1957), 211.

68. Heidegger, "What Are Poets For?" in *Poetry, Language, Thought.*

69. Heidegger, *Discourse on Thinking*, 55.

70. Heidegger, "The Age of the World Picture," in *The Question Concerning Technology and Other Essays*, 131.

71. For more on these stages see H. Dreyfus, *Heidegger and Foucault on the Ordering of Things* (Berkeley: University of California Press, 1991).

72. In his notes on the history of metaphysics, Heidegger stresses the difference between *Being and Time* and Kierkegaard's Christian demand for passionate commitment, which he no longer claims to have secularized and ontologized. He also admits the equivocal relation of *Being and Time* to metaphysics, which he now sees as nihilistic. The question in *Being and Time* "is profoundly different from Kierkegaard's passion which is at bottom theological. But it does remain in the essential critical dialogue with metaphysics" (Heidegger, *The End of Philosophy*, 71).

73. Heidegger, *The Question Concerning Technology*, 33. We read for "*im Geringen*," "in humble things" rather than "in little things," as in the published translation. The idea is: in things that are insignificant, given our technological understanding of reality.

74. Heidegger, "The Origin of the Work of Art," in *Poetry, Language, Thought*, 42.

Index